Chambers
Dates

Chambers Dates

Second Edition

G. L. Hough

Chambers

© 1989 G. L. Hough

First published 1983

This second edition published 1989 by W & R Chambers Ltd, 43–45 Annandale Street, Edinburgh EH7 4AZ

British Library Cataloguing in Publication Data

Hough, G. L. (George Leslie), *1921*–
   Chambers dates. – 2nd ed
   1. World, to 1977 – Encyclopaedias
   I. Title   II. Hough, G. L. (George Leslie), *1921* .
   Chambers dictionary of dates.
   909

   ISBN 0–550–11831–4

Cover design by David Sneddon

Typeset by Buccleuch Printers Ltd, Hawick
Printed in Great Britain

Preface

Chambers Dates is a reference book that everyone will find at once informative and enjoyable. It provides a fascinating summary of events for each and every day of the year throughout history – from early times to the present day.

The book is much more than the traditional list of historical dates. It contains information related to a wide diversity of fields such as sport, entertainment, transport and politics, as well as history and literature.

It is essentially a book of interesting snippets – when was alcohol prohibition introduced in the USA? When did breakfast television start in Britain? When was the Paris Bastille stormed? When did Neil Armstrong set foot on the moon? When was Canadian ice hockey star Wayne Gretzky born? When did Amundsen reach the South Pole? Where was legendary jockey Lester Piggott born? When does the oyster season begin? When was the Cullinan diamond discovered? You will find all this information – and so much more – in this invaluable reference book.

The comprehensive index adds another dimension to the book's usefulness. Browsing through it will stimulate your curiosity about topic after topic that you would not otherwise have thought of. The index will also direct you with ease to the point in the book where your curiosity will be satisfied.

People of all ages will find *Chambers Dates* useful. Everyone has occasion, from time to time, to check up on a date, whether for purposes of work or leisure. The book will be invaluable to all quiz enthusiasts and to after-dinner speakers searching desperately for a suitable topic.

National day of Cuba, Sudan and Haiti.

1660 Samuel Pepys began his famous diary—written in Shelton's system of shorthand—was discontinued on 31 May 1669.

1735 Paul Revere, American patriot famous for his ride from Charlestown to Lexington to warn of the British advance on Concord, born in Boston, Massachusetts.

1766 James Stuart, the 'Old Pretender' and father of Bonnie Prince Charlie, died in Rome.

1785 The British daily newspaper *The Times* was founded as the *Daily Universal Register*, and published by John Walter. Was re-titled *The Times* three years later.

1801 Ceres, the largest of the minor planets, was discovered by Giuseppe Piazzi at Palermo, in Sicily.

1863 Pierre de Coubertin, responsible for the revival of the Olympic Games in 1896, born.

1879 (Edward Morgan) E. M. Forster, English novelist, born in London.
William Fox, film impresario and founder of 20th Century Fox, born in Hungary as William Friedman.

1881 Postal orders were first issued in Britain.

1889 The State of New York adopted the electric chair for capital punishment.

1894 The 35-mile Manchester Ship Canal, linking Manchester with the Mersey estuary and the Irish Sea, was opened to traffic—was officially opened by Queen Victoria on 21 May.

1895 J. Edgar Hoover, American criminologist and founder and head of the FBI, born in Washington, DC.

1900 Xavier Cugat, American musician and Latin bandleader born in Barcelona, Spain.

1901 The six states and two territories federated to form the Commonwealth of Australia.

1904 The first motor vehicle registration plate in Britain, A1, was secured by Earl Russell for his 'Napier'.

1909 Barry Goldwater, American politician and Senator, born in Phoenix, Arizona.
The first payments of old age pensions were made in Britain—five shillings (25p) a week to persons over 70 years of age.
Dana Andrews, American film actor, born in Collins, Mississippi.

1913 Film censorship in Britain came into operation.

1921 The Navy, Army and Air Force Institute, more commonly called 'NAAFI', was founded in Britain.
Car tax discs for obligatory display on windscreens were introduced in Britain.

1944 Sir Edwin Lutyens, English architect, designer of the Cenotaph in London and planner of New Delhi, died in London.
1947 The British coal industry became nationalised.
All British 'silver' coins, except Maundy money, to be struck from cupro-nickel—an alloy of copper (75 parts) and nickel (25 parts).
1948 British railways became nationalised.
1951 The steel industry in Britain became nationalised.
1953 Hank Williams, American country-music singer and composer who could not read music, died.
1956 Sudan became an independent Republic after joint Anglo-Egyptian administration.
1957 Nancy Lopez, American international lady golfing champion, born in Torrance, California.
1959 Fidel Castro seized power in Cuba, overthrowing the right-wing government of Fulgencio Batista.
1961 The birth-control pill was launched in Britain.
1970 The British half-crown coin ceased to be legal tender.
1972 Maurice Chevalier, French singer and musical comedy star in films, died aged 83.
1973 Britain, Ireland and Denmark became members of the European Economic Community.
1974 New Year's Day was celebrated in Britain as a national public holiday for the first time.
1981 Greece became the tenth member of the European Economic Community.
1985 The new British decimal ½p ceased to be legal tender.

---

2 JANUARY   [2]

1727 James Wolfe, British Army general and commander at the capture of Quebec from the French, born at Westerham vicarage in Kent, the son of a general.
1788 Georgia, the Peach or Empire State of the South, became the 4th state of the Union.
1839 Frenchman Louis Daguerre took the first photograph of the moon.
1892 Sir George Airy, English Astronomer Royal who modernised the Greenwich Observatory, died in Alnwick, Northumberland.
1895 Count Folke Bernadotte, nephew of the King of Sweden, born.
1896 The Jameson raid into the Boer colony of Transvaal to support the British settlers ended in failure.
1901 The first municipal crematorium was opened in Hull, England, by the Lord Mayor.

1905 Sir Michael Tippett, English composer, born in London, the son of a lawyer.

1936 Roger Miller, American singer whose hits include *King of the Road*, born in Fort Worth, Texas.

1938 David Bailey, British photographer, born the son of a tailor.

1946 King Zog of Albania was deposed *in absentia*—the country declared a republic on 11th.

1950 Emil Jannings, US film actor and the first male winner of the Oscar award, for his role in *The Way of All Flesh*, died.

1959 *Lunik I*, Russia's first solar satellite, was launched as a moon rocket at Tyuratam.

1971 Ibrox Park football ground at Glasgow in Scotland was the scene of an ugly accident, when a barrier collapsed and 66 were crushed to death.

1974 Tex Ritter, American singing cowboy of stage and screen, died.

1976 Internal self-government was granted by Britain to the Solomon Islands of the west Pacific.

3 JANUARY [3]

1777 The Battle of Princeton took place in the War of American Independence, in which Washington defeated the British forces under Lord Cornwallis.

1795 Josiah Wedgwood, English potter and creator of blue jasper ware, died.

1823 Robert Whitehead, English engineer and inventor of the naval torpedo, born in Bolton-le-Moors, Lancashire.

1840 Father Damien, Belgian priest and RC missionary, born as Joseph de Veuster.

1850 Work began in London's Hyde Park on the glass and iron Crystal Palace to house the Great Exhibition.

1870 Work began on the Brooklyn-New York bridge over the East River.

1883 Clement Attlee, British statesman, Labour Party leader and Prime Minister, born in Putney, Greater London.

1888 Herbert Morrison, British Labour politician and statesman, born in Lambeth, London.
James Bridie, British playwright, born in Glasgow as Osborne Henry Mavor.

1892 J. R. R. Tolkien, British author, notably of *The Lord of the Rings*, born in Bloemfontein in the Orange Free State in South Africa.

1894 Elizabeth Peabody, American educator and founder in 1860 of the first kindergarten in the US, died aged 89.

1908 Ray Milland, American film actor and Oscar winner for *The Lost Weekend* in 1945, born in Neath, Wales as Reginald Truscott-Jones.

1909 Victor Borge, American comedian and pianist, born in Copenhagen, Denmark, as Borge Rosenbaum.

1915 Tear gas was used for the first time in warfare—by the Germans against the Russians in Poland.

1931 Joseph Joffre, French marshal and commander-in-chief of the French armies on the Western Front, died.

1946 William Joyce, British Nazi propagandist, known as 'Lord Haw Haw', was hanged in London for treason.

1958 Sir Edmund Hillary, with a New Zealand party, reached the South Pole, the first man to do so overland since Captain Scott.

1959 Alaska became the 49th state of America—and the largest.

1967 Jack Ruby, who shot Lee Harvey Oswald, the alleged assassin of President Kennedy, died of natural causes in hospital in Dallas while awaiting the retrial of his murder case.

1971 The Open University was inaugurated. The regular courses commenced the following Sunday, 10 January.

1979 Conrad Hilton, American hotelier and founder of the Hilton Hotels Corporation, died aged 91.

1980 Joy Adamson, famous for her work with wildlife, especially the lioness Elsa, described in *Born Free*, was murdered in Shaba Game Park in Kenya.

1981 The Countess of Athlone, the longest ever lived British 'Royal', died aged 97.

4 JANUARY   *[4]*

National day of Burma.

1785 Jacob Grimm, the elder of the two German brothers famous for fairy tales, born in Hanau.

1809 Louis Braille, French benefactor of the blind, born in Coupvray, near Paris.

1813 Isaac Pitman, English pioneer of phonetic shorthand, born in Trowbridge, Wiltshire.

1838 Charles Sherwood Stratton was born; he later became known as 'Tom Thumb', a midget exhibited by Phineas Barnum.

1878 Augustus John, Welsh portrait painter, born in Tenby.

1896 Utah, the Beehive State, became the 45th state of the Union.

1910 The first Juvenile Courts in Britain opened in London.

1914 Jane Wyman, American film actress and Oscar winner in 1948 for *Johnny Belinda*, born in St Joseph, Missouri as Sarah Jane Faulks.

1935 Floyd Patterson, American boxer, born in Waco, North Carolina.

1936 The first pop music chart was compiled, based on record sales published in New York in *The Billboard*.
1937 Dyan Cannon, American film actress, born in Tacoma, Washington as Samile Diane Friesen.
1948 Burma became an independent Republic outside the Commonwealth.
1958 *Sputnik I* disintegrated after completing 1367 circuits of the Earth and travelling some 43 million miles on its 92-day flight.
1961 Barry Fitzgerald, American film character actor, died.
1965 (Thomas Stearns) T. S. Eliot, American-born English poet, playwright and Nobel Prize winner in 1948, died in London.
1967 Donald Campbell was killed on Coniston Water, Cumbria, in *Bluebird K 7* attempting to break his own world water speed record.
1981 The Broadway show *Frankenstein* opened and closed on the same night, losing an estimated two million dollars.
1985 Mrs Kim Cotton, believed to be the first commercial surrogate mother in Britain, gave birth to a girl.

---

5 JANUARY   [5]

1066 Edward the Confessor, King of England, died.
1855 King Camp Gillette, American inventor of the safety razor about 1900, born in Fond du Lac, Wisconsin.
1858 Joseph Radetsky, Austrian field marshal, commander and national hero, died in Milan aged 91.
1876 Konrad Adenauer, West German statesman and Chancellor, born in Cologne.
1922 Sir Ernest Shackleton, British Antarctic explorer, died on the island of South Georgia in the South Atlantic, on his expedition to Enderby Land.
1925 Nellie Taylor Ross was installed as the first US woman Governor of Wyoming, after the death of her husband.
1928 Walter Mondale, American politician and Vice-President, born in Ceylon, Minnesota.
1933 Calvin Coolidge, American Republican statesman and 30th President from 1923 to 1929, died of a heart attack in Northampton, Massachusetts.
1938 King Juan Carlos I, Head of State of Spain in succession to General Franco, born in Rome.
1941 Amy Johnson, English aviator and first woman to fly solo from England to Australia in 1930, was mysteriously lost in a crash in the Thames estuary on a routine flight.
1964 The first automatic ticket barrier on the London Underground Railway was installed at Stamford Brook.

The Christian festival of Epiphany.

1367 King Richard II was born at Bordeaux in France, the son of Edward the Black Prince and grandson of King Edward III.

1840 Fanny Burney, English novelist and diarist, died aged 87.

1852 Louis Braille, French inventor in 1829 of the raised-dot system of writing used by the blind, died.

1880 Tom Mix, American film actor in Westerns, born in El Paso, Texas.

1882 Richard Dana Jnr, American novelist, writer of the classic *Two Years Before the Mast* based on his own voyage around Cape Horn, died.

1884 Gregor Mendel, Augustine monk and botanist who pioneered the study of biological heredity, died in Brunn, Bavaria.

1901 Philip Armour, American meat packer, one of the first to use refrigerator transport and to make canned-meat products, died.

1912 New Mexico, the Sunshine State became the 47th state of the Union.

1913 Loretta Young, American film actress and Oscar winner, born in Salt Lake City, Utah, as Gretchen Young.

1919 Theodore Roosevelt, American Republican statesman and 26th President from 1901 to 1909 and Nobel Prize winner in 1906, died at Sagamore Hill, Oyster Bay in the State of New York.

1931 The New Sadler's Wells Theatre in London was opened.

1945 The 'Battle of the Bulge' ended.

1949 Victor Fleming, American film director, notably of *The Wizard of Oz*, died in Phoenix, Arizona.

1959 Kapil Dev, Indian Test cricketer, born.
Work began on the seven-mile Mont Blanc road tunnel between France and Italy.

1964 Pope Paul VI finished his three-day tour of the Holy Land, the first Pope to visit there since Christianity began, and the first to leave Italy in over 150 years.

1981 (Archibald Joseph) A. J. Cronin, Scottish novelist, author of *Hatter's Castle* and *The Citadel*, died in Switzerland aged 84.

1536 Catherine of Aragon, the first of Henry VIII's six wives and mother of Queen Mary I, died in Kimbolton Palace, Huntingdonshire.

1558 Calais, the last English possession on the mainland of France, was regained by the French.
1768 Joseph Bonaparte, eldest brother of Napoleon, born on the Mediterranean island of Corsica.
1785 Jean Pierre Blanchard and his sponsor American doctor John Jeffries made the first aerial crossing of the English Channel, from Dover to Calais, in a hydrogen-filled balloon.
1789 The first national election took place in America.
1800 Millard Fillmore, American Whig statesman and 13th President, born in Summerhill in the State of New York, the son of a farmer.
1830 The first railway station was opened, at Mount Clare, Baltimore.
1904 The 'CQD' distress call signal was introduced—'CQ' meant 'seek you', with 'D' for danger added. Was replaced by 'SOS' in 1906.
1925 Gerald Durrell, British zoologist and writer, born in Jamshedpur, India.
1927 The famous American basketball team, the 'Harlem Globetrotters', was founded at Hinckley, Illinois by Abraham Saperstein of Chicago.
     The transatlantic telephone service between London and New York opened, charging £15 for three minutes.
1937 Juliana, Queen of the Netherlands from 1948, married Prince Bernhard.
1988 Trevor Howard, British film actor, died in Bushey, Hertfordshire.

---

8 JANUARY [8]

1642 Galileo, Italian mathematician, physicist and astronomer, died.
1798 The Eleventh Amendment to the US Constitution was ratified, dealing with judicial powers.
1815 The Battle of New Orleans took place—the last battle between England and America—in which Andrew Jackson defeated General Sir Edward Pakenham's British forces.
1824 Wilkie Collins, English detective story writer, notably *The Woman in White*, born in London.
1825 Eli Whitney, American inventor of the cotton gin facilitating separation of fibre and seed, died in New Haven, Connecticut.
1862 Frank Doubleday, American publisher and editor, born in New York.
1863 Yorkshire County Cricket Club was founded at a meeting in the Adelphi Hotel, Sheffield.
1868 Sir Frank Dyson, British astronomer, born in Measham, then in Derbyshire.
1885 John Curtin, Australian Labour statesman, born.
1886 The Severn tunnel, joining England and Wales and the longest in Britain at four miles 624 yards, was opened.

1897 Dennis Wheatley, English novelist, born.
1899 Solomon Bandaranaike, Prime Minister of Sri Lanka, born in the capital, Colombo.
1902 Georgi Malenkov, Soviet politician, born in Orenburg.
1916 The final withdrawal of Allied troops from Gallipoli took place, after an unsuccessful expedition to capture Constantinople.
1918 Recruiting began in Britain for the WRNS—Women's Royal Naval Service.
1921 Lloyd George became the first Prime Minister to occupy 'Chequers', a country mansion near Wendover in Buckinghamshire, given to the nation by Lord Lee of Fareham.
1935 Elvis Presley, born in Tupelo, Mississippi, the surviving brother of twins.
1937 Shirley Bassey, British singer and entertainer, born in Cardiff, South Wales.
1940 Food rationing began in Britain.
1941 Robert Baden-Powell, British soldier, Boer War hero and founder of the Boy Scout movement in 1908, died aged 83.
1947 David Bowie, British musician and rock star, born in London as David Jones.
1948 Richard Tauber, Austrian-born British tenor, died in Sydney, Australia.
1959 Charles de Gaulle was installed as the first President of the Fifth French Republic.
1961 Calvin Smith, American athlete and sprint champion, born.
1976 Chou En-Lai, Chinese Communist statesman and Prime Minister since 1949, died—succeeded by Hua Kuo-Feng.

9 JANUARY [9]

1788 Connecticut, the Constitution or Nutmeg State, became the 5th state of the Union.
1793 Jean Pierre Blanchard made the first ascent in a balloon in America, near Woodbury in New Jersey.
1799 Prime Minister William Pitt the Younger introduced income tax, at two shillings in the £, to raise funds for the Napoleonic Wars.
1806 Lord Nelson, famous British Admiral, was buried in St Paul's Cathedral.
1873 Napoleon III, Emperor of France and nephew of Bonaparte, died in exile, in Chislehurst, Kent.
1878 Victor Emmanuel, the first King of Italy in 1861, died and was succeeded by his son Humbert.
1898 Gracie Fields, English singer, comedienne and music-hall performer, born in Rochdale, Lancashire as Grace Stansfield.

1904   George Balanchine, Russian-American choreographer, born in St Petersburg (now Leningrad).
1913   Richard Nixon, American Republican statesman and 37th President, born in Yorba Linda, California.
1914   Gypsy Rose Lee, American entertainer famed for her striptease act, born in Seattle in the State of Washington as Rose Louise Hovick.
1923   Juan de la Cierva, Spanish aeronaut and inventor of the autogyro, made the first successful flight, at Getafe in Spain.
1941   Joan Baez, American folk singer, born in Staten Island, New York.
1942   Susannah York, English film actress, born in London.
1949   Tommy Handley, Liverpool comedian, died.
1957   Sir Anthony Eden resigned as Prime Minister, Harold Macmillan was appointed the following day.
1960   Work began on the Aswan High Dam in Egypt.
1969   The first trial flight of supersonic airliner *Concorde* took place at Bristol.
1972   The liner *Queen Elizabeth*, after being removed to Hong Kong to serve as a floating marine university and renamed *Seawise University*, sank after catching fire.
1978   The daily newspaper *The Trib* was launched in New York.

---

10 JANUARY   [10]

1645   William Laud, English churchman and Archbishop of Canterbury from 1633, was beheaded on Tower Hill for treason.
1769   Michel Ney, French Army marshal, the most famous of Napoleon's marshals, born in Saarlouis, the son of a cooper.
1778   Carl Linnaeus, Swedish botanist who devised a modern system of naming and classifying plants, died in Uppsala.
1840   The Penny Post came into force in Britain, as a result of the efforts of Sir Rowland Hill.
1862   Samuel Colt, American gunsmith and patentee in 1835 of a revolver that bears his name, died in Hartford, Connecticut.
1863   The first section of the London Underground Railway system was opened to passengers by Mr Gladstone—from Paddington to Farringdon Street.
1880   Grock, Swiss circus clown and entertainer, born as Adrien Wettach.
1903   Barbara Hepworth, English abstract sculptor, born in Wakefield, Yorkshire.
1912   The first flying boat, designed by Glenn Curtiss, made its maiden flight at Hammondsport, New York.

1917 William Frederick Cody, the army scout, Indian fighter and showman known as 'Buffalo Bill', died in Denver, Colorado.

1920 The League of Nations came into being, holding its first meeting at Geneva.

1922 Arthur Griffith was elected President of the newly formed Irish Free State.

1927 Johnnie Ray, American pop singer, born in Dallas, Oregon.

1928 Aviators Hood and Moncrieff were lost attempting the first flight from Australia to New Zealand across the Tasman Sea.

1930 The first New Zealand v England cricket Test match started at Lancaster Park, Christchurch; the visitors ended up winning by eight wickets.

1945 Rod Stewart, British rock singer, born in London of Scots parentage.

1946 The League of Nations was dissolved after 26 years, and was superseded by the United Nations.

1951 Sinclair Lewis, American novelist, author of *Babbitt* and Nobel Prize winner in 1930, died near Rome.

1952 The German freighter *Flying Enterprise* finally sank off Falmouth, having been wrecked by enormous seas on the previous 27 December—Captain Kurt Carlsen remained on board until only minutes before it finally succumbed.

1957 Harold Macmillan was appointed British Prime Minister as a result of the resignation of Sir Anthony Eden.
Eddie Cheever, American motor racing driver, born.

1961 Dashiell Hammett, American writer and creator of the character 'Sam Spade', died.

1971 'Coco' Chanel, French fashion designer and one of the most influential couturiers of the twentieth century, died aged 87.

1985 Ravi Shastri, for Bombay v Baroda, hit six sixes off one over bowled by Tilak Raj.

---

11 JANUARY [11]

1753 Sir Hans Sloane, British physician and naturalist whose collection formed the nucleus of the British Museum, died .

1807 Ezra Cornell, American philanthropist, born at Westchester Landing, New York.

1843 Francis Scott Key, American lawyer and poet who wrote the words of the US national anthem *The Star-Spangled Banner* in 1814, died.

1857 Fred Archer, English champion jockey, born in Prestbury, Gloucestershire.

1864 Charing Cross railway station in London was formally opened.
Harry Gordon Selfridge, American merchant, born in Ripon,
Wisconsin.
1922 Leonard Thompson became the first diabetic patient treated with
insulin, administered at Toronto General Hospital.
1928 Thomas Hardy, English poet and novelist, notably *Tess of the
D'Urbervilles*, died in his native Dorset, aged 87.
1930 Rod Taylor, film actor in America and Europe, born in Sydney,
Australia.
1938 Arthur Scargill, trade unionist and President of the National
Union of Mineworkers, born.
1946 Albania was proclaimed a People's Republic, under General
Enver Hoxha.
1952 Ben Crenshaw, American international golfer, born.
1957 Bryan Robson, English international footballer, born.
1959 Cricketer Hanif Mohammad completed a record-breaking innings
of 499 at Karachi, Pakistan. His time at the crease totalled ten
hours 40 minutes.
1963 The first disco, called the 'Whisky-a-go-go', opened in Los
Angeles.
1974 The first sextuplets to survive were born, to Mrs Sue Rosen-
kowitz in Cape Town, South Africa.
1982 Steve Davis scored the maximum break of 147, televised in the
Lada Snooker Classic at Oldham.
1988 Isidor Rabi, American physicist and Nobel laureate, died aged
89.

12 JANUARY   *[12]*

1628 Charles Perrault, French writer and collector of fairy tales, born
in Paris.
1729 Edmund Burke, British statesman, orator and political writer,
born in Dublin.
1737 John Hancock, American patriot and politician, born in Quincy,
Massachusetts.
1746 Johann Pestalozzi, Swiss teacher and educational reformer, born
in Zurich.
1852 Joseph Joffre, French Army marshal and commander-in-chief on
the Western Front, born in Rivesaltes.
1864 Lancashire County Cricket Club was founded in Manchester.
1876 Jack London, American novelist, notably *Call of the Wild*, born in
San Francisco.
1893 Hermann Goering, German Nazi leader and creator of the
Luftwaffe, born in Rosenheim, Bavaria.
1896 Tommy Handley, English comedian, born in Liverpool.

1897 Sir Isaac Pitman, English inventor of a phonetic shorthand system of writing in 1837, died in Somerset aged 84.
1899 Paul Müller, Swiss chemist who formulated the insecticide DDT, born.
1907 Tex Ritter, American singing cowboy of stage and screen, born in Murvaul, Texas as Woodward Maurice Ritter.
1912 Luise Rainer, American film actress and Oscar winner, born in Vienna, Austria.
1916 Pieter Botha, South African statesman and President, born in Paul Roux in the Orange Free State.
1940 Bob Hewitt, international tennis player, born in Sydney, Australia.
1947 Joe Frazier, American world heavyweight boxing champion, born.
1948 The first full-size supermarket in Britain was opened—the London Co-op at Manor Park.
      Brendan Foster, British middle-distance athlete, born.
1950 The British submarine *Truculent* sank in a Thames collision, with the loss of 65 lives.
1952 John Walker, New Zealand middle-distance athlete, Olympic gold medallist and record holder, born in Papukura.
1956 Nel Tarleton, British featherweight boxing champion, died.
1960 Nevil Shute, English novelist, author of *A Town like Alice*, died.
1970 A Boeing 747 jumbo-jet touched down at Heathrow Airport after its first transatlantic proving flight from New York.
1976 Dame Agatha Christie, English mystery story writer and creator of the Belgian detective Hercule Poirot, died.

13 JANUARY   [13]

1691 George Fox, English religious leader and founder of the Society of Friends, commonly called the 'The Quakers', died in London.
1864 Stephen Foster, American composer of minstrel songs and popular ballads, died in New York an alcoholic, in poverty and obscurity.
1884 Sophie Tucker, American singer and vaudeville star, born in Russia as Sophia Abuza.
1904 Richard Addinsell, English composer of music for films, notably the *Warsaw Concerto* for the film *Dangerous Moonlight*, born.
1918 Lord Ted Willis, English scriptwriter for television and films, born.
1919 Robert Stack, American film and TV actor, known for his portrayal of Eliot Ness, born in Los Angeles.
1929 Wyatt Earp, American marshal famous for law enforcement by the use of a gun, died aged 80.
1941 James Joyce, Irish novelist, author of *Ulysses*, died in Zurich.

1969 Stephen Hendry, British snooker champion, born in Scotland.
1978 Hubert Humphrey, US senator, Democratic Party leader and vice-President to Lyndon Johnson from 1965 to 1969, died.
1979 John Spencer scored the maximum break of 147 at Slough in Berkshire, the first in a major snooker tournament, although the table had oversized pockets.

14 JANUARY   [14]

1741 Benedict Arnold, American general and traitor during the American Revolution, born in Norwich, Connecticut.
1742 Edmond Halley, English astronomer and Astronomer Royal, died in Greenwich aged 85.
1847 Wilson Carlile, English clergyman and founder of the Church Army, born in Buxton, Derbyshire.
1858 Felice Orsini, an Italian revolutionary, led an unsuccessful attempt on Napoleon III's life in Paris—an act for which he and another were executed.
1875 Albert Schweitzer, French medical missionary, born in Kaysersberg, Upper Alsace, the son of a Lutheran pastor.
1876 Essex County Cricket Club was formed at a meeting in The Shire Hall, Chelmsford.
1886 Hugh Lofting, American writer of children's stories, born in Maidenhead, England.
1897 Aconcagua (22 834ft/6960m), Argentina, the highest peak in the western hemisphere, was first climbed by William Martin, Baron Conway of Allington, a British mountaineer and art critic.
1898 Lewis Carroll, English writer, author of *Alice in Wonderland*, died in Guildford, Surrey.
1904 Cecil Beaton, English photographer and theatrical designer, born in London.
1906 Nel Tarleton, British featherweight boxing champion, born.
1937 The first Gallup opinion poll in Britain took place, conducted by Dr Henry Durant.
1941 Faye Dunaway, American film actress and Oscar winner for *Network* (1976), born in Bascom, Florida.
1943 The Casablanca Conference, between President Roosevelt and Winston Churchill, began—ended on 26th.
1953 Tito assumed office as President of the Republic of Yugoslavia.
1957 Humphrey Bogart, American film actor and Acadamy Award (Oscar) winner in 1951 for his part in *The African Queen*, died.
1965 Jeanette MacDonald, American singer and film actress with Nelson Eddy, died.
1972 Queen Margrethe II acceded to the throne of Denmark, in succession to her father King Frederick IX.

1977 Peter Finch, English film actor and posthumous Oscar winner for his part in *Network*, died in Los Angeles.
Sir Anthony Eden—Earl of Avon, British statesman and Conservative Prime Minister from 1955 to 1957, died aged 79.

1980 André Kostelanetz, American international conductor, died.

---

15 JANUARY [15]

1559 The coronation of Queen Elizabeth I took place.

1622 Molière, French dramatist, born in Paris as Jean Baptiste Poquelin, the son of an upholsterer.

1759 The British Museum at Montague House in Bloomsbury, London, was opened to the public.

1797 The top hat first appeared in London, worn by haberdasher James Hetherington, an act for which he was fined £50.

1815 Emma, Lady Hamilton, mistress of Lord Nelson, died in Calais in poverty.

1880 The first telephone directory in Britain was published, by the London Telephone Company, with 255 names.

1893 Ivor Novello, British actor, playwright and composer, born in Cardiff as David Ivor Davies.

1898 Uffa Fox, English yachtsman, born in Cowes on the Isle of Wight.

1906 Aristotle Onassis, Greek ship-owner, born in Smyrna, Turkey.

1909 Gene Krupa, American drummer and bandleader, born in Chicago, Illinois.

1913 The first sickness benefit (10 shillings per week), unemployment benefit (7 shillings) and maternity benefit (30 shillings) were introduced in Britain.

1918 Gamal Nasser, Egyptian statesman and his country's first President, born in Alexandria.

1926 Chuck Berry, American singer and songwriter, born in San Jose, California.

1929 Martin Luther King, American clergyman and Negro civil rights leader, born in Atlanta, Georgia.

1943 The Pentagon, headquarters of the US Department of Defense, in Arlington County on the Virginia side of the Potomac River, was completed.

1951 Sir Ernest Swinton, British soldier, inventor and one of the originators of the military tank, died.

1964 Jack Teagarden, American trombonist and orchestra leader, died.

1971 ½p, 1p and 2p decimal coins were issued in Britain.
The Aswan High Dam on the Nile, built with Soviet finance and technological assistance, was opened by Presidents Sadat and Podgorny.

1988 Sean MacBride, Irish politician, human rights advocate and Nobel Peace Prize winner, died aged 83.

---

16 JANUARY   *[16]*

1547 Ivan the Terrible, the first Russian to assume the title of 'Tsar', was crowned.
1794 Edward Gibbon, English historian and author of *The Decline and Fall of the Roman Empire*, died.
1809 The Battle of Corunna took place, in which the British won a rearguard action against the French under Nicolas Soult during the Peninsular War.
Sir John Moore, British Commander, was killed during the above battle at Corunna.
1851 Sir William Hall-Jones, New Zealand Liberal statesman, born in Folkestone, England.
1853 André Michelin, French tyre manufacturer, born in Paris.
1886 Amilcare Ponchielli, Italian composer of operas, notably *La Gioconda*, died.
1891 Léo Delibes, French composer, notably of ballet music including *Coppelia*, died in Paris.
1906 Diana Wynyard, British actress, born as Dorothy Cox.
1908 Baden-Powell's fortnightly magazine *Scouting for Boys* first appeared in the shops.
1909 Ethel Merman, American singer in Broadway musicals, born in Astoria, New York as Ethel Zimmerman.
The Shackleton expedition located the magnetic South Pole.
1919 The Eighteenth Amendment to the US Constitution was ratified, prohibiting the sale of intoxicating liquors, effective after one year.
1920 Prohibition came into force in America, ratified by the 18th amendment to the Constitution—was repealed by the 21st amendment on 5 December 1933.
1929 The British periodical *The Listener* was first published.
1948 Cliff Thorburn, Canadian snooker player and a world champion, born.
1957 Arturo Toscanini, Italian-born conductor and musical director, died in New York aged 89.
The Royal Ballet—the title by which The Sadler's Wells Ballet, Sadler's Wells Theatre Ballet and The Sadler's Wells School were incorporated.

1612   Thomas Fairfax, English commander of the Parliamentary Army in the Civil War, born in Denton, Yorkshire.

1706   Benjamin Franklin, American statesman, scientist and writer, born in Boston, Massachusetts, the 15th of 17 children.

1773   Captain Cook's ship *Resolution* became the first to cross the Antarctic circle.

1820   Anne Brontë, English novelist and youngest of the 3 literary sisters, born in Thornton, Yorkshire.

1860   Anton Chekhov, Russian dramatist, notably *The Cherry Orchard*, and short-story writer, born in Taganrog, the son of a shopkeeper.

1863   David Lloyd George, British Liberal statesman and Prime Minister, born in Manchester.

1871   David, Earl Beatty, British admiral and fleet commander in World War I, born in Nantwich, Cheshire.

1874   The original Siamese twins, Chang and Eng Bunker, died within three hours of each other, aged 62.

1880   Mack Sennet, film director in America, born in Richmond in the Canadian province of Quebec as Michael Sinnott.

1883   Compton Mackenzie, British writer, born in West Hartlepool as Edward Montague Compton, the older brother of actress Fay Compton.

1893   Rutherford Hayes, American Republican statesman and 19th President from 1877 to 1881, died in Fremont, Ohio.

1899   Al Capone, American gangster and racketeer in Chicago, born in Naples, Italy.
      Nevil Shute, English novelist, born in Ealing, Greater London as Nevil Shute Norway.

1911   Sir Francis Galton, English anthropologist and writer on heredity and eugenics, died aged 88.

1918   Sir Keith Joseph, British politician and minister, born.

1926   Moira Shearer, British ballerina, born in Dunfermline, Scotland as Moira King, the daughter of a civil engineer.
      Clyde Walcott, West Indian Test cricketer, born in Bridgetown, the capital of Barbados.

1928   Vidal Sassoon, English hair stylist, born in London.

1942   Muhammad Ali, American heavyweight boxing champion, born in Louisville, Kentucky as Cassius Clay.

1961   Ex-Premier Lumumba of independent Congo was murdered in Katanga.

1977   Gary Gilmore was executed by a firing squad at the Utah State prison, thus ending a ten-year suspension of capital punishment in the US.

1983   Breakfast television started in Britain.

1778 Captain Cook discovered Hawaii (originally known as the Sandwich Islands).

1849 Sir Edmund Barton, Australian statesman and the country's first Prime Minister in 1901, born in Glebe, Sydney.

1862 John Tyler, American Whig statesman and 10th President from 1841 to 1845, died in Richmond, Virginia.

1871 In the Hall of Mirrors at Versailles William I of Prussia was proclaimed the first Emperor of Germany—Deutscher Kaiser.

1879 The first England v Wales football international was played at Kennington Oval in London—England winning 2-1.

1882 A. A. Milne, English writer of children's books and creator of 'Winnie-the-Pooh', born at St John's Wood in London.

1892 Oliver Hardy, American comedian of Laurel and Hardy cinema fame, born in Atlanta, Georgia.

1904 Cary Grant, American film actor, born in Bristol, England as Alexander Archibald Leach.

1911 US pilot Eugene Ely, in a Curtiss aircraft, made the first landing on the deck of a ship, the cruiser *Pennsylvania* moored in San Francisco Bay.

1912 British explorer Captain Scott reached the South Pole with Lawrence Oates, Lieutenant Bowers, Edward Wilson and Edgar Evans—only to find that Amundsen had arrived 35 days earlier—all five died on the return journey.

1913 Danny Kaye, American comedy film actor, born in Brooklyn, New York as David Daniel Kaminsky.

1933 David Bellamy, English botanist and broadcaster, born.

1936 Rudyard Kipling, English poet and novelist and Nobel Prize winner in 1907, died.

1943 Leningrad was relieved, having been besieged by the Germans for sixteen months.

1954 Sydney Greenstreet, British actor remembered in the film *The Maltese Falcon*, died.

1963 Hugh Gaitskell, British statesman and leader of the Parliamentary Labour Party from 1955 to 1963, died.

1972 The first plastic warship, minehunter HMS *Wilton*, was launched at Southampton.

1977 In the worst rail disaster in Australian history 82 people died when a Sydney-bound train was derailed.

1980 Cecil Beaton, English photographer and theatrical designer, died.

1736 James Watt, Scottish engineer and inventor, born in Greenock.

1785 The first balloon ascent in Ireland was made, in Dublin's Ranelagh Gardens.

1798 Auguste Comte, French philosopher, social reformer and founder of modern sociology, born in Montpellier.

1807 Robert E. Lee, American general and Confederate Army commander-in-chief in the Civil War, born in Stratford, Virginia.

1809 Edgar Allan Poe, American writer, best known for his macabre stories and poems, born in Boston, Massachusetts of theatrical parents.

1813 Sir Henry Bessemer, English metallurgist and inventor of a blast furnace method for converting cast iron into steel, born in Charlton, Hertfordshire.

1833 Louis Herold, French composer, noted for his *Zampa Overture*, died in Les Ternes, France.

1839 Paul Cézanne, French artist, born at Aix-en-Provence in the south of France.

1848 Matthew Webb, the first English Channel swimmer, was born in Dawley, Shropshire, the son of a doctor.

1915 The first casualties were sustained in an air raid over Britain, when bombs were dropped on Great Yarmouth in Norfolk by the German L3 Zeppelin.

1922 Arthur Morris, Australian Test cricketer, born.

1938 Phil Everly, American pop singer with his elder brother Don, born in Brownie, Kentucky.

1942 Michael Crawford, British comedy actor, born in Salisbury, Wiltshire as Michael Dumble-Smith.

1946 Dolly Parton, American 'country and western' singer and entertainer, born in Sevierville, Tennessee.

1966 Mrs Indira Gandhi became Prime Minister of India, following in the footsteps of her father, Jawaharlal Nehru.
Stefan Edberg, the Swedish winner of the 1988 Wimbledon men's singles title, born in Vastervik.

20 JANUARY [20]

Terms of office of US President and Vice-President end at noon.

1779 David Garrick, English actor and theatre manager, died, and was buried in Westminster Abbey.

1805 The London docks were opened.

1837 Sir John Soane, English architect notably responsible for the design of the Bank of England building in Threadneedle Street, died in London.

1841 Hong Kong ceded by China, in what they term the 'Unequal Treaties', after the Opium Wars was first occupied by Britain. Hong Kong island plus Kowloon is technically owned by UK (since ceded to us) but 'New Territories', the bulk of the area of the colony, where the water supplies are, is only leased; lease runs out in 1997, so UK has agreed to hand back all the Hong Kong colony in that year.

1875 Jean François Millet, French painter of rural scenes, notably *The Gleaners*, died.

1886 The Mersey Railway tunnel was formally opened at James Street station by the Prince of Wales.

1892 The game of basketball, devised by Canadian doctor James Naismith, was first played at the YMCA in Springfield, Massachusetts.

1896 George Burns, American comedy actor, born in New York City as Nathan Birnbaum.

1900 John Ruskin, English art and social critic, died near Coniston in the Lake District, aged 80.

1910 Canberra officially became the capital of Australia.

1914 Roy Plomley, creator of *Desert Island Discs*, was born. Started his career as a copywriter for an advertising agency, became actor then an announcer with French-based commercial radio station. Appointed OBE in 1975.

1920 Federico Fellini, Italian film director, born in Rimini.

1924 Slim Whitman, American pop singer, born.

1926 Patricia Neal, American film actress and Oscar winner, born in Packard, New York.

1930 Edwin 'Buzz' Aldrin, American astronaut and the second man to set foot on the moon, born in Glen Ridge, New Jersey.

1936 Death of King George V at Sandringham in Norfolk, aged 70—accession of his eldest son as Edward VIII.

1937 Franklin D. Roosevelt began his record 4th term of office.

1961 John F. Kennedy, American Democrat statesman, was inaugurated as the 35th President—the first Roman Catholic.

1981 Ronald Reagan, American Republican statesman, was inaugurated as the 40th President—at 69, the oldest to take such office.

1984 Johnny Weissmuller, American champion swimmer and actor noted for his role as Tarzan, died in Acapulco.

1987 Terry Waite, the Archbishop of Canterbury's special envoy in the Middle East, disappeared on a peace mission in Beirut.

1793 Louis XVI, King of France since 1774, was guillotined in the Place de la Révolution after being found guilty of treason; the executioner was named Sanson.

1824 Thomas Jonathan Jackson, American soldier and Confederate general, called 'Stonewall', born in Clarksburg, West Virginia.

1892 John Couch Adams, English astronomer associated with the discovery of the planet Neptune, died.

1901 Elisha Gray, American inventor who claimed to have invented the telephone, died.

1905 Christian Dior, French designer, born in Granville.

1911 The first Monte Carlo Rally was held, won seven days later by Henri Rougier from France.

1924 Lenin, Soviet Communist leader and founder of Bolshevism, died of a brain haemorrhage at Gorki outside Moscow.

1925 Benny Hill, English comedian, born in Southampton.

1927 Telly Savalas, American film actor, best known as 'Kojak', born in Garden City, New York.

1928 George Washington Goethals, American and chief engineer of the Panama Canal, died.

1940 Jack Nicklaus, American international golf champion, affectionately called 'The Golden Bear', born in Columbus, Ohio.

1941 Placido Domingo, Spanish international operatic tenor, born in Madrid.

1950 George Orwell, British writer, notably *Animal Farm* and *Nineteen Eighty-four*, died.

1954 *Nautilus*, the first US nuclear submarine, was launched at Groton in Connecticut.

1955 Peter Fleming, American international tennis player and champion, born.

1959 Cecil B. De Mille, American film producer and director, died.

1976 'Concorde' airliner entered supersonic service with simultaneous take-offs, from London to Bahrain and Paris to Rio de Janeiro.

1988 Microlight pilot Brian Milton touched down in Darwin, Australia 51 days after leaving London dockland in his 440c.c. aircraft *Dalgety Flyer*.

22 JANUARY *[22]*

1561 Francis Bacon, English statesman, essayist and philosopher, born at York House in London's Strand.

1775 André Ampère, French mathematician, physicist and founder of
the study of electromagnetics, born in Lyons, the son of a rich
merchant.

1778 Lord Byron, English Romantic poet, born in London.

1875 David Wark Griffith, American film producer and director, born
in Floydsfork, Kentucky.

1887 Sir Joseph Whitworth, English mechanical engineer who stand-
ardised screw threads, died in Monte Carlo.

1901 Death of Queen Victoria at Osborne House on the Isle of Wight,
aged 81—the longest lived and longest reigning of all British
monarchs, having reigned for over 63 years—accession of her
eldest son as Edward VII.

1905 'Bloody Sunday', the massacre by troops of St Petersburg
workers led by Priest Georgi Gapon.

1907 Dixie Dean, the legendary English footballer, born in Birkenhead
on Merseyside as William Ralph Dean.

1909 U Thant, diplomat and later Secretary-General of the United
Nations, born in Pantanaw, Burma.

1912 Ann Sothern, American film actress, born in Valley City, North
Dakota, as Harriette Lake.

1920 Sir Alf Ramsey, English international footballer and manager,
born.

1924 Ramsay MacDonald took office as Britain's first Labour Prime
Minister—on the resignation of Stanley Baldwin.

1927 The Football League game between Arsenal and Sheffield United
was the first to be broadcast.

1934 Bill Bixby, American film actor, born in San Francisco.

1941 Tobruk, a harbour and small town in Libya, was captured by
British and Allied forces.

1944 The Allied Army landings at Anzio in Italy began.

1948 George Foreman, American heavyweight boxing champion, born
in Marshall, Texas.

1959 Mike Hawthorn, British motor racing driver and world champion
in 1958, was killed in a motor accident near Guildford.

1973 Lyndon Johnson, American Democrat statesman and 36th
President from 1963 to 1969, died of a heart attack in San
Antonio, Texas.
George Foreman became world heavyweight boxing champion,
beating Joe Frazier in a second-round knockout in Kingston,
Jamaica, on his 25th birthday.

1978 Herbert Sutcliffe, Yorkshire and England opening batsman, died
aged 83 in a nursing home in Crosshills.

1556 An earthquake took place in the Shensi Province of China, killing an estimated 830 000 people.

1571 The Royal Exchange in London, founded by financier Sir Thomas Gresham as a bankers' meeting house, was opened.

1622 William Baffin, British navigator and explorer who searched for the North-west Passage and gave his name to Baffin Island and Baffin Bay, died.

1783 Stendhal, French novelist, born in Grenoble as Marie Henri Beyle.

1806 William Pitt the Younger, British Tory statesman and Prime Minister on two occasions, first when only 25, died in Putney, Greater London, and was buried in Westminster Abbey.

1832 Edouard Manet, French painter and printmaker, born in Paris.

1849 Elizabeth Blackwell, born in Bristol, UK, graduated from The Medical School of Geneva, New York State, to become the first woman doctor.

1875 Charles Kingsley, English clergyman and novelist, author of *Westward Ho!* and *The Water Babies* died in London.

1879 The stand made by a handful of British soldiers at Rorke's Drift in the Zulu War ended. Eleven V.C.s were awarded for the action.

1899 Lord Denning, British judge and Master of the Rolls, born.

1903 Randolph Scott, American film actor, born in Orange County, Virginia as Randolph Crance.

1930 Mervyn Rose, Australian international tennis player, born in Coffs Harbour, New South Wales.

1931 Anna Pavlova, Russian prima ballerina famous as the 'Dying Swan', died in The Hague.

1933 The Twentieth Amendment to the US Constitution was ratified, outlining the office terms of the President, Vice-President, Senators and Representatives.

1941 Nylon was first produced in Britain, at Coventry.

1956 Sir Alexander Korda, Hungarian-born film producer and a major figure in the British film industry, died in London.

1960 The US Navy bathyscaphe *Trieste*, manned by Dr Piccard and Lt Walsh, reached a record depth of 35 820 feet in the Challenger Deep of the Marianas Trench in the Pacific Ocean.

1964 The Twenty-fourth Amendment to the US Constitution was ratified, barring poll tax in Federal elections.

1968 The USS *Pueblo* and an 83-man crew were seized by the North Koreans in the Sea of Japan.

1976 Paul Robeson, American Negro bass baritone singer of stage and films, died.

1978 Jack Oakie, American comedy film actor, died.

1712 Frederick the Great, Prussian king and military leader, born in Berlin.

1732 Pierre Beaumarchais, French playwright, best known for *The Barber of Seville* and *The Marriage of Figaro*, born in Paris as Pierre Augustin Caron, the son of a watchmaker.

1749 Charles James Fox, British Whig statesman and brilliant orator, born in London.

1818 John Mason Neale, English churchman and hymn writer, born in London.

1848 Gold was first discovered in California, at Sutter's Mill near Coloma, by James Marshall.

1895 Lord Randolph Churchill, British statesman and Conservative Party leader, died.

1917 Ernest Borgnine, American film actor and Oscar winner in 1955, born in Hamden, Connecticut as Ermes Borgnino.

1935 Beer in cans was first sold, in Richmond, Virginia, by the Krueger Brewing Company.
Bamber Gascoigne, English author and TV presenter, born in London.

1941 Neil Diamond, American singer and songwriter, born in Brooklyn, New York.

1965 Death of Sir Winston Churchill aged 90—exactly 70 years after his father's death—was buried in Bladon Churchyard, within view of Blenheim Palace, his birthplace.

1975 Dr Donald Coggan was enthroned as the 101st Archbishop of Canterbury, succeeding Michael Ramsey.

1978 An orbiting Russian satellite crashed near Yellow Knife, North West Territory, Canada.

25 JANUARY   *[25]*

Burns night.

1533 King Henry VIII and Anne Boleyn were secretly married by the Bishop of Lichfield—to become the parents of the future Queen Elizabeth I.

1627 Robert Boyle, Irish chemist and physicist, born at Lismore Castle in Munster in the Republic of Ireland.

1759 Robert Burns, Scottish poet, born in Alloway near Ayr, Ayrshire, the son of a poor farmer.

1874 W. Somerset Maugham, British novelist and short-story writer, born in Paris.

1882 Virginia Woolf, English novelist, notably *To the Lighthouse*, and playwright, born in London as Virginia Stephen.

1895 The first hockey international took place at Rhyl, with Ireland beating the hosts Wales by three goals to nil.

1917 USA purchased the Virgin Islands, formerly the Danish West Indies, for 25 million dollars.

1924 The First Winter Olympics were inaugurated at Chamonix in the French Alps.

1947 Al Capone, American gangster and leader of organised crime in Chicago during Prohibition, died as a result of a massive brain haemorrhage—and virtually penniless.

1954 Kim Hughes, Australian Test cricketer, born.

1971 Idi Amin became President of Uganda, deposing Milton Obote while he was absent abroad.

1980 *QE 2* became the largest liner to pass through the Panama Canal.

---

26 JANUARY [26]

National day of both Australia and India.

1788 The first consignment of convicts from England arrived in Australia, at Sydney Cove.

1823 Edward Jenner, English physician and pioneer in vaccination, died in Berkeley, Gloucestershire.

1828 The Duke of Wellington became Tory Prime Minister.

1837 Michigan, the Wolverine or Great Lake State, became the 26th state of the Union.

1871 The Rugby Football Union was founded in England, in London by 20 clubs.

1880 Douglas MacArthur, American general and commander in SW Pacific, born near Little Rock in Arkansas.

1885 General Gordon, British commander and Governor of the Sudan, was killed by a spear flung by a Muslim soldier while besieged at Khartoum.

1905 The Cullinan diamond, weighing over 1¼ pounds, was found at the Premier Mine in Pretoria, South Africa, by Captain Wells.
Cardinal Heenan, Roman Catholic Archbishop of Westminster, born.

1907 Henry Cotton, English golf champion, born in Holmes Chapel, Cheshire.

1908 The 1st Glasgow Boy Scout Troop was registered, to become the first such troop.

1913 Jimmy Van Heusen, American composer of film and stage scores, born in Syracuse, New York.

1922 Michael Bentine, British actor and comedian, born in Watford, Hertfordshire.

1925 Paul Newman, American film actor, born in Cleveland, Ohio.
1928 Eartha Kitt, American international singer and actress, born in North, South Carolina.
1950 India became a democratic Republic within the Commonwealth.
1956 The 7th Winter Olympic Games were opened at Cortina d'Ampezzo, Italy.
1961 Wayne Gretzky, North American ice hockey league star with Canadian team Edmonton Oilers, born.
1973 Edward G. Robinson, Hungarian-born American film actor, usually in gangster roles, died aged 79.
1979 Nelson Rockefeller, American Republican politician, Governor of New York and vice-President to Gerald Ford, died.

---

27 JANUARY [27]

1731 Bartolommeo Cristofori, Italian harpsichord maker who developed the first pianos about 1710, died in Florence.
1756 Wolfgang Amadeus Mozart, Austrian composer, born in Salzburg, the son of a musician.
1832 Lewis Carroll, English mathematician and children's book author, notably *Alice in Wonderland*, born at the vicarage in Daresbury near Warrington as Charles Lutwidge Dodgson, the first son of a family of 12.
1859 Kaiser Wilhelm II born in Potsdam near Berlin, the son of the German Emperor and the grandson of Queen Victoria.
1885 Jerome Kern, American composer for Broadway musicals and films, born in New York City.
1901 Giuseppe Verdi, Italian opera composer, notably *La Traviata* and *Il Trovatore*, died in Milan aged 87.
1903 Sir John Eccles, Australian physiologist and Nobel Prize winner in that field, born in Melbourne.
1926 Scottish inventor John Logie Baird gave the first public demonstration of true television, to members of the Royal Institution in his workshop in Soho, London.
1938 Jack Sharp, double English cricket and football international, died.
1943 The US Air Force made its first bombing raid on Germany.
1951 Carl Mannerheim, Finnish soldier, statesman and President who secured his country's independence from Russia, died aged 83.
1967 Queen Elizabeth conferred the knighthood on Francis Chichester at Greenwich, with Sir Francis Drake's sword.
    Fire occurred aboard the spacecraft *Apollo I* during the ground test at Cape Kennedy, killing Virgil Grissom, Edward White and Roger Chaffee.
1973 The Vietnam cease-fire agreement was signed.

1457 King Henry VII was born at Pembroke Castle—the founder of the Tudor dynasty.

1547 Death of King Henry VIII at Whitehall Palace aged 55—accession of his 9-year old son Edward VI.

1596 Sir Francis Drake, the most renowned seaman of the Elizabethan era, died of dysentery and was buried at sea off Porto Bello.

1725 Peter the Great, Tsar of Russia from 1682, died in St Petersburg.

1791 Louis Hérold, French composer of operas and ballets, born in Paris.

1833 General Gordon, British Army commander and administrator, born in Woolwich, Greater London.

1841 Sir Henry Stanley, British journalist and explorer, born in Denbigh, North Wales as John Rowlands.

1878 America's first commercial telephone switchboard exchange opened in New Haven, Connecticut.

1884 Auguste Piccard, Swiss deep-sea explorer and balloonist, born in Basle.
The first Ireland v Scotland football international took place in Belfast—Scotland ending as winners by five goals to nil.

1887 Artur Rubinstein, concert pianist in American, born in Lodz, Central Poland.

1912 Jackson Pollock, American abstract painter, born in Cody, Wyoming.

1935 A law was passed in Iceland legalising abortion on medical-social grounds, the first country to introduce such legislation.

1936 Alan Alda, American film actor and director, notably in *M.A.S.H.*, born in New York City.

1939 (William Butler) W. B. Yeats, Irish poet, playwright and Nobel Prize winner in 1923, died in the south of France.

1953 James Scullin, Australian Labour statesman and 13th Prime Minister from 1929 to 1932, died.

1965 Alfred Percy 'Tich' Freeman, Kent and England cricketer, died

1984 Canada's Kirk Stevens scored a televised maximum 147 snooker break at Wembley.

1986 The US space shuttle *Challenger* exploded shortly after lift off from Cape Canaveral, killing the five men and two women on board.

29 JANUARY [29]

1737 Thomas Paine, English social and political philosopher and pamphleteer, born in Thetford, Norfolk.

1782 Daniel Auber, French composer of operas, born in Caen.
1820 Death of George III at Windsor Castle aged 81—the longest lived and the longest-reigning British King—having reigned over 59 years. Accession of his son as George IV.
1843 William McKinley, American Republican statesman and 25th President, born in Niles, Ohio, the son of an iron manufacturer.
1850 Sir Ebenezer Howard, originator of the Garden City movement, born in London.
1856 The Victoria Cross, Britain's highest military decoration, was instituted by Queen Victoria.
1861 Kansas, the Sunflower State, became the 34th state of the Union.
1862 Frederick Delius, English composer, born in Bradford, Yorkshire.
1879 W. C. Fields, American comedy film actor, born in Philadelphia, Pennsylvania, as William Claude Dukenfield.
1886 The first successful petrol-driven car, built by Karl Benz, was patented.
1916 British military tanks had their first trials, at Hatfield in Hertfordshire.
     Victor Mature, American film actor, born in Louisville, Kentucky.
1928 Earl Haig, Army commander and founder of the British Legion in 1921, died in London and was buried at Dryburgh Abbey.
1939 Germaine Greer, Australian writer, born in Melbourne.
1942 *Desert Island Discs*, a BBC Radio 4 programme devised and presented by Roy Plomley until 11 May, 1985. He died 17 days later on 28 May. Each week a well-known person is interviewed and gives his or her choice of the eight records which he or she would most like to have as a castaway on a desert island. The first castaway was the comedian, Vic Oliver.
1950 Jody Scheckter, motor racing champion, born in South Africa.
1951 James Bridie (Osborne Henry Mavor), British playwright, died in Edinburgh aged 63.
1962 Fritz Kreisler, Austrian-born violin virtuoso, died in New York four days before his 87th birthday.
1964 Alan Ladd, American film actor, died.
     The 9th Winter Olympic Games were opened in Innsbruck, Austria.
1965 Jack Hylton, English dance-band leader and impresario, died in London.
1980 Jimmy Durante, American comedian and vaudeville performer, affectionately called 'Schnozzle', died aged 86.

30 JANUARY   [30]

1649 King Charles I died on the scaffold outside the Banqueting House of London's Whitehall Palace, having been convicted of treason; the executioner was Richard Brandon.

1790 The first purpose-built lifeboat, appropriately called *The Original*, was launched at South Shields on the River Tyne.
1857 The naval uniform for ratings in the Royal Navy was authorised.
1858 The Hallé Orchestra, Manchester, performed its first regular public concert.
1882 Franklin Delano Roosevelt, American Democrat statesman and 32nd President, born near Hyde Park, New York.
1888 Edward Lear, English artist and author, noted for his *Book of Nonsense*, died in San Remo, Italy.
1913 Percy Thrower, English gardener and broadcaster on the subject, born in Winslow, Buckinghamshire.
1931 Gene Hackman, American film actor and Oscar winner, born in San Bernardino, California.
1933 Adolf Hitler was appointed German Chancellor by President von Hindenburg.
1934 Frank Doubleday, American publisher and editor, died.
1937 Vanessa Redgrave, English film actress, born in London the daughter of Sir Michael.
Boris Spassky, Russian chessmaster and a world champion, born in Leningrad.
1948 Orville Wright, the younger of the two American airplane pioneers, died.
'Mahatma' Gandhi, Indian political and religious leader was assassinated in his own garden in New Delhi by a Hindu fanatic, Nathuran Vinayak Godse—ten days after a previous attempt on his life.
The 5th Winter Olympic Games were opened in St Moritz, Switzerland.
1965 The state funeral of Sir Winston Churchill took place—was buried in Bladon Churchyard, within view of Blenheim Palace, where he was born 90 years previously.
1972 'Bloody Sunday' in Londonderry in Northern Ireland, when 13 protest marchers were killed by British troops.
1982 Stanley Holloway, English actor and singer, best known for his role as Alfred Doolittle in *My Fair Lady*, died aged 91.

31 JANUARY [31]

1606 Guy Fawkes, English conspirator involved in the unsuccessful Gunpowder Plot to blow up the Parliament building, was executed.
1788 Bonnie Prince Charlie, leader of the Jacobite rebellion to depose King George II, died in Rome.
1797 Franz Schubert, Austrian composer, born near Vienna, the son of a schoolmaster.

1858 The five-funnelled 692 foot long *Great Eastern*, designed by Isambard Brunel and John Scott Russell, was eventually launched at Millwall, after three months of setbacks.

1868 Theodore Richards, American chemist, born in Germantown, Pennslyvania.

1875 Zane Grey, American writer of western novels, notably *Riders of the Purple Sage*, born in Zanesville, Ohio.

1880 The Sydney *Bulletin* was published for the first time.

1885 Anna Pavlova, Russian prima ballerina, born in St Petersburg.

1892 Eddy Cantor, American comedian and song-and-dance man, born in New York City as Edward Israel Iskowitz.

1903 Tallulah Bankhead, American actress, born in Huntsville, Alabama.

1910 Dr Crippen poisoned his wife Cora, for which he was executed at Pentonville on 23 November.

1914 Jersey Joe Walcott, American heavyweight boxing champion, born in Merchantville, New Jersey as Arnold Raymond Cream.

1915 Garry Moore, American TV personality, born in Baltimore as Thomas Garrison Morfit.

1921 Mario Lanza, American tenor singer and actor, born in Philadelphia as Alfredo Arnold Cocozza.

1923 Norman Mailer, American novelist and journalist, born in Long Branch, New Jersey.

1929 Jean Simmons, English film actress, born in London.
Leon Trotsky was exiled from Russia by Stalin, and found asylum in Mexico.

1931 Christopher Chataway, British athlete and later Conservative Member of Parliament, born.

1933 John Galsworthy, English novelist, noted for *The Forsyte Saga* and Nobel Prize winner in 1932, died.

1938 Queen Beatrix of the Netherlands born, the eldest daughter of Queen Juliana.

1947 Nolan Ryan, American baseball player and the fastest pitcher, born in Refugio, Texas. His fastest pitch was recorded at 100.9 mph.

1951 Sir C. B. Cochran, British theatrical producer, knighted in 1948, died.

1956 A. A. Milne, English writer of children's books, notably *Winnie-the-Pooh*, died in Hartfield, Sussex.

1958 America's first earth satellite, *Explorer I*, was launched by the Army at Cape Canaveral.

1971 *Apollo 14* was launched with Alan Shepard, Stuart Roosa and Edgar Mitchell—Shepard and Mitchell making the 3rd moon landing.

1974 Sam Goldwyn, Polish-born American film producer, died aged 91.

1983 In Great Britain the wearing of seat belts in cars became compulsory.

The partridge and pheasant shooting season ends.

1851 Mary Shelley, English novelist, best known as the author of *Frankenstein*, died.

1859 Victor Herbert, Irish-American conductor and composer of light opera, born in Dublin.

1895 John Ford, American director of action-adventure and western films, born in Cape Elizabeth, Maine, as Sean O' Feeney or O'Fearna.

1900 Stephen Potter, British writer of humorous books, born.

1901 Clark Gable, American film actor and Oscar winner for *It Happened One Night* (1934), born in Cadiz, Ohio, the son of an oil man.

1908 Carlos I, King of Portugal, was assassinated.

1911 HMS *Thunderer*, the last battleship built on the Thames, was launched from the old Thames Ironworks in Silvertown.

1915 Stanley Matthews, the legendary English footballer, born in Hanley, Staffordshire.
Passport photographs were first required in Britain.

1920 The North West Mounted Police changed their name to the Royal Canadian Mounted Police.

1930 *The Times* newspaper published its first crossword.

1937 Don Everly, American singer with his younger brother Phil, born in Brownie, Kentucky.

1941 The Air Training Corps, the junior branch of the Royal Air Force, was formed.

1949 The name of the Auxiliary Territorial Service (ATS) was changed to Women's Royal Army Corps (WRAC).

1957 The first turbo-prop airliner, the Bristol Britannia, entered into scheduled service in Britain.

1958 The State known as the United Arab Republic was formed by the union of Egypt and Syria.

1965 Prescriptions on the National Health Service became free of charge. A charge was re-introduced on 10 June 1968.

1966 Joseph Francis 'Buster' Keaton, American silent film comedian, died.

Candlemas—feast of the purification of the Virgin Mary.

1650 Nell Gwyn, English comic actress, favourite and mistress of Charles II, by whom she had two children, born as Eleanor Gwyn, the daughter of a fishwife.

1801 The Parliament of the United Kingdom of Great Britain and Ireland assembled for the first time.
1852 The first public flushing lavatory for men was opened in London's Fleet Street.
1864 Middlesex County Cricket Club was founded at a meeting in the London Tavern, Bishopsgate.
1875 Fritz Kreisler, Austrian-American violin virtuoso and composer, born in Vienna.
1876 The Welsh Football Association was formed.
1880 The first frozen meat imported into Britain, arrived in London from Sydney, aboard SS *Strathleven*.
1882 James Joyce, Irish novelist notably *Ulysses*, born in Dublin.
1901 Jascha Heifetz, violin virtuoso in America, born in Vilna, Russia.
1914 Cub Scouts were founded in England, in Robertsbridge, Sussex.
1918 John L. Sullivan, American boxer and world heavyweight champion from 1882 to 1892—the last bareknuckle champion—died.
1926 Giscard D'Estaing, French statesman and President, born.
1952 61905 spectators attended Liverpool's FA cup tie with Wolverhampton Wanderers, to create a club record.
1959 Buddy Holly, American singer, guitarist and major influence in early rock-and-roll, died aged 22.
1970 Bertrand Russell, British philosopher, mathematician and Nobel Prize winner in 1950, died aged 97.
1972 The British Embassy in Dublin was burnt down by besieging crowds.
1976 The Queen opened the 310-acre National Exhibition Centre at Bickenhill, Birmingham.
1986 Women voted for the first time in Liechtenstein.
1987 Alistair Maclean, Scottish novelist and writer of best sellers, died.

3 FEBRUARY   [34]

1399 John of Gaunt, Duke of Lancaster, fourth son of Edward III and father of King Henry IV, died.
1809 Felix Mendelssohn, German composer and pianist, born in Hamburg, the son of a banker.
1811 Horace Greeley, American newspaper editor and founder of *The New York Tribune*, born in Amherst, New Hampshire.
1821 Elizabeth Blackwell, English-American physician, the first woman in US to gain an MD degree, born in Bristol.
1913 The Sixteenth Amendment to the US Constitution was ratified, authorising the power to impose and collect taxes on incomes.
1919 The League of Nations held its first meeting, in Paris, with Woodrow Wilson as chairman.

1924 Woodrow Wilson, American Democrat statesman, 28th President from 1913 to 1921 and Nobel Prize winner, died, and was buried in Washington Cathedral.

1926 Shelley Berman, American stand-up comic and actor, born in Chicago.

1928 Frankie Vaughan, English singer and entertainer, born in Liverpool as Frank Abelson.

1929 Val Doonican, Irish singer and entertainer, born in Waterford in the Republic of Ireland.

1936 Bobby Simpson, Australian Test cricketer, born.

1960 Harold Macmillan made his 'wind of change' speech in Cape Town, South Africa.

1962 The liner *France* made her official maiden voyage, from Le Havre to New York City.

1966 The first 'soft' landing on the Moon was made by Russia's *Luna IX*, in the area of the Ocean of Storms.

1969 Boris Karloff, London-born American actor, best known for horror-film roles, died aged 81.

1972 The 11th Winter Olympic Games were opened in Sapporo, Japan.

4 FEBRUARY [35]

National day of Sri Lanka.

1881 Voroshilov, Russian Army marshal and political leader, born in the Ukraine.

1893 The first stretch of Liverpool's Overhead Railway—from Alexandra Dock to the Herculaneum Dock   was opened by Lord Salisbury.

1902 Charles Lindbergh, American aviator, noted for his historic solo flight across the Atlantic in 1927, born in Detroit, Michigan.

1912 Byron Nelson, American champion golfer, born in Fort Worth, Texas.

1918 Ida Lupino, English film actress, born in London.

1920 Norman Wisdom, English comedy actor, born as Norman Wisden.

1932 The 3rd Winter Olympic Games were opened in Lake Placid, New York.

1945 The Yalta Conference in the Crimea between Allied leaders Roosevelt, Churchill and Stalin, began.

1948 Ceylon became a self-governing dominion within the Commonwealth, having been a British Crown Colony since 1802. Alice Cooper, bizarre American rock singer, born in Detroit as Vince Furnier.

1953 Sweet rationing ended in Britain.

1962 *The Sunday Times* became the first British newspaper to issue a colour supplement.

Two Swiss climbers made the first winter ascent of the north face of the Matterhorn, on the Swiss-Italian border.

1976 Roger Livesey, British actor, died.

The 12th Winter Olympic Games were opened in Innsbruck, Austria.

1983 Karen Carpenter, sister of Richard in the pop singing duo 'The Carpenters', died.

1985 The border between Spain and Gibraltar was re-opened.

1987 Liberace, flamboyant American pianist, died.

The United States regained the America's Cup; *Stars and Stripes* beating the Australian challenger *Kookaburra III* off Perth.

5 FEBRUARY [36]

1788 Sir Robert Peel, British Tory statesman, Prime Minister and founder of the Metropolitan Police Force, born in Bury, Lancashire, the son of a cotton millionaire.

1811 The Prince of Wales became Prince Regent on the established insanity of George III.

1837 Dwight Moody, American evangelist, born in Northfield, Massachusetts.

1840 Sir Hiram Stevens Maxim, American inventor of the first fully automatic machine-gun, named after him, born in Sangersville, Maine.

John Boyd Dunlop, Scottish veterinary surgeon and patentee of the pneumatic bicycle tyre, born in Dreghorn, Ayrshire.

1881 Thomas Carlyle, Scottish essayist and historian, called the 'sage of Chelsea', died at 5 Cheyne Row in Chelsea aged 85.

1889 Patsy Hendren, Middlesex and England cricketer and England football international, born in Chiswick.

1900 Adlai Stevenson, American Democrat statesman, born in Los Angeles, California, the grandson of a vice-President.

1920 Frank Muir, British comedy writer and broadcaster, born.

Royal Air Force College at Cranwell opened and had its first intake of apprentices.

1924 The BBC 'pips' or time-signals from Greenwich Observatory, were heard for the first time. They are sent out by a clock, called the Mean Solar (sun) Time Clock. This is corrected frequently from another clock, which keeps sideral (star) time, and is itself corrected by observations of the stars. The actual sending of the signals is done automatically by a special mechanism in the clock. Signals are sent every fifteen minutes to the offices of the BBC, but are broadcast only every hour.

1934 Henry 'Hank' Aaron, American legendary baseball player, born in Mobile, Alabama.
1941 Andrew 'Banjo' Paterson, Australian journalist and poet who adapted *Waltzing Matilda* from a traditional ditty to become the country's premier national song, died.
1946 George Arliss, British stage and film actor and Academy Award (Oscar) winner in 1930 for the leading role in *Disraeli*, died aged 77.
1961 The British newspaper the *Sunday Telegraph* began publication.
1982 Laker Airways collapsed with debts of over £210 million.

---

6 FEBRUARY [37]

National day of New Zealand—Waitangi Day.

1564 Christopher Marlowe, English poet and dramatist notably *Doctor Faustus*, born in Canterbury, Kent, the son of a shoemaker.
1665 Queen Anne was born at St James's Palace, the second daughter of James II by his first wife Anne Hyde.
1685 Death of King Charles II, stricken with apoplexy—accession of his brother as James II.
1783 Lancelot Brown known as 'Capability' Brown, English landscape gardener, noted especially for the gardens at Blenheim and Kew, died.
1788 Massachusetts, the Bay State, became the 6th state of the Union.
1802 Sir Charles Wheatstone, English physicist and pioneer of telegraphy, born in Gloucester.
1804 Joseph Priestley, English clergyman and chemist who discovered oxygen, died in Northumberland, Pennsylvania.
1838 Sir Henry Irving, English actor, born in Keinton Mandeville, Somerset as John Henry Brodribb, the son of a shopkeeper.
1840 The Treaty of Waitangi was concluded by Captain Hobson, between Britain and the Maori chiefs of New Zealand—proclaiming British sovereignty and protection.
1895 'Babe' Ruth, the legendary American baseball player, born in Baltimore, Maryland as George Herman Ruth.
1899 Ramon Novarro, Mexican-US actor, born in Durango as Ramon Samaniegos.
1911 Ronald Reagan, American Republican statesman and 40th President, born in Tampico, Illinois.
1918 A Parliamentary candidature deposit of £150 was introduced in Britain.
Women were first permitted to vote in elections to the Parliament at Westminster—their first vote actually came in the General Election on 14 December 1918.

34

1924 Billy Wright, English footballer and international with 105 caps, born in Ironbridge, Shropshire.
1931 Fred Trueman, Yorkshire and England cricketer, born in Scotch Springs.
1936 The 4th Winter Olympic Games were opened in Garmisch-Partenkirchen, Germany.
1950 Natalie Cole, American singer, born in Los Angeles, the daughter of Nat King Cole.
1952 Death of King George VI at Sandringham aged 56—accession of his daughter as Elizabeth II.
1958 Manchester United lost eight of their players when the aircraft bringing the team home from Belgrade crashed on take-off at Munich airport—also killed were three club officials and eight sporting journalists.
1968 The 10th Winter Olympic Games were opened in Grenoble, France.

---

7 FEBRUARY [38]

1301 The first Prince of Wales was created—Edward of Caernarvon, who later became King Edward II.
1478 Sir Thomas More, English statesman and Lord Chancellor to Henry VIII, born in London, the son of a judge.
1812 Charles Dickens, English novelist notably *Bleak House*, born in Landport, Portsmouth, the son of a clerk in the Navy pay office.
1845 The Portland Vase, a 10-inch Roman dark blue cameo glass vessel, was smashed by a stone from a maniac, while on loan to the British museum—has been skilfully restored.
1870 Alfred Adler, Austrian psychiatrist pioneer, born in Vienna.
1878 Pope Pius IX died after reigning for over 31½ years—was succeeded by Leo XIII (Gioacchino Vincenzo Pecci).
1885 Sinclair Lewis, American novelist and Nobel Prize winner, born in Sauk Centre, Minnesota.
1912 Sir George Russell Drysdale, Australian artist, born in Bognor Regis, Sussex.
1924 Dora Bryan, English comedy actress, born as Dora Broadbent.
1959 Daniel Malan, South African politician and creator of his country's apartheid policy, died in Stellenbosch, Cape Province aged 84.
1974 Grenada, in the Windward Islands of the West Indies, became a fully independent state within the Commonwealth, with Eric Gairy its first Prime Minister—having been a British colony since 1783.
1984 Bruce McCandless, from *Challenger*, became the first to walk in space without being attached to his space craft.

1587 After nearly 19 years of confinement Mary, Queen of Scots was executed in the Great Hall of Fotheringhay Castle in Northamptonshire, for her implication in the Babington plot to overthrow Queen Elizabeth and restore Roman Catholicism in England.

1819 John Ruskin, English writer and art critic, born in Dulwich, Greater London, the son of a wine merchant.

1820 General William Sherman, American Union Army commander during the Civil War, born in Lancaster, Ohio.

1828 Jules Verne, French novelist and early exponent of science fiction, born in the seaport of Nantes.

1861 The Confederate States joined together to fight the American Civil War and chose Jefferson Davis as provisional President.

1888 Dame Edith Evans, English actress, especially Shakespearean roles, born in London.

1904 The Russo-Japanese War broke out—provoked by Russian penetration into Manchuria and Korea.

1910 The Boy Scout movement in America was founded by W. Boyce.

1920 Lana Turner, American film actress, called the original 'sweater girl', born in Wallace, Idaho as Julia Turner.

1924 The gas chamber was used for the first time in America—in the Nevada State Prison, Carson City—the victim was Gee Jon.

1925 Jack Lemmon, American film actor and Oscar winner for *Mister Roberts* (1955), born in Boston, Massachusetts.

1931 James Dean, American film actor, born in Marion, Indiana as James Byron.

1967 Sir Victor Gollancz, British writer and publisher, died.

1974 America's final Skylab mission, with Gerald Carr, Edward Gibson and William Pogue, returned after 84 days.

1984 The 14th Winter Olympic Games were opened in Sarajevo, Yugoslavia.

1540 The first recorded horserace meeting in Britain was held, at the Roodeye Field, Chester—now called the Roodee.

1649 The funeral of King Charles I took place—was taken to his final resting place in the Garter Chapel in St George's, Windsor.

1773 William Henry Harrison, American Whig statesman and 9th President, born in Berkeley in Charles City County, Virginia.

1863 Anthony Hope, English novelist, author of *The Prisoner of Zenda*, born in London as Anthony Hope Hawkins.
1881 Fyodor Dostoyevsky, Russian novelist, died.
1891 Ronald Colman, film actor in America and Oscar winner, born in Richmond, England.
1894 Adolphe Saxe, Belgian musical instrument maker and designer of the saxophone, died in Paris.
1897 Sir Charles Kingsford Smith, airman of distinction, born in Brisbane, Australia.
1909 Dean Rusk, American government official and Secretary of State, born in Cherokee County, Georgia.
1916 Military conscription was first effective in Britain.
1922 Jim Laker, Surrey and England cricketer, born in Frizinghall, West Yorkshire.
1923 Brendan Behan, Irish playwright, born in the Dublin slums.
     The Soviet State Airline was instituted, called 'Dobrolet'—was re-named 'Aeroflot' in 1932.
     Kathryn Grayson, American actress and singer in musical films, born in Winston-Salem, North Carolina as Zelma Hedrick.
1926 Dr Garret Fitzgerald, Irish statesman and Prime Minister, born in Dublin.
1942 Soap rationing began in Britain.
     The French passenger liner *Normandie* was gutted by fire in New York harbour. There was extensive damage but no loss of life.
1945 Mia Farrow, American film actress, born in Los Angeles, California, the daughter of Maureen O'Sullivan.
1958 Sandy Lyle, British golfer, born.
1969 The Boeing 747 jumbo-jet made its maiden flight. Entered service on 21 January 1970.
1981 Bill Haley, American rock and roll singer remembered for his *Rock around the clock*, died.
1983 Shergar, the 1981 Derby winner, was stolen from his stable in County Kildare.
1984 Yuri Andropov, Soviet leader, died after only 15 months in office, and was succeeded by Konstantin Chernenko.

10 FEBRUARY [41]

1567 Lord Darnley, second husband of Mary, Queen of Scots and father of James VI of Scotland and I of England, was murdered in the early hours of the morning at Kirk o' Field, a house near Edinburgh.
1763 Canada was ceded to Britain by the Peace of Paris.
1775 Charles Lamb, English essayist, born in the Temple, London, the son of a clerk.

1824 Samuel Plimsoll, British mercantile marine benefactor, born in Bristol.

1837 Alexander Pushkin, poet, novelist and a leading figure in Russian literature, was killed in a duel.

1840 Queen Victoria and Prince Albert were married in the Chapel Royal of St James's Palace, both aged 20.

1890 Boris Pasternak, Russian writer, author of *Dr Zhivago*, born in Moscow.

1893 Jimmy Durante, American vaudeville performer and comedian, born in New York City.
Bill Tilden, American international tennis player, born in Germantown, Pennsylvania.

1894 Harold Macmillan, British statesman and Conservative Prime Minister, born in London.

1910 Joyce Grenfell, English actress and broadcaster, born in London.

1912 Lord Lister, English surgeon and founder of antiseptic surgery, died in Walmer, Kent aged 84.

1914 Larry Adler, American harmonica player and composer, born in Baltimore, Maryland.

1923 Wilhelm Konrad von Röntgen, German physicist who discovered X-rays in 1895, died in Munich.

1932 Edgar Wallace, English writer, noted as an author of thrillers, died in Hollywood.

1939 Roberta Flack, American rock singer, born in Black Mountain, North Carolina.

1942 The first actual golden disc was presented to Glenn Miller, for *Chattanooga Choo Choo*. It was a disc sprayed with gold by RCA Victor.

1950 Mark Spitz, American swimmer and Olympic champion of distinction, born in Modesto, California.

1955 Greg Norman, Australian international golfing champion, born.

1964 The Australian destroyer *Voyager* sank after colliding with the Australian aircraft carrier *Melbourne* off New South Wales, with the loss of 82 lives.

1966 Sophie Tucker, American singer known as 'the last of the red hot mammas', died aged 82.

1967 The Twenty-fifth Amendment to the US Constitution was ratified, dealing with Presidential disability and succession.

1984 Harold Macmillan was awarded an earldom. He chose the name of Stockton from the name of his first Parliamentary constituency in 1924.

1800 William Fox Talbot, English photographic pioneer, born in Evershot.

1847 Thomas Alva Edison, prolific American inventor, born in Milan, Ohio.

1852 The first public flushing lavatory for women was opened in London's Bedford Street. The cost of 'spending a penny' was 'tuppence'.

1858 Virgin Mary is said to have appeared to a peasant girl, Bernadette Soubirous in a grotto in Lourdes.

1868 Jean Foucault, French physicist, inventor of the gyroscope and first to measure the speed of light, died in Paris.

1878 The Meteorological Office published its first *Weekly weather report*.

1908 Sir Vivian Fuchs, English geologist and Antarctic explorer, born in Kent, the son of a farmer of German origin.

1909 Max Baer, American heavyweight boxer, born in Omaha, Nebraska.

1920 Farouk, the last King of Egypt, born in Cairo, the son of King Fuad I.

1924 Edward 'Budge' Patty, American tennis champion, born in Arkansas.

1928 The 2nd Winter Olympic Games were opened in St Moritz, Switzerland.

1929 Vatican City became an independent Papal State within the city of Rome by the Lateran Treaty, signed by Benito Mussolini and Pietro Gasparri.

1931 Sir Charles Parsons, English engineer and inventor of the first practical steam turbine in 1884, died in Kingston, Surrey.

1934 John Surtees, British motorcycle and motor racing champion, born.
Mary Quant, English fashion designer, including the miniskirt, born in Blackheath, London.

1936 Burt Reynolds, American film actor, born in Waycross, Georgia.

1937 Bill Lawry, Australian Test cricketer, born.

1940 John Buchan, Scottish novelist, (*The Thirty-Nine Steps* and others), latterly Governor-General of Canada, died.

1941 Sergio Mendes, Brazilian musician and arranger, born in Niteroi.

1945 The Yalta Conference, in the Crimea, of Allied leaders ended, at which the final defeat of Germany was planned, together with agreement on the founding of the United Nations.

1968 The current Madison Square Garden, situated over Pennsylvania station on New York's 7th Avenue, was opened.

1970 Japan launched her first earth satellite.

1976 Lee J. Cobb, American actor in films and television series, died.

1554   Lady Jane Grey, Queen of England for nine days, was executed on Tower Green for high treason.

1797   The last invasion of Britain occurred when the Irish-American General William Tate landed in Pembrokeshire on the coast of Wales with 1400 French troops, who subsequently surrendered.

1804   Immanuel Kant, German philosopher and idealist, died in Königsberg.

1809   Charles Darwin, English naturalist, born in Shrewsbury, Shropshire.
Abraham Lincoln, American Republican statesman and 16th President, born in a log cabin on a farm near Hodgenville in Hardin County, Kentucky, the son of a carpenter.

1818   Chile proclaimed independence from Spain after a revolutionary war led by San Martin and Bernardo O'Higgins.

1828   George Meredith, English novelist and poet, born in Portsmouth.

1851   The gold rush began in Australia, after Edward Hargraves made the discovery at Summerhill Creek, about 20 miles north of Bathurst in New South Wales.

1870   Marie Lloyd, English star of the music halls, born as Matilda Alice Victoria Wood.

1893   Omar Bradley, American general and commander, born in Clark, Missouri.

1915   Lorne Greene, film actor in America, born in Ottawa, Ontario, Canada.
Emile Waldteufel, French composer, notably of *The Skaters' Waltz*, died in Paris.

1929   Lillie Langtry, British actress and entertainer, died in Monte Carlo.

1935   Escoffier, famous French chef known as the 'King of Cooks', died aged 88.

1956   The first yellow 'no parking' lines in Britain were introduced, in Slough, Buckinghamshire.

1973   The first group of American prisoners was released from North Vietnam.

1986   The Channel Tunnel agreement was signed at Canterbury.

13 FEBRUARY [44]

1542   Catherine Howard, the fifth wife of Henry VIII, accused of adultery, was executed on Tower Green.

1689 William III of Orange and Mary, daugher of James II of England became joint sovereigns of Great Britain. William was born in The Hague.

1692 The Glencoe massacre took place in the Scottish Highlands, in which the MacDonalds were massacred by their traditional enemies, the Campbells—38 butchered bodies were later found in the glen.

1849 Lord Randolph Churchill, British Conservative statesman and father of Winston, born at Blenheim Palace in Woodstock, Oxfordshire.

1859 The Corps of Commissionaires was founded in London by Captain Sir Edward Walter, for the employment of ex-regular service men.

1873 Fyodor Chaliapin, Russian operatic bass singer of great power, born in Kazan.

1883 Richard Wagner, German opera composer, died in Venice.

1885 Elizabeth Truman, wife of America's 33rd President, born in Independence, Missouri as Elizabeth Wallace.

1903 Georges Simenon, Belgian detective story writer and creator of 'Maigret' of the Paris police, born in Liège as Georges Sim.

1923 Charles 'Chuck' Yeager, American pilot and first to fly at supersonic speed in 1947, born.

1933 Kim Novak, American film actress, born in Chicago, Illinois as Marilyn Novak.

1943 The Nuffield Foundation for research was established in London.

1958 Dame Christabel Pankhurst, British suffragette and daughter of Emmeline, died.

1974 Alexander Solzhenitsyn, Russian novelist and Nobel Prize winner in 1970, was expelled from the Soviet Union.

1980 The 13th Winter Olympic Games were opened in Lake Placid, New York.

1988 The 15th Winter Olympic Games were opened in Calgary, Alberta, Canada.

14 FEBRUARY [45]

St Valentine's Day. There were two possible St Valentines, both of whom were martyred in or around Rome in the 3rd century. The tradition of sending love letters on this day is more likely to be connected to the medieval belief that birds paired on this day.

1779 Captain Cook was stabbed to death by natives at Kealakekua Bay in the Sandwich Islands—now Hawaii.

1797 The naval Battle of St Vincent took place off SW Portugal, in which the British under Admiral Jervis defeated the Spanish fleet.

1819   Christopher Sholes, American inventor of the modern typewriter, born near Mooresburg, Pennsylvania.

1852   The first patient, Eliza Armstrong, was admitted to the Children's Hospital in Great Ormond Street, London.

1859   Oregon, the Beaver State, became the 33rd state of the Union.

1891   William Sherman, Union Army general and military commander in the American Civil War, died in New York City.

1894   Jack Benny, American comedian and actor, born in Chicago, Illinois as Benjamin Kubelsky.

1907   Johnny Longden, American jockey who rode 6032 winners, born in Wakefield, England.

1912   Arizona, the Apache State, became the 48th state of the Union.

1916   Jimmy Wilde of Wales, nicknamed the 'mighty atom', won the world flyweight boxing title, which he held for over seven years.

1929   The St Valentine's Day massacre took place in a warehouse in Chicago when seven members of Bugsy Moran's gang were gunned down.

1930   Sir Thomas Mackenzie, New Zealand statesman and Prime Minister for a short time in 1912, died.

1933   The first telephone speaking clock went into operation in the Paris area.

1938   The British naval base at Singapore opened.

1951   Kevin Keegan, English international footballer, born in Armthorpe, Yorkshire, the son of a miner.

1952   The 6th Winter Olympic Games were opened in Oslo, Norway.

1975   (Pelham Grenville) P. G. Wodehouse, English novelist and creator of the characters 'Bertie Wooster' and 'Jeeves', died aged 93.

---

15 FEBRUARY   [46]

1564   Galileo, Italian astronomer and physicist, born in Pisa as Galileo Galilei.

1809   Cyrus Hall McCormick, American inventor of the first mechanical crop reaper, born in Rockbridge County, Virginia.

1820   Susan Anthony, American social reformer and pioneer of Women's suffrage, born in Adams, Massachusetts.

1857   Mikhail Glinka, Russian composer, best known for his opera *Russlan and Ludmilla*, died in Berlin.

1874   Sir Ernest Shackleton, British Antarctic explorer, born in Kilkee, County Clare in the Republic of Ireland.

1878   Jack Sharp, an England double cricket and football international, born.

1882 The first shipment of frozen meat left New Zealand for England on SS *Dunedin*.
John Barrymore, American stage actor and star of the silent screen, born in Philadelphia as John Blythe, the younger brother of Lionel and Ethel.

1898 The US battleship *Maine*, sent to Havana on a goodwill tour, was blown up by a mine—resulting in the short Spanish-American War.

1922 The Permanent Court of International Justice held its first sitting at The Hague, in the Netherlands.

1928 Herbert Henry Asquith, British Liberal Party leader and Prime Minister from 1908 to 1916, died.

1929 Graham Hill, British international motor racing champion, born in London.

1931 Claire Bloom, English actress, born in London as Claire Blume.

1933 Italian immigrant and anarchist Giuseppe Zangara failed in his attempt to assassinate President Franklin D. Roosevelt in Miami's Bayfront Park.

1942 The British naval base of Singapore surrendered to the Japanese forces.

1952 The funeral of King George VI took place at Windsor.

1965 Nat King Cole, American singer and pianist, died.

1970 Lord Dowding, British Air Chief Marshal and chief of Fighter Command during the Battle of Britain, died aged 87.

1971 The decimal currency system came into operation in Britain.

1978 New Zealand secured their first ever cricket victory over England, in Wellington.

1981 Football League games were first played on a Sunday.

1982 Professor Richard Feynman, US physicist and Nobel laureate died aged 69.
The 'Ocean Ranger' oil rig, owned by Ocean Drilling and Exploration Co., USA, sank off Newfoundland, with the loss of all 84 on board.

1988 The death was reported of Frederick Loewe, American composer of musicals notably *My Fair Lady* and *Paint Your Wagon*, in Palm Springs, California, aged 86.

---

16 FEBRUARY

1659 The date on the first cheque known to have been drawn on a British bank—the original cheque is preserved in the archives of the National Westminster Bank.

1740 Giambattista Bodoni, Italian printer and typographer, born in Saluzzo.

1822 Sir Francis Galton, English scientist famous for his pioneer work in eugenics, born in Birmingham, a cousin of Charles Darwin.

1852 Charles Taze Russell, American religious leader, born in Pittsburgh.

1903 Edgar Bergen, American ventriloquist, born in Chicago as John Edgar Bergren.

1937 Nylon, developed by a research team in America under the direction of Dr Carothers, was patented.

1940 HMS *Cossack* took off 299 British prisoners from the German naval auxiliary ship *Altmark* in Norwegian waters.
Sonny Bono, American singer with ex-wife Cher in popular duo, born in Detroit, Illinois.

1949 Chaim Weizmann was sworn in at Jerusalem as the first President of the State of Israel.

1957 Sir Leslie Hore-Belisha, British statesman and Minister of Transport responsible for the introduction of Belisha beacons, the Highway Code and driving tests, died.

1959 Fidel Castro became Prime Minister of Cuba after overthrowing the regime of Fulgencio Batista.
John McEnroe, American international tennis champion, born in Wiesbaden, West Germany.

1978 Leon Spinks beat Muhammad Ali to win the world heavyweight boxing championship in Las Vegas.

---

17 FEBRUARY [48]

1673 Molière (Jean Baptiste Poquelin), French dramatist and writer of comedies, died of a brain haemorrhage from the bursting of a blood vessel after a coughing fit on stage.

1781 René Laennec, French physician who invented and named the stethoscope, born in Quimper, Brittany.

1827 Johann Pestalozzi, Swiss educationalist and pioneer in progressive elementary school teaching, died in Brugg, aged 81.

1862 Edward German, British composer, born in Whitchurch, Shropshire as Edward German Jones.

1863 The International Red Cross, an organisation for the prevention and alleviation of human suffering in time of war or disaster, was promoted in Geneva by Swiss philanthropist Jean Henri Dunant.

1864 Andrew Barton Paterson, Australian journalist nicknamed 'Banjo', born.

1890 Christopher Sholes, American inventor of the modern typewriter, died in Milwaukee, Wisconsin.

1909 Geronimo, the last Apache chief to surrender, died in custody in Fort Sill, Oklahoma.

1916 Don Tallon, Queensland and Australian Test wicket-keeper, born.

1919 Sir Wilfrid Laurier, Canadian Liberal statesman and Prime Minister from 1896 to 1911, died.

1923 The inner chamber of the tomb of Tutankhamun was opened in the presence of officials of the Egyptian Government and leading archaeologists.

1934 Albert I, King of the Belgians since 1909, was killed in a climbing accident near Namur.
Barry Humphries, Australian comedy actor, noted for his Dame Edna Everage character, born.

1941 Gene Pitney, American singer and songwriter, born in Hartford, Connecticut.

1959 Queen Elizabeth II gave Marlborough House to the nation for use as a Commonwealth centre.

1968 Sir Donald Wolfit, English stage and film actor, died.

1980 Graham Sutherland, British artist and designer of the tapestry in Coventry Cathedral, died.

---

18 FEBRUARY [49]

National day of both Nepal and Gambia.

1455 Fra Angelico, Italian Dominican friar and painter of religious subjects, died in Rome.

1516 Queen Mary I, born in Greenwich Palace, the daughter of Henry VIII and Catherine of Aragon—became known as 'Mary Tudor' and 'Bloody Mary'.

1546 Martin Luther, German Augustinian friar and leader of the Protestant reformation, died in Eisleben.

1564 Michelangelo, Italian artist of the Renaissance, died in Rome aged 88.

1745 Alessandro Volta, Italian physicist, born in Como.

1838 Ernst Mach, Austrian physicist and scientist, born in Moravia.

1882 England scored 13 goals against Ireland at Belfast—the highest margin in an international football match in the British Isles.

1892 Wendell Wilkie, American Republican politician, born in Elwood, Indiana.

1894 Andres Segovia, Spanish classical-guitar virtuoso, born in Linares.

1895 Timoshenko, Soviet Army marshal, born in Furmanka Village, Bessarabia.

1920 Jack Palance, American film actor, born in Lattimer, Pennsylvania as Walter Palanuik.

1933   James Corbett, American pugilist and world heavyweight
       champion from 1892 to 1897, known as 'Gentleman Jim', died.
       Bobby Robson, ex-professional footballer and manager since 1982
       of England's national team, born.
1934   Yoko Ono, the widow of John Lennon, born.
1954   John Travolta, American film actor, born in Englewood, New
       York State.
1960   The 8th Winter Olympic Games were opened in Squaw Valley,
       California.
1965   Gambia, the smallest country in Africa, became an independent
       monarchy within the Commonwealth—having been a British
       colony since 1843.
1967   Robert Oppenheimer, American physicist who developed the US
       atomic bomb, died in Princeton, New Jersey.
1980   Pierre Trudeau returned to power in the Canadian General
       Election after nine months out of office.
1982   Ngaio Marsh, writer of murder mysteries and created a Dame of
       the British Empire in 1948, died.

19 FEBRUARY   [50]

1473   Nicolaus Copernicus, Polish astronomer, born in Torun.
1717   David Garrick, English actor and theatre manager, born in
       Hereford, the son of an Army captain.
1843   Adelina Patti, Italian soprano opera singer, born in Madrid, the
       daughter of a Sicilian tenor.
1878   US patent number 200521 was issued to Edison for his
       phonograph.
1893   Sir Cedric Hardwick, stage and film actor, born in Lye,
       Worcestershire.
1897   Charles Blondin, famous tightrope walker who crossed Niagara
       Falls many times, died aged 72.
       The 'Women's Institute' organisation was founded at Stoney
       Creek in Ontario by Mrs Hoodless—its first meeting was held on
       25 September. The idea was brought to England during World
       War I by a Mrs Watt.
1910   Manchester United played their first Football League game in
       their new ground at Old Trafford.
1911   Merle Oberon, film actress in America, born in Tasmania as
       Estelle Merle O'Brien Thompson.
1912   Stan Kenton, American musician, born in Wichita, Kansas.
1916   National Savings certificates first went on sale in Britain.
       Ernst Mach, Austrian physicist after whom the speed of sound in
       air is named, died the day after his 78th birthday.

1924 Lee Marvin, American film actor and Oscar winner in 1965 for *Cat Ballou*, born in New York City.
1945 Iwo Jima was invaded by US Marines. The island was conquered on 16 March with the loss of 4590 killed.
1960 Prince Andrew (Andrew Albert Christian Edward), third child and second son of Queen Elizabeth II, born in Buckingham Palace.
1985 The first episode of BBC TV's *EastEnders* was broadcast.

20 FEBRUARY   [51]

1473 James I, King of Scotland, was murdered in Perth by a band of assassins led by Sir Robert Graham.
1547 The coronation of nine-year-old King Edward VI took place in Westminster Abbey.
1878 Pope Leo XIII (Gioacchino Vincenzo Pecci) was elected at the third ballot, upon the death of Pius IX.
1893 Pierre Beauregard, American Confederate Army general, died.
1898 Enzo Ferrari, Italian car manufacturer, born in Modena.
1904 Alexei Kosygin, Soviet Communist leader and Premier, born in Leningrad.
1920 Robert Peary, American Arctic explorer and first man to reach the North Pole, in 1909, died in Washington, DC.
1927 Sidney Poitier, American film actor and first male black Oscar winner for *Lilies of the Field* (1963), born in Miami, Florida.
1934 Bobby Unser, American motor racing champion driver, born in Albuquerque, New Mexico.
1940 Jimmy Greaves, English international footballer, born.
1961 Percy Grainger, Australian-born composer and pianist, died.
1962 John Glenn became the first American in orbit when he circled the earth three times in the Mercury capsule *Friendship 7*.
1966 Chester Nimitz, American admiral and Pacific fleet commander in World War II, died in San Francisco four days short of his 81st birthday.
1972 Walter Winchell, American journalist and gossip columnist, died.

21 FEBRUARY   [52]

1728 Peter III, Tsar of Russia, born in Kiel, the grandson of Peter the Great.
1741 Jethro Tull, English agricultural pioneer and inventor of the seed drill about 1701, died near Hungerford in Berkshire.

1801 Cardinal Newman, English theologian, born in London, the son of a banker.

1836 Léo Delibes, French composer of opera and ballet music, born in St Germain-du-Val.

1852 Nikolai Gogol, Russian short-story writer and novelist, died in Moscow.

1859 George Lansbury, British Labour politician and Party leader, born near Lowestoft in Suffolk.

1910 Douglas Bader, World War II fighter pilot and squadron commander, born in London.

1916 The Germans launched an all out attack on the French fortress of Verdun. Pétain took over the defence, drove back the enemy and achieved victory in June.

1937 Ron Clark, Australian middle-distance runner, born.

1938 George Ellery Hale, American astronomer responsible for the operation of the Mount Wilson and the Mount Palomar observatories, died.

1941 Sir Frederick Banting, Canadian scientist who, with Charles Best in 1921, isolated insulin, was killed in an air crash.

1952 Identity cards were abolished in Britain.

1965 Malcolm X (Malcolm Little), American militant black Muslim leader, was murdered by persons unknown in New York City.

1968 Lord Florey, Australian-born British pathologist who helped to produce penicillin on a large scale, died.

---

22 FEBRUARY

1512 Amerigo Vespucci, Italian navigator and explorer of the New World, died.

1732 George Washington, American soldier, Federalist statesman and President, born in Wakefield, Westmoreland County, Virginia.

1810 Frédéric Chopin, Polish composer and pianist, born in Zelazowa Wola near Warsaw, the son of a Frenchman.

1819 Florida was purchased by the United States from Spain.

1857 Lord Baden-Powell, British Army officer and founder of the Boy Scout movement in 1908, born in London, the son of an Oxford professor.

1879 F. W. Woolworth opened the first 'nothing over five cents' store, in Utica, New York.

1886 *The Times* became the first newspaper to institute a 'personal column' on its classified page.

1908 John Mills, English film actor, born in Felixstowe, Suffolk.

1920 Owen Patrick Smith opened the first greyhound racing stadium, in Emeryville, California.

1932 Edward Kennedy, American senator and younger brother of President Kennedy, born in Brookline, Massachusetts.
1949 'Niki' Lauda, motor racing driver and world champion, born in Vienna, Austria.
1956 At Fratton Park, Portsmouth, the local team and Newcastle United took part in the first Football League game to be played under lights.
1980 Robin Cousins won a figure skating gold medal in the Lake Placid Olympics.
1987 Andy Warhol, American pop artist known for his paintings of soup cans etc., died.

23 FEBRUARY [54]

1468 Johann Gutenberg, German inventor of printing from movable type, died.
1633 Samuel Pepys, famous English diarist, born in Salisbury Court, Fleet Street, London, the son of a tailor.
1685 George Frederick Handel, German composer, born in Halle, the son of a barber-surgeon.
1792 Sir Joshua Reynolds, English portrait painter and first President of the Royal Academy, died in London.
1820 The Cato Street conspiracy—an unsuccessful plot to assassinate British Cabinet ministers—took place in London, led by Arthur Thistlewood.
1821 John Keats, English poet famous for his odes, died of tuberculosis in Rome, only 25 years of age.
1836 The Siege of the Alamo, a fort in San Antonio, Texas, by the Mexican Army under Santa Anna, began during the Texas Revolution.
1848 John Quincy Adams, American statesman and 6th President from 1825 to 1829, died in the White House.
1874 The game of lawn tennis was patented by an Englishman—Major Walter Wingfield (1832 to 1912)—under the name of 'Sphairistike'.
1883 Victor Fleming, American film director, born in Pasadena, California.
1905 The Rotary Club was founded by Paul Harris and others, in offices in Dearborn Street, Chicago.
1906 Tommy Burns won the world heavyweight boxing title with a points win over Marvin Hart in Los Angeles.
1908 Sir William 'Bill' McMahon, Australian Liberal statesman and the 25th Prime Minister, born.
1931 Dame Nellie Melba (Helen Porter Mitchell), Australian operatic soprano, died.

1934 Sir Edward Elgar, English composer and a major figure in British music, died of pneumonia in Worcester.

1939 Peter Fonda, American film actor, born the son of Henry Fonda in New York City.

1944 Leo Hendrik Baekeland, Belgian-born American chemist and inventor of one of the first plastics, Bakelite®, died.

1950 Election returns were televised in Britain for the first time.

1953 British World War II deserters were granted amnesty.

1965 Stan Laurel, English-born American film comedian with Oliver Hardy, died aged 74.

1970 Guyana, the former colony of British Guiana on the NE coast of South America, became a Republic, with Arthur Chung its first President.

The passenger service on the railway linking Perth and Sydney in Australia opened, a distance of 2461 miles.

1976 (Laurence Stephen) L. S. Lowry, English artist noted for his 'matchstick people', died in Glossop, Derbyshire.

1983 Sir Adrian Boult, English conductor, died in Tunbridge Wells, Kent aged 93.

---

24 FEBRUARY [55]

1582 Pope Gregory XIII announced the introduction of the new Gregorian calendar, replacing the Julian calendar—was not adopted by Britain until 1752, when it resulted in a loss adjustment of 11 days.

1786 Wilhelm Grimm, German philologist and collector of fairy tales with his brother Jacob, born in Hanau.

1810 Henry Cavendish, English scientist who discovered the properties of hydrogen and other gases, died.

1815 Robert Fulton, American engineer and designer of submarines and steamships, died.

1866 Sir Arthur Pearson, English newspaper owner, born in Wookey, near Wells, Somerset.

1885 Chester Nimitz, American admiral and commander of the Pacific fleet during World War II, born in Fredericksburg, Texas.

1887 The telephone link between Paris and Brussels was inaugurated—the first between capitals.

1905 The 12.3 mile Simplon Tunnel through the Alps was completed.

1914 David Langdon, British cartoonist, born.

1920 Viscountess Astor became the first woman to speak in the British Parliament.

1925 Joseph Rowntree, owner of the cocoa manufacturing business in York, died in that city.

1931 Brian Close, Yorkshire cricketer and England's youngest Test player, born.
1932 Michel Legrand, French musician, composer and conductor, born in Paris.
1938 Toothbrush bristles were manufactured in Arlington, New Jersey to become the first commercially produced nylon product.
1940 Denis Law, Scottish international footballer, born in Aberdeen.
Jimmy Ellis, US heavyweight boxer and a world champion, born in Louisville, Kentucky.
1946 Juan Peron was elected President of Argentina.
1955 Alain Prost, French motor racing driver, born.
1964 Henry Cooper beat Brian London to win his second Lonsdale belt.
1966 Kwame Nkrumah, President of Ghana since independence in 1957, was overthrown by an army coup, and went into exile in Guinea.
1975 Nikolai Bulganin, Soviet statesman and Prime Minister from 1955 to 1958, died.
1981 Prince Charles and Lady Diana Spencer announced their engagement.
1987 The London evening newspapers *London Daily News* and *Evening News* were launched.

25 FEBRUARY [56]

National day of Kuwait.

1308 The coronation of Edward II of England took place.
1723 Sir Christopher Wren, English architect and designer, notably of St Paul's Cathedral, died in London and was buried in the crypt of his Cathedral.
1841 Pierre Auguste Renoir, French Impressionist painter, born in Limoges, the son of a tailor.
1845 Sir George Reid, Australian statesman, born in Johnstone, Scotland.
1862 'Greenbacks', American bank notes, were first issued during the Civil War by Abraham Lincoln.
1873 Enrico Caruso, Italian operatic tenor, born in Naples.
1882 The first Wales—Ireland football international took place at Wrexham, the home side winning by 7 goals to 1.
1883 Princess Alice Mary, later Countess of Athlone, born.
1888 John Foster Dulles, American government official and diplomat, born in Washington, DC.
1890 Dame Myra Hess, English concert pianist, born in London.
1899 Paul Julius Reuter, German founder of the news agency that bears his name, died in Nice.

1901 'Zeppo' Marx, the youngest of the Marx brothers who later became their agent, born in New York City as Herbert.

1914 John Arlott, British radio and television cricket commentator, born in Basingstoke, Hampshire.

1917 Anthony Burgess, English novelist, best known for *A Clockwork Orange*, born in Manchester as Burgess Wilson.

1918 Bobby Riggs, American international tennis player, born in Los Angeles.

1937 Tom Courtenay, British stage and film actor, born in Hull.

1938 Herb Elliott, Australian middle-distance athlete and record holder, born in Subiaco near Perth.

1940 The first ice hockey match to be televised was played at Madison Square Garden, between New York Rangers and Montreal Canadians.

1941 David Puttnam, British film producer, born.

1943 George Harrison of the pop group 'The Beatles', born in Liverpool.

1955 HMS *Ark Royal*, Britain's largest ever aircraft carrier, was completed.

1964 Cassius Clay (later Muhammad Ali) won the world heavyweight boxing title for the first time—knocking out Sonny Liston in round 7 in Miami.

1969 *Mariner 6*, for a Mars fly-by, was launched from Cape Kennedy.

1983 Tennessee Williams, American controversial playwright notably *A Streetcar Named Desire*, died in a New York hotel.

---

26 FEBRUARY   [57]

1797 £1 notes were first issued by the Bank of England.

1802 Victor Hugo, French poet and novelist, born in Besançon, the son of a professional soldier.

1815 Napoleon escaped from exile on the island of Elba and returned to France.

1839 The first official Grand National Steeplechase was run at Aintree, Liverpool—won by Jem Mason on 'Lottery'.

1846 'Buffalo Bill', American Army Scout and showman, born on a farm in Scott County in Iowa as William Frederick Cody.

1903 Richard Gatling, American inventor of the revolving battery gun that bears his name, died aged 84.
Orde Wingate, British general, born in Naini Tal, India, the son of an Army colonel.

1916 Jackie Gleason, American comic film actor, born in Brooklyn, New York.

1922 Margaret Leighton, British stage and film actress, born.

1925 Everton Weekes, West Indian Test cricketer, born in Barbados.
1928 Fats Domino, American pianist, singer and songwriter, born in New Orleans, Louisiana as Antoine Domino.
1932 Johnny Cash, American 'country' singer, born in Kingsland, Arkansas, the son of a cotton farmer.
1935 'RADAR'—RAdio Detection And Ranging—was first demonstrated in Daventry, by Robert Watson-Watt.
1950 Sir Harry Lauder, Scottish music hall and vaudeville comedian, died aged 79.
1961 Hassan II acceded as King of Morocco on the death of his father, King Mohammad V.

27 FEBRUARY [58]

1706 John Evelyn, English writer whose diary covered the last 65 years of his life, died in Wotton near Dorking, Surrey.
1807 (Henry Wadsworth) H. W. Longfellow, American poet, born in Portland, Maine.
1847 Ellen Terry, English stage actress, born in Coventry, the daughter of a provincial actor.
1848 Sir Hubert Parry, English composer, born in Bournemouth, Dorset.
1879 The discovery of saccharin was reported by chemists Constantine Fahlberg and Ira Remsen of the Johns Hopkins University in Baltimore.
1881 The British were defeated by the Boers at the Battle of Majuba in Northern Transvaal.
1899 Charles Best, Canadian co-discoverer of insulin for the treatment of diabetes, born in West Pembroke, Maine.
1901 Gene Sarazen, US champion golfer, born in Harrison, New York.
1902 John Steinbeck, American novelist and Nobel Prize winner notably for *The Grapes of Wrath*, born in Salinas, California.
1907 The Central Criminal Court, on the site of Newgate Prison, commonly called The Old Bailey, was opened.
1930 Joanne Woodward, American film actress and Oscar winner, born in Thomasville, Georgia.
1932 Elizabeth Taylor, English film actress and Oscar winner in 1960 for *Butterfield 8* and 1966 for *Who's Afraid of Virginia Woolf?*, born in London.
1933 The Reichstag, the imposing German Parliament building in Berlin, was destroyed by fire, believed deliberately set by Nazis.
1951 The Twenty-second Amendment to the US Constitution was ratified, limiting Presidential terms of office.
1985 Henry Cabot Lodge, American politician, diplomat and senator, died aged 82.

1824   Charles Blondin, French tightrope walker famous for his crossings of Niagara Falls, born in Hesdin near Calais as Jean Francois Gravelet.

1854   The United States Republican Party was formed, in Ripon, Wisconsin.

1865   Sir Wilfred Grenfell, English medical missionary in Labrador, born.

1887   Alexander Borodin, Russian composer, notably the opera *Prince Igor*, died in St Petersburg.

1900   Ladysmith in West Natal was relieved by a force under Sir Redvers Buller—British troops having been besieged since the previous 2 November by Transvaal forces during the Boer War.

1901   Dr Linus Pauling, American biochemist and twice winner of a Nobel Prize, born in Portland, Oregon.

1910   Vincente Minnelli, American film director, born in Chicago, Illinois.

1916   Henry James, American novelist notably for *Portrait of a Lady*, died in Rye, Sussex.

1922   The British Protectorate over Egypt ceased, when Ahmed Fuad was proclaimed King.

1931   Peter Alliss, British golfer and golf commentator, born in Berlin.

1940   Mario Andretti, motor racing champion, born in Trieste, Italy.
         The first basketball match to be televised was played at Madison Square Garden, between Fordham University and the University of Pittsburgh.

1941   Alfonso XIII, ex-King of Spain, died in Rome, having been forced into exile on the establishment of a Republic in 1931.

1961   'Barry' McGuigan, British boxer and former world flyweight champion, born in the Irish border town of Clones, County Monaghan, with the christian name Finbar.

1967   Henry Luce, American editor, publisher and founder of *Time* and *Life*, died.

1975   Britain suffered its worst underground train disaster in London's Moorgate tube station, when 42 were killed.

29 FEBRUARY   [60]

Leap Year day.

1736   Ann Lee, English religious leader, born in Manchester.

1792 Gioacchino Rossini, Italian composer of many operas, including *The Barber of Seville* and *William Tell*, born in Pesaro on the Adriatic coast, the son of a strolling horn player.

1840 John Philip Holland, American inventor who pioneered the modern submarine, born in County Clare in the Republic of Ireland.

1880 The cutting of the 9¼ mile St Gotthard tunnel in Switzerland was completed—the work of engineer Louis Favre—linking the Swiss and Italian railways.

1904 Jimmy Dorsey, American musician and band leader, born in Shenandoah, Pennsylvania, the younger brother of Tommy.

1960 Agadir, seaport of Morocco in North Africa, was devastated by an earthquake, with an estimated 12 000 deaths.

---

1 MARCH

St David's Day—national day of Wales.

1498 Mozambique, on the SE African coast, was discovered by Vasco de Gama.

1711 The first number of the British periodical *Spectator* was published.

1803 Ohio, the Buckeye State, became the 17th state of the Union.

1810 Sweden appointed Lars Mannerheim as Ombudsman; he was the first in the world to hold such a position.

1839 Sussex County Cricket Club was founded, to become the oldest.

1859 Kent County Cricket Club was founded at Maidstone, but was substantially reorganised on 6 December 1870.

1867 Nebraska, the Cornhusker State, became the 37th state of the Union.

1872 Yellowstone, the oldest and largest park in America—over two million acres in Wyoming, Montana and Idaho—was designated.

1904 Glenn Miller, American band leader and trombonist, born in Clarinda, Indiana.

1910 David Niven, film actor in America and Oscar winner in 1958, born in London.

1912 Captain Albert Berry made the first parachute descent from an aeroplane, at 1500 feet over Jefferson Barracks, St Louis, America.

1913 The International Lawn Tennis Federation (I.L.T.F.), the world's governing body for tennis, was founded at a meeting in Paris with representatives from thirteen countries.

1921 Dinah Shore, American pop singer, born in Winchester, Tennessee.

1927 Harry Belafonte, American singer, born in New York City.

1932   The 20-month-old son of Charles Lindbergh was kidnapped from the nursery of their home at Hopewell in New Jersey—was found dead on 12th May—Bruno Hauptmann was convicted and electrocuted.

1935   Herb Alpert, American musician and trumpeter, born in Los Angeles, California.

1940   David Broome, British show-jumping champion, born.

1946   The Bank of England passed to public ownership by Act of Parliament.

1947   The International Monetary Fund began operations.

1949   Joe Louis retired as world heavyweight boxing champion—having defended his title 25 times.

1958   Gary Sobers reached a score of 365 not out at Sabina Park, Kingston, Jamaica, to establish a cricket record for a Test Match.

1966   Russia's *Venus III* made a hard landing on Venus to become the first spacecraft to land on another planet. Was launched on the previous 16 November.

1980   William Ralph Dean, the legendary English footballer called 'Dixie', died as a spectator at the ground of his old club Everton.

1986   Tommy Farr, British heavyweight boxer and world title challenger in 1937, died.
Ely Cathedral became the first in Britain to levy an admission charge.

---

2 MARCH   *[62]*

1717   The first ballet, *The Loves of Mars and Venus*, was presented at The Theatre Royal, Drury Lane in London.

1791   John Wesley, English evangelist and theologian who founded the movement that became the Methodist Church, died in London aged 87.

1793   Sam Houston, American politician and soldier, born in Lexington, Virginia.

1810   Pope Leo XIII was born in Carpineto as Gioacchino Vincenzo Pecci, the son of a Count.

1824   Bedrich Smetana, Czech composer, conductor and pianist, born in Litomysl, Bohemia.

1836   The first point-to-point horseracing meeting was held, at the Madresfield Estate, by the Worcester Hunt.
Texas proclaimed independence from Mexico.

1855   Tsar Nicholas I of Russia died during hostilities in the Crimean War.

1876   Pope Pius XII was born in Rome as Eugenio Pacelli.

1882   An attempt to assassinate Queen Victoria was made at Windsor by R. MacLean.

1917 Nicholas II, the last Tsar, was forced to abdicate after Russian setbacks in World War I.

1919 Jennifer Jones, American film actress and Oscar winner in 1943, born in Tulsa, Oklahoma as Phyllis Isley.

1923 Cardinal Basil Hume, British Roman Catholic Archbishop of Westminster from 1976, born.

1930 (David Herbert) D. H. Lawrence, English novelist, notably *Women in Love*, and short story writer, died.

1931 Mikhail Gorbachev, Soviet statesman and party leader, born in Stavropol in the North Caucasus.

1939 Howard Carter, British egyptologist who discovered the tomb of Tutankhamun in 1922, died.

1949 Captain James Gallagher, in a USAF B50 *Lucky Lady II*, completed the first non-stop round-the-world flight from Fort Worth in Texas—refuelling four times in flight.
J. P. R. Williams, Welsh Rugby Union player and winner of 55 caps, born.

1950 Karen Carpenter, American pop singer, born at New Haven, Connecticut.

1958 Ian Woosnam, Welsh golfer and British Ryder Cup player, born.
Vivian Fuchs and a party of 12 completed the first crossing of the Antarctic, covering 2158 miles from Shackleton Station on the Weddell Sea to Scott Station on the Ross Sea in 99 days.

1962 Wilt Chamberlain scored all of Philadelphia's 100 points in the basketball game against New York.

1969 The French-built supersonic airliner *Concorde* made its maiden flight from Toulouse.

1970 Southern Rhodesia, a colony of Britain, styled itself the Republic of Rhodesia. It became fully independent and became Zimbabwe in 1980. See entry for 17 April.

1987 Joan Greenwood, British film actress, died.
Randolph Scott, American film actor, died aged 84.

---

3 MARCH [63]

National day of Morocco.

1703 Robert Hooke, English scientist, contributor to astronomy, chemistry and biology, died.

1792 Robert Adam, Scottish architect and interior designer, son of William Adam, died.

1803 The Duke of Bridgewater, pioneer of British inland waterways, died.

1831 George Pullman, American inventor of Pullman railway carriages, born in Brocton, New York State.

1845 Florida, the Peninsula or Sunshine State, became the 27th state of the Union.

1847 Alexander Graham Bell, Scottish-American scientist and inventor of the telephone, born in Edinburgh, the son of a teacher of elocution.

1865 Worcestershire County Cricket Club was founded during a meeting at the Star Hotel, Worcester.

1869 Sir Henry Wood, English conductor and founder of the Promenade Concerts, born in London.

1878 The Treaty of San Stefano was signed, ending the Russo-Turkish War.

1911 Jean Harlow, American film actress nicknamed the 'platinum blonde', born in Kansas City, Missouri, as Harlean Carpentier.

1918 Peter O'Sullevan, British racing correspondent and commentator, born in Ireland.

1920 Ronald Searle, English artist and creator of the schoolgirls of 'St Trinian's', born in Cambridge.

1923 The American magazine *Time* was first issued.

1931 *The Star-Spangled Banner*, written by Francis Scott Key on 14 September 1814, was designated the United States national anthem by Act of Congress. Music was adapted from an English song *Anacreon in Heaven* written by John Stafford Smith.

1953 James J. Jeffries, US heavyweight boxer and world champion from 1899 to 1903, died in Burbank, California.

1961 Fatima Whitbread, British javelin champion and a world record holder, born.

1969 *Apollo 9* was launched, with James McDivitt, David Scott and Russell Schweickart.

1982 The Barbican Arts Centre in London opened.

1985 British miners agreed to call off their strike against pit closures without an agreement having been reached.

1987 Danny Kaye, American film actor, died.

1988 Dick Chipperfield, circus man in Britain, died aged 83.

---

4 MARCH [64]

1678 Antonio Vivaldi, Italian composer and violinist, born in Venice.

1789 The first meeting of Congress was held, at Federal Hall in New York City.

1791 Vermont, the Green Mountain State, became the 14th state of the Union.

1824 The Royal Naval Lifeboat Institution was founded by Sir William Hillary.

1882 The first electric tramcars ran in London, at Leytonstone.

1889 Pearl White, American actress, born in Green Ridge, Missouri.

1890 The 1710-feet Forth Railway cantilever bridge, the longest in Britain, designed and constructed by Benjamin Baker and John Fowler, was officially opened by the Prince of Wales—57 having been killed during its construction.

1923 Patrick Moore, English astronomer, born in Pinner, Middlesex.

1928 Alan Sillitoe, English author, especially *Saturday Night and Sunday Morning*, born in Nottingham.

1936 Jim Clark, British motor racing champion driver, born in Duns, Scotland.

1951 Kenny Dalglish, Liverpool and Scotland footballer and holder of the record number of appearances for his country, born in Glasgow.

1967 The first North Sea gas was pumped ashore, at Easington, Co. Durham.

1968 Boxing was seen for the first time at the new Madison Square Garden.

1970 The *Eurydice*, a French submarine, was lost off the coast of Toulon in the Mediterranean, with the loss of its entire crew of 57.

1974 Edward Heath resigned as Prime Minister and a minority Labour Government, led by Harold Wilson, took office.

1975 Charles Chaplin was knighted by the Queen.

1986 The first issue of Eddy Shah's new national newspaper *Today* was published.

---

5 MARCH [65]

1133 Henry II, the first Plantagenet King of England, born in Le Mans, the eldest son of Matilda, daughter of Henry I.

1461 Henry VI was deposed as King of England—accession of Edward IV.

1512 Gerardus Mercator, Flemish cartographer and mathematician, born in the Flanders region as Gerhard Kremer.

1575 William Oughtred, English mathematician and inventor of the slide rule, born in Eton, Berkshire.

1770 The Boston massacre took place, in which British troops fired into a mob, killing five—one of the incidents leading up to the War of Independence.

1778 Thomas Arne, English composer, including *Rule Britannia*, died in London.

1790 Flora Macdonald, Scottish Jacobite heroine who helped the Young Pretender to escape from the Hebridean island of Benbecula, died.

1815 Friedrich Mesmer, German physician who developed the theory of animal magnetism (mesmerism) for curing disease, died aged 80.

1827 Alessandro Volta, Italian physicist who invented the first electric battery, died in Como, Lombardy, aged 82.

1850 The Menai tubular bridge, joining Wales and Anglesey and constructed by Robert Stephenson, was opened.

1908 Rex Harrison, English stage and film actor and Oscar winner in 1964, born in Huyton, Liverpool, as Reginald Carey.

1912 John Marshall, New Zealand statesman and Prime Minister in 1972, born in Wellington.

1936 The Spitfire was first flown by Captain J. Summers from Eastleigh Airport, Southampton.

1946 Winston Churchill made his 'iron curtain' speech at Westminster College, Fulton, Missouri.

1953 Joseph Stalin, Soviet Communist leader, died in mysterious circumstances. He thought he was being poisoned and several 'Jewish doctors' were arrested.
Sergei Prokofiev, Russian composer, notably the orchestral fairytale *Peter and the Wolf*, died.

1956 The telephone weather forecasting service began in Britain.

1983 Robert Hawke became Australia's Prime Minister, ending the seven-year premiership of Malcolm Fraser.

1984 Tito Gobbi, Italian international operatic baritone, died at his home in Rome.

---

6 MARCH [66]

National day of Ghana.

1475 Michelangelo, Italian painter, sculptor, artist and poet, born in Capresse, Tuscany, as Michelagniolo di Lodovico Buonarroti.

1619 Cyrano de Bergerac, French novelist and playwright, born in Paris.

1806 Elizabeth Barrett Browning, English poet and wife of Robert Browning, born in Coxhoe Hall, Durham.

1834 George du Maurier, English novelist and artist, born in Paris.

1836 The Siege of the Alamo ended after 12 days—the garrison included William Travis, Jim Bowie and Davey Crockett, who died defending the mission fort against Mexican forces under Santa Anna.

1888 Louisa M. Alcott, American novelist and author of *Little Women* and *Little Men*, died in Concord.

1900 Gottlieb Daimler, German motor engineer who improved the internal combustion engine and made the first motorcycle, died.

1906 Lou Costello, American comedy film actor, born in Paterson, New Jersey, as Louis Cristillo.

1926 The Shakespeare Memorial Theatre at Stratford-on-Avon was engulfed by flames, leaving only a blackened shell.

1929 David Sheppard, Bishop of Liverpool and former Sussex and England Test cricketer, born.

1930 Frozen foods, developed by Clarence Birdseye, were first put on sale in stores in Springfield, Massachusetts.

1932 John Philip Sousa, American bandmaster and composer of famous marches, especially *The Stars and Stripes Forever* and *El Capitan*, died in Reading, Pennsylvania.

1937 Valentina Tereshkova, Russian astronaut and first woman in space in 1963, born.

1941 Gutzon Borglum, American sculptor noted for his work on Mount Rushmore of the heads of Presidents Washington, Jefferson, Lincoln and Theodore Roosevelt, died.

1944 From bases in Britain US bombers began daytime attacks on Berlin.
Dame Kiri Te Kanawa, New Zealand opera singer, born in Gisborne, North Island.

1947 Dick Fosbury, American high jumper, born in Portland, Oregon.

1951 Ivor Novello, Welsh-born actor and composer, died in London.

1957 Ghana, formerly the Gold Coast, became the first British colony in Africa to achieve independence, with Kwame Nkrumah its first Premier.

1961 Mini cabs were first introduced in London.
George Formby, British comedian and singer of songs to his own ukulele accompaniment, died in Preston.

1964 Constantine II acceded to the throne as King of the Hellenes, succeeding his father Paul.

1965 Herbert Morrison, British Labour statesman, died.

1967 Nelson Eddy, American singer, famed for operetta films with Jeanette MacDonald, died.

1973 Pearl Buck, American novelist, notably *The Good Earth*, and Nobel Prize winner in 1938, died aged 80.

1983 Australian Christopher Massey attained a water skiing record speed of 143.08 m.p.h., on Hawkesbury River in New South Wales.

1987 The Townsend Thoresen ferry *Herald of Free Enterprise* capsized with her bow door open leaving Zeebrugge harbour, resulting in the loss of 193 lives.

1792   Sir John Herschel, English astronomer, born in Slough, Buckinghamshire.

1802   Sir Edwin Landseer, English painter, especially of animals, born in London, the son of an engraver.

1809   Jean Pierre Blanchard, French balloonist and first to cross the English Channel by air, from Dover to Calais in 1785, was killed at La Haye during practice jumps from a balloon.

1849   Luther Burbank, American botanist and plant breeder, born in Lancaster, Massachusetts.

1850   Thomas Masaryk, Czech statesman and his country's first President in 1918, born in Hodonin, Moravia.

1866   The Albert Medal, for gallantry in saving life at sea and on land, was instituted.

1872   Michael Savage, New Zealand Labour statesman, born in Benalla, Victoria, Australia.

1875   Maurice Ravel, French composer, born in Ciboure, in the Basque country.

1917   Reginald Maudling, British Conservative statesman, born in London.

1930   The Earl of Snowdon, born, as Antony Charles Robert Armstrong-Jones.

1945   Allied troops crossed the Rhine, by the Ludendorff Bridge at Remagen.

1952   Viv Richards, West Indian Test cricketer, born in St John's, Antigua.

1960   Ivan Lendl, international tennis player, born in Czechoslovakia.

1969   The Victoria Line of London's underground was opened.

1702   Death of King William III, caused by the stumbling of his horse Sorrel over a molehill in the Park at Hampton Court—leaving no children; the crown passed to Anne, daughter of James II.

1717   Abraham Darby, English ironmaster and first to use coke to smelt iron, died in Worcester.

1726   Richard Howe, British admiral and commander of distinction, born in London.

1859   Kenneth Grahame, Scottish author of children's books, especially *The Wind in the Willows*, born in Edinburgh.

1869   Hector Berlioz, French composer, died in Paris.

1874 Millard Fillmore, American Whig statesman and 13th President from 1850 to 1853, died in Buffalo in the State of New York.

1889 John Ericsson, Swedish-born American ship designer and inventor of the first successful screw propeller, died.

1910 The first pilot's licence in Britain was issued by the Royal Aero Club to J. T. C. Moore Brabazon (later Lord Brabazon).

1917 Graf von Zeppelin, German airship pioneer, died in Charlottenburg, near Berlin.
The 'February' Revolution began at Petrograd, ending on 14 March.

1923 Cyd Charisse, American dancing star of the 1950s musicals, born in Amarillo, Texas, as Tula Ellice Finklea.

1930 William Howard Taft, American Republican statesman and 27th President from 1909 to 1913, died in Washington.

1943 Michael Grade, British Television controller and executive, born.

1945 Mickey Dolenz, American musician, actor and member of 'The Monkees', born in Los Angeles.

1950 John Charles, at 18 years 3 months of age, became the youngest footballer to play for Wales, in the home international against Ireland.

1961 Sir Thomas Beecham, English conductor and founder of the London Philharmonic Orchestra, died aged 81.

1971 Harold Lloyd, US comedian and film actor of the silent era, died.
Muhammad Ali suffered his first professional defeat, being outpointed by Joe Frazier.

1974 The inauguration of the third Paris airport—the Charles de Gaulle—took place.

1983 Sir William Walton, English composer, died on the island of Ischia.

9 MARCH [69]

1454 Amerigo Vespucci, Italian explorer and navigator of many voyages to the New World, born in Florence.

1763 William Cobbett, English political journalist and historian, born in Farnham, Surrey, the son of a farmer.

1796 Napoleon Bonaparte married Josephine, the widow of the Vicomte de Beauharnais.

1831 The French Foreign Legion was founded by King Louis Philippe, with headquarters at Sidi-Bel-Abbes in Algeria—moved to Aubagne in France in 1962.

1862 The first battle of iron-clad ships took place during the American Civil War. *Merrymack* was forced to withdraw at Hampton Roads by the Union's *Monitor*.

1876 Graham Bell filed his patent for the first telephone—only three hours ahead of a similar one by Elisha Gray.

1881 Ernest Bevin, British union leader, politician and minister, born in Winsford, Somerset.

1890 Molotov, Soviet political leader and diplomat, born in Kukaida with the surname Skriabin.

1918 Mickey Spillane, America writer of detective novels and creator of 'Mike Hammer', born in Brooklyn, New York, as Frank Morrison.

1932 Eamon de Valera was elected President of the Republic of Ireland.

1934 Yuri Gagarin, Russian astronaut and the first man in space, born near Smolensk, the son of a collective farmer.

1943 Bobby Fischer, chess champion and first American to hold the world title, born in Chicago.

1946 Day of tragedy at Burnden Park, Bolton, before an English FA Cup tie against Stoke City, with 33 killed and over 400 injured, as a result of broken crush-barriers.

1950 Andy North, American international golfer, born.

1956 Archbishop Makarios, implicated in terrorism in Cyprus, was deported by the British to the Seychelle Islands.

1974 Britain returned to a five day working week, having been on three days since December 1973 to conserve fuel. Supplies from the Middle East had been reduced due to the Arab-Israeli War.

1987 Bobby Locke, South African international golfer, died.

10 MARCH   [70]

1854 Sir Thomas Mackenzie, New Zealand statesman, born in Edinburgh.

1863 King Edward VII, when he was Prince of Wales, married Princess Alexandra of Denmark in St George's Chapel, Windsor.

1872 Giuseppe Mazzini, Italian revolutionary who fought for his country's unity and independence, died in Pisa.

1876 Alexander Graham Bell transmitted the first coherent telephone message from 5 Exeter Place, Boston, Massachusetts to his assistant Thomas Watson, consisting of the words 'Come here, Watson, I want you'.

1886 The first Cruft's dog show was held in London—the first ever took place in 1859 in Newcastle.

1888 Barry Fitzgerald, American film character actor, born in Dublin as William Joseph Shields.

1906 The Bakerloo Line of London Underground was opened.

1935 Hitler renounced the Versailles Treaty of 1919 and ordered conscription in Germany.

1948 Jan Masaryk, Czech statesman and minister, died in Prague under suspicious circumstances after the Communists gained control.

1964 Prince Edward (Edward Antony Richard Louis), born in Buckingham Palace, the third son of Elizabeth II.

1969 Jimmy Wilde, Welsh flyweight boxer and world champion from 1916 to 1923, died aged 76.

1985 Konstantin Chernenko, Soviet party leader, died. Mikhail Gorbachev was named as successor.

1986 Ray Milland, American film actor and Oscar winner in 1945 for *The Lost Weekend*, died.

---

11 MARCH

1682 The Royal Chelsea Hospital was founded by Charles II. It was built by Wren and opened in 1692.

1702 The *Daily Courant*, the first successful English newspaper, published by E. Mallet as a single sheet, had its first issue.

1751 Dr Hill, under the name of 'The Inspector' was the first newspaper columnist, contributing to the *London Advertiser and Literary Gazette*.

1770 William Huskisson, British Tory statesman, born in Worcestershire.

1801 Paul I, Tsar of Russia, was strangled in a scuffle with his own officers who were conspiring to compel him to abdicate.

1819 Sir Henry Tate, English philanthropist whose money and pictures founded the Tate Gallery in 1897, born in Chorley.

1885 Sir Malcolm Campbell, English racing driver who established world records on land and water, born in Chislehurst, Kent.

1907 Jessie Matthews, English actress, born in London.

1916 Sir Harold Wilson, British statesman and Labour Prime Minister, born in Huddersfield, Yorkshire.

1923 Louise Brough, American tennis champion, born in Oklahoma City.

1930 *The Intimate Revue* at the Duchess Theatre, London, opened and closed on the same night to create the shortest run on record.

1931 Rupert Murdoch, Australian newspaper proprietor, born.

1932 Nigel Lawson, British Conservative politician and a Chancellor of the Exchequer, born.

1936 Earl Beatty, British admiral and cruiser commander at the Battle of Jutland, died.

1941 The United States Lend-Lease Bill was signed by President Roosevelt.

1947 Geoff Hunt, Australian world amateur and open squash champion, born.

1955 Sir Alexander Fleming, Scottish bacteriologist, discoverer of penicillin in 1928 and Nobel prizewinner in 1945, died.

1957 Richard Byrd, American admiral, aviator and Polar explorer, died.

1969 Golda Meir became Prime Minister of Israel after the death of Levi Eshkol, a post she held until her resignation in 1974.

1970 Erle Stanley Gardner, American crime writer and creator of the character 'Perry Mason', died.

12 MARCH

1710 Thomas Arne, English composer, notably of *Rule Britannia*, born in London, the son of an upholsterer.

1789 The United States Post Office was established.

1869 George Forbes, New Zealand statesman, born in Lyttleton, South Island.

1881 Kemal Ataturk, Turkish general, statesman and President, born in Salonika, Greece, as Mustafa Kemal Pasha.

1889 The first South Africa *v.* England cricket Test match started at St George's Park, Port Elizabeth, South Africa, the visitors ended up winners by eight wickets.

1890 Vaslav Nijinsky, Russian ballet dancer and choreographer, born in Kiev.

1912 The Girl Scouts movement in America was founded by Juliette Gordon Low.

1914 George Westinghouse, American engineer, inventor and patentee of the Westinghouse railway brake in 1868, died in New York City.

1917 *Izvestia*, the official daily newspaper of the USSR, was founded after the February Revolution.

1923 The foundation stone of the Australia Federal Parliament Building at Canberra was laid.
Walter Schirra, American astronaut, born in Hackensack, New Jersey.

1925 Sun Yat-Sen, Chinese revolutionary leader and national hero, died of cancer in Peking.

1935 A speed limit of 30 m.p.h. was introduced for towns and built-up areas in Britain.

1946 Liza Minnelli, American entertainer, film actress and Oscar winner in 1972, for *Cabaret*, born in Los Angeles, the daughter of Judy Garland.

1955 Charlie Parker, American jazz saxophonist, died.

1968 The volcanic island of Mauritius in the Indian Ocean became an independent member of the Commonwealth, having been a British colony since 1810.

1984 The first day of the British miners' strike against pit closures.
1985 Eugene Ormondy, American conductor of the Philadelphia Orchestra from 1936, died aged 85.
1988 Bank of England pound notes, replaced by coins in 1983, were no longer legal tender.

13 MARCH

1733 Joseph Priestley, English scientist who discovered gases, notably oxygen, born in Leeds, the son of a cloth dresser.
1781 The planet Uranus, 7th in distance from the sun, was discovered by the German-born English astronomer Sir William Herschel.
1855 Percival Lowell, American astronomer, born in Boston, Massachusetts.
1858 Felice Orsini, Italian revolutionary, was executed for his part in the assassination attempt on the life of Napoleon III in Paris.
1873 The Scottish Football Association was formed at a meeting attended by the representatives of eight clubs.
1881 Alexander II, Tsar of Russia from 1855, died from injuries received when a bomb was thrown at him near his Palace.
1884 Sir Hugh Walpole, British novelist, born in Auckland, North Island of New Zealand.
1894 The first public striptease act was performed at a Paris music hall, consisting of a girl getting ready for bed.
1901 Benjamin Harrison, American Republican statesman and 23rd President from 1889 to 1893, died in Indianapolis, Indiana.
1906 Susan Anthony, pioneer and leader of Women's Suffrage and named in the hall of fame for great Americans, died aged 86.
1930 The discovery of the planet Pluto, at the Lowel Observatory in Arizona, was announced by Clyde Tombaugh—although its existence had been predicted earlier by Percival Lowell.
1936 Sir Francis Bell, New Zealand statesman and Prime Minister for only 16 days, died aged 84.
1938 Nazi Germany invaded Austria, after which it was incorporated in the German Reich under the name of Ostmark.
1939 Neil Sedaka, American singer and songwriter, born in New York City.
1944 HMS *Thunderbolt*, the new name of the salvaged submarine *Thetis*, was sunk off Sicily.
1948 The Lincolnshire Handicap, an English horserace, had a record 58 runners.
1950 Joe Bugner, British heavyweight boxing champion, born in Hungary.

1961 The old black and white Bank of England £5 notes ceased to be legal tender.

1967 Sir Frank Worrell, West Indian Test cricketer, died.

---

14 MARCH

1757 Admiral John Byng was shot by a firing squad on the *Monarque* at Portsmouth for his failure to relieve the island of Minorca, threatened by the French fleet.

1804 Johann Strauss the elder, Austrian composer and conductor, born in Vienna, the son of an inn-keeper.

1820 Victor Emmanuel II, the first king of united Italy, born.

1836 Mrs Beeton, English writer on cookery and household management, born.

1844 Umberto I, King of Italy, born in Turin, the son of Victor Emmanuel (above), whom he succeeded in 1878.

1864 Lake Albert in Africa was discovered and named by Sir Samuel Baker.

1879 Albert Einstein, German scientist known for his theory of relativity, born in Ulm, Bavaria, of Jewish parents.

1883 Karl Marx, German social philosopher and radical leader, died in London and was buried in Highgate Cemetery.

1918 John McCallum, Australian film actor, born in Brisbane.

1928 Frank Borman, American astronaut, born in Gary, Indiana.

1932 George Eastman, American photographic pioneer, died by his own hand.

1933 Michael Caine, English film actor, born in London as Maurice Micklewhite.

1934 Eugene Cernan, American astronaut and one of the sixth pair to land on the moon, born in Chicago, Illinois.

1936 The London to Hong Kong airline service was inaugurated.

1939 The Test between England and South Africa at Kingsmead, Durban ended, having started on 3 March, to become the lengthiest recorded cricket match. It was finally abandoned because the team had to rejoin their ship, the *Athlone Castle*, at Cape Town.

1945 The heaviest bomb of the war, 'Grand Slam' weighing 22 000 pounds, was dropped by the RAF on Bielefeld railway viaduct.

1961 The New Testament was published in a revised form after many years work.

1975 Susan Hayward, American film actress and Academy Award (Oscar) winner in 1958 for her part in *I Want to Live*, died.

1976 Busby Berkeley, American film director and choreographer, died.

1767 'Old Hickory', Andrew Jackson, American general, Democrat statesman and 7th President, born in the Waxhaws District, South Carolina, the son of Irish immigrants.

1779 Viscount Melbourne, British Whig statesman and Prime Minister, born in London as William Lamb.

1820 Maine, the Pine Tree State, became the 23rd state of the Union.

1824 Work on the construction of John Rennie's London Bridge began.

1869 Cincinnati Red Stockings, the first professional baseball club, played their first match, against Great Western.

1877 Australia played England at Melbourne in the first cricket Test match—the hosts ended up winners by 45 runs, and Charles Bannerman scoring the first Test century with 165.

1892 The first escalator, called The Reno Inclined Elevator, was patented by Jesse Reno and installed at the Old Iron Pier on Coney Island four years later.

1898 Sir Henry Bessemer, English metallurgist and inventor of an economical process for converting cast iron into steel in 1856, died aged 85.

1909 Selfridge's, American-owned department store in London's Oxford Street, was opened.

1916 Harry James, American trumpeter and bandleader, born in Albany, Georgia.

1919 The American Legion was founded.

1920 Billy Meredith became the oldest player to appear in a football international when he played for Wales against England at Highbury in London when well over 45.

1937 America set up its first blood bank, at Cook County Hospital in Chicago.

1945 Album-record charts were first published in America, by *Billboard*, with *King Cole Trio*, number one.

1947 Floods in England were the worst recorded.

1949 Clothes rationing ended in Britain.

1975 Aristotle Onassis, Greek shipping magnate and Olympic Airways operator, and second husband of Jacqueline Kennedy, died.

1983 Rebecca West, British novelist, died.

1751 James Madison, American Republican statesman and 4th President, born in Port Conway, Virginia, the first of 12 children.

1774 Matthew Flinders, English naval officer and navigator, born in Donington, near Boston in Lincolnshire, the son of a surgeon.

1787 Georg Ohm, German physicist specialising in electricity, born in Bavaria.

1802 The United States Military Academy was established at West Point in New York State.

1872 The first English FA Cup final took place, Wanderers, a team formed by ex-public school and university men, beating Royal Engineers 1–0 at the Oval, London.

1878 William Banting, English pioneer of slimming by diet control, died.

1904 Books of stamps were first issued in Britain by the GPO, containing 24 at one penny.

1912 Thelma Nixon, wife of America's 37th President, born in Ely, Nevada, as Thelma Ryan.

1920 Leo McKern, Australian actor, born in Sydney.

1926 Jerry Lewis, American comedy actor, born in Newark, New Jersey, as Joseph Levitch.

1937 Sir Austen Chamberlain, British Conservative statesman who negotiated the signing of the Locarno Pact in 1925 and Nobel Prize winner in the same year, died.

1966 Spacecraft *Gemini 8* was launched, with Neil Armstrong and David Scott.

1970 The Old Testament was published in a revised form after many years work.

1973 The second London Bridge was opened by H.M. The Queen.

1976 Harold Wilson resigned as Prime Minister of Britain.

17 MARCH [77]

St Patrick's Day—national day of Ireland.

1337 Edward, Duke of Cornwall, was the first to be created a Duke.

1787 Edmund Kean, English Shakespearean actor, born in London.

1816 The 38-ton *Elise* left Newhaven and made a stormy 17-hour journey to Le Havre to become the first steamboat to cross the English Channel.

1834 Gottlieb Daimler, German engineer who improved the internal combustion engine, born in Schorndorf.

1846 Kate Greenaway, English artist and illustrator of children's books, born in London, the daughter of a wood engraver.

1861 Victor Emmanuel was declared King of Italy at Turin by the country's first Parliament.

1897 Bob Fitzsimmons became the only British-born boxer to win the world heavyweight title, defeating Jim Corbett at Carson City in Nevada.

1902 Bobby Jones, the legendary American golf champion, born in Atlanta, Georgia.

1912 Lawrence Oates, Putney-born explorer with Captain Scott, died on the return journey from the South Pole—on his 32nd birthday—'I am just going outside, and may be some time'.

1919 Nat 'King' Cole, American singer and entertainer, born in Montgomery, Alabama, as Nathaniel Adams Coles.

1938 Rudolf Nureyev, Russian ballet dancer, born in Irkutsk, Siberia.

1939 Robin Knox Johnston, yachtsman and the first to complete the non-stop solo circumnavigation of the earth, born.

1948 The Brussels Treaty, a pact of economic, political, cultural and military alliance, was signed by Britain, France and the Benelux countries.

1963 The first of the Tristan da Cunha islanders returned home from Britain.

1978 The oil-tanker *Amoco Cadiz* ran aground on the coast of Brittany, broke in half and subsequently disgorged some 220 000 tons of crude oil.

1986 Sir John Glubb (Glubb Pasha), founder and commander of the modern Arab Legion, died.

18 MARCH [78]

1584 Ivan IV, called 'the Terrible', the first to assume the title of Tsar, died of sorrow for his son, whom he had killed in a mad fit of rage some three years earlier.

1745 Sir Robert Walpole, British Whig statesman and Chief Minister from 1721 to 1742, died in London, having been created Earl of Orford.

1768 Laurence Sterne, Irish-born clergyman and novelist, notably *The Life and Opinions of Tristram Shandy*, died in poverty in London.

1837 Grover Cleveland, American Democrat statesman and President on two occasions, born in Caldwell, New Jersey, the son of a Presbyterian minister.

1844 Rimsky-Korsakov, Russian composer, born in Tikhvin, Novgorod.

1858 Rudolf Diesel, German engineer and inventor of the engine that bears his name, born in Paris.

1869 Neville Chamberlain, British statesman and Conservative Prime Minister, 1937 to 1940, born in Birmingham.

1891 The London–Paris telephone system opened, with communications between the Prince of Wales and President Carnot. The service became available to the general public on 1 April.

1905 Robert Donat, English film actor and Oscar winner for *Goodbye Mr Chips* (1939), born in Manchester.

1913 George I, King of Greece from 1863, was assassinated at Salonika.

1926 Peter Graves, American film actor, born at Minneapolis as Peter Aurness, the younger brother of James Arness.

1939 Charley Pride, American country singer, born in Sledge, Missouri.

1949 Alex 'Hurricane' Higgins, snooker champion, born in Northern Ireland.

1952 Pat Eddery, English champion jockey, born.

1965 Farouk I, King of Egypt from 1936 to 1952, died in exile in Italy.
Aleksei Leonov left *Voshkod II* and made the first space walk, lasting about ten minutes.

1967 The oil tanker *Torrey Canyon* was wrecked on the Pollard Rock between the Isles of Scilly and Land's End.

1983 King Umberto II of Italy, in exile since 1946, died in a Geneva clinic aged 78.

1984 The Oxford and Cambridge University boat race was run on a Sunday for the first time, having been abandoned for a day because the Cambridge boat had been damaged in a collision.

1988 Percy Thrower, horticulturist, writer and broadcaster on the subject, died.

---

19 MARCH

1813 David Livingstone, Scottish explorer and medical missionary in Africa, born at 9 Shuttle Row, Blantyre, near East Kilbride.

1821 Sir Richard Burton, much-travelled English explorer and writer, born in Torquay, Devon, the son of a colonel.

1834 Six labourers, known as the Tolpuddle Martyrs, were convicted at Dorchester of trade union activity, and sentenced to seven years transportation.

1848 Wyatt Earp, American law officer and gunfighter, born in Monmouth, Illinois.

1872 Sergei Diaghilev, Russian ballet impresario and artistic director, born in Novgorod.

1883 Joseph Stilwell, American Army general, born in Palatka, Florida.

1906 Adolf Eichmann, German Nazi official responsible for the execution of millions of Jews during World War II, born in Solingen.

1930 Arthur James Balfour, British statesman and Conservative Prime Minister from 1902 to 1905, died aged 81.

1932 The 1650-feet span Sydney Harbour Bridge—the world's widest —was officially opened.

1950 Edgar Rice Burroughs, American popular novelist, best known for the series of Tarzan books, died.

1986 The engagement between Prince Andrew and Miss Sarah Ferguson was announced.

---

20 MARCH [80]

1413 King Henry IV died of a stroke in the Jerusalem Chamber at Westminster Abbey—having prophesied he would die in Jerusalem—accession of his eldest son as Henry V.

1602 The Dutch East India Company was founded by the Netherlands Government to trade with the East Indies—was wound up in 1798.

1727 Sir Isaac Newton, outstanding British scientist and mathematician, died in London aged 84, and was buried at Westminster Abbey.

1806 The foundation stone of Dartmoor Prison, at Princetown in Devon, was laid. Originally built to house French prisoners of war—was used as a convict prison from 1850.

1828 Henrik Ibsen, Norwegian playwright, notably *Hedda Gabler*, the father of modernist drama, born in the seaport of Skien.

1890 Beniamino Gigli, Italian tenor, born in Rencanati, near Ancona, the son of a shoemaker.

1908 Michael Redgrave, English state and film actor, born in Bristol.

1917 Dame Vera Lynn, English vocalist and 'Forces Favourite', born in London as Vera Welch.

1929 Ferdinand Foch, French Army marshal and commander-in-chief of the allied armies in France, died.

1937 Harry Vardon, British international golfer and six times winner of the British Open, died in Totteridge, London.

1939 Brian Mulroney, Canadian statesman and Prime Minister, born.

1956 Tunisia became an independent sovereign state, after being a Protectorate of France since 1881.

1964 Brendan Behan, Irish playwright notably *The Quare Fellow*, died in a Dublin hospital.

1974 An attempt to kidnap Princess Anne was made in The Mall in London.

1980 Radio Caroline, the British pop pirate radio station, finished when the station's home, the ship *Mi Amigo*, ran aground and sank after sixteen years of illegal broadcasting.

73

1556 Thomas Cranmer, the first Protestant Archbishop of Canterbury in 1533, was condemned as a traitor and heretic and burnt at the stake in Oxford.

1685 Johann Sebastian Bach, German composer and organist, born in Eisenach, Thuringia, now in East Germany.

1839 Modest Moussorgsky, Russian composer, born in Karevo (now Pskov).

1843 Robert Southey, English poet and Poet Laureate from 1813, died in Keswick, Cumbria.

1869 Florenz Ziegfeld, American theatre manager, impresario and creator of the fabulous *Follies*, born in Chicago, Illinois.

1933 Michael Heseltine, British Conservative politician, born.

1935 Brian Clough, English footballer and club manager, born.

1958 The London Planetarium in Marleybone Street was opened—the first of its kind in Britain.

1960 The Sharpeville shootings in the Transvaal, South Africa took place, when police fired on an African demonstration against Pass Laws—about 70 were killed.

1961 Henry Cooper out-boxed Joe Erskine to win his first Lonsdale belt.

1963 Davey Moore, defending his world featherweight boxing title against Sugar Ramos in Los Angeles, was taken to hospital after the fight—died four days later.
Alcatraz, the prison on the island in San Francisco Bay, was closed, having been a maximum security Federal prison since 1934.

1985 Sir Michael Redgrave, English actor of stage and screen, knighted in 1959, died.

The earliest date on which Easter can fall.

1599 Sir Anthony van Dyck, Flemish artist and court painter to King Charles I, born in Antwerp, the son of a cloth manufacturer.

1832 Johann von Goethe, German poet and novelist, author of *Faust*, died aged 82.

1857 Paul Doumer, French statesman and President, born in Aurillac, Cantal.

1887 'Chico' Marx, the piano-playing member of the Marx brothers, born in New York City as Leonard.

1888 The English Football League was formed at a meeting at Anderton's Hotel in Fleet Street, London—with 12 clubs.
1895 The earliest demonstration of a celluloid cinematograph film was given in Paris by Auguste and Louis Lumière.
1896 Thomas Hughes, English reformer and author, known for his *Tom Brown's Schooldays*, died.
1903 Frederic William Farrar, English clergyman and writer of school stories, particularly *Eric*, or *Little by Little*, died.
1908 John Crawford, Australian international tennis player, born.
1910 Nicholas Monsarrat, English author of sea novels, notably *The Cruel Sea*, born in Liverpool.
1913 Karl Malden, American film actor, born in Chicago, as Malden Sekulovich.
1923 Marcel Marceau, French actor and mime artist, born in Strasbourg, France.
1929 The Grand National Steeplechase at Aintree, Liverpool had a record sixty-six runners.
1930 Stephen Sondheim, American composer and lyricist, born in New York City.
1931 William Shatner, stage and film actor, born in Montreal, Canada.
1936 Roger Whittaker, British singer and songwriter, born in Nairobi, Kenya.
1941 The Grand Coulee dam of the Columbia River in Washington State began operating.
1946 Jordan became an independent Kingdom, having been under British protection.
1948 Andrew Lloyd Webber, English songwriter, born in London.
1958 Mike Todd, American film producer who was also responsible for the development of Todd-Ao and Cinerama widescreen processes, died.

23 MARCH

National day of Pakistan.

1842 Stendahl (Marie Henri Beyle), French novelist, died in Paris.
1891 Goal nets, the invention of J. A. Brodie of Liverpool, were used for the first time in an FA Cup final.
1908 Joan Crawford, American film actress and dancer, born in San Antonio, Texas, as Lucille Le Sueur.
1912 Wernher von Braun, German engineer and pioneer of rocketry in Germany and America, born in Wirsitz.
1919 The Fascist Party was founded by Benito Mussolini in Milan.

1921 (Ernest William) E. W. Hornung, English novelist and creator of 'Raffles' the gentleman burglar, died.
Donald Campbell, British racing driver and water speed record holder, born.

1929 Roger Bannister, British athlete and first to run a mile in under 4 minutes (3 minutes 59.4 seconds), born in Harrow, Greater London.

1938 Norman Breedlove, American speed racing driver, born in Los Angeles.

1945 Steve Donoghue, English champion jockey who rode six Derby winners, died suddenly in London.

1956 Pakistan was proclaimed an Islamic Republic within the Commonwealth.
Queen Elizabeth laid the foundation stone of the new Coventry Cathedral.

1964 Peter Lorre, Hungarian-born American film character actor, died.

1965 Spacecraft *Gemini 3* was launched, with Virgil Grissom and John Young.

1981 Mike Hailwood, British international motorcycling racing champion, died.

---

24 MARCH [84]

1603 Queen Elizabeth died in Richmond Palace aged 69, after nearly 45 years as Queen—accession of James I, the son of Mary, Queen of Scots.

1776 John Harrison, English watchmaker and inventor of the chronometer, died in London.

1877 The only dead-heat in the history of the Oxford–Cambridge University boat race took place.

1882 (Henry Wadsworth) H. W. Longfellow, American poet, author of *The Song of Hiawatha*, died in Cambridge, Massachusetts.

1905 Jules Verne, French novelist and pioneer of science fiction, died in Amiens, aged 77.

1909 Clyde Barrow, one half of outlaws Bonnie and Clyde, born in Teleco, Texas.

1930 Steve McQueen, American actor in action-adventure films, born in Indianapolis, Indiana.

1944 Orde Wingate, British Army commander who created and led the famous Chindits in Burma, was killed in a plane crash in the jungle in Assam.

1953 Queen Mary, wife of George V, died at her London home, Marlborough House in Pall Mall.

1956 The Queen Mother's horse 'Devon Loch', when in the lead, inexplicably collapsed fifty yards from the finish of the Grand National Steeplechase to deny a Royal victory.

1958 Elvis Presley joined the Army, his call-up having been postponed to enable him to finish *King Creole*, the film he was making.

1961 Dean Jones, Australian Test cricketer, born.

1962 Benny Paret, defending his world welterweight boxing title against Emile Griffith in New York, was taken to hospital after the fight with brain injury sustained in the fight—died on 3 April.
Auguste Piccard, French deep-sea explorer and balloonist, died in Lausanne.

1964 Stansted, in Essex, was provisionally chosen as the site of London's third airport.

1976 Isabel Peron was ousted as President of Argentina by a military coup.
Bernard, Viscount Montgomery, Irish-born British Army field marshal and successful commander, died aged 88.

25 MARCH [85]

National day of Greece.

1802 The Peace Treaty of Amiens was signed, settlement in which Britain returned most of its gains from the Revolutionary Wars.

1807 The slave trade in England was abolished.

1843 The 1300-feet Thames Tunnel, linking Wapping with Rotherhithe, was formally opened.

1867 Arturo Toscanini, Italian conductor and musical director, born in Parma, the son of a tailor.

1871 Gutzon Borglum, American sculptor, born near Bear Lake in Idaho.

1876 The first Scotland *v.* Wales football international was played in Glasgow—the hosts won easily by four goals to nil.

1879 Leicestershire County Cricket Club was founded in Leicester.

1881 Bela Bartok, Hungarian composer and pianist, born.

1906 A. J. P. Taylor, English historian, born.

1908 David Lean, British film director, born in Croydon, Greater London.

1918 Claude Debussy, French composer, including *Clair de Lune* and *La Mer*, died of cancer in Paris.

1928 James Lovell, American astronaut, born in Cleveland, Ohio.

1936 The longest ice hockey match, of 2 hours 56½ minutes, was played when Detroit Red Wings beat Montreal Maroons 1–0 in the sixth period of extra time at the Forum, Montreal.

1942 Aretha Franklin, American rhythm-and-blues singer, born in Memphis, Tennessee.

1944 Paul Michael Glaser, American actor, best known for his part as 'Starsky' in the TV series *Starsky and Hutch*, born.

1947 Elton John, British musician and pop singer, born in Pinner, Middlesex, as Reginald Kenneth Dwight.

1957 European Economic Community, an organisation usually called the 'Common Market', was formed by the Treaty of Rome.

1974 *The Mousetrap* moved after 8862 performances to St Martin's Theatre, London.

1975 King Faisal of Saudi Arabia was assassinated by his nephew Prince Museid, in the Royal Palace at Riyadh.

1978 The Cambridge boat sank in the Oxford and Cambridge University boat race.

1980 Robert Runcie was enthroned as the 102nd Archbishop of Canterbury.

26 MARCH [86]

1726 Sir John Vanbrugh, English architect of Blenheim Palace, died of a quinsy in Whitehall, London.

1827 Ludwig van Beethoven, German composer of outstanding genius, died in Bonn.

1839 The annual Henley Rowing Regatta at Henley-on-Thames in Oxfordshire, was inaugurated.

1856 William Massey, New Zealand statesman, born at Limavady in County Derry.

1885 The first cremation in Britain took place, at Woking Crematorium in Surrey.

1902 Cecil Rhodes, British statesman, financier and colonial administrator, died in Cape Town.

1914 Tennessee Williams, American playwright, born in Columbus, Mississippi, as Thomas Lanier Williams.
William Westmoreland, American Army general and chief of staff, born in Spartanburg County, South Carolina.

1916 Bill Edrich, Middlesex and England cricketer, born.

1923 Sarah Bernhardt, versatile French actress, died aged 78.
BBC broadcast its first daily weather forecast.

1925 Hindenburg was elected President of the German Republic.

1931 Leonard Nimoy, American film actor known for his role as 'Doctor Spock' in TV's *Star Trek*, born in Boston, Massachusetts.

1940 Michael Savage, New Zealand Labour statesman and Prime Minister from 1935 to 1940, died.

1944 Diana Ross, American singer and actress, born in Detroit, Michigan.

1945 David Lloyd George, British statesman and Liberal Prime Minister from 1916 to 1922, died in Llanystumdwy near Criccieth in North Wales, aged 82.

1957 Edouard Herriot, French radical statesman and twice Prime Minister, died.

1959 Raymond Chandler, American detective storywriter and creator of the character 'Philip Marlowe', died.
Mushtaq Mohammad became the youngest man to play in a cricket Test match, at 15 years 124 days, when he played for Pakistan against the West Indies at Lahore.

1973 Sir Noel Coward, English playwright, notably *Blithe Spirit*, actor and songwriter, died.
Mrs Susan Shaw became the first woman to set foot on the floor of the London Stock Exchange in the 171 years of its existence.

---

27 MARCH   *[87]*

1625 Death of King James I, the 'wisest fool in Christendom', at Theobalds Park, Cheshunt, Hertfordshire—accession of his son as Charles I.

1794 The United States Navy was created. It was operated under the Secretary for War. Prior to this time American Congress had only fitted out naval forces to respond to aggressive action, but from this date they decided they needed a permanent naval force.

1845 Wilhelm von Röntgen, German physicist and discoverer of X-rays, born in Lennep, Prussia.

1863 Sir Frederick Henry Royce, English car manufacturer, of Rolls-Royce Ltd, born in Alwalton, the son of a miller.

1871 The first Rugby International was played, Scotland defeating England in Edinburgh.

1889 John Bright, British radical statesman and reformer who worked with Richard Cobden for the repeal of the Corn Laws, died.

1894 Dashiell Hammett, America writer, born in St Mary's County, Maryland.

1912 James Callaghan, British statesman and Labour Prime Minister from 1976 to 1979, born in Portsmouth.

1917 Cyrus Vance, American Government official, born in Clarksburg, West Virginia.

1923 Sir James Dewar, Scottish chemist and physicist, inventor of the vacuum flask, died aged 80.

1931 Arnold Bennett, English novelist who wrote of the Staffordshire potteries, died of typhoid.

1968 Yuri Gagarin, the first man in space in 1961, was killed in a jet plane crash near Moscow on a routine training flight.

1975 Sir Arthur Bliss, English composer and Master of the Queen's Musick from 1953, died.
1977 The world's worst aviation disaster took place, when two aircraft collided and exploded on the foggy single airstrip at Los Rodeos Airport at Tenerife on the Canary Islands, with 582 deaths.

28 MARCH [88]

1483 Raphael, Italian painter, born in Urbino, as Raffaello Sanzio or Santi.
1660 George I, the first Hanoverian King of Great Britain, born in Osnabrück Castle, Hanover.
1845 The oldest Beagle hunt—the Royal Rock Beagles, of Wirral, Merseyside—had its first outing.
1868 The Earl of Cardigan, British leader of the disastrous cavalry charge at Balaklava in the Crimean War in 1854, died.
1881 Modest Moussorgsky, Russian composer, died as a result of chronic alcoholism.
1891 Paul Whiteman, American musician and bandleader, born in Denver, Colorado.
1902 Dame Flora Robson, English actress, born in South Shields, Tyneside.
1910 The first seaplane, designed by Frenchman Henri Fabre, took off from water near Marseilles.
1917 The Women's Army Auxiliary Corps was founded in Britain.
1921 Dirk Bogarde, English film actor, born in Hampstead, London.
1924 Freddie Bartholomew, English actor famed as a Hollywood child actor, born in London as Frederick Llewellyn.
1941 The Battle of Matapan took place off the south coast of Greece, with victory for the British Navy over an Italian fleet.
     Virginia Woolf, English novelist and critic, died—ending her life by drowning near Rodmell in Sussex.
1942 British commandos made a dawn raid on the French port of St Nazaire—called 'Operation Chariot'—in which an old destroyer, the *Campbeltown*, full of explosives, rammed the main dock gate and put it out of action for the rest of the war.
     Neil Kinnock, British politician, MP for Bedwellty and leader of the Labour opposition, born in Tredegar, South Wales.
1943 Sergei Rachmaninov, Russian-American composer and piano virtuoso, died in Beverly Hills, California.
1955 The lowest cricket Test score was recorded—26 by New Zealand against England at Eden Park, Auckland.
1969 Dwight D. Eisenhower, American Army commander, Republican statesman and 34th President from 1953 to 1961, affectionately called 'Ike', died in Washington.

1977 Eric Shipton, British mountaineer who made five assaults on Mount Everest, died in Salisbury, Wiltshire.
Breakfast TV in Britain started as an experiment, on Yorkshire TV, hosted by Bob Warman.

1979 A radiation leak occurred at the Three Mile Island nuclear station in Pennsylvania.

1983 Ian MacGregor was appointed chairman of the British National Coal Board.

---

29 MARCH

1461 The Battle of Towton took place in North Yorkshire in a snowstorm during the Wars of the Roses—the bloodiest battle fought on British soil, in which it was said that over 28 000 died.

1769 Nicolas Soult, French marshal serving under Napoleon, born.

1788 Charles Wesley, English evangelist, hymn writer and younger brother of John, died.

1790 John Tyler, American Whig statesman and 10th President, born in Greenway, Virginia.

1866 John Keble, English cleric who inspired the start of the Oxford Movement (a revivial in the Church of England), died in Hursley, Hampshire.

1869 Sir Edwin Lutyens, English architect, born in London.

1871 The Royal Albert Hall at Kensington, built in memory of Prince Albert, was opened by Queen Victoria.

1902 Sir William Walton, English composer, born in Oldham, Lancashire, to musical parents.

1912 Captain Scott perished in Antarctica returning from his expedition to the South Pole.

1918 Pearl Bailey, American singer, born in Newport News, Virginia.

1920 After 42 years service in the British Army Sir William Robertson attained the rank of field marshal—the only British soldier to rise through the ranks from private.

1931 Norman Tebbit, British Conservative politician and a chairman of the party, born.

1939 The Spanish Civil War was declared to have ended, Franco was named Caudillo, or leader of the nation.

1940 Metal strips were introduced into the Bank of England £1 notes, as an anti-forgery device.

1961 The Twenty-third Amendment to the US Constitution was ratified, dealing with the Presidential vote for the District of Columbia.

1972 J. Arthur Rank, industrialist and builder of a British film organisation, created a Peer in 1957, died.

1973 The last US troops left South Vietnam.
1980 Mantovani, Anglo-Italian conductor famous for his harmonious orchestral arrangements, died.
1981 The first London marathon was run, and won by Norwegian Inge Simonsen.

30 MARCH   [90]

1746 Francisco de Goya, Spanish painter, born in Fuendetodos, near Saragossa, the son of a master gilder.
1820 Anna Sewell, English author, notably *Black Beauty*, born in Great Yarmouth, Norfolk.
1840 George Bryan ('Beau') Brummell, English dandy and leader of fashion, died in Caen, France, in the pauper lunatic asylum.
1842 Dr Crawford Long of Jefferson, Georgia, performed the first surgical operation using an anaesthetic. James Venable had a cyst removed from his neck while under ether.
1853 Vincent van Gogh, Dutch painter, born in the village of Groot-Zundert, the son of a Lutheran pastor.
1856 The Treaty of Paris was signed, ending the Crimean War.
1867 Through the efforts of Secretary of State William H. Seward, Alaska was acquired by America from Russia for 7.2 million dollars—the 375 million acres worked out at less than 2 cents an acre, including all rights.
1870 The Fifteenth Amendment to the US Constitution was ratified, stating that race was no bar to voting rights.
1884 Sean O'Casey, Irish playwright, notably *Juno and the Paycock*, born in a poor part of Dublin.
1913 Frankie Laine, American singer, born in Chicago, Illinois, as Frank Paul Lo Vecchio.
1927 Wally Grout, Queensland and Australian Test cricketer, born.
1929 The first commercial air route between London and Karachi was inaugurated by Imperial Airways.
1930 Rolf Harris, Australian entertainer, born.
1938 Warren Beatty, American film actor and director, born in Richmond, Virginia, the older brother of Shirley MacLaine.
1950 Léon Blum, French Socialist statesman and Prime Minister, died.
1967 The wrecked oil tanker *Torrey Canyon*, off Land's End was bombed to destruction.
1981 An attempt to assassinate President Reagan was made by John Hinckley, outside Washington's Hilton Hotel.
1986 James Cagney, American film actor and Oscar winner in 1942 for *Yankee Doodle Dandy*, died aged 86.
1987 'Sunflowers' by Vincent van Gogh was sold at auction by Christie's in London for £24 750 000.

1732 Franz Joseph Haydn, Austrian composer, born in Rohrau, the son of a wheelwright.

1809 Edward Fitzgerald, English scholar and poet, born near Woodbridge, Suffolk.

Nikolai Gogol, Russian novelist, born in Sorochinsty, Poltava.

1811 Robert Bunsen, German chemist, physicist and inventor, born in Göttingen, Lower Saxony.

1837 John Constable, English landscape painter, notably *The Hay Wain*, died.

1851 Sir Francis Bell, New Zealand statesman, born in Nelson, South Island.

1855 Charlotte Brontë, the oldest of the three literary sisters, author of *Jane Eyre*, died during pregnancy.

1872 Sergei Diaghilev, Russian music and ballet impresario, born in Novgorod.

Arthur Griffith, Irish nationalist leader and President of the Irish Free State, born in Dublin.

1878 Jack Johnson, Negro American heavyweight boxing champion, born in Galveston, Texas.

1889 The 300-metre Eiffel Tower was completed in readiness for the Universal Exhibition in Paris, and inaugurated by Premier Tirard.

1900 Henry, Duke of Gloucester, third son of King George V, born.

1921 Gordon Richards rode 'Gay Lord' at Leicester, the first of 4870 winners in his career.

1935 Richard Chamberlain, American film actor, born in Beverly Hills, California.

1938 David Steel, British politician and Liberal Party leader, born.

1946 General Gort, British Commander of the British Expeditionary Force in France in 1939 and the retreat in 1940, died.

1949 Newfoundland, with its dependency of Labrador, became the tenth Province of the Dominion of Canada.

1970 Timoshenko, Soviet Army marshal of World War II, died.

1973 'Red Rum' won the Grand National Steeplechase of thirty jumps and 4½ miles in a record time of 9 minutes 1.9 seconds.

1979 The British Navy was finally withdrawn from Malta.

1980 Jesse Owens, distinguished American athlete, died in Tucson, Arizona.

1986 Captain Scott's ship *Discovery*, after 51 years in London, left for Dundee, where she was built.

1988 Sir William McMahon, Australian Prime Minister (1971–72), died aged 80.

1578 William Harvey, English physician who discovered the circulation of the blood, born in Folkestone, Kent.

1810 Napoleon, desirous of an heir, married Marie Louise of Austria.

1815 Otto von Bismarck, German statesman and first Chancellor, born in Schönhausen, Brandenburg.

1875 *The Times* became the first newspaper to publish a daily weather chart.

1883 Lon Chaney, American silent-screen actor, born in Colorado Springs, Colorado.

1893 Cicely Courtneidge, British actress, born in Sydney, Australia.

1898 Henry Luce, American editor and publisher, born in Tengchow, China.

1902 The use of the treadmill in British prisons was finally suspended.

1917 Scott Joplin, American ragtime pianist and composer, of such as *Maple Leaf Rag*, died.

1918 The Royal Air Force was formed, by the amalgamation of the Royal Flying Corps and the Royal Naval Air Service.

1932 Debbie Reynolds, American singer and film actress, born in El Paso, Texas, as Mary Frances Reynolds.

1945 Okinawa, the principal Japanese base in the Ryukyu group, was invaded in the final campaign in the Far East. Victory was achieved after 83 days of fighting.

1947 King George II of Greece died, and was succeeded by his brother as Paul I.
     The school leaving age in Britain was raised to 15.

1948 Britain's electricity industry was nationalised.

1954 The US Air Force Academy was created at Colorado Springs in Colorado.

1957 David Gower, Leicestershire cricketer and an England captain, born in Tunbridge Wells, Kent.

1960 America launched the first meteorological satellite, *Tiros I*.

1965 Greater London came into being, comprising the City of London and 32 metropolitan boroughs.

1967 Sir Edmund Compton took office as Britain's first Ombudsman.

1973 Value Added Tax came into operation in Britain.

1974 Changes were made in many names and boundaries of the counties of England and Wales.

1725 Giovanni Casanova, Italian adventurer, born in Venice.

1792 The first United States Mint was established at Philadelphia, then the nation's capital.

1801 The naval Battle of Copenhagen took place, in the course of which Nelson, aboard the *Elephant*, put the telescope to his blind eye and so 'did not see' Admiral Parker's signal to break off the fight—the Danish fleet was destroyed.

1805 Hans Christian Andersen, Danish writer of fairy tales, born in Odense, the son of a shoemaker.

1827 Holman Hunt, English painter and member of the Pre-Raphaelite Brotherhood, born in London.

1840 Emile Zola, French novelist, born in Paris, the son of an Italian engineer.

1865 Richard Cobden, British statesman who worked for the repeal of the Corn Laws with John Bright, died in London.

1868 The murderess Frances Kidder was hanged outside Maidstone Jail—the last public execution of a woman.

1872 Samuel Morse, American inventor of the telegraphic Morse Code, died in New York City aged 80.

1873 Sergei Rachmaninov, Russian composer and piano virtuoso, born in Nijni-Novgorod.

1908 Buddy Ebsen, American stage and film actor, born in Belleville, Illinois.

1914 Sir Alec Guinness, English actor and Oscar winner in 1957, born in Marylebone, London.

1926 Jack Brabham, motor racing champion and car builder, born in Sydney, Australia.

1928 Theodore Richards, American chemist, who in 1914 became the country's first winner of the Nobel Prize for chemistry, died.

1939 Marvin Gaye, American soul singer, born in Washington, D.C.

1940 Metal strips were introduced into the Bank of England ten-shilling notes, as an anti-forgery device.
Mike Hailwood, British motorcycle racing champion, born in Oxford.
Donald Jackson, Canadian world ice skating champion, born.

1946 The Royal Military Academy was established at Sandhurst in Berkshire, having been at Woolwich since 1741.

1955 Duncan Edwards, at 18 years and 6 months, became the youngest footballer to play for England, against Scotland in the home international championship.

1966 (Cecil Scott) C. S. Forester, British novelist and writer of the 'Hornblower' series, died.

1974 Georges Pompidou, French statesman, Prime Minister and President from 1969, died in office.

1977 The English racehorse 'Red Rum' won the Grand National steeplechase for a record third time, ridden by Tommy Stack.

1982 Argentinian forces invaded and occupied the British Falkland Islands in the South Atlantic.

1367 Henry IV, the first Lancastrian King of England, born in Bolingbroke Castle, Lincolnshire, the son of John of Gaunt.

1721 Robert Walpole became Britain's first Prime Minister, an office he held continuously until 12 February 1742.

1783 Washington Irving, American writer, born in New York City.

1860 The Pony Express, founded by William Russell, was first run— 1980 miles between St Joseph in Missouri and Sacramento in California—ended on 24 October 1861 when the first trans-continental telegraph line was completed.

1866 (James Barry) J. B. Hertzog, South African statesman and nationalist Prime Minister, born in Wellington, Cape Colony.

1882 Jesse James, American outlaw and robber, was shot in the back at close range by one of his own gang, Robert Ford, in St Joseph, Missouri.

1893 Leslie Howard, British film actor, born in London as Leslie Steiner.

1897 Johannes Brahms, German composer and pianist, died in Vienna.

1901 Richard D'Oyly Carte, English theatrical impresario who staged the Gilbert and Sullivan operettas, died.

1924 Marlon Brando, American film actor and twice Oscar winner for *On the Waterfront* (1954) and *The Godfather* (1972) born in Omaha, Nebraska.
Doris Day, American singer and film actress, born in Cincinnati, Ohio as Doris Kappelhoff.

1925 Anthony Wedgwood Benn, British Labour politician, born.

1926 Virgil Grissom, American astronaut and the third man to enter space, born in Mitchell, Indiana.

1930 Haile Selassie was proclaimed Emperor of Ethiopia, a country he ruled for 44 years.
Helmut Kohl, Chancellor of the Federal Republic of Germany, born.

1933 Two British planes made history by becoming the first to fly over Mount Everest.

1954 Oxford won the 100th University Boat Race.

1978 The first regular BBC radio broadcasts of the proceedings in the British Parliament commenced.

1982 Dick Saunders, at 48, became the oldest winner of the Grand National steeplechase, riding 'Grittar'—in the same race Geraldine Rees on 'Cheers' became the first female jockey to finish the 4½ mile course of 30 fences.

National day of Hungary.

1581 Francis Drake was knighted on board the *Golden Hind* at Deptford, on the River Thames.

1617 John Napier, Scottish mathematician and first to publish logarithm tables, in 1614, died at Merchiston Castle, Edinburgh.

1774 Oliver Goldsmith, Irish writer, notably *The Vicar of Wakefield*, died in London.

1841 William Harrison, American statesman and 9th President, died after only 31 days in office, as a result of catching pneumonia during his inauguration—his term of office was finished by vice-President John Tyler.

1887 Susanna Salter was elected at Argonia in Kansas to become the world's first woman mayor.

1922 Elmer Bernstein, American composer and writer of film scores, born in New York City.

1929 Karl Benz, German engineer and pioneer of early motor cars with internal combustion engines, died aged 84.

1933 America's helium-filled airship *Akron* crashed into the sea off the coast of New Jersey during a violent storm.

1934 The first 'cats-eye' studs were laid in the road at a notorious accident blackspot, a crossroads near Bradford.

1941 André Michelin, French industrialist who built the first factories for the mass-production of rubber motor tyres, died in Paris.

1949 The North Atlantic Treaty Organisation was created in a treaty signed at Washington.

1958 Members of Campaign for Nuclear Disarmament held their first protest march, setting out from Hyde Park Corner marching to the Atomic Weapons Research Establishment in Aldermaston, Berkshire.

1968 Martin Luther King, American Negro civil rights leader and Nobel Peace Prize winner in 1964, was assassinated at his motel in Memphis, Tennessee—the alleged assassin was James Earl Ray.

1979 Ali Bhutto, Prime Minister of Pakistan, was hanged for allegedly conspiring to murder a political opponent.

1981 Bob Champion won the English Grand National steeplechase on 'Aldaniti'.

1983 Gloria Swanson, American stage and film actress, died in a New York hospital aged 84.

1988 The last episode of British TV soap opera *Crossroads*, number 4510, was shown, the first having been seen in December 1964.

1614 The Addled Parliament began sitting—was dissolved on 7 June without having passed a Bill—hence its name.

1648 Elihu Yale, American philanthropist, born in Boston, Massachusetts of British parents.

1732 Jean Fragonard, French painter and engraver, born in Grasse.

1793 The plan for the building of the Capitol, Washington DC, USA, drawn by William Thornton, was accepted.

1794 Georges Jacques Danton, French revolutionary leader, guillotined for treason.

1811 Robert Raikes, English philanthropist and founder of the Sunday School movement, died in Gloucester.

1818 Chile achieved independence from Spanish rule after a revolutionary war led by Bernardo O'Higgins.

1827 Joseph Lister, English surgeon and pioneer of disinfection and antiseptics, born in London.

1884 John Wisden, Sussex cricketer and compiler of the record books that bear his name, died in London.

1894 Chesney Allen, English comedian and member of the famous Crazy Gang, born.

1900 Spencer Tracy, American film actor, born in Milwaukee, Wisconsin.

1901 Melvyn Douglas, American film actor, born in Macon, Georgia, as Melvyn Hesselberg.

1908 Bette Davis, American film actress and twice Oscar winner, for *Dangerous* (1935) and *Jezebel* (1938), born in Lowell, Massachusetts.

1915 Jess Willard won the world heavyweight boxing title, knocking out Jack Johnson in Havana, Cuba.

1916 Gregory Peck, American film actor, born in La Jolla, California.

1922 Tom Finney, English footballer with 76 international caps, born.

1933 Earl Biggers, American mystery-story writer and creator of 'Charlie Chan', died.

1955 Sir Winston Churchill resigned as Prime Minister.

1964 Douglas MacArthur, American general and commander in the Pacific in World War II, died in Washington, DC aged 84.
Driverless tube trains began regular trials on the Central Line of the London Underground between Woodford and Hainault.

1971 Mrs Fran Phipps became the first woman to reach the North Pole.

1975 Chiang Kai-Shek, Chinese military and political leader, died aged 87.

1976 Howard Hughes, American multi-millionaire industrialist, died on board his private jet en route to hospital at Houston, Texas aged 71.
James Callaghan succeeded Harold Wilson as Prime Minister, defeating Michael Foot in the final ballot for the leadership of the Labour Party.

1982   The British Fleet set sail from Portsmouth for the Falklands.

6 APRIL

1199   King Richard I, called the Lion Heart, died from a wound
        received while besieging the Castle of Chaluz.
1520   Raphael (Raffaello Sanzio or Santi), Italian Renaissance painter,
        died in Rome.
1528   Albrecht Dürer, German artist and engraver, died in Nuremberg.
1830   The Mormon Movement or Church of Jesus Christ of Latter Day
        Saints was founded by Joseph Smith in Fayette, New York State.
1843   William Wordsworth was appointed Poet Laureate.
1874   Harry Houdini, American magician and escapologist, born in
        Appleton, Wisconsin as Ehrich Weiss, the son of a rabbi from
        Budapest.
1896   Modern Olympic Games were revived by Pierre de Coubertin, at
        Athens, with James Connolly of America winning the first Gold
        medal, in the triple jump event.
1906   Sir John Betjeman, English writer and Poet Laureate, born in
        London.
1909   Robert Peary became the first man to reach the North Pole—at
        his sixth attempt in 15 years—with his negro servant Matthew
        Henson and four Eskimos.
1917   The United States of America declared war on Germany.
1926   Rev. Ian Paisley, British politician and MP for Antrim, born.
1929   André Prévin, conductor, composer and musical director, born
        in Berlin.
1944   Pay As You Earn income tax came into force in Britain. The
        system was devised by Sir Cornelius Gregg.
1955   Sir Anthony Eden succeeded Sir Winston Churchill as Prime
        Minister.
1965   The communications satellite *Early Bird* was launched by USA.
1971   Igor Stravinsky, Russian-born composer best known for his
        ballets, died in New York City aged 88.
1984   Sir Arthur Harris, Britain's wartime bomber commander, died
        aged 91.
1985   Henrietta Shaw became the first woman to cox Cambridge in the
        Oxford and Cambridge University boat race.
1988   Sir John Clements CBE, British actor-manager, died aged 77.

7 APRIL

1506   St Francis Xavier, Spanish Jesuit missionary, born near Sanguesa.

1739 The notorious highwayman Dick Turpin was hanged in York for the murder of a keeper from Epping—was buried in York as 'John Palmer'.

1770 William Wordsworth, English poet, born in Cockermouth, Cumbria, the son of an attorney.

1827 Friction matches, the invention of Stockton chemist John Walker, were first sold.

1853 Queen Victoria became the first Royal to accept the use of chloroform, for the birth of her eighth child, Prince Leopold.

1862 The Federal Army under Grant defeated the Confederates under General Joseph Johnson on the second day of the Battle of Shiloh, near the Tennessee river.

1891 Phineas T. Barnum, American showman who created 'The Greatest Show on Earth' in 1871, died aged 80.
David Low, British political cartoonist, born in Dunedin on the South Island of New Zealand.

1897 Walter Winchell, American gossip columnist and radio commentator, born in New York City.

1914 Middleweight Al McCoy knocked out George Chip in 45 seconds in Brooklyn, New York, to record the shortest world title fight win.

1915 Billie Holiday, American jazz-blues singer, born in Baltimore, Maryland, to be christened Eleanora.

1928 James Garner, American film actor, born in Norman, Oklahoma as James Baumgarner.

1939 Italy invaded and seized Albania and placed it under the rule of the King of Italy.
Joseph Lyons, Australian statesman and 14th Prime Minister from 1932, died.
David Frost, British TV interviewer and presenter, born in Tenterden, Kent.

1947 Henry Ford, American motor car manufacturer, the father of 'mass-production' died aged 83.

1948 WHO—the World Health Organisation—was established 'with the aim of attaining the highest possible level of health for all people', with headquarters at Geneva.

1968 Jim Clark, British motor racing champion driver, was killed during a race on the Hockenheim track in West Germany.

---

8 APRIL

1614 El Greco, Greek-born Spanish painter, sculptor and architect, died.

1838 Brunel's 236 foot steamship *Great Western* left Bristol for New
York on her maiden voyage, under the command of Captain
James Hosken.
1861 Elisha Graves Otis, American inventor of the first safe elevator in
1852, died in Yonkers, New York.
1875 Albert I, King of the Belgians, born.
1882 Warwickshire County Cricket Club was founded at a meeting in
the Queen's Hotel, Coventry.
1889 Sir Adrian Boult, English conductor and musical director, born in
Chester.
1893 Mary Pickford, American film actress, born in Toronto in the
Canadian Province of Ontario as Gladys Marie Smith.
1908 Herbert Henry Asquith became Liberal Prime Minister and held
office until 7 December 1916.
1912 Sonja Henie, Olympic and world skating champion and film
actress in America, born in Oslo, Norway.
1913 The Seventeenth Amendment to the US Constitution was
ratified, dealing with the method of election of State Senators.
1915 The Croix de Guerre, France's military decoration for bravery in
battle, was instituted.
1918 Elizabeth Ford, wife of America's 38th President, born in
Chicago, Illinois, née Bloomer.
1919 Ian Smith, Rhodesian Prime Minister, born in Selukwe, Southern
Rhodesia.
1930 Dorothy Tutin, English actress, born.
1946 The League of Nations held its final meeting.
1950 Vaslav Nijinsky, legendary Russian ballet dancer, died in
London.
1963 Julian Lennon, British musician, born the son of John Lennon.
Lester Pearson became Labour Prime Minister of Canada defeating John Diefenbaker's Conservative Party.
1973 Pablo Picasso, Spanish painter and founder of the Cubist
movement, died aged 91.
1986 Clint Eastwood, renowned film actor, was elected Mayor of
Carmel in California.

9 APRIL   *[100]*

1483 Death of King Edward IV—accession of his young son as
Edward V.
1626 Francis Bacon, English philosopher and statesman, died near
Highgate in London, as Lord Verulam.
1649 The Duke of Monmouth, son of King Charles II and Lucy Walter,
born in Rotterdam.

1806 Isambard Brunel, English engineer, born in Portsmouth, the son of a refugee from the French Revolution.
1835 Leopold II, King of the Belgians, born in Brussels.
1838 The National Gallery in London's Trafalgar Square was opened.
1865 Confederate General Robert E. Lee surrendered to General Grant at Appomattox Court House in Virginia, bringing the American Civil War to an end.
1867 John Watson, Australian Labour statesman, born in Valparaiso.
1872 Léon Blum, French Socialist statesman and Prime Minister, born in Paris.
1882 Dante Gabriel Rossetti, English poet and painter, co-founder of the Pre-Raphaelite Brotherhood with Millais and Hunt, died in Kent.
1893 Sir Victor Gollancz, British publisher, born in London.
1898 Paul Robeson, American negro singer, born in Princeton, New Jersey, the son of a minister.
1906 Hugh Gaitskell, British politician and leader of the Labour Party, born in London.
1909 Robert Helpmann, Australian ballet dancer and choreographer, born in Mount Gambier in the State of South Australia.
1957 Severiano Ballesteros, Spanish international golf champion, born in Santander.
1959 Frank Lloyd Wright, one of the most influential US architects in history, died in Phoenix, Arizona aged 89.
1969 The British supersonic airliner *Concorde* made its maiden flight, from Bristol to Fairford in Gloucestershire.
1983 Jenny Pitman became the first woman to train an English Grand National steeplechase winner, with 'Corbiere'.

10 APRIL [101]

1790 The US Congress inaugurated the first American patent system.
1820 The first British settlers arrived in South Africa, at Algoa Bay near Port Elizabeth in Cape Province.
1829 William Booth, English evangelist preacher and founder of the Salvation Army, born in Nottingham, the son of a builder.
1834 John MacArthur, known as 'the father of New South Wales', died.
1841 The American newspaper *New York Tribune*, founded by Horace Greeley, was first published.
1847 Joseph Pulitzer, American newspaper publisher, born in Mako, Hungary.
1849 The safety pin was patented by New Yorker Walter Hunt.

1858 Big Ben, the bell within the world's most famous clock, was cast in Whitechapel in the East End of London. The bell weighs 13.5 tons (12 metric tonnes). It was named after Sir Benjamin Hall, the then Commissioner of Works, who was a large, tall man known as 'Big Ben'.

1864 Maximilian, an Austrian Archduke, was made Emperor of Mexico.

1868 George Arliss, American film actor, born in London as Augustus George Andrews.

1870 Lenin, Russian Communist leader and founder of Bolshevism, born in Simbirsk (now Ulyanovsk) as Vladimir Ilyich Ulyanov, the son of a schools inspector.

1908 Vic Feather, British trade union leader, born.

1917 Vimy Ridge, in northern France, was taken by Canadian forces with heavy casualties in an epic assault during the Battle of Arras, in the First World War.

1929 Mike Hawthorn, British motor racing driver, born in Mexborough, Yorkshire.

1932 Omar Sharif, film actor, born in Alexandria, Egypt as Michel Shaboub (or Shalhouz).

1937 Stan Mellor, English National Hunt jockey, born in Manchester.

1954 Auguste Lumière, French pioneer of cinematography with his brother Louis, died in Lyons.

1963 The US Navy atomic submarine *Thresher* sank off Cape Cod, with the loss of 129 lives.

1966 Evelyn Waugh, English novelist, died near Taunton in Somerset.

1988 Sandy Lyle became the first British golfer to win the US Masters tournament, in Atlanta, Georgia, together with the coveted Green Jacket.

---

11 APRIL [102]

1689 King William III and Queen Mary II were crowned as joint sovereigns of Great Britain by the Bishop of London—the Archbishop of Canterbury refused to perform the service.

1713 The Treaty of Utrecht was signed, ending the hostilities in the War of the Spanish Succession.

1770 George Canning, British Tory statesman and Prime Minister, born in London.

1814 Napoleon abdicated as Emperor, and was exiled to the island of Elba—Louis ascended the throne of France on his return from refuge in England.

1819 Sir Charles Hallé, British pianist, conductor and founder of the famous Hallé orchestra, born in Hagen, Germany.

1855 London's first six pillar boxes were installed, and were painted green.
1884 Charles Reade, English novelist, notably *The Cloister and the Hearth*, died.
1893 Dean Acheson, American politician and Secretary of State, born in Middletown, Connecticut.
1899 By a treaty of ratification Puerto Rico was ceded by Spain to the USA.
1908 Dan Maskell, British tennis champion, coach and commentator, born.
1926 Luther Burbank, American botanist and plant breeder, died.
1930 The British newspaper *Daily Express* became the first to publish television programmes.
1945 The German concentration camp at Buchenwald, near Weimar, was liberated by the Americans.
1961 The trial of the Nazi war criminal Adolf Eichmann opened in Jerusalem.
1970 *Apollo 13* was launched, with James Lovell, Fred Haise and John Swigert.
The English FA Cup final at Wembley Stadium, between Leeds United and Chelsea, ended in a draw—the first since 1912.
1982 The trans-globe expedition reached the North Pole, to complete the first circumnavigation of the world via the Poles.

12 APRIL [103]

1606 The Union Jack was adopted as the flag of England, Wales and Scotland.
1684 Niccolo Amati, the most famous of a family of violin makers in Cremona, died.
1709 The English magazine *The Tatler* was first published.
1861 The American Civil War, a conflict between the 23 northern states and the 11 southern states, began with the bombardment of Fort Sumter in South Carolina by the Confederate Army under General Pierre Beauregard.
1903 The first municipal motor omnibus service in the world was inaugurated in England between Eastbourne Station and Meads, Sussex.
1912 Clara Barton, founder of the American Red Cross and called the 'Angel of the Battlefield' during the Civil War, died aged 90.
1913 Lionel Hampton, American musician and bandleader, born in Birmingham, Alabama.
1930 Wilfred Rhodes became the oldest man to play in a cricket Test match, aged 52 years and 165 days, when he played for England v the West Indies in Kingston, Jamaica.

1938 Fyodor Chaliapin, Russian operatic bass singer considered one of opera's greatest performers, died.

1941 Bobby Moore, English international footballer with 108 appearances for his country, born in Barking, London.

1945 Franklin D. Roosevelt, American Democrat statesman and 32nd President from 1933, died of cerebral haemorrhage in Warm Springs, Georgia—the remainder of his term of office was completed by vice-President Harry S. Truman.

1954 *Rock Around the Clock*, the best selling pop record of all time, was recorded by Bill Haley.

1961 Yuri Gagarin was launched in *Vostok I* from Tyuratam in Kazakhstan and made a single orbit of the earth, and landed near Engels in the Saratov region.

1965 The Astrodome at Houston, the first indoor stadium, the home of the Houston Astros baseball team, was opened.

1981 Joe Louis, American legendary heavyweight boxing champion, died in a Las Vegas hospital.
The United States launched its pioneering space shuttle *Columbia* from Cape Canaveral, with Robert Crippen and John Young.

13 APRIL [104]

1668 John Dryden was appointed the first Poet Laureate, an appointment he kept until 1689.

1732 Lord North, British statesman and Tory Prime Minister, born in London.

1741 The Royal Military Academy was established at Woolwich—is now at Sandhurst, Berkshire.

1743 Thomas Jefferson, American statesman and 3rd President, born in Shadwell, Virginia, the son of a civil engineer.

1771 Richard Trevithick, English engineer and designer of steam engines, born in Illogan, Redruth, Cornwall.

1852 Frank Winfield Woolworth, American merchant and founder of the chain of stores which bears his name, born in Rodman, Jefferson County in the State of New York.

1892 Sir Arthur Harris, British wartime bomber commander, born.

1919 The Amritsar massacre took place in the Punjab, in which General Dyer's British troops shot 380 of Gandhi's followers and wounded over 1200.
Howard Keel, American actor and leading man in musical comedy films, born in Gillespie, Illinois.

1922 John Braine, English author, born in Bradford, Yorkshire.

1935 The London to Australia airline service was inaugurated by Imperial Airways and QANTAS.

1936 Joe Payne scored ten goals, for Luton Town against Bristol Rovers, on his debut as a centre forward. This is a record for one man in one game.

1937 Britain's aircraft carrier *Ark Royal* was launched from Cammell Laird's shipyard in Birkenhead.

1951 The Coronation Stone (Stone of Destiny), stolen on the previous Christmas Day by Scottish nationalists, was returned to Westminster Abbey.

1952 Jonjo O'Neill, champion National Hunt jockey in Britain and now trainer, born in Ireland.

1963 Gary Kasparov, Russian chess player and a world champion, born.

1964 Ian Smith became Prime Minister of Southern Rhodesia on the resignation of Winston Field.

---

14 APRIL [105]

1629 Christian Huygens, Dutch scientist and astronomer, born in The Hague, the son of a poet.

1759 George Frederick Handel, German composer, best known for his *Messiah*, died in London aged 74.

1828 *Webster's Dictionary* was first published—properly named 'American Dictionary of the English language'.

1865 Abraham Lincoln, America's 16th President from 1861, was shot in Ford's Theatre by John Wilkes Booth. He died the following day—the remainder of his term of office was completed by vice-President Andrew Johnson, sworn in as President.

1894 Thomas Edison's 'Kinetoscope', invented in 1887, was given its first public showing at 1155 Broadway, New York City.

1904 Sir John Gielgud, English Shakespearean actor, born in London.

1917 Dr Zamenof, Polish linguist and creator of the international language of Esperanto, died.

1925 Rod Steiger, American film actor and Oscar winner in 1967 for *In the Heat of the Night*, born in Westhampton in the State of New York.

1929 The Monaco Grand Prix was first run, 76 laps round the narrow streets and the harbour of Monte Carlo.

1931 *The Highway Code* was first issued in Britain by the Ministry of Transport.
Alfonso XIII, the last king of Spain, abdicated in favour of a Republic.

1941 Julie Christie, British film actress and Oscar winner, born in India.

96

1951 Ernest Bevin, British Labour statesman and trade union leader, died.

1975 Fredric March, American film actor and twice Academy Award (Oscar) winner for *Dr Jekyll and Mr Hyde*, in 1932 and for *The Best Years of our Lives*, in 1946, died.

1981 The first American space shuttle landed at Edwards Air Force Base in California after a successful mission.

15 APRIL [106]

1755 Dr Samuel Johnson's famous dictionary was published, after eight years' work and containing 40 000 words.

1764 Madame de Pompadour, French courtier and mistress of Louis XV, died in Versailles.

1793 The first Bank of England £5 notes were issued.

1797 British naval personnel mutinied at Spithead, in the Solent off Portsmouth.

1843 Henry James, American novelist, notably *The Wings of A Dove*, born in New York.

1845 The building of the new House of Lords was completed, after the fire of 1834, to the designs of Sir Charles Barry and Augustus Pugin.

1865 Andrew Johnson was sworn in as President of the United States on the death of Abraham Lincoln.

1875 James J. Jeffries, American heavyweight boxer, born in Carroll, Ohio.

1883 Stanley Bruce, Australian statesman, born.

1888 Matthew Arnold, English poet and educationalist, died suddenly in Liverpool.

1889 Father Damien, Belgian RC priest and missionary, died on the Hawaiian island of Molokai.

1894 Bessie Smith, American blues singer, born in Chattanooga, Tennessee.

1901 Joe Davis, many times world snooker and billiards champion, born in Whitwell, near Chesterfield, Derbyshire.

1912 The 'unsinkable' White Star passenger liner *Titanic* sank in 2½ hours on her maiden voyage from Southampton to New York City, hitting an iceberg off Newfoundland, with the loss of over 1500 lives.

1940 Jeffrey Archer, British politician and author, born.

1942 The island of Malta was awarded the George Cross for its heroism during heavy German and Italian bombardments.

1949 Wallace Beery, American film actor and Academy Award (Oscar) winner for his part in *The Champ*, died.

1955 McDonald's, the world's largest hamburger chain, was founded in De Plaines, Chicago by Ray Kroc.

1961 England defeated Scotland 9–3 at Wembley in a record-scoring football match between the two countries.

1980 Jean-Paul Sartre, French dramatist and novelist who refused the Nobel Prize in 1964, died.

---

16 APRIL

1746 The Battle of Culloden took place near Inverness—the last battle in Britain—in which the Jacobites were defeated by the Duke of Cumberland's forces, terminating attempts of the Stuarts to regain the English throne.

1828 Francisco de Goya, Spanish painter and etcher, died in France aged 82.

1850 Madame Tussaud, Swiss founder of the famous wax museum in London, died.

1867 Wilbur Wright, the elder of the two American aviation pioneers, born near Millville in Indiana.

1875 The English Hockey Association was founded at Cannon Street Hotel, London.

1881 Earl of Halifax, British Conservative statesman and diplomat, born in Devon as Edward Frederick Lindley Wood.

1889 Charlie Chaplin, film actor, producer and director, born in Kennington, London, the son of two music hall entertainers.

1911 Guy Burgess, English civil servant and Russian spy, born in Devonport. He died in August 1963 in a Moscow hospital.

1912 American pilot Harriet Quimby became the first woman to fly the English Channel, from Dover to Hardelot.

1918 Spike Milligan, English comedy actor, born in Ahmaddnagar, India as Terence Alan Milligan.

1921 Peter Ustinov, English actor and producer, born in London.

1922 Kingsley Amis, English novelist, Booker Prize winner in 1986 with *The Old Devils*, born in London.

1924 Henry Mancini, American pianist and composer of many songs and film scores, born in Cleveland, Ohio.

1938 Bertram Mills, English circus proprietor, died in Chalfont St Giles, Buckinghamshire.

1939 Dusty Springfield, English pop singer, born in Hampstead as Mary O'Brien.

1940 Queen Margrethe II, Queen of Denmark, born.

1951 The British submarine *Affray* sank in the English Channel, with the loss of 75 lives.

1953 The Royal yacht *Britannia* was launched.
1954 Stock car racing was seen for the first time in Britain, at the Old Kent Road Stadium, New Cross in London.
1972 *Apollo 16* was launched with John Young, Charles Duke and Thomas Mattingley—Young and Duke making the 5th moon landing.

17 APRIL   *[108]*

National day of Syria.

1790 Benjamin Franklin, American scientist and statesman who helped draft the Declaration of Independence, died in Philadelphia aged 84.
1876 Ian Hay, Scottish writer, born as John Hay Beith.
1888 The first formal meeting of the Football League took place in the Royal Hotel, Manchester.
1894 Nikita Khrushchev, Russian political leader, born in Kalinovka, near Kursk.
1897 Thornton Wilder, American novelist and playwright, born in Madison, Wisconsin.
1916 Sirimavo Bandaranaike, Sri Lankan stateswoman and Prime Minister, born in Ratnapura.
1918 William Holden, American film actor and Oscar winner, born in O'Fallon, Illinois as William Beedle.
1929 James Last, international musician and arranger, born in Germany.
1937 A British attendance record at a football match was set when 149 547 watched Scotland v England at Hampden Park, Glasgow.
1946 Clare Francis, British round-the-world yachtswoman, born.
1957 Archbishop Makarios arrived back in Athens from his 13 month exile in the Seychelle Islands.
1961 An attempt by Cuban exiles and US forces to invade Cuba at the Bay of Pigs and overthrow Castro's Communist regime, was repulsed.
1969 In Britain all those over the age of 18 were allowed to vote—21 having been the age since 1928.
Bernadette Devlin became the youngest woman MP when elected for Mid Ulster, six days short of her 22nd birthday.
1980 Rhodesia became the independent nation of Zimbabwe.
1984 General Mark Clark, American military Commander of the 5th Army in Italy, died aged 87.
WPC Yvonne Fletcher was shot dead by terrorists outside the Libyan Embassy in London.

1480 Lucrezia Borgia, Italian noblewoman, born in Rome, the illegitimate daughter of Rodrigo Borgia (later Pope Alexander VI).

1689 Judge Jeffreys, Lord Chancellor notorious for his harshness at the 'Bloody Assizes' following the Monmouth Rebellion of 1685, died in the Tower of London.

1775 The night of Paul Revere's famous ride from Charlestown to Lexington, accompanied by William Dawes, to warn the Massachusetts colonists of the arrival of British troops at the outbreak of the War of American Independence.

1820 Franz von Suppé, Austrian composer, born in Spalato.

1867 Sir Robert Smirke, British architect who designed the front facade of the British Museum at Bloomsbury, died.

1874 David Livingstone's remains were interred in Westminster Abbey—he having died in Africa on 1 May 1873.

1882 Leopold Stokowski, American conductor and musical director, born in London of Polish origin.

1903 Bury beat Derby County 6–0 at Crystal Palace to record the most decisive victory in an FA Cup final.

1906 The San Francisco earthquake and resulting fire started just before dawn.

1923 Yankee Stadium, the home of the New York Yankees baseball team, was opened.

1932 Business reply-paid envelopes were introduced in Britain by the GPO.

1934 The first launderette was opened in Fort Worth, Texas by J. F. Cantrell, and called a 'Washateria'.

1946 Hayley Mills, English actress, born in London, the daughter of Sir John Mills.

1949 The start of the first Scout 'bob-a-job' week in Britain.
Will Hay, English comedy film actor, died.
The Republic of Ireland was proclaimed, severing ties with Britain by leaving the Commonwealth.

1955 Albert Einstein, naturalised-American physicist who propounded the theory of relativity and Nobel Prize winner in 1921, died in Princeton, New Jersey.

1978 The death penalty was abolished in Spain.

1661 Postmarks were introduced in Britain by the Post Office.

1775   The Battle of Lexington, the opening engagement in the War of
       American Independence, took place near Boston.
1824   Lord Byron died of marsh fever at Missolonghi while aiding the
       Greek insurgents who had risen against the Turks in their fight
       for independence, aged only 36.
1873   Sydney Barnes, Lancashire and England cricketer, born in
       Smethwick in the West Midlands.
1881   Benjamin Disraeli, British Conservative statesman, twice Prime
       Minister and as a novelist wrote *Coningsby*, died and was buried
       in Hughenden near High Wycombe, Buckinghamshire. The date
       became known as 'Primrose Day' from his liking for this flower.
1882   Charles Darwin, English naturalist who developed the theory of
       evolution, died near Orpington, Kent, and was buried in
       Westminster Abbey.
1903   Eliot Ness, American Government special agent, born in Chicago,
       Illinois.
1905   Jim Mollison, Scottish aviator, born in Glasgow.
1906   The San Francisco earthquake ended, resulting in 452 deaths.
       Pierre Curie, French physicist who discovered radium, was run
       over and killed in Paris.
1932   Jayne Mansfield, American film actress, born in Bryn Mawr,
       Pennsylvania as Vera Jane Palmer.
1933   Harold 'Dickie' Bird, England's foremost cricket umpire, born.
1935   Dudley Moore, English actor and composer, born in London.
1942   Alan Price, English pop singer, musician and composer, born.
1951   The initial Miss World contest took place, at the Lyceum
       Ballroom off the Strand in London—the winner was Miss
       Sweden—Kiki Haakonson.
1954   Trevor Francis, English soccer international and first to be
       involved in a million pound transfer fee, born.
1956   Prince Rainier of Monaco married Grace Kelly.
1958   Bobby Charlton made the first of his 106 football international
       appearances for England—against Scotland—and scored the first
       of his record 49 goals scored in international matches.
       Billy Meredith, Welsh international footballer with 48 caps, died
       aged 83.
1967   Konrad Adenauer, West German statesman and Chancellor from
       1949 to 1963, died aged 91.
1971   Russia launched the first space station, *Salyut*.
1989   Daphne du Maurier, English author, notably *Rebecca*, died at her
       home in Cornwall aged 81.

1768 Canaletto, Italian painter and a pioneer of architecturally accurate cityscapes, died in Venice.

1889 Adolf Hitler, German dictator and Nazi leader, born in Braunau, Austria, the son of a customs official, who had changed his name from Schicklgrüber.

1893 Harold Lloyd, American comedian of the silent film era, born in Burchard, Nebraska.

1902 Sir Donald Wolfit, English actor, born in Newark-on-Trent, Nottinghamshire.

1912 Bram Stoker, Dublin-born writer of the classic horror tale *Dracula* in 1897, died in London.
Fenway Park, the home of Boston Red Sox baseball team, was opened.

1916 Wrigley Field, the home of Chicago Cubs baseball team, was opened. It is the oldest in the National League and the only major League stadium without floodlights.

1938 Betty Cuthbert, Australian athlete and sprint champion, born.

1939 Battledress blouses and gaiters were first issued in the British Army.

1947 Christian X, King of Denmark since 1912, died.

1949 The first 3-day Badminton horse trials were held, at that village in Gloucestershire, the seat of the Duke of Beaufort—won by John Shedden on 'Golden Willow'.

1955 Two pairs of brothers, L. and I. Allchurch and J. and M. Charles, set a record by appearing in the same soccer international side for Wales at Windsor Park, Belfast.

1957 *Mayflower II*, a replica of the Pilgrim Father's ship, sailed from Plymouth to Cape Cod, the landfall of the 1620 original.

1968 Pierre Trudeau became Liberal Prime Minister of Canada for the first time.

1509 Death of King Henry VII in Richmond, Surrey—accession of his second son as Henry VIII.

1634 Jan van Riebeck, Dutch surgeon and founder of Cape Town, born in the Netherlands.

1782 Friedrich Froebel, German educational pioneer and founder of the kindergarten system, born in Oberweissbach.

1816 Charlotte Brontë, English novelist, born in Thornton, the eldest of three literary daughters of a Yorkshire clergyman.

1910 Mark Twain, American writer, especially of *Tom Sawyer* and *Huckleberry Finn*, died in Reading, Connecticut.

1916 Anthony Quinn, American film actor, born in Chihuahua, Mexico.

1918 The legendary German air ace Manfred von Richthofen, known as the 'Red Baron', was shot down in his bright red tri-plane, and died behind the British lines.

1926 Queen Elizabeth II was born at 17 Bruton Street in London— Elizabeth Alexandra Mary—the elder daughter of King George VI.

1932 Angela Mortimer, British tennis player and Wimbledon champion in 1961, born in Plymouth.

1952 Sir Stafford Cripps, British statesman, died in Switzerland.

1960 Brasilia was inaugurated as the new capital of Brazil—planned by Lucio Costa.

1964 BBC's second television channel opened.

1966 The opening of British Parliament was televised for the first time.

1967 A military coup took place in Greece, resulting in King Constantine II fleeing in exile to Rome.

1970 Bobby Charlton made his 100th football international appearance for England—against Northern Ireland at Wembley Stadium— and scored a goal.

1977 Milton 'Gummo' Marx, a Marx brother who became the family's agent and manager, died in Palm Springs, California.

1983 One pound coins went into circulation in Britain replacing the paper notes in England and Wales, but not in Scotland and Northern Ireland.

22 APRIL [113]

1500 Brazil was discovered by Pedro Alvarez Cabral, who claimed it on behalf of the King of Portugal.

1662 The Royal Society was constituted by Royal Charter from Charles II.

1707 Henry Fielding, English novelist, born at Sharpham Park, Glastonbury, the son of an Army general.

1724 Immanuel Kant, German philosopher, born in Königsberg, East Prussia, the son of a saddler.

1778 James Hargreaves, English inventor of the spinning jenny in 1764, died in Nottingham.

1806 Villeneuve, French admiral, died in Rennes, having stabbed himself on his way home after captivity in England.

1833 Richard Trevithick, English engineer and pioneer of the steam railway locomotive, died in Dartford, Kent.

1838 The British ship *Sirius* reached Sandy Hook, New York to become the first to cross the Atlantic under steam power only—having left Queenstown, now Cobh, on 4 April.

1876 Boston beat Philadelphia 6–5 in the first National League baseball game, and major League baseball dates from this game.

1881 Alexander Kerensky, Russian politician and Prime Minister until overthrown by the Bolsheviks, born in Simbirsk (now Ulyanovsk).

1884 An earthquake occurred in East Anglia, killing four.

1904 Robert Oppenheimer, American physicist who developed the US atomic bomb at Los Alamos, born in New York City.

1908 Sir Henry Campbell-Bannerman, British statesman and Liberal Prime Minister, died.
Eddie Albert, American actor known for 'nice guy' film roles, born in Rock Island, Illinois as Edward Albert Heimberger.

1912 Kathleen Ferrier, British contralto singer, born in Higher Walton, Lancashire.

1915 Germany introduced poison gas, at Ypres.

1916 Yehudi Menuhin, American violin virtuoso and child prodigy, born in New York City.

1917 Sir Sidney Nolan, Australian artist noted for his interpretation of the outback, born in Melbourne.

1933 Sir Frederick Henry Royce, English car manufacturer of Rolls Royce Ltd., died.

1938 Glen Campbell, American singer and entertainer, born in Billstown, Arkansas.

1960 Lloyd Honeyghan, British boxer and a world welterweight champion, born.

1968 The first open lawn tennis championship, amateurs and professionals alike, was the Hard Court Championship of GB held at the West Hants Club, Bournemouth, finishing on 27 April.

1969 Robin Knox Johnston arrived back at Falmouth in his yacht *Suhaili* after 312 days, having completed the earliest non-stop solo circumnavigation of the earth.

1972 John Fairfax and Sylvia Cook in their 35 ft *Britannia II* arrived at Hayman Island, Australia to become the first to row across the Pacific—having left San Francisco on the previous 26 April.

23 APRIL [114]

St George's Day—national day of England.

1564 The traditional date of the birth of William Shakespeare in Stratford-on-Avon, the third of eight children of a tanner.

1616 Miguel de Cervantes, Spanish novelist, best known for his masterpiece *Don Quixote*, died in Madrid.
William Shakespeare, playwright and poet, died.

1661 The coronation of King Charles II took place.

1697 George Anson, English admiral, born in Shugborough Park, Staffordshire.

1702 The coronation of Queen Anne took place.

1775 Joseph Turner, English landscape and seascape painter, born in Covent Garden, London, the son of a barber.

1791 James Buchanan, American Democrat statesman and 15th President, born in Stony Batter near Mercersburg, Pennsylvania, the son of a farmer.

1850 William Wordsworth, English poet and Poet Laureate from 1843, died at Rydal Mount, Grasmere in the Lake District aged 80.

1861 Viscount Allenby, British Army commander, born in Brackenhurst, Nottinghamshire.

1879 The Shakespeare Memorial Theatre, in Stratford-on-Avon, was opened.

1891 Sergei Prokofiev, Russian composer of *Peter and the Wolf*, born in Sontsovka in the Ukraine.

1893 Billy Smart, British circus proprietor, born in London the son of a fairground owner.

1897 Lester Pearson, Canadian statesman and Liberal Prime Minister, born in Newtonbrook, Ontario.

1899 Ngaio Marsh, mystery writer, born in Christchurch, New Zealand.

1915 Rupert Brooke, English poet, died of blood poisoning on the Greek island of Skyros on his way to the Dardanelles.

1924 The Empire Exhibition opened at the Wembley Stadium in London.

1927 Cardiff City beat Arsenal 1–0 in the FA Cup final to become the first club to take the Cup out of England.

1928 Shirley Temple, American child film star, born in Santa Monica, California—is now Mrs Charles Black.

1936 Roy Orbison American singer and composer, born in Wink, Texas.

1940 Lee Majors, American TV film actor, born in Wyandotte, Michigan.

1942 Sandra Dee, American film actress, born in Bayonne, New Jersey as Alexandra Zuck.

1965 The Pennine Way—250 miles long from Edale in Derbyshire to Kirk Yetholm in Roxburghshire—opened.

1967 Russian *Soyuz I* was launched, and after completing 17 orbits crashed on re-entry, 'on the Steppes of Orenburg', killing Vladimir Komarov.

1968 5p and 10p decimal coins were issued in Britain.

1983 Cliff Thorburn scored the first televised maximum break of 147 in the World Snooker championships, at Crucible Theatre, Sheffield.

1985 Princess Anne made her flat-racing debut, at Epsom.
1986 Otto Preminger, US film director, died.
Jim Laker, English Test cricketer and broadcaster, died.

---

24 APRIL

1743 Edmund Cartwright, British inventor of the power loom in 1785, born in Marnham, Nottinghamshire.

1800 The United States Library of Congress, the largest in the world, was founded, on Capitol Hill in Washington, DC.

1815 Anthony Trollope, English post-office official and novelist, born in London.

1856 Philippe Pétain, French statesman and Army marshal, born in Cauchy-à-la-Tour.

1882 Lord Dowding, British Air Force commander, responsible for victory in the Battle of Britain, born in Moffat, Scotland.

1889 Sir Stafford Cripps, British statesman, born in London.

1892 Jack Hulbert, English actor, born in Ely, Cambridgeshire.

1895 Captain Joshua Slocum set out on his single-handed voyage round the world, from Boston in the 36 ft sloop *Spray*—completed the circumnavigation on 27 June 1898.

1900 The first publication of the *Daily Express*, founded by C. Arthur Pearson, appeared in London.

1906 William Joyce, British traitor and Nazi collaborator, born in Brooklyn, New York City.

1916 Roger Casement was arrested in Ireland after landing from a German submarine.
The Easter rebellion took place in Dublin against British rule in Ireland—ended on 29th—was followed by reprisals by British troops, called the 'Black and Tans'.

1927 The English Table Tennis Association was formed.

1934 Shirley MacLaine, American film actress, born in Richmond, Virginia as Shirley Beaty *(sic)*, the younger sister of fellow actor Warren Beatty.

1941 John Williams, international guitarist, born in Melbourne, Australia.

1942 Barbra Streisand, American singer and film actress, born in Brooklyn, New York.

1970 After a national referendum Gambia became a Republic within the Commonwealth—having been a British colony since 1843.
China launched her first satellite.

1971 The Russian *Soyuz 10* spacecraft linked up with the orbiting space station *Salyut*.

1974 Bud Abbott, comedian and straight-man of the Abbott and Costello team, died.

1986 Her Grace The Duchess of Windsor died in Paris aged 89.
Bill Edrich, English Test cricketer of distinction, died.

---

25 APRIL [116]

Anzac day in Australia.
The last date on which Easter can fall.

1284 King Edward II born in Caernarvon Castle, the third son of Edward I.

1599 Oliver Cromwell, British soldier, statesman and Lord Protector of England, born in Huntingdon, Cambridgeshire.

1744 Anders Celsius, Swedish astronomer who devised the centigrade temperature scale in 1742, died.

1769 Sir Marc Isambard Brunel, British engineer, born in Hacqueville near Rouen, France.

1792 The guillotine was first used, in Paris at the Place de Grève—the victim was a young highwayman named Pelletier.
Rouget de Lisle, a French Army captain, completed the words and music for his country's national anthem *La Marseillaise*, when stationed in Strasbourg.

1800 William Cowper, English poet and writer of hymns, died in East Dereham, Norfolk.

1843 The Royal yacht *Victoria and Albert* was launched at Pembroke in South Wales.

1859 Work began on the construction of the 100-mile Suez Canal, under the direction of its planner Ferdinand de Lesseps—was opened on 16 November 1869.

1872 C. B. Fry, English all-round sportsman, born in Croydon, Surrey.

1873 Walter de la Mare, English poet and novelist, born in Charlton, Kent.

1874 Guglielmo Marconi, Italian physicist and radio pioneer, born in Bologna.

1878 Anna Sewell, English authoress, best remembered for her book *Black Beauty*, died.

1895 Sir Stanley Rous, English football administrator, born.

1908 Ed Murrow, American broadcaster, born in Greensboro, North Carolina.

1915 Australian and New Zealand troops landed in Gallipoli.

1918 Ella Fitzgerald, American jazz singer, born in Newport News, Virginia.

1939 Patrick Lichfield, Royal photographer, born.

1947 Johann Cruyff, Dutch international footballer, born.

1957 Eric Bristow, world-ranked darts champion, born.
1959 The St Lawrence Seaway, linking the Great Lakes to the Atlantic, was opened jointly by Queen Elizabeth II and President Eisenhower.
1960 US nuclear submarine *Triton* surfaced at St Paul's Rock after a three-month submerged circumnavigation of the earth.
1975 Elections were held in Portugal, the first for 50 years.
1976 Sir Carol Reed, British film director, died.

---

26 APRIL [117]

1731 Daniel Defoe, English writer, best known as author of *Robinson Crusoe* and *Moll Flanders*, died.
1765 Emma, Lady Hamilton, mistress of Lord Nelson, born as Emily Lyon in the village of Ness, Cheshire.
1812 Alfred Krupp, German armaments manufacturer, born in Essen in the Ruhr.
1856 Sir Joseph Ward, New Zealand Liberal statesman, born.
1865 John Wilkes Booth, the assassin of Abraham Lincoln, died of a bullet wound resisting arrest in a burning barn on a farm near Bowling Green, Virginia.
1880 Michel Fokine, Russian-American dancer, choreographer and founder of modern ballet, born in St Petersburg.
1894 Rudolf Hess, Nazi leader and Hitler's deputy, born in Alexandria, Egypt.
1916 Morris West, Australian novelist best known for his best-selling *The Devil's Advocate*, born in Melbourne.
1918 Fanny Blankers-Koen, Dutch athlete of distinction, born in Amsterdam.
1923 King George VI, then the Duke of York, married Lady Elizabeth Bowes-Lyon in Westminster Abbey.
1928 Madame Tussaud's waxworks re-opened in Marylebone Road after its previous address in Baker Street burnt down.
1937 Guernica, in the Basque country, was largely destroyed by German Air Force bombers supporting the Nationalists during the Spanish Civil War.
1938 Duane Eddy, American rock and roll guitarist and songwriter, born in Corning, New York State.
1942 The world's worst mine disaster took place, in Honkeiko Colliery in China, resulting in 1572 deaths.
1947 The FA Cup final between Charlton Athletic and Burnley was the first to be televised from start to finish.
1957 The BBC TV programme *Sky at Night*, presented by Patrick Moore, was first transmitted.

1964 The Republic of Tanzania was formed by the union of Tanganyika and Zanzibar, with Julius Nyerere as its first President.
1970 Gypsy Rose Lee, American entertainer famed for her striptease act, died.
1980 Cicely Courtneidge, British actress, died aged 87.
1984 Count Basie, American jazz pianist and big-band leader, died.
1986 A major nuclear power accident occurred at Chernobyl near Kiev, Russia.
Broderick Crawford, American film actor and Oscar winner in 1949 for *All the King's Men*, died.

27 APRIL [118]

National day of both Sierra Leone and Togo.

1521 Ferdinand Magellan, Portuguese navigator, was killed by natives on the island of Mactan in the Philippines on his voyage round the world.
1737 Edward Gibbon, English historian, born in Putney, London, the son of a country gentleman.
1791 Samuel Morse, American portrait painter and inventor of the famous code, born in Charlestown, Massachusetts.
1822 Ulysses Grant, American general of the Union Army, Republican statesman and 18th President, born in Point Pleasant, Ohio, the son of a tanner.
1828 Regent's Park of 464 acres in north west London was opened.
1840 Edward Whymper, English mountaineer and first person to climb the Matterhorn in 1865, born in London.
1882 Ralph Waldo Emerson, American philosopher and poet, died in Concord, Massachusetts.
1904 C. Day-Lewis, British novelist, poet and Poet Laureate, born in Sligo in the Republic of Ireland.
1908 The annual Football Association Charity Shield was first played for—Manchester United being the initial winners.
1927 Coretta King, civil-rights leader and wife of Martin Luther King, born in Marion, Alabama, née Scott.
Sheila Scott, British aviator and first woman to fly solo round the world, born.
1932 The London to Cape Town airline service was inaugurated.
1937 The National Maritime Museum, beside the Thames at Greenwich, was opened by King George VI.
1939 Conscription for World War II was introduced in Great Britain.
1947 Thor Heyerdahl set sail on a balsa wood raft from Callao in Peru to Raroia in Polynesia to establish that Peruvian Indians could have settled in Polynesia.

1956 Rocky Marciano retired as undefeated world heavyweight boxing champion.

1961 Sierra Leone, Republic of West Africa, achieved full independence within the Commonwealth.

1967 Expo 67 opened in Montreal—closing on October 30.

1968 Jimmy Ellis won the world heavyweight boxing title at Oakland, beating Jerry Quarry on points.
Legalised abortion in Britain came into effect.

1972 Kwame Nkrumah, ex-Ghanaian Prime Minister and President, died.

---

28 APRIL [119]

1442 King Edward IV born in Rouen, the son of Richard, Duke of York.

1603 The funeral of Queen Elizabeth I took place at Westminster Abbey.

1758 James Monroe, American Republican statesman and 5th President, born in Westmoreland County, Virginia.

1770 Captain Cook in the *Endeavour* reached Australia, at a point in New South Wales they named Sting Ray Bay—found to be a botanist's paradise, it was later re-named Botany Bay.

1788 Maryland, the Old Line or Free State, became the 7th state of the Union.

1789 The mutiny on the *Bounty* took place in the early hours off Tofua in the Friendly Islands in the South Seas, led by Fletcher Christian. Captain Bligh and 17 men reached Timor—the mutineers settled on and colonised Pitcairn Island.

1795 Charles Sturt, British soldier and explorer in Australia, born in Bengal.

1801 Lord Shaftesbury, British social reformer, born in London as Anthony Ashley Cooper.

1865 Samuel Cunard, Canadian shipowner and founder of the British steamship company bearing his name, died.

1878 Lionel Barrymore, American film actor, born in Philadelphia as Lionel Blythe—the eldest of the acting trio.

1889 Antonio Salazar, Portuguese long-serving Prime Minister and dictator, born in Vimiero near Coimbra.

1908 Jack Fingleton, Australian Test cricketer, born.

1923 The first English FA Cup final at Wembley Stadium in London was staged—Bolton Wanderers defeating West Ham United 2–0.

1924 Kenneth Kaunda, Zambia's first President, born in Lubwa.

1936 Farouk became King of Egypt on the death of his father, King Fuad I.

1937 Jack Nicholson, American actor and Oscar winner for *One Flew Over the Cuckoo's Nest*, born in Neptune, New Jersey.
1942 Mike Brearley, Middlesex and England cricketer, born.
1945 Benito Mussolini, Italian dictator and creator of Fascism, was executed with his mistress Claretta Petacci near Azzano by Italian partisans as they tried to flee the country.
1967 Muhammad Ali was stripped of his title by the World Boxing authorities for refusing to serve in the US forces.

29 APRIL   *[120]*

National day of Japan.

1769 The Duke of Wellington, British soldier of distinction, statesman and public official, born in Dublin as Arthur Wellesley. (Some authorities say 1 May.)
1818 Alexander II, Tsar of Russia, born in St Petersburg, the son of Tsar Nicholas I.
1863 William Randolph Hearst, American newspaper editor and publisher, born in San Francisco.
1879 Sir Thomas Beecham, English conductor, born in St Helens, Lancashire, the son of a manufacturer of patent medicines.
1895 Sir Malcolm Sargent, English conductor, born.
1899 'Duke' Ellington, American jazz musician and composer, born in Washington, DC as Edward Kennedy Ellington, the son of a butler in the service of the White House.
1901 Hirohito, Emperor of Japan, born in Tokyo.
1913 The improved version of the zip fastener as we know it today, was patented by a young Swedish engineer Gideon Sundback from Hoboken, New Jersey.
1929 Jeremy Thorpe, British politician and leader of the Liberal Party, born.
1931 Lonnie Donegan, British singer and entertainer, born.
1933 Players were first numbered, in the English FA Cup final at Wembley Stadium—the numbers running from 1 to 22—with Manchester City having the higher set of numbers.
1947 Johnny Miller, American golf champion, born in San Francisco.
Jim Ryun, American athlete and a record holder at middle distances, born in Wichita, Kansas.
1980 Sir Alfred Hitchcock, London-born director known for suspense thriller films, died in Hollywood aged 80.
1986 The funeral of Her Grace The Duchess of Windsor took place in St George's Chapel, Windsor Castle.
1988 Andrew Cruikshank, MBE, British actor, died aged 80.

National day of the Netherlands.

1789 George Washington was inaugurated as the first President of the USA, on the balcony of New York's Federal Hall, with John Adams as vice-President.

1803 USA purchased Louisiana from France, the deal was completed by President Thomas Jefferson—working out at a little under three cents an acre.

1804 Shrapnel was first used in warfare, by the British against the Dutch in Surinam.

1812 Louisiana, the Pelican State, became the 18th state of the Union.

1870 Franz Lehar, Hungarian composer, born in Komarom, the son of a military bandmaster.

1883 Edouard Manet, French Impressionist painter, died in Paris.

1909 Juliana, Queen of the Netherlands, born in The Hague.

1938 The English FA Cup final at Wembley Stadium, between Preston North End and Huddersfield Town, was the first to be televised live.

1945 Adolf Hitler committed suicide with his wife Eva Braun, in his underground bunker beneath the Chancellory in Berlin. He married very shortly before this incident.

1975 The Vietnamese War ended—having been the longest conflict of the twentieth century.

1979 London's new Jubilee Underground Line, which runs from Charing Cross to Stanmore, was opened by Prince Charles.

1980 Juliana abdicated as Queen of the Netherlands in favour of her daughter Beatrix.
Armed terrorists seized the Iranian Embassy in London, taking 20 hostages and threatening to blow it up if their demands were not met.

1988 Peter Shilton made his 825th Football League appearance, in Derby's game at Watford, beating Terry Paine's long-standing record.

1672 Joseph Addison, English poet, essayist and co-founder of *The Spectator*, born the son of the rector of Milston in Wiltshire.

1700 John Dryden, English poet and Poet Laureate for over 20 years, died in London.

1707 The Union of Scotland and England was proclaimed.

1841   47 persons left Independence in Missouri on the first emigrant wagon train—reached Stanislaus River in California on 4 November.

1851   The Great Exhibition, housed in the Crystal Palace in London's Hyde Park, was opened by Queen Victoria.

1873   David Livingstone was found dead at Chitambo—kneeling by his bedside in an attitude of prayer.
       The first US postal card was issued.

1896   General Mark Clark, US Army commander, born in Madison Barracks, New York of a military father.

1904   Antonin Dvorak, Czech composer, noted for his symphony *From the New World*, died.

1916   Glenn Ford, American film actor, born in Quebec, Canada.

1928   Sir Ebenezer Howard, founder of Letchworth and Welwyn Garden cities, knighted in 1927, died in his Welwyn creation.

1931   The Empire State Building on New York's 5th Avenue was completed—its 102 floors rising to 1250 feet.

1933   The Britain to India telephone service was inaugurated.

1945   Joseph Goebbels, Nazi leader and propagandist, committed suicide in a Berlin bunker after killing his wife and six children.

1949   Britain's gas industry was nationalised.

1952   William Fox, American film impresario and founder of 20th Century Fox, died in New York.

1960   Steve Cauthen, US jockey riding in England, born in Covington, Kentucky.
       The U-2 reconnaissance plane of the United States, piloted by Gary Powers, was shot down in the Soviet Union.

1961   Betting shops opened in Britain.

1965   Spike Jones, American musician and bandleader whose forte was zany variations on popular songs, died.

1971   Amtrak, the new rail passenger service of America, went into operation.

1978   The May Day holiday was celebrated in Britain for the first time.

2 MAY   *[123]*

1519   Leonardo da Vinci, Italian artist and man of science, noted for his painting of the *Mona Lisa*, died at the Château Cloux near Amboise.

1729   Catherine the Great, Empress of Russia, born in Stettin, Germany.

1859   Jerome K. Jerome, English humorous writer, born in Walsall, Staffordshire.

1860 Theodor Herzl, Hungarian Jew, founder of Zionism, born in the capital Budapest.

1892 Baron Manfred von Richthofen, German air ace of World War I, known as the 'Red Baron', born in Schweidnitz in Prussia to aristocratic parents.

1895 Lorenz Hart, American lyricist, born in New York City.

1903 Dr Benjamin Spock, American pediatrician, born in New Haven, Connecticut.

1904 Bing Crosby, born in Tacoma, Washington as Harry Lillis Crosby.

1926 Clive Jenkins, British trade union leader, born.

1942 HMS *Edinburgh* was sunk in the Barents Sea off northern Norway on its way to Russia. The cruiser and its valuable cargo of gold bars lay in 803 feet of water until salvaged in 1981.

1952 A British DH Comet flew from London to Johannesburg, thus inaugurating the first turbo-jet airline service.

1953 King Hussein II formally acceded as King of Jordan, succeeding his father, King Talal, deposed the previous August.
      Blackpool came from 3–1 down to beat Bolton Wanderers 4–3 in a thrilling FA Cup final, dubbed the 'Matthews final'.

1957 Senator Joe McCarthy, American politician and Republican Senator noted for his campaign against Communism, died.

1959 Chapelcross nuclear power station, the first in Scotland, opened.

1962 Jimmy White, British snooker champion, born.

1964 Nancy, Lady Astor, the first woman to sit in the House of Commons, in 1919, died aged 84.

1965 The 'Early Bird' communications satellite went into operation, transmitting television programmes to 24 countries.

1969 The British passenger liner *QE 2* (*Queen Elizabeth* 2) went on its maiden voyage.

1972 J. Edgar Hoover, American founder and head of the FBI from 1924, died in Washington, DC.

1982 The Argentinian cruiser *General Belgrano* was sunk by the British submarine HMS *Conqueror*: some 350 men were lost.

1984 HM The Queen opened the Liverpool Garden Festival.

3 MAY [124]

1814 Napoleon made his home in exile on the island of Elba.

1844 Richard D'Oyly Carte, English theatrical impresario, known for his productions of Gilbert and Sullivan operettas, born.

1845 Thomas Hood, English poet and humorist, died in Finchley Road, London after a long illness.

1898 Golda Meir, Israeli Prime Minister, born in Kiev, Russia as Golda Mabovitch (Mabovitz), the daughter of a carpenter.

1903 The first electric train ran in the Mersey Railway tunnel between Liverpool and Birkenhead, England.

1920 Sugar Ray Robinson, American boxer and world middleweight champion, born in Detroit, Michigan as Walker Smith.

1934 Henry Cooper, British long-reigning heavyweight boxing champion, born in Camberwell, London.

1936 Engelbert Humperdinck, British pop singer, born in Madras, India as Arnold George Dorsey.

1939 The British battleship *Prince of Wales* was launched at Cammell Laird's shipyard in Birkenhead.

1948 Peter Oosterhuis, British golfer, born.

1951 The Festival of Britain in London was opened by King George VI—ended on 30 September.

1952 Alan Wells, British sprinter and champion, born.

4 MAY [125]

1471 The Battle of Tewkesbury took place in Gloucestershire, the scene of a Yorkist victory in the last encounter in the War of the Roses.

1494 The West Indian island of Jamaica was discovered by Columbus.

1655 Bartolommeo Cristofori, Italian craftsman who developed the first piano, born in Padua.

1780 The first Derby horse race classic for 3-year-olds over a distance of 1½ miles was run at Epsom—won by Sir Charles Bunbury's 'Diomed'.

1820 Joseph Whitaker, English publisher, born in London, the son of a silversmith.

1896 The British newspaper *Daily Mail*, founded by Lord Northcliffe, was first published.

1926 The General Strike in England started, in response to the national lockout of the coalminers—ended on 12th.

1929 Audrey Hepburn, British actress and Oscar winner in 1953 for *Roman Holiday*, born in Brussels, Belgium.

1938 Douglas Hyde became the first President of Eire.

1953 The Duke of Edinburgh received his pilot's wings.

1973 Sears Tower in Chicago, the tallest office building in the world at 1454 feet with 110 storeys, was 'topped out', when the highest storey was completed.

1974 Geraldo, English orchestra leader and entrepreneur, died on holiday in Vevey, Switzerland.

1979 Margaret Thatcher became Britain's first female Prime Minister.

1980 Marshal Tito, President of Yugoslavia since 1953, died after a long illness aged 87.

1982 The British destroyer HMS *Sheffield* was sunk off the Falklands after being hit by an Exocet missile: 20 men were lost.

1984 Diana Dors, English film actress and sex symbol, died.

---

5 MAY

1760 The hangman's drop was used for the first time, in Tyburn, London, for the execution of Earl Ferrers.

1818 Karl Marx, German social philosopher, radical leader and 'Father of Communism', born in Trier, the son of a Jewish lawyer.

1821 Napoleon Bonaparte died of cancer in exile on the Atlantic island of St Helena.

1835 Belgium's national railway first ran—from Brussels to Malines.

1883 Lord Wavell, British field marshal, born in Colchester into an Army family.

1904 Sir Gordon Richards, 26 times English champion jockey, born in Oakengates, Shropshire, the son of a miner.

1906 Mary Astor, American film actress, born in Quincy, Illinois as Lucille Langehanke.

1913 Tyrone Power, American film actor, born in Cincinnati, Ohio.

1915 Alice Faye, American singer and film actress, born in New York City as Alice Leppert.

1923 Roy Dotrice, British actor, born on the Channel Island of Guernsey.

1928 Dixie Dean of Everton scored three goals against Arsenal to take his season's total to a record 60.

1930 Amy Johnson took off from Croydon on her historic solo flight to Australia in a Gypsy Moth named *Jason*—arrived on 24th.

1941 Emperor Haile Selassie returned to Ethiopia from exile in England after the liberation of his country by British forces.

1942 Tammy Wynette, American country singer, born in Red Bay, Alabama.

1952 HM The Queen took up residence at Buckingham Palace.

1954 Austin Reed, owner of many London and provincial men's outfitting shops, died in Gerrard's Cross, Buckinghamshire.

1961 Alan Shepard became the first American spaceman, in a Mercury capsule *Freedom VII*.

1967 Britain's first satellite *Ariel III* was launched from Vandenburg Air Base in California.

1975 The *Scottish Daily News*, the first workers co-operative national newspaper, was published.

1980 SAS commandos stormed the beseiged Iranian Embassy and released the hostages—all but one of the gunmen were killed.

1626 Manhattan Island, a borough of New York City, was bought from the local Red Indians by Peter Minuit for goods and trinkets to the equivalent value of 24 dollars.

1758 Robespierre, French Revolutionary leader, born in Arras.

1840 The first adhesive British stamps, the penny black and the twopenny blue, introduced by Sir Rowland Hill, were officially issued by the GPO.

1851 Linus Yale patented the lock that bears his name.

1856 Robert Peary, American Arctic explorer, born in Cresson Springs, Pennsylvania.
Sigmund Freud, Austrian neurologist and pioneer of psycho-analysis, born in Freiburg, Moravia.

1882 Epping Forest in Essex, was opened as a Park by Queen Victoria.
The Phoenix Park murders by the 'Irish Invincibles' took place in Dublin—the victims were Lord Cavendish and Thomas Burke.

1894 Sir Alan Cobham, British aviator, born.

1895 Rudolph Valentino, American film actor and romantic idol, born in Castellaneta, Southern Italy, the son of a vet.

1910 Death of King Edward VII after a short illness—accession of his son as George V.

1913 Stewart Granger, British film actor, born in London as James Stewart.

1915 Orson Welles, American film actor, director and producer, born in Kenosha, Wisconsin.

1919 Frank Baum, American writer of children's stories, notably *The Wonderful Wizard of Oz*, died.

1937 The 804-foot German airship *Hindenburg* was burned at its moorings in Lakehurst, New Jersey, killing 36 of the 97 people aboard.

1954 Roger Bannister ran the first sub four-minute mile, on the Iffley Road track in Oxford, in 3 minutes 59.4 seconds.

1960 Princess Margaret was married to Antony Armstrong-Jones in Westminster Abbey.

1966 Ian Brady and Myra Hindley, the 'Moors murderers', were found guilty at Chester Crown Court, in England.

1972 The first all-ladies race under Jockey Club rules was run, the Goya Stakes over nine furlongs at Kempton Park.

7 MAY [128]

1765 The *Victory*, a British battleship, was launched at Chatham. Is now preserved in Portsmouth.

1812 Robert Browning, English poet, born in Camberwell, London.
1832 Greece was proclaimed an independent kingdom, with Otto I as King.
1833 Johannes Brahms, German composer and pianist, born in Hamburg, the son of a poor orchestral musician.
1840 Peter Ilyich Tchaikovsky, Russian composer, born in Votkinsk, the son of a Government mines inspector.
1847 Lord Rosebery, British Liberal statesman and Prime Minister, born in London.
1876 Samuel Courtauld, English industrialist and art patron, born in Braintree, Essex.
1890 James Nasmyth, Scottish engineer and inventor of the first steam hammer, died in London.
1901 Gary Cooper, American film actor and twice Oscar winner, born in Helena in Montana as Frank James Cooper.
1909 Edwin Land, American inventor of the Polaroid lens and the instant camera, born in Bridgeport, Connecticut.
1915 The 762-foot Cunard passenger liner *Lusitania*, captained by William Thomas Turner, was torpedoed by a German submarine about ten miles off Old Head of Kinsale, Ireland, and sank in 18 minutes with the loss of 1198 lives.
Scobie Breasley, a successful and champion jockey in England, born in Australia.
1921 Thirteen paid to see a Division Two soccer match between Stockport County and Leicester City at Old Trafford. Stockport County's ground was under suspension.
1925 William Lever, English manufacturer and builder of the great Lever Brothers enterprise, died as Viscount Leverhulme.
1931 Teresa Brewer, American pop singer, born in Toledo, Ohio.
1932 French President Paul Doumer was assassinated by a Russian émigré.
1940 George Lansbury, British politician and Labour Party leader, died in London aged 81.
1957 Eliot Ness, US Government agent, best known as the special FBI agent who headed the investigation of Al Capone in Chicago, died.
1980 Paul Geidel was released from the Fishkill Correctional Facility in Beacon, New York having served 68 years and 8 months – the longest recorded term in US history.

8 MAY [129]

The festival of the Floral Dance is held annually in Helston, Cornwall.

1701 'Captain' Kidd was tried at London's Old Bailey for piracy—was hanged on 23rd.
1794 Antoine Lavoisier, French chemist who identified and named oxygen, was guillotined in Paris.
1828 John Henri Dunant, Swiss philanthropist and founder of the International Red Cross, born in Geneva.
1884 Harry S. Truman, American Democrat statesman and 33rd President, born in Lamar, Missouri.
1886 Dr John Pemberton first produced the world's top-selling soft drink Coca-Cola® in Atlanta, Georgia.
1896 Yorkshire's score against Warwickshire at Edgbaston reached 887 to record the highest innings total in a county cricket championship game.
1902 The volcano of Mount Pelée on the French Caribbean island of Martinique erupted—within three minutes the town of St Pierre was totally destroyed and about 30 000 people killed.
1903 Paul Gauguin, French post-Impressionist painter, died.
1912 Pilot Lt. Samson, in a Short S.38, made the first take-off from a ship under way, HMS *Hibernia* at Weymouth moving at ten knots.
1921 Sweden abolished capital punishment.
1926 David Attenborough, British broadcaster, born.
1927 Speedway racing took place in Britain for the first time, at Camberley Heath.
1932 Sonny Liston, American heavyweight boxing champion, born.
1936 Jack Charlton, English football international and club manager, born in Ashington, Northumberland.
1940 Peter Benchley, American novelist, notably *Jaws*, born in New York City.
Rick Nelson, American singer and songwriter, born in Teaneck, New Jersey.
1942 The naval battle of the Coral Sea ended, during which the US lost the aircraft carrier *Lexington*. It was the first allied success in the Pacific, resulting in saving Australia from invasion.
1945 The war in Europe officially ended.
1947 Harry Gordon Selfridge, American merchant and store owner, died.
1955 The European Cup for the football league champions of the respective nations was approved by FIFA.
1962 Trolleybuses ran for the last time in London.
1984 The Thames Barrier at Woolwich was opened.
1986 Lord 'Manny' Shinwell, British politician and Labour Minister, died aged 101.
1988 Robert Heinlein, US science fiction writer, died aged 80.

National day of Czechoslovakia.

1671 Disguised as a clergyman, Colonel Thomas Blood attempted to steal the Crown jewels from the Tower of London.

1800 John Brown, American anti-slavery crusader, born in Torrington, Connecticut.

1850 Joseph Gay-Lussac, French chemist and physicist, died.

1860 (James Matthew) J. M. Barrie, Scottish playwright and novelist, born at 9 Brechin Road, Kirriemuir, the son of a weaver.

1870 Harry Vardon, British international golfer, born in Grouville on the island of Jersey.

1873 Howard Carter, English Egyptologist who discovered the tomb of King Tutankhamun in 1922, born in Swaffham, Norfolk.

1926 Richard Byrd, American explorer, made the first flight over the North Pole, with pilot Floyd Bennett.

1927 Canberra was inaugurated as the new capital of Australia, replacing Melbourne.

1928 Ricardo 'Pancho' Gonzalez, American international tennis champion, born in Los Angeles.

1931 Albert Michelson, American physicist, who in 1907 became the country's first winner of the Nobel Prize for physics, died.

1936 Glenda Jackson, English film actress and twice Oscar winner for *Women in Love* (1970) and *A Touch of Class* (1973), born in Hoylake, Merseyside.
Terry Downes, British boxer and former world middleweight champion, born in Paddington, London.
Albert Finney, British film actor, born in Salford, Greater Manchester.

1946 Victor Emmanuel III, King of Italy since 1900, abdicated—the monarchy being replaced by a Republic.
Candice Bergen, American film actress, born in Beverly Hills, California, the daughter of ventriloquist Edgar Bergen.

1949 Prince Rainier III became Head of State of Monaco, succeeding his grandfather Prince Louis II.
The first self-service launderette was opened in Britain, in Queensway, London.
Billy Joel, American singer and songwriter, born in the Bronx, New York.

1955 Gordon Richards, England's most successful jockey, gained his first winner as a trainer, 'The Saint' at Windsor.

1986 Tenzing Norgay, or Tensing as he was known, the joint first conqueror of Everest, died.

1655 Jamaica was taken by the British, having been in Spanish hands for 161 years after its discovery by Columbus.

1798 George Vancouver, British navigator, explorer and surveyor of the Pacific coast of North America, died.

1818 Paul Revere, American patriot famed for his night ride in 1775 to warn of the advance of British troops, died in Boston, Massachusetts aged 83.

1838 John Wilkes Booth, American actor and assassin of President Abraham Lincoln, born in Baltimore, Maryland.

1850 Sir Thomas Lipton, British grocer and philanthropist, born in Glasgow.

1857 The Indian Mutiny or Sepoy Rebellion, when Sepoy soldiers rebelled against biting off the greased end of the cartridges for the new Lee Enfield rifles, broke out in Meerut—ended in July 1858.

1863 Thomas Jonathan 'Stonewall' Jackson, American Confederate general, was killed by his own soldiers near Chancellorsville in Virginia.

1869 The US transcontinental railroad was completed. A golden spike was driven in at Promontory Point, Utah, marking the junction of the Central Pacific and Union Pacific railways.

1886 The issuing of football international caps was approved by the FA Council.

1899 Fred Astaire, American film actor and dancer, born in Omaha, Nebraska as Frederick Austerlitz, the son of Austrian immigrants.

1904 Sir Henry Morton Stanley, British journalist and explorer in Africa, died in London.

1907 Mother's Day, initiated in America by Miss Anna Jarvis, was first held in Philadelphia.

1914 Sir William Alexander Smith, founder of the Boys Brigade, died.

1915 Denis Thatcher, husband of Britain's Prime Minister, born.

1919 The first airline in Britain started, flying the 50 miles between Alexander Park, Manchester and Blackpool in a two-seater single-engine Avro biplane.

1920 John Wesley Hyatt, American inventor and discoverer of celluloid, the first synthetic plastic, died.

1925 William Massey, New Zealand statesman and Prime Minister from 1912, died in office.

1934 The Police Training College in Hendon, London was opened.

1937 Britain's first frozen food went on sale: asparagus, the product of Smedley's of Wisbech, Cambridgeshire.

1938 Manuel Santana, Spanish international tennis player and champion, born in Madrid.

1940   Neville Chamberlain resigned as Prime Minister.
Belgium was invaded and occupied by German forces.

1941   Rudolf Hess, German Nazi leader and Hitler's deputy, parachuted and landed in Eaglesham, Scotland, apparently hoping to negotiate a separate peace, but was imprisoned.
Part of the House of Commons in Westminster was destroyed by enemy bombs.

1954   George Hirst, Yorkshire and England cricketer, died in Huddersfield.

1955   Tommy Burns, Canadian heavyweight boxer and world champion from 1906 to 1908, died in Vancouver.

1974   Anatoly Karpov defeated Boris Spassky to become world chess champion.

1976   Jeremy Thorpe resigned as leader of the British Liberal Party.

1977   Joan Crawford, American film actress and Academy Award (Oscar) winner in 1945 for her part in *Mildred Pierce*, died in New York.

1978   Liverpool won the European Cup in football for the second successive year.

1980   Paul Allen, at 17 years and 256 days, became the youngest footballer to appear in a FA Cup final, playing for West Ham United against Arsenal.

1981   François Mitterrand won the French Presidential election, defeating Giscard D'Estaing.

---

11 MAY   *[132]*

National day of Laos.

1745   The Battle of Fontenoy took place in Belgium, the scene of Marshal de Saxe's French victory over British and allied forces during the War of the Austrian Succession.

1778   William Pitt the Elder, British statesman and chief minister who became Earl of Chatham, died in Hayes.

1811   The original Siamese twins, Chang and Eng Bunker, were born in Maklong, Siam, joined at the chest.

1812   Spencer Perceval, British Tory Prime Minister from 1809, was assassinated in the Lobby of the House of Commons by a merchant named Francis Bellingham.

1818   The Old Vic theatre opened in Waterloo Road, London as the Royal Coburg.

1858   Minnesota, the Gopher or North Star State, became the 32nd state of the Union.

1871   Sir John Herschel, English astronomer and pioneer of celestial photography, died in London.

1888   Irving Berlin, American composer, born in Tyumen, Eastern Russia as Israel Baline.
1892   Margaret Rutherford, English stage and film actress, born in London.
1904   Salvador Dali, Spanish Surrealist painter, born in Figueras, Upper Catalonia.
1908   The foundation stone of Liverpool's Liver Building was laid.
1912   Phil Silvers, American comedy film actor, born in Brooklyn, New York as Philip Silversmith.
1922   The British radio station '2LO' was established, at Marconi House in London's Strand.
1940   Winston Churchill became head of the wartime Coalition Government.
1941   Ian Redpath, Victoria and Australian Test cricketer, born.
1955   Gilbert Jessop, English cricketer in 18 Test matches, died in Fordington, near Dorchester, aged 80.
1964   John Parrott, British snooker champion, born in Liverpool.
1981   Bob Marley, born in Kingston, Jamaica and leading exponent of reggae music, died.
1985   Fire broke out in the main stand at Bradford City football ground, resulting in the death of 56 spectators. The club resumed its fixtures there on 14 December 1986.

12 MAY   [133]

1812   Edward Lear, English 'nonsense' poet and artist, born in Highgate, London.
1820   Florence Nightingale, English hospital reformer and founder of the modern nursing profession, born in Italy in Florence—after which place she was named.
1828   Dante Gabriel Rossetti, English poet and painter, born in London to exiled Italian parents as Gabriel Charles Dante.
1860   Sir Charles Barry, English architect responsible for the new Palace of Westminster, died.
1870   Manitoba, previously called the Red River Colony and controlled by the Hudson Bay Company, was purchased by Canada and made a province.
        Rules were drafted for the game of water polo, by the London Swimming Association.
1871   Daniel Auber, French composer of operas, died in Paris.
1880   Lincoln Ellsworth, American polar explorer, born in Chicago, Illinois.
1884   Bedrich Smetana, Czech composer, notably the opera *The Bartered Bride*, died in a Prague mental hospital.
1903   Wilfrid Hyde White, British film actor, born.

1906 Horatio Bottomley began the publication of the British weekly magazine *John Bull*.

1907 Leslie Charteris, crime story writer and creator of the character 'The Saint', born in Singapore as Leslie Charles Yin.

1924 Tony Hancock, British comedy actor, born in Birmingham.

1926 The General Strike in England ended after nine days.

1928 Burt Bacharach, American pianist and composer, born in Kansas City, Missouri, the son of a newspaper columnist.

1935 'Alcoholics Anonymous', a self-help organisation, was founded by William Wilson in Akron, Ohio.

1937 The coronation of King George VI took place.
Beryl Burton, British cyclist and a world champion, born.

1942 Susan Hampshire, English actress, born in London.

1949 The Russians lifted the blockade of Berlin.

1957 Erich Von Stroheim, one of the silent screen's greatest directors, whose career waned with the 'talkies', died.

1967 John Masefield, English poet and Poet Laureate from 1930, died.

1969 The voting age in Britain was lowered to 18.

1982 The *QE 2* liner sailed south to join the Falklands Task Force.

13 MAY [134]

1607 Captain John Smith and 105 Cavaliers in three ships landed on the Virginia coast and started the first permanent English settlement in the New World, in Jamestown.

1717 Maria Theresa, Empress of Austria, born in Vienna.

1787 A fleet of 11 ships, consisting of two men-o-war, three with stores and six transporters containing about 730 convicts, set out from England to Australia, under the command of Captain Arthur Phillip, on a journey which lasted until the following January. The convicts disembarked at Sydney Cove, 40 less in number.

1835 John Nash, English architect, especially of Regent's Park and Brighton Pavilion, died on the Isle of Wight.

1842 Sir Arthur Sullivan, English composer of light operas in collaboration with W. S. Gilbert, born in Lambeth, London, the son of a bandmaster.

1884 Cyrus Hall McCormick, American inventor of the first successful reaping machine, died in Chicago.

1907 Daphne du Maurier, British novelist, author of *Rebecca*, born in London.

1914 Joe Louis, American heavyweight boxer and world champion known as 'The Brown Bomber', born in Lafayette, Alabama as Joseph Louis Barrow.

1930 Fridtjof Nansen, Norwegian Arctic explorer and later statesman and Nobel Prize winner in 1922, died in Lysaker, Norway.

1949 Britain's first jet bomber, the *Canberra*, was test flown at Warton in Lancashire.

1950 Stevie Wonder, American singer and composer, born in Saginaw, Michigan as Steveland Morris.

1961 Gary Cooper, American film actor and twice Academy Award (Oscar) winner—1941 for the title role in *Sergeant York* and 1952 for his part in *High Noon*—died.

1981 An attempt was made on the life of Pope John Paul II in St Peter's Square in Rome—the would-be assassin was Nehmet Ali Hagca.

---

14 MAY [135]

National day of Paraguay.

1643 Louis XIV ascended the throne of France, aged 4 years 231 days, on the death of his father Louis XIII—and reigned for over 72 years.

1686 Gabriel Fahrenheit, German physicist and inventor of the mercury thermometer, born in Danzig.

1727 Thomas Gainsborough, English landscape and portrait painter, born in Sudbury, Suffolk, the son of a cloth merchant.

1771 Robert Owen, British industrialist and social reformer, born in Newtown, Wales, the son of a saddler.

1796 Edward Jenner made his first vaccination against smallpox, and laid the foundation for modern immunology.

1804 Meriwether Lewis and William Clark set out from St Louis on the first expedition to find an overland route to the Pacific.

1842 The British periodical *Illustrated London News* was first published.

1862 The ship which was to be renamed *Alabama* was launched into the River Mersey at Birkenhead and was named *Enrica* that day.

1885 Otto Klemperer, German musical director and conductor, born in Breslau.

1912 The Royal Flying Corps was created.

1919 Henry John Heinz, American food manufacturer and founder of the company that bears his name, died.

1921 The British Legion was founded in London by Earl Haig—became the Royal British Legion in 1971.

1925 Sir Rider Haggard, English novelist, notably *King Solomon's Mines*, died.

1926 Eric Morecambe, English comedian of the Morecambe and Wise team, born in Morecambe, Lancashire as Eric Bartholomew.

1936 Viscount Allenby, British army commander in Palestine in World War I, died.

Bobby Darin, American singer of the rock and roll era, born in New York City as Walden Robert Cassoto.

1940 Local Defence Volunteers (later called Home Guard) was formed in Britain as a makeshift anti-invasion force.

1948 Israel was established as a Jewish state following the partition of Palestine.

1965 HM the Queen unveiled a memorial to the late President John F. Kennedy in Runnymede.

1967 Liverpool's Roman Catholic Cathedral was opened.

1970 Sir William Dobell, Australian artist and portrait-painter, knighted in 1966, died.

1973 America's Skylab I was launched—eventually returning to earth on 11 July 1979, after 34 981 orbits.

1977 Bobby Moore retired from professional football on his 1000th appearance in all matches, for West Ham United, Fulham and England.

1988 John Aldridge of Liverpool became the first player not to score from a penalty awarded in a Wembley FA Cup final.

15 MAY [136]

1718 The world's first machine gun was patented by its designer James Puckle.

1800 At the theatre in Drury Lane an attempt to assassinate King George III was made by James Hatfield.

1847 Daniel O'Connell, Irish Catholic political leader, called 'The Liberator' died in Genoa.

1856 Frank Baum, American writer, born in Chittenango, New York.

1858 The present Royal Opera House at Covent Garden in London (the third on the present site) was opened.

1859 Pierre Curie, French physicist, born in Paris the son of a French physician.

1892 Jimmy Wilde, British flyweight boxing champion known as the 'Mighty Atom', born in Wales.

1895 Joseph Whitaker, English publisher who founded *Whitaker's Almanack* in 1869, died.

1905 Joseph Cotton, American film actor, born in Petersburg, Virginia.

1909 James Mason, British film actor, born in Huddersfield, Yorkshire.

1918 USA inaugurated the world's first regular air mail service, between New York and Washington, operated for the US Post Office by the US Navy.

1928 The Flying Doctor Service was inaugurated in Australia, at Cloncurry in Queensland—Dr Vincent Welsh was the first.

1935 The first quiz programme was broadcast in Canada.
1937 Philip Snowden, British Labour statesman, died in Tilford, Surrey.
1940 Nylon stockings were first launched in the United States.
1941 Britain's first jet-propelled aircraft, designed by Frank Whittle, flew for the first time, at Cranwell.
1948 In one day's cricket Australia scored a record 721 runs, against Essex at Southchurch Park, Southend.
1949 At Los Angeles Shroeder and Falkenburg beat Gonzalez and Stewart after a record 135 games in tennis, the first set ended 36–34 and the last 19–17.
1957 Britain dropped her first hydrogen bomb, over Christmas Island in the South Pacific.
1972 Governor George Wallace of Alabama was seriously crippled after being shot in an assassination attempt in Laurel, Maryland.
1978 Sir Robert Menzies, Australia's Liberal Prime Minister, died in his home in Melbourne, aged 83.
1981 HRH Princess Anne gave birth to a daughter, Zara Anne Elizabeth.
1987 Rita Hayworth, American film actress and dancer, died.
1988 Russia began evacuating her troops from Afghanistan after more than eight years of occupation.

16 MAY   [137]

1568 Mary, Queen of Scots sailed from Port Mary across the Solway Firth to begin her exile in England.
1703 Charles Perrault, French author and writer of fairy tales, including *Little Red Ridinghood* and *Cinderella*, died in Paris.
1804 Elizabeth Peabody, American educator, born in Billerica, Massachusetts.
1811 The Battle of Albuera took place in Spain, the scene of a combined English, Portuguese and Spanish victory over the French under Marshal Soult.
1831 David Hughes, Anglo-American inventor of the teleprinter and the microphone, born in London.
1832 Philip Armour, American meat packer, born in Stockbridge, New York.
1835 Felicia Hemans, English poet who wrote *The boy stood on the burning deck*, died in Dublin.
1888 Emile Berliner demonstrated the first gramophone in Philadelphia.
1905 Henry Fonda, American film actor, born in Grand Island, Nebraska.
1908 Britain's first diesel submarine, appropriately called *D 1*, was launched at Barrow.

1911 The Queen Victoria Monument in front of Buckingham Palace was unveiled.

1913 Woody Herman, American jazz clarinettist and bandleader, born in Milwaukee, Wisconsin, as Woodrow Charles.

1919 Liberace, American pianist and entertainer, born into a musical family in West Allis, Wisconsin as Wladziu Valentino Liberace.

1929 Film Academy Awards were first presented in Hollywood—the name 'Oscar' for the trophy was first issued in 1931, after a Mr Oscar Pierce of Texas.

1938 The WVS (Women's Voluntary Service) was started in Britain by the Marchioness of Reading—it became 'Royal' in 1966.

1943 The Mohne, Eder and Sorpe Dams in Germany were breached by 19 Lancaster bombers of 617 Squadron from Scampton, led by Guy Gibson, using special 'skip' bombs invented by Dr Barnes Wallis.

1955 Olga Korbut, Soviet gymnast and Olympic gold medal winner, born in Grodno.

1966 The Seaman's strike began, and ended on 1 July, to become the largest (man-days lost) strike in Britain since World War II and the first of its kind since 1911.

1969 The Russian spacecraft *Venus 5* touched down on Venus.

1975 Junko Tabei of Japan became the first woman to reach the summit of Everest.

1983 London police began fitting wheel clamps to illegally-parked

---

17 MAY   *[138]*

National day of Norway.

1673 Jacques Marquette, a French missionary, discovered the Mississippi river.

1749 Edward Jenner, English physician and pioneer in vaccinations, born in Berkeley vicarage in Gloucestershire.

1861 The very first 'package holiday', arranged by Thomas Cook, set out from London Bridge on a six day trip to Paris.

1875 The first Kentucky Derby was run, at Churchill Downs, Louisville, Kentucky.

1889 'Tich' Freeman, Kent and England cricketer, born in Lewisham.

1890 *Comic Cuts*, the first comic paper, was issued in London.

1900 A small British force under Baden-Powell in Mafeking in the Cape Province of South Africa, was relieved after holding out for 217 days during the siege by the Boers under General Piet Cronje.

1911 Maureen O'Sullivan, American film actress, born in Bayle, Ireland.

1920 KLM, the national airline of the Netherlands, opened its first
scheduled service—Amsterdam to London.
1934 Cass Gilbert, American architect, noted for his skyscrapers,
especially the Woolworth Building in New York City, died.
1935 Paul Dukas, French composer, best known for *The Sorcerer's
Apprentice*, died in Paris.
Dennis Potter, British author, playwright and screenwriter, born.
1945 Tony Roche, Australian international tennis player, born in
Tarcutta, New South Wales.
1956 'Sugar' Ray Leonard, American boxing champion at welterweight,
born in Wilmington, North Carolina.
1960 The Kariba Dam, on the Zambesi River, was opened by Queen
Elizabeth, the Queen Mother.
1965 'Early Bird' transmitted its first transatlantic programme in
colour.
1970 Nigel Balchin, English novelist, died.

18 MAY

1804 Napoleon Bonaparte was proclaimed Emperor of France.
1868 Nicholas II, the last Tsar of Russia, born the son of Alexander III.
1872 Bertrand Russell, British philosopher and mathematician, born in
Ravenscroft near Trelleck, Monmouthshire, Wales.
1882 The present Eddystone lighthouse, the fourth in existence, built
by Sir James Douglass, was opened.
1897 Frank Capra, American film director, born in Palermo, Italy.
1905 Hedley Verity, Yorkshire and England cricketer, born in
Headingley, Leeds.
1909 Fred Perry, English tennis champion, born in Stockport, Cheshire.
George Meredith, English novelist and poet, died in Boxhill,
Surrey, aged 81.
1911 Gustav Mahler, Czech-Austrian composer, conductor and musical
director, died in Vienna.
1912 Perry Como, American singer and entertainer, born in
Canonsburg, Pennsylvania.
1919 Margot Fonteyn, English prima ballerina, born in Reigate, Surrey
as Margaret Hookham.
1920 Pope John Paul II was born as Karolum Wojtyla in the market
town of Wadowice near Cracow in Poland, the son of a junior
officer in the Polish army.
1947 George Forbes, New Zealand statesman and Prime Minister from
1930 to 1935, died.
1953 Jacqueline Cochrane, piloting a North American F-86 Sabre,
became the first woman to fly faster than sound.

1960 Real Madrid beat Eintracht-Frankfurt 7–3 in a football match at Hampden Park, Glasgow to win the European Cup for the fifth year in succession.

1968 Dennis Clarke became the first substitute to be used in an FA Cup final, for West Bromwich Albion in their victory over Everton.

1969 *Apollo 10* was launched with Thomas Stafford, John Young and Eugene Cernan.

1980 Eruption of Mount St Helen's volcano, in the US State of Washington, began.

1985 Kevin Moran of Manchester United became the first player in the history of the FA Cup final to be sent off.

---

19 MAY [140]

1536 Anne Boleyn, the second of Henry VIII's wives and mother of Queen Elizabeth I, was executed on Tower Green for alleged adultery.

1795 James Boswell, Scottish diarist and biographer of Dr Johnson, died in London.

1799 Pierre Beaumarchais, French playwright, notably *The Marriage of Figaro*, died in Paris.

1802 The French 'Légion d'Honneur', an order of distinction for civil or military service, was created by Napoleon.

1849 An attempt to assassinate Queen Victoria was made by William Hamilton.

1861 Dame Nellie Melba, Australian operatic singer, born in Melbourne as Helen Mitchell, the daughter of a brick-maker.

1864 Nathaniel Hawthorne, American novelist and short story writer, died in Plymouth, New Hampshire.

1874 Gilbert Jessop, English cricketer, born in Cheltenham, Gloucestershire.

1879 Lady Astor, English politician and the first lady to take a seat in the House of Commons, born in Greenwood, Virginia—née Langhorne.

1896 Sir Malcolm Balcon, English film producer, born in Birmingham.

1898 William Ewart Gladstone, British statesman and four times Liberal Prime Minister, died at Hawarden Castle in north Wales, aged 88.

1906 The 20 kilometre Simplon rail tunnel, between Switzerland and Italy, was officially opened.

1912 Aeroplane International Registration numbers were introduced.

1925 Malcolm X, US militant black civil rights leader, born in Omaha, Nebraska as Malcolm Little.

1926 David Jacobs, British radio and TV broadcaster, born.
1935 (Thomas Edward) T. E. Lawrence, known as Lawrence of Arabia, died as a result of a motor cycle accident six days previously in a Dorset country lane.
1939 Sandy Macpherson presented the first British radio request programme, called *From my Post-Bag*.
1958 Ronald Colman, British-born film actor and Academy Award (Oscar) winner in 1947 for his part in *A Double Life*, died.
1971 Ogden Nash, American poet known for his humorous verse, died in Baltimore, Maryland.
1984 Sir John Betjeman, writer and Poet Laureate since 1972, died.

20 MAY [141]

1506 Christopher Columbus, Italian navigator and discoverer of the New World in 1492, died in Valladolid, Spain.
1588 The Spanish Armada, comprising 129 ships, under the command of the Duke of Medina, sent by Philip II in an attempt to invade England, set sail from Lisbon.
1799 Honoré de Balzac, French novelist, born in Tours, the son of the deputy Mayor.
1818 William George Fargo, co-founder of Wells-Fargo Express Co., born in Pompey in the State of New York.
1834 Lafayette, French general and statesman, died aged 76.
1851 Emile Berliner, American inventor, born in Germany.
1867 The foundation stone of the Royal Albert Hall in London was laid.
1881 Wladyslaw Sikorski, Polish general and Prime Minister, born in the Galicia region.
1908 James Stewart, American film actor and Oscar winner for *The Philadelphia Story* (1940), born in Indiana, Pennsylvania.
1913 The first Chelsea Flower Show opened in London.
1915 Moshe Dayan, Israeli military commander and minister, born in Deganya.
1939 The first regular North Atlantic airmail service was inaugurated by flyingboats of Pan American Airways, flying between New York and Lisbon/Marseilles.
1941 The island of Crete in the East Mediterranean was invaded by German airborne forces.
1946 Cher, American singer with husband as Sonny and Cher, born in El Centro, California, as Cherilyn La Pierre.
1956 Sir Max Beerbohm, English writer and caricaturist, died aged 83.
     The Americans dropped their first hydrogen bomb, over the Bikini Atoll in the Marshall Islands of the Pacific.

1962 Bobby Moore made the first of his record 108 football international appearances for England, against Peru in Lima.

1967 Substitutes were allowed for the first time in the FA Cup final, but Cliff Jones of Tottenham Hotspur and Joe Kirkup of Chelsea were never used.

1970 Bobby Charlton scored his record 49th goal for England, against Colombia in the World Cup competition.

1975 Barbara Hepworth, English abstract sculptor, died in St Ives, Cornwall.

1977 The Orient Express, from Paris to Istanbul, ran for the last time.

21 MAY [142]

1471 Albrecht Dürer, German artist and engraver, born in Nuremberg, the son of a goldsmith.

Henry VI, King of England, was murdered in the Tower of London.

1502 The South Atlantic island of St Helena was discovered by the Portuguese explorer Joao de Nova.

1688 Alexander Pope, English poet, born in London, the son of a linen draper.

1780 Elizabeth Fry, English prison reformer, born in Norwich, the daughter of a Quaker banker John Gurney.

1840 New Zealand was declared a colony of Britain.

1844 Henri Rousseau, French painter known as 'Le Douanier', born in Laval.

1878 Glenn Curtiss, American aviation pioneer, born in Hammondsport, New York.

1884 The Statue of Liberty was finished, work having been begun by Auguste Bartholdi about 1874 in Paris.

1894 The 35-mile Manchester Ship Canal was formally opened by Queen Victoria.

1895 Franz von Suppé, Austrian composer who wrote the overture *Poet and Peasant*, died in Vienna.

1904 The Football Federation FIFA was founded in Paris, for the better control of the game on an international basis.

Fats Waller, American musician and jazz pianist, born in New York City.

1916 Daylight saving, advocated by William Willett, was introduced in Britain.

Harold Robbins, American novelist, born in New York as Harold Rubin.

1917 Raymond Burr, American film actor, born in New Westminster in the Canadian province of British Columbia.

1927 Charles Lindbergh, US air-mail pilot, became the first to fly the Atlantic solo—from Roosevelt Field, Long Island, New York to Le Bourget airfield, Paris, in 33½ hours in a single-engine monoplane *Spirit of St Louis*, to win a prize of 25 000 dollars.

1929 Lord Rosebery, British statesman and Liberal Prime Minister, died.

1930 Malcolm Fraser, Australian politician and Liberal Prime Minister, born in Melbourne in the State of Victoria.

1932 Amelia Earhart became the first woman to fly the Atlantic solo—flying from Harbor Grace in Newfoundland to Londonderry in Ireland in just under 15 hours.

1965 Sir Geoffrey de Havilland, British aircraft designer, knighted in 1944, died in Stanmore, Middlesex.

---

22 MAY   *[143]*

1783 William Sturgeon, English scientist who built the first practical electromagnet, born in Whittington, Lancashire.

1813 Richard Wagner, German operatic composer, born in Leipzig.

1859 Sir Arthur Conan Doyle, British novelist, creator of Sherlock Holmes, born of Irish parents in Edinburgh.

1874 Daniel Malan, South African politician responsible for the country's apartheid policy, born in Riebeck West, Cape Province.

1880 Sir Ernest Oppenheimer, South African mining magnate and philanthropist, born in Friedberg, Germany, the son of a Jewish cigar merchant.

1885 Victor Hugo, French poet and novelist, author of *Les Misérables*, died in Paris, aged 83.

1897 The Blackwall Tunnel under the Thames was officially opened by the Prince of Wales.

1906 Wilbur Wright patented his airplane.

1907 Laurence Olivier, English stage and film actor, born in Dorking, Surrey.

1915 The worst train disaster in the United Kingdom took place—a triple collision at Quintinshill, near Gretna Green, Dumfries, killing 227.

1923 Stanley Baldwin began the first of his three terms as Conservative Prime Minister.

1925 Sir John French, British general and commander of the British Expeditionary Force in France and Belgium, died.

1931 Kenny Ball, trumpeter and jazz-band leader, born in Ilford, Essex.

1946 Howard Kendall, English footballer and successful manager, born.

George Best, Northern Ireland football international, who helped Manchester United win the English League Championship and the European Cup, born in East Belfast.

Karl Hermann Frank, the Nazi ruler in Czechoslovakia, was hanged in Prague for ordering the massacre in Lidice.

1972 Ceylon became the Republic of Sri Lanka within the Commonwealth.

C. Day-Lewis, English poet and Poet Laureate from 1967, died.

Margaret Rutherford, British character actress, died aged 80.

Richard Nixon arrived in Moscow, the first visit of a US President.

1979 Pierre Trudeau lost the General Election to Joe Clark's Progressive Conservative Party, ending his 11 year rule.

---

23 MAY [144]

1701 'Captain' William Kidd, Scottish privateer, was hanged at Execution Dock in London for piracy.

1706 The Battle of Ramillies took place near Louvain in Belgium, the scene of the French defeat by the allied British, Dutch and Danish armies under Marlborough in the War of the Spanish Succession.

1707 Carl Linnaeus, Swedish botanist, born as Carl Linné, the son of the parish clergyman of Rashult.

1734 Franz Anton Mesmer, Austrian physician and founder of mesmerism, born near Constance, the son of a gamekeeper.

1788 South Carolina, the Palmetto State, became the 8th state of the Union.

1795 Sir Charles Barry, English architect and designer of the new Palace of Westminster, born in London.

1797 The Nore mutiny, led by Richard Parker, against bad food and inadequate pay was started—collapsed on 30 June.

1799 Thomas Hood, English poet, born in London, the son of a bookseller.

1868 Kit Carson, American frontiersman, soldier and Indian agent, died.

1873 The North West Mounted Police were established in Canada—their name was changed to The Royal Canadian Mounted Police on 1 February 1920.

1883 Douglas Fairbanks, American film actor, born in Denver, Colorado, as Douglas Elton Thomas Ullman.

1890 Herbert Marshall, American film actor, born in London.

1906 Henrik Ibsen, Norwegian playwright, best known for *Peer Gynt*, died aged 78.

1908 John Bardeen, US physicist and the only person to win two Nobel Prizes in one field, born in Madison, Wisconsin.
1910 Artie Shaw, American clarinettist and bandleader, born in New York as Arthur Jacob Arshawsky.
      Sir Hugh Casson, British architect and town planner, born.
1918 Denis Compton, English international cricketer and footballer, born in Hendon, London.
1921 Humphrey Lyttelton, English jazz musician and trumpeter, born.
1928 Rosemary Clooney, American singer, born in Maysville, Kentucky.
1931 Whipsnade Zoo, a park in the Chiltern Hills in Bedfordshire, was opened.
1933 Joan Collins, film actress and author, born.
1934 Bonnie and Clyde (Bonnie Parker and Clyde Barrow), notorious murderers and outlaws, were killed in an ambush near Gibland, Louisiana.
1937 John D. Rockefeller, American philanthropist and founder of the Standard Oil Company, died in Florida aged 97.
1941 Herbert Austin, English motor mechanic and manufacturer of the car that bears his name, died near Bromsgrove.
1944 John Newcombe, international tennis champion, born in Sydney, Australia.
1945 Heinrich Himmler, German Nazi leader and notorious chief of police, committed suicide.
1946 David Graham, international golfer, born in Australia.
1949 The State of Germany, or the German Federal Republic, came into existence, with Bonn its capital.
1951 Anatoly Karpov, Russian chess player and world champion in 1975, born.
1954 Marvin Hagler, American world middleweight boxing champion, born.

24 MAY   [145]

1543 Nicolaus Copernicus, Polish founder of modern astronomy, died of apoplexy.
1743 Jean Paul Marat, French revolutionary, born in Boudry, near Neuchâtel, Switzerland.
1792 Lord Rodney, British admiral and victorious commander, died in Hanover Square, London.
1809 Dartmoor Prison at Princetown was opened—was built originally to house French prisoners of war—used for convicts from 1850.
1819 Queen Victoria was born at Kensington Palace, granddaughter of King George III and niece of King William IV.

1830 The first passenger railroad was opened in America—the Baltimore & Ohio.

1836 Joseph Rowntree, British cocoa manufacturer and philanthropist, born in York.

1844 The first morse message over the first telegraph line was sent from Washington to Baltimore, by its inventor Samuel Morse— 'What hath God wrought'.

1870 Jan Christiaan Smuts, South African soldier, statesman and Prime Minister, born in Malmesbury, Cape Colony.

1879 William Lloyd Harrison, American leader of slavery abolition and women's suffrage, died in New York.

1883 The 1595-feet Brooklyn Bridge over the East River, designed by John Augustus Roebling, was opened.

1895 The first stage knighthood was conferred on Sir Henry Irving in the Birthday Honours.

1899 Suzanne Lenglen, French tennis player and six times Wimbledon winner, born in Compiègne, Picardy.

1902 Empire Day was first celebrated in Britain.

1912 Joan Hammond, international soprano, born in New Zealand.

1930 Amy Johnson landed at Darwin in Northern Australia, having flown solo from London—in her Gypsy Moth, *Jason*—the first woman to do so.

1941 The battle cruiser HMS *Hood* was sunk by the *Bismarck* 13 miles off the coast of Greenland—only three of her 1421 crew survived.
Bob Dylan, American singer, born in Duluth, Minnesota, as Robert Zimmerman—chose the name in honour of Dylan Thomas.

1950 Lord Wavell, field marshal, commander in the Middle East and Viceroy of India, died in London.

1956 The first Eurovision song contest was held at Lugano, and was won by Switzerland, the host country.

1959 Empire Day was renamed Commonwealth Day.
John Foster Dulles, American Government official and diplomat, died.

1964 A riot broke out when the referee disallowed a goal by the home side in a soccer international against Argentina. The police used tear gas and during the ensuing panic to get out of the stadium 301 people were killed and over 500 injured in the biggest disaster in the history of sport, at the National Stadium, Lima, Peru.

1969 *The Black and White Minstrel Show*, at London's Victoria Palace, closed after 4354 performances in seven years to become the longest-running musical show in Britain.

1970 The Menai tubular railway bridge linking Wales and Anglesey was severely damaged by fire.

1972 'Spaghetti junction', the most complex interchange on the British road system, at Gravelly Hill, was opened.

1974 'Duke' Ellington, American jazz musician, composer and pianist, died aged 75.
Giscard d'Estaing became President of France.
1978 Princess Margaret obtained a divorce from Lord Snowdon.
1987 Hermione Gingold, English stage and film actress, died aged 89.
1988 Liverpool's Albert Dock was restored and re-opened as a business and leisure centre by HRH The Prince of Wales.

25 MAY [146]

National day of Jordan.

1803 Ralph Waldo Emerson, American poet and essayist, born in Boston, Massachusetts, the son of a minister.
1871 The Bank Holiday Act was passed in the House of Commons.
1879 Lord Beaverbrook, English statesman and newspaper owner, born in Maple in the Canadian province of Ontario as William Maxwell Aitken.
1889 Igor Sikorsky, American aviation engineer and pioneer of the helicopter, born in Kiev.
1892 Josip Broz (Marshal Tito), Yugoslav Communist leader and President, born in Kumrovec, near Klanjec.
(Some sources quote 7 May).
1897 Alan Kippax, New South Wales and Australian Test cricketer, born.
1898 Gene Tunney, American heavyweight boxing champion, born in Greenwich Village, New York City, as James Joseph Tunney.
1907 The first 24 hour motor race, called the Endurance Derby, was held in Philadelphia. The winning car covered a distance of 791 miles.
1913 Richard Dimbleby, English broadcaster, born.
1934 Gustav Holst, English composer of *The Planets*, died and was buried in Chichester Cathedral.
1935 Jesse Owens, American athlete, set six world records within 45 minutes, at Ann Arbor in Michigan.
1939 Sir Frank Dyson, English astronomer and director of Greenwich Observatory, died.
1951 Burgess and Maclean both escaped from England en route to Moscow.
1955 A British expedition, led by Charles Evans, became the first to climb the Himalayan peak Kangchenjunga, the third highest summit in the world.
1962 Coventry's new Cathedral was consecrated—after six years of building.

137

1965 When Muhammad Ali fought Sonny Liston at Lewiston, Maine, there were only 2434 spectators, the smallest attendance for a world heavyweight title fight.

1967 Celtic, the Scottish champions, became the first British football club to win the European Cup—beating Internazionale 2–1 in Lisbon.

1982 HMS *Coventry* and the merchant vessel *Atlantic Conveyor* were sunk in the Falklands conflict with the loss of 24 lives.

26 MAY [147]

1650 The Duke of Marlborough, British general and statesman, born as John Churchill, in Ashe, Devon.
(Some sources quote 24 June).

1703 Samuel Pepys, famous English diarist, died in Clapham, London.

1799 Aleksander Pushkin, Russian poet and novelist, born in Moscow.

1805 Napoleon was crowned King of Italy, in Milan Cathedral.

1863 Bob Fitzsimmons, British boxer, born in Helston, Cornwall.

1865 The American Civil War ended, with the surrender of General Kirby Smith in Texas.

1867 Queen Mary, wife of King George V, born in Kensington Palace as Princess Mary of Teck.

1868 The last public execution in England took place—Michael Barrett—outside Newgate Prison in London.

1886 Al Jolson, American entertainer, often in black face, born in Srednik, Lithuania, as Asa Yoelson.

1891 Paul Lukas, Hungarian-American film actor, born in Budapest.

1904 George Formby, English comedy actor and entertainer, born.

1906 Vauxhall Bridge over the River Thames was officially opened.

1907 John Wayne, American film actor, born in Winterset, Iowa, as Marion Michael Morrison.

1908 Robert Morley, English actor, born in Semley, Wiltshire.

1909 Sir Matt Busby, Scottish international footballer and club manager, born.

1913 Miss Emily Duncan was appointed a Justice of the Peace in West Ham to become the first British woman magistrate.

1920 Peggy Lee, American singer, born in Jamestown, South Dakota, as Norma Egstrom.

1923 The annual Le Mans 24-hour race for sports cars was first held, on the old Sarthe circuit.
James Arness, American film actor, born in Minneapolis, the elder brother of fellow actor Peter Graves.

1924 Victor Herbert, Irish-born American cellist, conductor and composer, died.

1938 The first Volkswagen motor car came off the assembly line at the factory at Wolfsburg, Germany.

1939 Charles Mayo, American surgeon and co-founder of the Mayo Clinic Foundation, died aged 78.

1943 Edsel Ford, President of the Ford Motor Company from 1919, died.

1947 Glenn Turner, Otago and New Zealand Test cricketer, born.

1950 Petrol rationing ended in Britain.

1951 Lincoln Ellsworth, American scientist and explorer of the Arctic and Antarctic, died.

1966 British Guiana, under Burnham, became fully independent and a member of the British Commonwealth, changing its name to Guyana.

Zola Budd, who was granted British citizenship in time for the 1984 Olympics, amid great controversy, born in South Africa.

---

27 MAY   [148]

National day of Afghanistan.

1564 John Calvin, French theologian who spread the Protestant Reformation, died.

1818 Amelia Bloomer, American campaigner for women's rights who popularised 'bloomers', born in Homer, New York.

1837 'Wild Bill' Hickok, American scout and frontier marshal, born in Troy Grove, Illinois, as James Butler Hickok.

1840 Niccolo Paganini, Italian violin virtuoso and composer, died in Nice.

1863 Broadmoor Asylum for the criminally insane, was established in Crowthorne, Berkshire.

1867 Arnold Bennett, English novelist, born near Hanley, Staffordshire, the son of a solicitor.

1878 Isadora Duncan, American dancer, born in San Francisco.

1887 Frank Woolley, Kent and England cricketer, born in Tonbridge.

1897 Sir John Cockcroft, English nuclear physicist, born in Yorkshire.

1910 Robert Koch, German bacteriologist and Nobel Prize winner who discovered the bacillus of tuberculosis, died.

1911 Vincent Price, American actor best known for his roles in horror movies, born in St Louis, Missouri.

Hubert Humphrey, American Democrat politician and Vice-President to Lyndon Johnson, born in Wallace, South Dakota.

1912 Sam Snead, American champion golfer, born in Hot Springs, Virginia.

1914 Sir Joseph Swan, English chemist, physicist and inventor, died in Surrey, aged 85.

1919 Lt Cdr Read and a crew of five in a Curtiss NC–4 seaplane, reached Lisbon via the Azores to complete the first transatlantic flight, having left Trepassey, Newfoundland, on 16 May.

1922 Christopher Lee, British actor, mainly in horror films, born in London.

1923 Henry Kissinger, American Secretary of State, born in Fürth, Germany.

1936 The open prison at New Hall near Wakefield, Yorkshire, was opened, as the first of its kind in Britain.

1937 The 4200-feet Golden Gate Bridge, over the Golden Gate waterway at San Francisco, was opened.

1940 'Operation Dynamo', the evacuation of British and French troops from the Dunkirk beaches began—ended on 4 June.

1941 The German battleship *Bismarck* was sunk by the battleships *Prince of Wales*, *King George V* and *Rodney*, afer torpedo attacks by Swordfish aircraft from the carrier *Ark Royal*.

1943 Cilla Black, English pop singer, born in Liverpool, as Priscilla White.
Joseph Coates, New Zealand statesman and Prime Minister from 1925 to 1928, died.

1951 John Conteh, a former world light heavyweight boxing champion, born in Liverpool.

1964 Pandit Nehru, Indian statesman and first Prime Minister of independent India in 1947, died.

1965 Pat Cash, Australian tennis player and a Wimbledon singles champion, born.

1975 Ezzard Charles, American heavyweight boxer and world champion from 1949 to 1951, died in Chicago.

1981 Willie Shoemaker rode 'War Allied' to victory at Hollywood Park in California to record his 8000th winner.

---

28 MAY [149]

1759 William Pitt the Younger, British statesman and Tory Prime Minister, born in Hayes, near Bromley, Kent.

1818 Pierre Beauregard, American Confederate Army general, born in St Bernard, near New Orleans, Louisiana.

1842 The first public library was opened, in Frederick Street, Salford, Manchester.

1843 Noah Webster, American lexicographer and originator of *Webster's Dictionary* in 1828, died in New Haven, Connecticut, aged 84.

1849 Anne Brontë, English novelist, author of *The Tenant of Wildfell Hall*, died in Scarborough, Yorkshire, aged 29.

1884 Eduard Beneš, Czech statesman and founder of modern Czechoslovakia, born in Kozlany, Bohemia.

1907 The first Isle of Man motor cycle TT race was held.
1908 Ian Fleming, English novelist and creator of the character 'James Bond', born in London.
1912 Patrick White, Australian novelist and Nobel Prize winner, born in London.
1934 The Dionne quins (Emilie, Yvonne, Cécile, Marie and Annette) were born in Callender, Ontario, to Mrs Oliva Dionne.
1937 Alfred Adler, Austrian psychiatrist and psychologist, died.
     A Coalition or National Government was formed under the leadership of Neville Chamberlain.
1940 Belgian King Leopold III surrendered to Germany.
1944 Gladys Knight, American soul singer, born in Atlanta, Georgia.
1959 The Mermaid Theatre in London opened at Puddle Dock.
     Billy Wright, soccer player, made his 105th and final appearance for England, in the 8–1 win over the USA at Los Angeles.
1967 Francis Chichester arrived back at Plymouth after sailing around the world single-handed in *Gipsy Moth IV*.
1972 The Duke of Windsor, the abdicated King Edward VIII, died in Paris aged 77.
1982 When John Paul II arrived at Gatwick airport he became the first reigning Pope to visit Great Britain.
1984 Eric Morecambe, English comedian of the Morecambe and Wise team, died in Cheltenham.

29 MAY   [150]

Memorial Day, USA.
Oak apple day. Charles II fleeing after the Battle of Worcester (1651) is said to have hidden up an oak tree in Boscobel. Loyal subjects wear oak leaves on this day to commemorate the event.

1500 Bartolomeu Diaz, Portuguese explorer who discovered the Cape of Good Hope in 1488, was drowned during a storm at sea.
1630 King Charles II was born in St James's Palace, the son of Charles I and Henrietta Maria of France.
1660 After nearly nine years of wandering in exile Charles II returned to England and entered London in triumph, and was restored to the English throne.
1790 Rhode Island, the Ocean State, became the 13th state of the Union—and the smallest.
1829 Sir Humphry Davy, English chemist who invented the miners' safety lamp in 1815, died in Geneva.
1848 Wisconsin, the Badger State, became the 30th state of the Union.
1871 Whit Monday became the first Bank Holiday in Britain.

1874 (Gilbert Keith) G. K. Chesterton, English novelist and poet, born in Kensington, London.

1898 Beatrice Lillie, American actress, born in Toronto in the Canadian province of Ontario as Constance Sylvia Munston.

1903 Bob Hope, American comedian and film actor, born in Eltham, London as Leslie Townes Hope—emigrated to USA when he was four.

1911 Sir William Gilbert, English writer of comic operas in collaboration with Sir Arthur Sullivan, died.

1917 John F. Kennedy, American Democrat statesman and 35th President, born in Brookline, Massachusetts, the second of nine children.

1939 Al Unser, American motor racing champion driver, born the younger brother of Bobby.

1942 John Barrymore, American film actor, called the 'Great Profile', died.
White Christmas, the world's best selling gramophone record single was recorded by Bing Crosby.

1951 Fanny Brice, American singer, long associated with the Ziegfeld Follies, died.

1953 Everest, the world's highest mountain, was conquered by Edmund Hillary and Sherpa Tensing.

1968 Manchester United became the first English football club to win the European Cup—beating Benfica of Portugal 4–1 at Wembley Stadium in London.

1979 Mary Pickford, Canadian-born film actress and Academy Award (Oscar) winner in 1929 for her part in *Coquette*, died aged 86.

1985 39 were killed after a wall collapsed as a result of soccer crowd violence at Heysel Stadium, Brussels, before the Liverpool v Juventus match.

1987 Mathias Rust, a German teenager, flew his small plane into Russia and landed in Moscow's Red Square.

30 MAY [151]

1431 Joan of Arc, French peasant girl of Domrémy who became a national heroine, was burned at the stake in Rouen for heresy— was made a saint in 1920.

1536 King Henry VIII married Jane Seymour, the third of his six wives, in the Queen's Chapel, Whitehall—11 days after the execution of Anne Boleyn.

1593 Christopher Marlowe, English poet and playwright, author of *Doctor Faustus*, was mysteriously killed in a tavern brawl in Deptford, London, aged 29.

1640   Peter Paul Rubens, Flemish baroque painter, died in Antwerp.
1656   The Grenadier Guards, the senior regiment of the British Army, was formed.
1672   Peter the Great, Tsar and Emperor of Russia, born in Moscow the son of Tsar Alexei.
1744   Alexander Pope, English poet, died in Twickenham, London.
1766   The 'Royal' in Bristol, the oldest theatre still in use in Britain, was opened.
1778   Voltaire, the name adopted by Francois Marie Arouet, French philosopher and historian, died in Paris, aged 83.
1842   An attempt was made on the life of Queen Victoria as she was driving down Constitution Hill with Prince Albert—the would-be assassin was John Francis.
1896   Howard Hawks, American film director, born in Goshen, Indiana.
1908   Mel Blanc, American entertainer and the voice of many cartoon characters, born in San Francisco.
1909   Benny Goodman, American clarinettist and band leader, born in Chicago, Illinois.
        George Headley, West Indian Test cricketer, born in Panama.
1911   The 'Indianapolis 500' car race of 200 laps was inaugurated in the USA.
1912   Wilbur Wright, American airplane pioneer and first to make a controlled flight in 1903, died in Dayton, Ohio.
1922   The Lincoln Memorial at West Potomac Park was dedicated. It was designed by Henry Bacon, and the statue was made by Daniel Chester French.
1959   Auckland Harbour bridge on New Zealand's North Island was officially opened.
        The first full-sized experimental hovercraft, built by Saunders-Roe, was launched at Cowes on the Isle of Wight.
1960   Boris Pasternak, Russian poet and novelist, author of *Dr Zhivago* and Nobel Prize winner in 1958 (declined), died near Moscow.
1967   Claude Rains, British-born film actor, died aged 77.
1971   *Mariner 9* was launched by the US at Cape Kennedy for a Mars mission.

31 MAY   [152]

National day of South Africa.

1594   Tintoretto, the name adopted by Jacopo Robusti, one of the greatest of Italian painters, died in Venice.
1669   Samuel Pepys discontinued his diary, which began on 1 January 1660.

1809 Franz Josef Haydn, Austrian composer, died in Vienna.

1837 Joseph Grimaldi, English clown of Italian parentage, died.

1859 'Big Ben', in the clock tower of the Houses of Parliament in London, first began recording time.

1872 Heath Robinson, British humorous artist of complex machinery which performed simple tasks, born in London.

1902 The Peace of Vereeniging was signed, ending the Boer War.

1908 Don Ameche, American film actor, born in Kenosha, Wisconsin as Dominic Felix Amici.

1910 The colonies of the Cape of Good Hope, Natal, the Transvaal and the Orange River Colony became united to form the Union of South Africa.
Elizabeth Blackwell, English-born American physician, the first woman to gain an MD degree, in 1849, died.

1911 The ill-fated British liner *Titanic* was launched at the Harland and Wolff shipyard in Belfast.

1915 The first air raid on London took place.

1916 The Battle of Jutland was fought in the North Sea between the British fleet under Jellicoe and Beatty and the German fleet commanded by Scheer and von Hipper.

1923 Prince Rainier III, the ruling Prince of the House of Grimaldi, born in Monaco.

1927 The last 'Tin Lizzie' came off the production line, almost unchanged since it was introduced as the model T Ford in 1908.

1930 Clint Eastwood, American film actor and director, born in San Francisco.

1939 Terry Waite, the Archbishop of Canterbury's envoy, born.

1961 South Africa became a Republic and withdrew from the Commonwealth.

1962 Adolf Eichmann was executed inside Ramleh Prison near Tel Aviv for his part in the wartime mass execution of millions of Jews.

1970 The famous British steeplechaser 'Arkle' was put down.

1973 Erskine Childers succeeded De Valera as President of the Irish Republic, a position the latter had held since 1959.

1983 Jack Dempsey, world heavyweight boxing champion, died.

1 JUNE [153]

National Day of Tunisia.

1792 Kentucky, the Blue Grass State, became the 15th state of the Union.

1796 Tennessee, the Volunteer State, became the 16th state of the Union.

1801 Brigham Young, American influential Mormon religious leader, born in Whittingham, Vermont.

1804 Mikhail Glinka, Russian composer of operas, born in Novospasskoi, Smolensk.

1868 James Buchanan, American Democrat statesman and 15th President from 1857 to 1861—the only bachelor—died in Wheatland, near Lancaster, Pennsylvania, aged 77.

1874 Pullman carriages were introduced in Britain, by the Midland Railway, from London to Bradford.

1878 John Masefield, English poet and Poet Laureate, born in Ledbury, Herefordshire.

1880 The first telephone call-box for public use, installed in New Haven, Connecticut, went into service.

1907 Sir Frank Whittle, English inventor and pioneer of jet propulsion, born in Coventry.

1921 Nelson Riddle, American bandleader and composer, born in Hackensack, New Jersey.

1926 Marilyn Monroe, American film actress and sex symbol, born in Los Angeles, California, as Norma Jean Baker.

1927 Lizzie Borden, the alleged axe murderess, died.

1928 Bob Monkhouse, English comedian and TV presenter, born in Beckenham, Kent.

1930 Edward Woodward, English actor, born in Croydon, London.

1934 Pat Boone, American pop singer of the 1950s, born in Jacksonville, Florida.

1935 Driving tests in Britain were introduced by Leslie Hore Belisha, and 'L' plates were made compulsory.

1937 Colleen McCullough, Australian novelist noted for *The Thorn Birds*, born in Wellington, Australia.

1939 The British naval submarine *Thetis* sank while on trials in Liverpool Bay, with the loss of 99 lives. Was later raised and put back into service as HMS *Thunderbolt*.

1941 Hugh Walpole, English novelist, knighted in 1937, died in Brackenburn near Keswick.

1943 Leslie Howard, British film actor and director, was killed when the plane in which he was travelling was shot down.

1946 The first television licences were issued in Britain, at a fee of £2.

1953 Alex James, Scottish international footballer and player with Preston North End and Arsenal, died in London.

1957 The first Premium Bond prize winners were drawn by the computer 'ERNIE'—with a first prize of £1000.

1958 Charles de Gaulle became Prime Minister of France.

1968 Helen Keller, American author and lecturer, blind and deaf from the age of two, died aged 87.

1983 Lester Piggott rode his record ninth Epsom Derby winner, on the favourite 'Teenoso'.

National Day of Italy.

1780   The Gordon Riots took place when Lord George Gordon called his
        followers to St George's Field in London, and led them in protest
        at the cancellation of some of the restrictions on Roman Catholics.
1840   Thomas Hardy, English novelist and poet, born in Higher
        Bockhampton, Dorset, the son of a stonemason.
1850   Jesse Boot, English pharmacist and chemist, born in Nottingham.
1857   Sir Edward Elgar, English composer, born in Broadheath, near
        Worcester, the son of a music-seller and organist.
1868   The first Trades Union Congress was held in Manchester—
        finished on 6th.
1882   Giuseppe Garibaldi, Italian soldier and patriot who helped to form
        the Kingdom of Italy, died.
1883   The first floodlit baseball match took place at Fort Wayne in
        Indiana, the home team playing Quincy from Illinois.
1886   President Grover Cleveland married Frances Folsom in the White
        House.
1896   Marconi was granted the first patent (numbered 12039) for a
        system of communication by means of electromagnetic waves.
1903   Johnny Weismuller, American swimmer, holder of many world
        records and 'Tarzan' in 19 movies, born in Windber, Penn-
        sylvania.
1909   Mike Todd, American theatre and film producer, born in
        Minneapolis as Avron Hirsch Golbogen.
1910   Charles Stewart Rolls, in a Short-Wright biplane, flew from Dover
        to Sangatte to become the first Briton to fly the Channel.
1929   Ken McGregor, Australian international tennis player, born in
        Adelaide.
1930   Charles Conrad, American astronaut whose craft made the
        second landing on the Moon, born in Philadelphia, Pennsylvania.
1938   Regent's Park Children's Zoo in London was opened by Robert
        and Edward Kennedy.
1940   Constantine II, King of the Hellenes, born the son of King Paul.
1941   Clothes rationing started in Britain.
1953   The coronation of Queen Elizabeth II took place.
1966   The American *Surveyor* spacecraft made a soft landing on the
        Moon.
1970   Bruce McLaren, New Zealand motor racing driver, accidentally
        killed.

1657 William Harvey, English anatomist and physician who discovered and demonstrated the circulation of the blood, died near Saffron Walden, Essex.

1804 Richard Cobden, British statesman and economist, born in Heyshott, near Midhurst, Sussex, the son of a farmer.

1808 Jefferson Davis, American statesman and President of the Confederate States in the American Civil War, born in Fairview, Kentucky.

1851 The first baseball inter-club match took place, Knickerbocker Club v Washington Baseball Club, at Red House Grounds, New York.

1865 King George V, the second son of Edward VII and Queen Alexandra, born at Marlborough House, London.

1875 Georges Bizet, French composer, notably the opera *Carmen*, died in Bougival, near Paris.

1898 Samuel Plimsoll, English social reformer, known as 'The Sailors' Friend', who devised the Plimsoll line for the safe loading of ships, died in Folkestone, Kent.

1899 Johann Strauss the Younger, Austrian composer of light music, notably the *Blue Danube*, died in Vienna.

1915 Paulette Goddard, American film actress, born in Great Neck in the State of New York as Marion Levy.

1925 Tony Curtis, American film actor, born in New York City as Bernard Schwartz, the son of Hungarian-Jewish immigrant parents.

1936 Colin Meads, New Zealand international Rugby Union player and winner of 55 caps, born in Cambridge, Waikato.

1937 The Duke of Windsor, the abdicated King Edward VIII, married Mrs Wallis Warfield Simpson in Monts, France.

1945 Hale Irwin, American golf champion, born in Joplin, Missouri.

1950 The Himalayan peak of Annapurna was first climbed, by Herzog and Lachenal members of a French expedition.

1956 Third class rail travel was abolished on British Rail, to conform with continental practice.

1963 Pope John XXIII, Angelo Giuseppe Roncalli, died.

1965 *Gemini 4* was launched, with James McDivitt and Edward White—during the flight Ed White became the first American to walk in space.

1986 Dame Anna Neagle, British film and stage actress, died aged 81.

1987 Andrés Segovia, Spanish classical-guitar virtuoso, died aged 93.

1989 Ayatollah Sayyed Khomeini, political and religious leader of Iran, died aged 86.

1703 Samuel Pepys was buried at St Olave's in London's Hart Street.

1738 King George III, the grandson of George II, was born in lodgings in St James's Square, London.

1798 Giovanni Casanova, Italian adventurer, lover and romancer, died at his Castle of Dux, Bohemia.

1805 The first 'Trooping of the Colour' took place, at Horse Guards Parade, London.

1831 Prince Leopold of Saxe-Coburg was chosen as the first sovereign of independent Belgium.

1832 The Great Reform Bill passed into law.

1867 Carl Mannerheim, Finnish soldier, statesman and President, born in Vilnas.

1910 Christopher Cockerell, British engineer and inventor of the amphibious Hovercraft, born in Cambridge.

1911 Rosalind Russell, American film actress, born in Waterbury, Connecticut.

1913 The 'Suffragette' Derby took place, during which Emily Davidson was trampled to death when she threw herself in front of the King's horse 'Anmer' at Tattenham Corner.

1925 Dennis Weaver, American stage and TV film actor, born in Joplin, Missouri.

1940 The evacuation of allied forces from Dunkirk and St Valéry was completed—having started on 27 May.

1941 Kaiser Wilhelm II, German Emperor, died in exile in the Netherlands.

1944 Allied forces entered and liberated the city of Rome.

1948 Bob Champion, English jockey and Grand National winner on 'Aldaniti' in 1981, born.

1958 The first Duke of Edinburgh Awards were presented, at Buckingham Palace.

1968 Sir Walter Nash, New Zealand Labour statesman and Prime Minister from 1957 to 1960, died.

1970 Tonga or Friendly Islands became completely independent and a member of the Commonwealth, having been a British Protectorate since 1900.

5 JUNE   [157]

National Day of Denmark

1723 Adam Smith, Scottish economist and philosopher, born in the seaport of Kirkcaldy, the son of a Customs officer.

1819 John Couch Adams, English astronomer, co-discoverer of the planet Neptune, born near Launceston, Cornwall.
1826 Carl von Weber, German composer, pianist and musical director, died in London.
1878 'Pancho' Villa, Mexican guerrilla leader and revolutionary, born in San Juan del Rio as Doroteo Arango.
1907 Gilbert Harding, British radio and TV entertainer, born in Hereford.
1916 Lord Kitchener, British general and conqueror of the Sudan, was lost at sea when HMS *Hampshire* struck a mine off Orkney, en route to Russia.
1939 Joe Clark, Canadian Conservative statesman and Prime Minister, born.
1941 Harry Nilsson, American singer and songwriter, born in New York as Harry Nelson.
1946 The Victory Parade took place in London, at which King George VI took the salute in The Mall.
1947 Marshall Aid by America was inaugurated, for European post-war recovery.
1953 Bill Tilden, American international tennis champion, died.
1967 The 'Six-day War' between Israel and Egypt, Jordan, Syria and Iraq began.
1964 Britain made its first flight into space, with *Blue Streak* rocket, launched from Woomera in Australia.
1968 Robert Kennedy, American Senator and younger brother of the late President, was shot in the Hotel Ambassador in Los Angeles by a Jordanian-Arab, Sirhan Bishara Sirhan—died the following day.
1975 President Sadat re-opened the Suez Canal to all but Israeli shipping, after eight years of closure.
     British citizens voted in a referendum on the entry into the European Community—result 17 378 581 YES and 8 470 073 NO.
1988 Kay Cottee ended her six month voyage in Sydney Harbour to complete the first solo non-stop round the world voyage by a woman.

6 JUNE [158]

National day of Sweden.

1599 Diego Velasquez, Spanish court painter, born in Seville.
1683 The first museum in Britain, the Ashmolean Museum in Broad Street, Oxford, founded by Elias Ashmole, was opened to the public.
1727 The first boxing title fight took place, in London—James Figg defeating Ned Sutton.

1755 Nathan Hale, American soldier and Revolutionary hero, born in Coventry, Massachusetts.

1762 Admiral George Anson, a victor in battle and man responsible for naval reform, died.

1861 Count Cavour, Italian statesman primarily responsible for the unification of Italy, died.

1868 Robert Falcon Scott, British Antarctic explorer, born near Devonport in Devon.

1875 Thomas Mann, German novelist, born at the port of Lübeck.

1882 The three-mile coastal limit for territorial waters was established by the Hague Convention.

1900 Arthur Askey, English comedian, born in Liverpool.

1908 England played their first football international against a foreign country—winning 6-1 in Vienna against Austria.

1923 Steve Donoghue became the first and only jockey to win the English Derby three times in succession, riding the fleet-footed 'Papyrus'.

1933 The first drive-in cinema was opened on a site in Camden, New Jersey by Richard Hollingshead.

1942 The three day Battle of Midway Island was concluded with a US victory: the turning point in the Pacific.

1944 The allied landings on the coast of Normandy, called 'Operation Overlord', took place—the start of the biggest sea-borne invasion in history.

1953 Gordon Richards, at his 28th attempt, rode his first Derby winner, 'Pinza', at the odds of 5-1.

1954 The Eurovision television link-up was inaugurated.

1956 Bjorn Borg, Swedish international tennis champion, born in Stockholm.

1957 Mike Gatting, English cricketer and England captain, born.

1961 Carl Jung, Swiss psychologist, psychiatrist and associate of Freud, died aged 85.

1976 Paul Getty, American oil businessman and reputed to be the richest man in the world, died aged 83.

1977 Derby was designated a city to mark the Silver Jubilee of HM Queen Elizabeth II.

7 JUNE [159]

1329 Robert the Bruce, King of Scotland from 1306, died of leprosy at Cardross Castle, on the Firth of Clyde, and was buried in Dunfermline Abbey under the High Altar.

1614 The Addled Parliament was dissolved without having passed a Bill since it first sat on 5 April—hence its name.

1761 John Rennie, Scottish civil engineer, responsible for several bridges and docks in London, born in East Linton.

1778 'Beau' Brummell, English dandy and leader of fashion born in London as George Bryan Brummell.

1848 Paul Gauguin, French painter, born in Paris, the son of a journalist.

1866 E. W. Hornung, English novelist, born at Middlesbrough.

1905 Norway gained independence from Sweden.

1906 The British Atlantic passenger liner *Lusitania* was launched.

1910 Pietro Annigoni, Italian painter, born in Milan.

1917 Dean Martin, American actor, singer and entertainer, born as Dino Paul Crocetti, in Steubenville, Ohio.

1929 The Papal State, extinct since 1870, was revived as the State of Vatican City, as a result of the Lateran Treaty.
John Turner, Canadian Liberal statesman and Prime Minister, born.

1937 Jean Harlow, American film actress, died aged 26.

1939 HM King George VI, accompanied by HM Queen Elizabeth, crossed the border from Canada into America at Niagara Falls on their way to the World's Fair in New York, to become the first British monarch to visit the USA.

1940 Tom Jones, British entertainer, born in Pontypridd, South Wales as Thomas Jones Woodward.

1950 The BBC radio serial *The Archers*, created by Godfrey Basely, was first broadcast.

1965 Judy Holliday, American film actress and Oscar winner in 1950 for her role in *Born Yesterday*, died.

1970 (Edward Morgan) E. M. Forster, English novelist, died aged 91.

1980 Henry Miller, American novelist, author of *Tropic of Cancer* and *Tropic of Capricorn*, died in California.

1989 Peter Shilton made his record 109th appearance for England, against Denmark in Copenhagen, passing Bobby Moore's long-standing record.

---

8 JUNE   [160]

1695 Christiaan Huygens, Dutch physicist and astronomer who invented the pendulum clock, died.

1724 John Smeaton, English civil engineer, born in Austhorp near Leeds in Yorkshire.

1809 Thomas Paine, English radical and political reformer, author of *The Rights of Man*, died in poverty in New York.

1810 Robert Schumann, German composer, born in Zwickau where his father kept a book shop.

1814 Charles Reade, English novelist, born in Ipsden House, Oxfordshire, the youngest of 11 children.

1829 Sir John Millais, English painter who helped to form the Pre-Raphaelite brotherhood, born in Southampton.

1845 Andrew Jackson, American general, Democrat statesman and 7th President from 1829 to 1837, nicknamed 'Old Hickory', died at The Hermitage in Nashville, Tennessee.

1865 Sir Joseph Paxton, English ornamental gardener and architect who designed the Crystal Palace for the 1851 Great Exhibition, died in London.

1869 Frank Lloyd Wright, American architect, born in Richmond Center, Wisconsin.

1876 George Sand (Armandine Dupin), French novelist and mistress of Chopin and Musset, died in Nohant.

1924 George Mallory, on his third attempt to climb Everest, and Irvine, were last seen at a point some 800 feet below the summit.

1928 Charles Kingsford-Smith and Captain Ulm landed at Brisbane in Australia to become the first to fly across the Pacific. They flew in their *Southern Cross* from Oakland in California via Hawaii and Fiji.

1929 Margaret Bondfield became the first British woman Cabinet Minister when she was appointed Minister of Labour.

1930 Returning from Exile, King Carol II was restored to the throne of Romania.

1940 Nancy Sinatra, American entertainer, born in Jersey City, New Jersey, the daughter of Frank Sinatra.

1968 Bermuda achieved internal self-government.

1969 Robert Taylor, American film actor, died.

1978 Naomi James arrived back at Dartmouth in her Bermuda sloop *Express Crusader* after 267 days, to become the first woman to sail solo around the world via Cape Horn.

1986 Kurt Waldheim was elected President of Austria amid widespread international criticism. He was inaugurated on 8 July.

1988 Russell Harty, British broadcaster and writer, died aged 53.

9 JUNE [161]

1549 The Book of Common Prayer, compiled by Thomas Cranmer, was adopted in England.

1781 George Stephenson, English locomotive engineer, builder of the *Rocket*, born in Wylam-on-Tyne near Newcastle, the son of a colliery engine keeper.

1870 Charles Dickens, English novelist, author of many famous works, died in Gadshill near Rochester in Kent after a brain haemorrhage the previous evening.

1874 Cochise, Apache chief and war leader against white settlers, died.
1892 Cole Porter, American lyricist and composer of musicals, born in Peru, Indiana.
1898 Hong Kong was leased by Britain from China for 99 years.
1899 James J. Jeffries won the world heavyweight boxing title, knocking out Bob Fitzsimmons in the 11th round at Coney Island.
1904 The London Symphony Orchestra gave its first concert.
1915 The British troops in France were first issued with hand grenades.
1934 Donald Duck was 'born', in Walt Disney's *The Wise Little Hen*.
1958 Gatwick Aiport in Sussex was opened by the Queen.
      Robert Donat, British film actor and Academy Award (Oscar) winner in 1939 for his part in *Goodbye, Mr Chips*, died.
1959 The first Polaris submarine, *George Washington*, was launched at Groton in Connecticut.
1964 Lord Beaverbrook, Canadian-born statesman and newspaper magnate, died aged 85.
1976 Dame Sybil Thorndike, British stage and film actress, died aged 93.

10 JUNE   *[162]*

1688 James Stuart, the 'Old Pretender', born in St James's Palace, the only son of King James II and his second wife, Mary of Modena.
1727 King George I died on his way to Hanover in the castle at Osnabruck—in the very room in which he had been born.
1829 The first Oxford and Cambridge University boat race took place, 2¼ miles from Hambledon Lock to Henley Bridge—won easily by Oxford.
1836 André Ampère, French physicist noted for his work on electrodynamics, died.
1854 Queen Victoria opened the Crystal Palace on its new site at Sydenham, South London.
1901 Frederick Loewe, musical comedy composer of Lerner and Loewe fame, born in Vienna.
1909 The SOS distress signal was transmitted for the first time when the Cunard liner *Slavonia* was wrecked off the Azores.
1911 Terence Rattigan, English playwright, born in London.
1921 Royal Consort Prince Philip, Duke of Edinburgh, born on the Greek island of Corfu.
1922 Judy Garland, American film actress and singer, born in Minnesota as Frances Ethel Gumm, of vaudeville parents.
1923 Robert Maxwell, publisher of newspapers, born in Solotvino, East Czechoslovakia, as Ludvick Hoch.

1929 James McDivitt, American astronaut, born in Chicago, Illinois.
1934 Frederick Delius, English composer, died.
1937 Sir Robert Borden, Canadian Conservative statesman and Prime Minister from 1911 to 1920, died aged 82.
1942 The Germans destroyed the Czech mining village of Lidice as a reprisal for the assassination of Heydrich, the German Protector of Bohemia and Moravia.
1943 Ball-point pens, devised by Hungarian Laszlo Biro, were patented in the United States.
1946 Jack Johnson, American boxer, the first black to hold the world heavyweight title, died.
     Italy became a republic, replacing King Humbert II.
1967 Spencer Tracy, American film actor and twice Academy Award (Oscar) winner for *Captains Courageous* (1937) and *Boys' Town* (1938), died.
1969 Sir George Russell Drysdale, Australian artist known for his pictures of the outback, died.
1974 Henry, Duke of Gloucester, son of King George V, died.
1978 Larry Holmes won the world heavyweight boxing title at Las Vegas, defeating Ken Norton on points.
1986 Bob Geldof, for his fund-raising events, was made an Honorary Knight by the Queen.

11 JUNE   [163]

1509 Henry VIII married Spanish Princess Catherine of Aragon—the first of his six wives.
1572 Ben Jonson, English poet and dramatist, born in Westminster, London.
1727 Accession of King George II on his father's death the previous day.
1776 John Constable, the greatest of English landscape painters, born in East Bergholt, Suffolk, the son of a landowner and miller.
1847 Sir John Franklin, English Arctic explorer, died in Canada in an attempt to discover the Northwest Passage.
1864 Richard Strauss, German composer, born in Munich where his father was a horn player.
1895 Nikolai Bulganin, Russian military and political leader, born in Gorki.
1907 Northamptonshire scored a record low of 12, against Gloucestershire at Gloucester in the county cricket championship.
1910 Jacques Cousteau, French underwater explorer and inventor of the aqualung, born in Saint-André, Gironde.
1919 Richard Todd, British film actor, born in Dublin.
1930 The luxury liner *Empress of Britain* was launched at Clydebank in Scotland, by the Prince of Wales.

1939 Jackie Stewart, British motor racing driver and world champion, born in Milton, Dunbartonshire.
1967 'Bombardier' Billy Wells, British heavyweight boxer, died.
1970 Alexander Kerensky, Russian political leader overthrown by the Bolsheviks in 1917, died in New York City aged 89.
1975 The first oil was pumped ashore from Britain's North Sea oilfields.
1979 John Wayne, American film actor and Academy Award (Oscar) winner in 1969 for his part in *True Grit*, died.
1982 The *QE 2* liner returned to Southampton from the South Atlantic with survivors from three destroyed British warships.

12 JUNE [164]

National day of the Philippines.

1819 Charles Kingsley, English clergyman-author, born at Holne vicarage, Dartmoor.
1842 Thomas Arnold, English educationalist who reformed the Public School system, died one day before his 47th birthday, and was buried in Rugby Chapel.
1897 Anthony Eden, later Earl of Avon, British statesman and Tory Prime Minister, born at Windlestone Hall, Bishop Auckland, County Durham.
      Leon Goossens, English oboist, born in Liverpool of a musical family.
1901 Norman Hartnell, English couturier and court dressmaker, born.
1908 The Rotherhithe-Stepney road tunnel under the Thames was opened.
1921 The last occasion postmen delivered mail on a Sunday.
1924 George Bush, President of USA since 1989, born in Milton, Massachusetts.
1928 Vic Damone, American singer, born in Brooklyn, New York as Vito Farinola.
1930 Germany's Max Schmelling won the vacant world heavyweight boxing title, against Jack Sharkey in New York on a disqualification in round 4—the only man to win this title in such a manner.
1944 The first flying bomb fell in England.
1945 Pat Jennings, a goalkeeper for Northern Ireland and holder of the British record of 119 football caps, born in Newry.
1957 Jimmy Dorsey, American musician and bandleader, died.
1979 Bryan Allen, a Californian racing cyclist, pedalled all the way across the Channel from Folkestone to Cap Gris Nez in his flimsy craft *Gossamer Albatross*.
1980 Sir Billy Butlin, the holiday camp promoter, died in Jersey.

155

1752   Fanny Burney, English novelist and diarist, born in King's Lynn, Norfolk, the daughter of a musician.

1795   Thomas Arnold, English educationalist, born in East Cowes on the Isle of Wight.

1842   Queen Victoria. accompanied by Prince Albert, travelled from Slough to Paddington on the Great Western Railway, to become the first British monarch to use such transport.

1854   Sir Charles Parsons, English engineer who developed the steam turbine, born in London.

1865   (William Butler) W. B. Yeats, Irish poet and playwright, born in Sandymount near Dublin, the son of an artist.

1892   Basil Rathbone, English stage and film actor, best known for his role as Sherlock Holmes, born in Johannesburg.

1893   The first women's golf championship took place, at Royal Lytham—won by Lady Margaret Scott.
       Dorothy L. Sayers, English writer of detective novels, born in Oxford.

1897   Paavo Nurmi, Finnish distance runner and world record holder, born in Turku.

1900   The Boxer Rebellion in China began—an uprising by the Boxers, a secret society dedicated to the removal of foreign influence.

1910   Mary Whitehouse, General Secretary of the National Viewers and Listeners Association, born.

1915   Donald Budge, American international tennis champion, born in Oakland, California.

1930   Sir Henry Segrave, British racing driver, was killed when his speed boat *Miss England* crashed at nearly 100 mph on Lake Windermere—it was Friday the 13th.

1931   Jesse Boot, English pharmacist, druggist and philanthropist, created Baron Trent in 1929, died in Millbrook, Jersey, aged 81.

1935   James J. Braddock won the world heavyweight boxing title, beating Max Baer on points at Long Island.

1951   Joseph 'Ben' Chifley, Australian Labour statesman and the 20th Prime Minister from 1945 to 1949, died.

1956   The last British troops were removed from the Suez Canal zone.
       From an entry of only sixteen clubs Real Madrid emerged winners, beating Reims 4–3 in Paris, in the first final of the European Cup.

1967   Gerald Patterson, Australian international tennis player, died.

1981   Blanks were fired at the Queen during the Trooping of The Colour ceremony. Marcus Sarjeant was held and later charged with treason.

1986   Benny Goodman, American musician known as 'The King of Swing', died.

1987 Princess Anne was created Princess Royal in the Queen's Birthday Honours List.

---

14 JUNE [166]

1645 The Battle of Naseby took place in Northamptonshire during the Civil War, with the Parliamentarians, under Cromwell and Fairfax, victorious over the Royalists under the command of Prince Rupert.

1777 The 'Stars and Stripes' was adopted by Congress as the flag of the United States of America.

1789 Captain Bligh, cast adrift from the *Bounty* with 18 men, arrived at Timor near Java, having sailed the frail craft for 3618 miles.

1800 The Battle of Marengo took place near Alessandria in N.W. Italy, in which a French army under Napoleon crushed the Austrians during the French Revolutionary Wars.

1801 Benedict Arnold, American general best known as a traitor during the Revolution, died in obscurity in London.

1811 Harriet Beecher Stowe, American novelist noted for *Uncle Tom's Cabin*, born in Litchfield, Connecticut.

1839 The first Henley Regatta on the Thames took place.

1883 Edward Fitzgerald, English poet and translator of the *Rubaiyat* of Omar Khayyam, died in Suffolk.

1884 John McCormack, Irish operatic tenor, born in Athlone in the Republic of Ireland.

1894 French President Sadi Carnot was assassinated by Italian anarchists at Lyons.

1909 Burl Ives, American folk singer and film actor, born in Hull, Illinois as Burl Icle Ivanhoe.

1919 Sam Wanamaker, American actor, born in Chicago.

1927 Jerome K. Jerome, English author, notably *Three Men in a Boat*, died.

1928 Emmeline Pankhurst, English suffragette and founder of Women's Social and Political Union, died in London.
Ernesto 'Che' Guevara, Cuban Communist revolutionary leader, born in Rosario, Argentina.

1929 Alan Davidson, Australian test cricketer, born.

1934 Max Baer won the world heavyweight boxing title at Long Island, knocking out Primo Carnera in the 11th round.

1936 G. K. Chesterton, English author of the *Father Brown* detective stories, died.

1937 A Constitution was passed changing the name Irish Free State to Eire and making it a 'Sovereign and Democratic State' with a directly-appointed President.

1940 Paris was captured and occupied by German forces.

1941 Mike Yarwood, English impressionist and TV entertainer, born in Stockport, Cheshire.

1946 John Logie Baird, Scottish inventor and pioneer in the development of television, died.

1969 Steffi Graf, German tennis player and international champion, born.

1970 Bobby Charlton played his 106th and last football game for England, in the World Cup in Mexico City—his first having been on 19 April 1958 against Scotland.

1982 Argentinian forces formally surrendered to troops of the British task force in the Falkland Islands.

1986 Alan Jay Lerner, American lyricist and collaborator with Frederick Loewe on Broadway musicals, died.

---

15 JUNE   *[167]*

1215 King John stamped the Royal seal on the Magna Carta at Runnymede, near Windsor.

1381 Wat Tyler, English rebel and leader of the Peasants' Revolt against the poll tax imposed by Richard II, was beheaded at a meeting in Smithfield, London.

1744 Admiral George Anson returned to Spithead in the *Centurion*, having circumnavigated the globe, an expedition which lasted three years and nine months.

1804 The Twelfth Amendment to the US Constitution was ratified, dealing with the manner of choosing the President and Vice-President.

1836 Arkansas, the Wonder State, became the 25th state of the Union.

1843 Edvard Grieg, Norwegian composer, born in Bergen of Scots descent.

1849 James Knox Polk, American Democrat statesman and 11th President from 1845 to 1849, died in Nashville, Tennessee.

1864 Arlington Cemetery, the site of the unknown soldier, was established near Washington.

1869 Thermoplastic called celluloid, a technically improved version of that invented by the English chemist Alexander Parkes, was patented by American inventor John Wesley Hyatt of Albany, New York.

1884 Harry Langdon, American silent film comedian, born in Iowa.

1905 James Robertson-Justice, British film actor, born.

1910 Captain Scott set out on his second and fatal expedition to the South Pole, in the *Terra Nova*.

1914 Yuri Andropov, Soviet leader, born in the village of Nagutskyoye, north of the Caucasus mountains.

1919 John Alcock and Arthur Whitten Brown completed the first non-stop transatlantic flight, from Lester's Field, St Johns in Newfoundland, to Derrygimla Bog near Clifden in County Galway, in a Vickers Vimy in just over 16 hours.
1925 Richard Baker, BBC television news reader, born in Willesden, London.
1940 Ken Fletcher, Australian tennis champion, born.
1945 Family allowance payments were introduced in Britain—five shillings per week for the second child and subsequent children. No payment was made for the first born.
1977 A General Election was held in Spain, the first since 1936.
1980 Jack Nicklaus returned a US Open record low aggregate of 272, on the lower course at Baltusrol, Springfield, New Jersey.
1985 Percy Fender, the hard-hitting cricketer for Surrey and England, died aged 92.
1988 Peter Shilton won his 100th cap for England, in the European Championship game against Holland at Dusseldorf.

16 JUNE [168]

1722 The Duke of Marlborough, British general famed for his victories in the War of the Spanish Succession, died in Windsor.
1743 The Battle of Dettingen took place in Bavaria, with King George II's forces defeating the French in the War of the Austrian Succession.
1858 Gustav V, King of Sweden from 1907 to 1950, born the son of Oscar II.
1869 Charles Sturt, British explorer into the interior of Australia and discoverer of the Darling and Lower Murray Rivers, died in Cheltenham, Gloucestershire.
1874 Arthur Meighen, Canadian Conservative statesman, born in Perth County, Ontario.
1890 Stan Laurel, of Laurel and Hardy fame, born in Ulverston, Lancashire as Arthur Stanley Jefferson.
1892 Lupino Lane. English music hall entertainer, born in London as Henry Lupino.
1912 Enoch Powell, British politician, born in Stechford, Birmingham.
1930 Elmer Sperry, American inventor of the gyroscopic compass and a wide variety of electrical devices, died in Brooklyn, New York.
     Mixed bathing was first allowed in the Serpentine in London's Hyde Park.
1932 At cricket, Holmes and Sutcliffe made an English record first-wicket partnership of 555, for Yorkshire against Essex at Leyton.
1942 Giacomo Agostini, motor cycle champion, born in Lovere, Italy.

1948 The Cathay Pacific Airways' Catalina flying boat *Miss Macao*, on a scheduled flight to Hong Kong, was the first aeroplane to be hijacked, by a gang of Chinese bandits.

1963 Valentina Tereshkova blasted off from Tyuratam in *Vostok 6* to become the first woman in space—landed on 19 June after 48 orbits.

1969 Earl Alexander of Tunis, British army commander and leader of the invasion of Italy, died.

1972 America's biggest political scandal started when five burglars were caught breaking into the offices of the Democratic National Committee in the Watergate office complex in Washington, DC.

1977 Leonid Brezhnev became President of USSR.
Werner von Braun, German-born pioneer of rocketry in America's manned flights to the moon, died in Alexandria, Virginia.

1982 Bryan Robson scored the fastest goal in the finals of the World Cup competition, finding the net in 27 seconds, against France in Bilbao.

---

17 JUNE [169]

National day of Iceland.

1239 King Edward I was born at Westminster in London, the elder son of Henry III and Eleanor of Provence.

1703 John Wesley, English evangelist and founder of the Methodist movement, born in Epworth, Lincolnshire, the 15th of the rector's 19 children.

1719 Joseph Addison, English poet, essayist and founder of the *Spectator* in 1711 with Sir Richard Steele, died at Holland House.

1775 The Battle of Bunker Hill, actually fought on nearby Breed's Hill, took place, with victory for the British under General Howe over American rebel troops in the War of Independence.

1818 Charles Gounod, French composer of operas, born in Paris the son of a portrait painter.

1845 Richard Barham, English author of the *Ingoldsby Legends*, died.

1860 The 692-foot liner *Great Eastern*, designed by Brunel and Russell, began its first transatlantic voyage.

1867 Joseph Lister performed the first operation under antiseptic conditions—on his sister Isabella, at the Glasgow Infirmary.

1881 Tommy Burns, Canadian heavyweight boxer, born in Ontario.

1882 Igor Stravinsky, American composer, born in Oranienbaum near St Petersburg in Russia.

1920 Beryl Reid, English character actress, born in Hereford.

1939 German multiple-murderer Eugen Wiedmann was the last to be publicly guillotined—outside Versailles prison in Paris.

1940 The British troopship *Lancastria* was sunk by enemy bombing action off St Nazaire, when some 2500 crew and troops perished.
1944 Iceland became an independent Republic.
1946 Barry Manilow, American singer and songwriter, born in New York City.
1969 Boris Spassky became world chess champion, beating Tigran Petrosian.
1970 Decimal postage stamps (10p, 20p, 50p) went on sale in Britain.

18 JUNE [170]

1769 Viscount Castlereagh, British statesman, born in Ireland.
1812 American Congress, by a small majority, voted a declaration of war against Great Britain.
1815 The Battle of Waterloo took place south of Brussels, the scene of Napoleon's defeat by the troops of Wellington and Blücher.
1817 London's Waterloo Bridge, built by John Rennie, was opened.
1835 William Cobbett, English political journalist and radical reformer, died near Guildford in Surrey.
1884 Edouard Daladier, French statesman and Premier, born in Carpentras, Vaucluse.
1886 George Mallory, English mountaineer, born in Mobberley, Cheshire.
1887 Hammersmith Bridge, over the Thames, was opened.
1902 Samuel Butler, English novelist, best known for *The Way of all Flesh*, died.
1907 Jeanette MacDonald, American singer and actress, born in Philadelphia.
1915 Arthur Fagg, Kent cricketer and the only batsman to score double centuries in both innings, born.
1920 Ian Carmichael, English film actor, born in Hull on Humberside.
1928 Roald Amundsen, Norwegian explorer and first to reach the South pole in 1911, was lost in the North Sea after a flying accident.
     Amelia Earhart became the first woman to cross the Atlantic by air, as passenger to pilot Wilmar Stulz, flying from Newfoundland to Wales.
1929 Eva Bartok, film actress in America, born in Budapest as Eva Sjoke.
1942 Paul McCartney of the 'Beatles' pop group, born in Liverpool.
1953 On Farouk's abdication Egypt was proclaimed a Republic, with General Neguib its first President.
1958 Douglas Jardine, English cricketer and captain whose 'leg theory' and 'body-line' bowling caused acute controversy in Australia, died.

1959 Ethel Barrymore, American actress, sister of John and Lionel, called the 'First Lady of American Theatre', died aged 79.

1970 The Conservative Party won the British General Election with an overall majority of 30, Edward Heath became Prime Minister the following day.

1972 Stan Mellor retired as a jockey, with 1049 wins in 20 years.

1983 Dr Sally Ride became America's first woman in space when the shuttle *Challenger* blasted off from Cape Canaveral.

---

19 JUNE   [171]

1566 King James I of England and Scotland, born in Edinburgh Castle, the only son of Mary, Queen of Scots and Lord Darnley.

1623 Blaise Pascal, French mathematician and philosopher, born in Clermont.

1820 Sir Joseph Banks, English botanist who accompanied Cook on his voyage round the world in the *Endeavour*, died.

1829 The London Metropolitan Police was founded, and set up by Sir Robert Peel.

1846 The first baseball game was played at the Elysian Fields at Hoboken in New Jersey—New York Nine against Knickerbockers.

1861 Earl Haig, British army commander, born in Edinburgh.

1864 The British-built *Alabama*, a Confederate warship in the American Civil War, was sunk off Cherbourg by the USS *Kearsarge*, captained by John Winslow.

1867 Emperor Maximilian of Mexico was shot by the troops of Juarez.

1895 The 61-mile Kiel Canal, connecting the North Sea with the Baltic, was formally opened by the German Emperor Wilhelm II.

1896 Bessie Wallis Warfield, later the Duchess of Windsor, born in Blue Ridge Summit, Pennsylvania.

1902 Guy Lombardo, Canadian bandleader, born in London, Ontario.

1903 Walter Hammond, Gloucestershire and England cricketer, born in Dover.

1906 Ernst Boris Chain, British biochemist noted for his work on penicillin with Fleming and Florey, born in Berlin.

1910 *Deutschland*, the first zeppelin airliner, was launched—crashed on 28th.

Father's Day was initiated in America by Mrs John Bruce Dodd.

1921 Louis Jourdain, film actor in America and Europe, born in Marseilles as Louis Gendre.

1936 Sir William Hall-Jones, New Zealand Liberal statesman and Prime Minister for six weeks after Richard Seddon's death, died.

1937 (James Matthew) J. M. Barrie, Scottish writer best known for *Peter Pan*, died.

1953 Julius and Ethel Rosenberg were executed at Ossining, New York, to become the first US civilians to be executed for espionage.

---

20 JUNE

1756 146 British subjects were imprisoned in a dungeon by the Nawab of Bengal—only 23 survived overnight—known as the 'Black Hole of Calcutta'.

1789 The French Revolution began.

1819 Jacques Offenbach, French-Jewish composer of light operas, born in Cologne as Jakob Eberst.
The *Savannah* arrived in Liverpool to become the first steamship to cross the Atlantic, having left Savannah in Georgia on 24 May, under the command of Captain Moses Rogers.

1837 Death of William IV, the 'Sailor King', at Windsor—accession of his 18-year-old niece as Queen Victoria.

1863 West Virginia, the Panhandle or Mountain State, became the 35th state of the Union.

1887 The second Tay Bridge, the longest railway bridge in Britain, was opened.

1906 Catherine Cookson, English author, born.

1909 Errol Flynn, actor in action-adventure films, born in Hobart, Tasmania.

1911 The city of Leeds introduced Britain's first trolley-bus service.

1923 General 'Pancho' Villa, Mexican guerrilla leader and revolutionary, was assassinated at Parral (Chihuahua) in Mexico.

1924 Chet Atkins, American country musician, born in Luttrell, Tennessee.

1925 Doris Hart, American international tennis champion, born in St Louis.

1927 Greyhound racing at London's White City Stadium began.

1949 Lionel Ritchie, American singer and songwriter, born.

1954 Allan Lamb, Northants and England Test cricketer, born in South Africa.

1960 Floyd Patterson defeated Ingemar Johansson by a knockout in round five to become the first heavyweight in boxing history to regain the world title—having lost it to the Swede some 12 months earlier.
Nan Winton became the first woman to read the national news on BBC television.

1973 Juan Peron returned to his former office as President of Argentina after almost 20 years of exile.

1987 The final of the first Rugby Union World Cup competition was played in Auckland, and won by New Zealand, beating France 29–9.

1377 King Edward III of England died.

1652 Inigo Jones, designer and the first of the great English architects, died.

1675 Work began on the rebuilding of St Paul's Cathedral.

1788 New Hampshire, the Granite State, became the 9th state of the Union.

1813 The Battle of Vitoria took place, the scene of Wellington's decisive victory over the French in the Peninsular War.

1843 The Royal College of Surgeons was founded in London.

1852 Friedrich Froebel, German educationalist and founder of the kindergarten system in 1837, died.

1854 20-year-old Irishman Charles Lucas won the first VC, for his action aboard HMS *Hecla* at Bomarsund in the Baltic—throwing an unexploded Russian bomb over the side.

1905 Jean-Paul Sartre, French dramatist and novelist, born in Paris.

1908 Nikolai Rimsky-Korsakov, Russian composer, died at Lyubensk.

1913 Georgina Broadwick became the first woman to parachute from an aircraft, over Griffith Park, Los Angeles.

1919 72 warships of the German Fleet were scuttled in Scapa Flow in the Orkneys.

1921 Jane Russell, American film actress, born in Minnesota.

1932 Jack Sharkey won the world heavyweight boxing title at Long Island, defeating Max Schmelling on points.

1937 Lawn tennis at Wimbledon was televised for the first time.

1940 President Richard Nixon married Thelma 'Pat' Ryan.

1942 Tobruk was captured by the German forces.

1963 Giovanni Battista Montini was elected as Pope Paul VI.

1969 Maureen Connolly, American international tennis champion, affectionately called 'Little Mo', died aged 34.

1970 Brazil beat Italy at football in Mexico City to become World champions and win the Jules Rimet trophy for a record third time.
Tony Jacklin became the first Englishman since Ted Ray in 1920 to win the US Open golf championship, played at Chaska, Minnesota.

1971 Dom Mintoff became Prime Minister after a Labour Party victory in the Malta general election.

1974 The destroyer HMS *Coventry* was launched at the Cammell Laird shipyard in Birkenhead.

1977 Menachem Begin became Prime Minister of Israel.

1982 Prince William (Arthur Philip Louis) born in London to the Prince and Princess of Wales.

1377 King Richard II acceded to the throne of England on the death of his grandfather Edward III the previous day.

1757 George Vancouver, English naval captain and surveyor of the Pacific coast of North America, born in King's Lynn, Norfolk.

1805 Giuseppe Mazzini, Italian patriot and revolutionary, born in Genoa.

1814 The first cricket match was played at the present Lord's ground in London.

1856 Rider Haggard, English novelist known for adventure stories in African settings, born at Bradenham Hall, Norfolk.

1906 Billy Wilder, American film director and writer, born in Austria.

1910 John Hunt, leader of the successful British Everest climbing expedition in 1953, born.

1911 The coronation of King George V took place.
     Liverpool's Liver clock—'Great George'—first began recording time.

1936 Kris Kristofferson, American actor, singer and songwriter, born in Brownsville, Texas.

1937 Joe Louis won the world heavyweight boxing title by knocking out James J. Braddock in round eight in Chicago—the title he successfully defended 25 times before announcing his retirement on 1 March 1949.

1940 Esther Rantzen, British TV personality and presenter, born in Berkhamsted, Hertfordshire.
     France capitulated and accepted the armistice terms of Germany.

1949 Lindsay Wagner, American TV film actress, born in Los Angeles.
     Meryl Streep, American film actress and Oscar winner, born.
     Ezzard Charles won the world heavyweight boxing title, beating Jersey Joe Walcott on points in Chicago.

1956 Walter de la Mare, English poet and writer of fantasy, died aged 83.

1969 Judy Garland, American singer and film actress, died.

1984 The inaugural flight of Virgin Atlantic, the new cut-price airline, took place.

1987 Fred Astaire, American actor and dancer in many films, died aged 88.

23 JUNE [175]

National day of Luxembourg

1611 English navigator Henry Hudson was set adrift in James Bay by mutineers on his ship *Discoverie* and was never seen again.

1757 The Battle of Plassey took place in Bengal, with victory for the British, under Robert Clive, over the Indian forces—so laying the foundations of the British Empire in India.

1763 Empress Josephine, wife of Napoleon, born on the French island of Martinique as Marie Rose Josèphe Tascher de la Pagerie.

1894 King Edward VIII born at White Lodge, Richmond, Surrey, the eldest son of George V and Queen Mary.
A disaster took place at the Albion coal pit at Cilfynydd in South Wales, claiming the lives of 286 men.
Alfred Charles Kinsey, American zoologist, born at Hoboken, New Jersey.

1902 The award of the 'Order of Merit' was founded by King Edward VII—is limited in number to 24 at any one time.

1914 The Royal Naval Air Service was formed.

1916 Sir Leonard Hutton, England cricketer, born in Fulneck near Pudsey, Yorkshire.

1928 The first England v West Indies cricket test match started at the Oval, the hosts ended up convincing winners by an innings and 58 runs.

1940 Adam Faith, British pop singer, born as Terence Nelhams.
Wilma Rudolph, American sprinter and gold medal winner, born in St Bethlehem, Tennessee.

1956 Nasser assumed office as the first President of Egypt, after an election at which voting was compulsory, and he was the only candidate.

1970 Brunel's 320-foot *Great Britain*, the world's first all-metal liner, returned to Bristol from the Falkland Islands where it had lain rusting since 1886.

1973 The first graduates of the Open University received their degrees at a ceremony in Alexandra Palace.

24 JUNE [176]

Midsummer Day, a quarter day in England.

1314 The Battle of Bannockburn took place near Stirling Castle—Robert the Bruce inflicting a crushing defeat on King Edward II of England.

1497 John Cabot, on his discovery of unknown lands, arrived at Cape Breton Island.

1509 The coronation of King Henry VIII took place.

1519 Lucrezia Borgia, Italian noblewoman, long associated with the crimes and moral excesses of her father, died.

1650 The Duke of Marlborough, British general and statesman, born as John Churchill in Ashe, Devon (some sources quote 26 May).

1717 The first Freemason Lodge was inaugurated, in London.
1825 (William Henry) W. H. Smith, founder of the English bookselling chain, born in London.
1850 Lord Kitchener, British Army commander, administrator and statesman, born near Ballylongford, County Kerry in the Republic of Ireland.
1859 The Battle of Solferino took place in Lombardy, where the French, under Napoleon III, defeated the Austrians.
1877 St John's Ambulance Brigade was formed, as the Ambulance Association, by the Red Cross.
1895 Jack Dempsey, American boxer and world heavyweight champion, born in Manassa, Colorado with the Christian names William Harrison.
1906 Phil Harris, American bandleader, born in Linton, Indiana.
1908 Grover Cleveland, American Democrat statesman and both 22nd and 24th President between 1885 and 1897, died in Princeton, New Jersey.
1911 Juan Fangio, five times world motor racing champion, born near Balcarce in Argentina.
1912 Brian Johnston, British broadcaster and cricket commentator, born.
1931 Billy Casper, American golf champion, born in San Diego, California.
1941 Graham McKenzie, Australian Test cricketer, born.
1947 The series of 'flying saucer' stories started when a pilot, Kenneth Arnold, reported seeing nine disc-shaped objects over Mount Rainier, Washington.
1948 Russia began the blockade of Berlin, stopping all land traffic between the capital and the west.
1971 The first tube of the second Mersey road tunnel was opened.
1981 The bridge over the Humber estuary was opened to traffic, but its official opening by the Queen took place on 17 July.

25 JUNE [177]

1788 Virginia, the Old Dominion State, became the 10th state of the Union.
1867 The first patent for barbed wire was taken out by Lucien Smith of Kent, Ohio.
1876 In an attempt to drive the Indians out of the Black Hills, Colonel George Armstrong Custer and his 264 soldiers of the 7th Cavalry were killed in battle at Little Big Horn in Montana, by Sioux Indians led by Chiefs Gall and Crazy Horse.
1900 Earl Louis Mountbatten, British admiral and commander, born at Frogmore House, Windsor.

1903　George Orwell, English novelist, born in Motihari, Bengal as Eric Arthur Blair.
1906　Roger Livesey, British actor, born.
1920　The Hague was made the permanent seat of the International Court of Justice.
1932　The first England v India cricket Test match started, at Lord's in London—England ending winners by 158 runs.
1945　Carly Simon, American rock singer and composer, born in New York City.
1948　Joe Louis made the record 25th defence of his heavyweight boxing title, knocking out Joe Walcott, the 22nd challenger to meet such an end.
1950　The Korean War began, when the Communist forces of the North crossed the 38th parallel and invaded the south.
1959　Eamon de Valera assumed office as President of the Republic of Ireland.
1968　Tony Hancock, British comedy actor, committed suicide in Sydney, Australia.
1969　Pancho Gonzalez and Charlie Pasarell played a record 112-game singles match, on Wimbledon's centre court, lasting 5 hours 12 minutes.
1975　Mozambique became fully independent after a ten-year war against Portuguese colonial domination.
1976　Johnny Mercer, American writer of many popular songs, died.

26 JUNE [178]

1483　Richard III acceded to the throne of England.
1541　Francisco Pizarro, Spanish conquistador was assassinated in his palace at Lima by the followers of Diego Almagro.
1824　Lord Kelvin, British physicist and mathematician, born in Belfast as William Thomson.
1827　Samuel Crompton, English inventor of the 'spinning mule' in 1779 for spinning fine yarn, died in Bolton, Lancashire.
1830　Death of King George IV—was succeeded by his brother, as William IV.
1836　Rouget de Lisle, French Army officer and composer of *La Marseillaise* in 1792, died.
1854　Sir Robert Borden, Canadian Conservative statesman, born in Grand Pre.
1857　The first investiture ceremony of Victoria Crosses took place, at Hyde Park in London.
1892　Pearl Buck, American novelist, born in Hillsboro, West Virginia.
1898　Wilhelm Messerschmitt, German aviation engineer and designer, born in Frankfurt.

1904 Peter Lorre, Hungarian character actor in films, born in Rosenberg as Laszlo Loewenstein.
1905 The Automobile Association was established in Britain.
1906 The first motor racing Grand Prix was organised and run over 12 laps of a 65-mile triangular circuit at Le Mans in France.
1909 The Victoria and Albert Museum in South Kensington was officially opened.
1914 Laurie Lee, British author, notably *Cider with Rosie*, born in Slad, near Stroud, Gloucestershire.
1917 The first contingent of the American Expeditionary Force landed in France, with General John Pershing commander-in-chief.
1945 The United Nations Charter was adopted and signed at San Francisco, as a successor to the League of Nations.
1959 Ingemar Johansson knocked out Floyd Patterson in round five in New York to become the fourth and last European to hold the world heavyweight boxing title.
1960 The Indian Ocean island of Madagascar became independent, having been a French colony since 1896.
1977 Lady Baden-Powell, founder of the Girl Guide movement in 1910, died.

27 JUNE   [179]

1778 The Liberty Bell was moved back to Philadelphia after the British Army left.
1816 Samuel Hood, British admiral of distinction, died in Bath aged 91.
1829 James Smithson, English scientist whose bequest established the Smithsonian Institution at Washington to encourage scientific research, died in Genoa.
1844 Joseph Smith, American religious leader and founder of the Church of Jesus Christ of Latter-Day Saints (Mormons) in 1830, was killed in Carthage jail in Illinois, with his brother Hyrum.
1846 Charles Stewart Parnell, Irish politician and leader of the Home Rule movement, born in Avondale, County Wicklow.
1880 Helen Keller, American author and lecturer, born in Tuscumbia, Alabama.
1939 The first transatlantic airline was inaugurated by Pan American Airways Boeing flying-boat *Yankee Clipper*, between Botwood, Newfoundland and Southampton with 19 passengers.
1947 Richard Bennett, Canadian Conservative statesman and Prime Minister from 1932 to 1935, died.
1954 The world's first atomic power station at Obninsk near Moscow went into production.
1961 Dr Ramsey was enthroned as the 100th Archbishop of Canterbury in Canterbury Cathedral.

1461 The coronation of King Edward IV took place.
1491 King Henry VIII was born in Greenwich, London, the second son of Henry VII.
1712 Jean Jacques Rousseau, French writer and philosopher, born in Geneva.
1836 James Madison, American statesman and 4th President from 1809 to 1817, died in Montpelier, Virginia aged 85.
1838 The coronation of nineteen-year-old Queen Victoria took place in Westminster Abbey.
1855 Lord Raglan, British Army officer and commander of the Expeditionary Force in the Crimean War, died.
1859 The first dog show took place over two days at Newcastle-Upon-Tyne Town Hall with 60 entries, split into two classes of Pointers and Setters.
1861 Robert Burke, Irish traveller and one of the few to cross the Australian continent from south to north, died.
1883 Pierre Laval, French politician and Premier, born in Chateldon.
1902 Richard Rodgers, American composer, of the Rodgers and Hammerstein partnership, born in New York.
1910 *Deutschland*, the first zeppelin airliner, crashed.
1914 Archduke Franz Ferdinand, heir to the Austrian throne, was assassinated with his wife in the Bosnian town of Sarajevo, by terrorist Gavrillo Princip.
1915 Victor Trumper, Australian Test cricketer, died.
1918 William Whitelaw, British Conservative politician, born.
1919 Peace Treaty between German representatives and Allied powers was signed in the Palace of Versailles in northern France.
1926 Mel Brooks, American actor and film director, born in New York City as Melvin Kaminsky.
1928 Cyril Smith, British Liberal politician, born in Rochdale.
1948 Due to Russia's blockade of Berlin, allied planes began their 'air lift' of stores and supplies.
1976 Seychelles, the volcanic island group in the Indian Ocean, became an independent Republic within the Commonwealth—having been ceded to Britain in 1814.

29 JUNE *[181]*

1577 Peter Paul Rubens, Flemish painter, born in Siegen in Westphalia, the son of a lawyer.
1801 The figures of Britain's first census were published.

1855 The *Daily Telegraph* was published in London for the first time, with Alfred Bate Richards its first editor.

1858 George Washington Goethals, American engineer, born in Brooklyn, New York.

1861 William James Mayo, American surgeon and co-founder of the Mayo Clinic at Rochester, Minnesota, born at Le Sueur in that state.

1868 The Press Association, the News Agency, was founded in London.

George Ellery Hale, American astronomer, born in Chicago, Illinois.

1871 Labour Unions in Britain achieved guaranteed legal recognition, by Act of Parliament.

1886 Robert Schuman, French statesman and Prime Minister, born in Luxembourg.

1895 The foundation stone of London's Westminster Cathedral was laid.

1901 Nelson Eddy, American singer and film actor, born in Providence in the New England state of Rhode Island.

1911 Prince Bernhard, husband of Queen Juliana of the Netherlands, born in Jena, Germany.

1933 Primo Carnera won the world heavyweight boxing title, knocking out Jack Sharkey in round six in Los Angeles.

1941 Paderewski, Polish pianist, composer, statesman and Prime Minister in 1919, died in Switzerland aged 80.

1950 Amateurs and part-timers of a United States football team caused the biggest upset in England's football history, winning 1–0 at Belo Horizonte, Brazil in the World Cup.

1967 Jayne Mansfield, American film actress, was killed in a car crash on the road to New Orleans.

Primo Carnera, Italian heavyweight boxer and world champion 1933–34, died.

1986 Richard Branson's boat *Virgin Atlantic Challenger II* completed the fastest Atlantic crossing in 3 days 8 hours and 31 minutes.

30 JUNE [182]

1520 Montezuma, the last Mexican Emperor, was killed by his own subjects in Mexico City during the Spanish conquest of Mexico under Cortes.

1660 William Oughtred, English mathematician and inventor of the slide rule in 1622, died in Albury, Surrey.

1797 The Nore naval mutiny, led by Richard Parker against bad food and inadequate pay, was suppressed.

1859 Charles Blondin made the earliest crossing of the Niagara Falls on a tightrope—1100 feet long and 160 feet above the Falls.

1861 Elizabeth Barrett Browning, English poet and wife of Robert Browning, died in Florence, Italy.

1894 London's Tower Bridge, designed by Sir Horace Jones and Sir J. Wolfe Barry, was opened.

1917 Buddy Rich, American musician and drummer of distinction, born in Brooklyn, New York.
Lena Horne, American singer, born in Brooklyn, New York.

1919 Susan Hayward, American film actress and Oscar winner, born in Brooklyn, New York, as Edythe Marriner.
Lord Rayleigh, English physicist, co-discoverer of the inert gas argon in 1894 and Nobel Prize winner, died in Witham, Essex aged 76.

1934 Hitler's rival Ernst Rohm and hundreds of influential Nazis were murdered by the SS in what has been called the 'night of the long knives'.

1936 The German zeppelin *Hindenburg* set out on its Atlantic crossing, reaching Lakehurst in New Jersey on 2 July.

1939 The Mersey Ferry boat service between Liverpool and Rock Ferry was discontinued.

1951 England beat Australia 17–0 at Sydney to record the highest score in a soccer international.

1957 The 'Lion' was stamped on British eggs for the first time—the practice ceased on 31 December 1968.

1963 Giovanni Battista Montini was crowned as Pope Paul VI.

1966 Mike Tyson, American heavyweight boxer and world champion, born.

1971 Soviet spacecraft *Soyuz II* crashed on its re-entry into the earth's atmosphere, killing the crew of three.
The Twenty-sixth Amendment to the US Constitution was ratified, lowering the voting age to 18 years.

1980 The British sixpence ceased to be legal tender after midnight.

---

1 JULY

National day of Canada.

1690 The Battle of the Boyne took place, fought at Oldbridge near Drogheda in Ireland, in which William III of England defeated the Jacobites under James II.

1804 George Sand, French woman novelist, born in Paris as Amandine Dupin.

1837 Registration of births, marriages and deaths came into effect in England and Wales.

1847 The first adhesive US stamps went on sale—Benjamin Franklin 5 cent and George Washington 10 cent.

1860 Charles Goodyear, American inventor of the vulcanised-rubber process, died a pauper.

1867 Canada became a Dominion under the British North America Act.

1872 Louis Blériot, French aviator and plane designer, born.
The Albert Memorial in Kensington Gardens was unveiled by Queen Victoria.

1873 Prince Edward Island was made part of the Dominion of Canada.

1884 Allan Pinkerton, Scottish-born American detective and founder of the agency that bears his name, died in Chicago.

1896 Harriet Beecher Stowe, American novelist, best known as the author of *Uncle Tom's Cabin*, died in Hartford, Connecticut.

1899 Charles Laughton, film actor and Oscar winner for *The Private Life of Henry VIII* (1932–33), born in Scarborough, Yorkshire.
The first juvenile court sat, at the Cork County Court in Chicago.

1903 Amy Johnson, English record-breaking aviator, born in Hull, Yorkshire.

1907 The world's first Air Force was established with the founding of the Aeronautical Division of the US Army's Signals Office, under the command of Captain Chandler.

1910 Comiskey Park, the home of Chicago White Sox baseball team, was opened to become the oldest ballpark in US.

1912 The first Royal Command performance took place, at the Palace Theatre in London.

1916 Olivia de Havilland, American film actress, born in Tokyo, Japan, the older sister of Joan Fontaine.
President Dwight Eisenhower married Mamie Geneva Doud.

1921 Sir Seretse Khama, Botswanan politician and later President of the Republic, born in Serowe.

1933 Speke aerodrome at Liverpool was declared open.

1937 The telephone 999 emergency service came into operation in Britain.
The constitution of the Republic of Ireland was approved by a plebiscite.

1940 German forces occupied the island of Guernsey.

1941 The first television commercial was transmitted in the US—paid for by the Bulova Clock and Watch Company.

1944 The Bretton Woods Conference began with representatives of 44 nations formulating the International Monetary Policy.

1946 A US atomic bomb was tested when dropped over Bikini Atoll in the Marshall Islands in the Pacific.

1960 Ghana was proclaimed a Republic, with Kwame Nkrumah its first President.

1961 Lady Diana Spencer, to become the Princess of Wales, born in Park House, Sandringham.
Carl Lewis, American athlete and Gold Medal winner, born in New Jersey.

1967 Television in colour began on BBC2.
1969 Prince Charles was invested as Prince of Wales at Caernarvon Castle.
1971 Sir Learie Constantine, West Indian Test cricketer, knighted in 1969, died.
1974 Juan Peron, Argentinian political leader and President, died aged 78.
1977 Virginia Wade of Britian won the women's singles at the Centenary Wimbledon, beating Holland's Betty Stove.

---

2 JULY [184]

1489 Thomas Cranmer, English clergyman and Archbishop of Canterbury, born in Aslockton, Nottinghamshire.
1644 The Battle of Marston Moor took place near York, in which the Cromwellian victory over the Royalist Cavaliers under Prince Rupert was the turning-point in the Civil War.
1778 Jean Jacques Rousseau, Geneva-born French political philosopher, died insane in Ermenonville.
1821 Sir Charles Tupper, Canadian Conservative statesman, born.
1850 Sir Robert Peel, British statesman, twice Tory Prime Minister and founder of the Police Force in 1829, died in London as a result of a horse-riding accident.
1865 The Salvation Army was originated by William Booth, with a revival meeting at London's Whitechapel.
1881 James Garfield, American Republican statesman and 20th President, was shot by Charles Guiteau in Washington, DC—died on 19 September in Elberon, New Jersey.
1892 Jack Hylton, British bandleader and impresario, born.
1900 The 2nd Olympic Games opened in Paris.
     Count Ferdinand von Zeppelin flew his first airship, from a field on the outskirts of Berlin.
1903 Sir Alec Douglas-Home, statesman and Conservative Prime Minister, born in London.
     King Olav V of Norway, born in Sandringham, England, the only child of King Haakon VII.
1921 Jack Dempsey fought and defeated Georges Carpentier in Jersey City in the first boxing match to take over a million dollars at the gate.
1937 Amelia Earhart Putnam, American aviator, and co-pilot Fred Noonan, were lost near Howland Island in the Pacific during their attempt to fly round the world.
     Richard Lee Petty, American motor racing champion driver, born in Randleman, North Carolina.

1938 David Owen, British politician and leader of the newly founded Social Democratic Party, born in Plympton, South Devon.

1940 The Vichy Government was formed after the collapse of France, with Henri Pétain as Head of State.

1950 American troops landed in South Korea.

1961 Ernest Hemingway, American novelist and Nobel prizewinner in 1954, fearing ill-health, shot himself in Ketchum, Idaho.

1965 Walter Hammond, Gloucestershire and England Test cricketer, died in Durban, South Africa.

1973 Betty Grable, American film actress and pin-up girl of World War II, died.

1985 Andrei Gromyko became President of the USSR.

---

3 JULY [185]

1608 Quebec was founded by the French explorer Samuel de Champlain.

1728 Robert Adam, Scottish architect and house interior designer, born in Kirkcaldy, Fifeshire.

1863 General Meade's Union Army defeated the Confederacy under the command of Robert E. Lee at Gettysburg, Pennsylvania.

1866 The Battle of Sadowa took place in North Czechoslovakia, in which the Austrians were defeated by the Prussians.

1890 Idaho, the Gem State, became the 43rd state of the Union.

1898 Captain Joshua Slocum arrived back at Newport Harbour on Rhode Island in his 36¾-feet *Spray*, having sailed 46000 miles to complete the first solo circumnavigation of the earth—started on 24 April 1895.

1904 Theodor Herzl, Hungarian-born journalist and founder of Zionism, died in Vienna.

1908 Joel Chandler Harris, American writer of the 'Uncle Remus' stories, died.

1920 The first RAF air display took place at Hendon.

1926 The new horseracing course at Washington Park opened.

1927 Ken Russell, English director and documentary film maker, born in Southampton.

1928 The world's first television transmission in colour was made by John Logie Baird, at the Baird Studios in London.

1937 Tom Stoppard, English playwright, born in Czechoslovakia.

1938 *Mallard* of LNER achieved a speed of 126 m.p.h. on the Stoke bank stretch of line between Grantham and Peterborough heading south, the world record for a steam locomotive.

1951 Richard Hadlee, Nottinghamshire and New Zealand Test cricketer, born.

1954 Food rationing ended in Britain.

1962 After a referendum President de Gaulle declared Algeria independent, with Ben Bella its first Prime Minister.

1976 Israeli commandos rescued 103 hostages held in the Entebbe Airport in Uganda by pro-Palestinian terrorists.

1986 Rudy Vallee, American singer with his band 'The Connecticut Yankees', died aged 84.

1987 Richard Branson and Per Lindstrand abandoned their hot-air balloon *Virgin Atlantic Flyer* in the Irish Sea off Rathlin Island near the Ulster coast, having flown it across the Atlantic from Maine, setting a world distance record.

---

4 JULY   *[186]*

Independence Day, USA.

1631 The first employment agency opened in Paris, charging a registration fee of three sous to both employee and employer.

1761 Samuel Richardson, English novelist, author of *Pamela* and *Clarissa*, died in Parsons's Green, Middlesex.

1776 The Declaration of Independence was adopted in Philadelphia—was actually signed on and after 2 August 1776.

1804 Nathaniel Hawthorne, American novelist and short story writer, born in Salem, Massachusetts, the son of a merchant captain.

1807 Giuseppe Garibaldi, Italian military leader and patriot, born in Nice, the son of a sea captain.

1817 Work began on the construction of the Erie Canal—properly named the New York State Barge Canal—opened on 26 October 1825.

1826 Stephen Foster, American composer of minstrel songs and popular ballads, born in Pittsburgh, Pennsylvania.

John Adams, American Federalist statesman and 2nd President from 1797 to 1801, died in Quincy, Massachusetts, aged 90.

Thomas Jefferson, American statesman and 3rd President from 1801 to 1809, died aged 83, and was buried near Charlottesville, Virginia.

1829 The first regular scheduled bus service was introduced in Britain, in London by George Shillibeer.

1831 James Monroe, American statesman and 5th President from 1817 to 1825, died in New York City.

1845 Thomas Barnardo, British founder of homes for destitute children, born in Dublin.

1872 Calvin Coolidge, American Republican statesman and 30th President, born in Plymouth, Vermont, the son of a storekeeper.

1884 The Statue of Liberty was formally presented to US Minister Morton by Frenchman Ferdinand de Lesseps.

1898 Gertrude Lawrence, British actress, born in London, as Alexandra Lawrence-Klasen.

1900 Louis Armstrong, American jazz trumpeter, born in New Orleans.

1904 Work began on the construction of the 40-mile long Panama Canal—was opened to traffic on 15 August 1914.

1919 Jack Dempsey won the world heavyweight boxing title at Toledo, his opponent Jess Willard retired after three rounds.

1928 Gina Lollobrigida, Italian film actress, born in Subiaco.
Stephen Boyd, film actor in England and America, born in Belfast, as William Millar.

1934 Marie Curie, Polish-born French scientist and pioneer in the medicinal use of radioactivity, died.

1938 Suzanne Lenglen, French tennis champion, called the 'Pavlova of tennis', died aged 39.

1943 Wladyslaw Sikorski, Polish solider, statesman and Prime Minister, was killed in an aircrash over Gibraltar.

1946 The Philippine Islands were given independence by USA, Manual Roxas being elected the first President of the new Republic.

1948 René Arnoux, French motor racing champion, born.

1962 Pam Shriver, American international tennis player, born.

1968 Alec Rose landed at Portsmouth after sailing single-handed round the world in *Lively Lady*.

1970 Margaret Court beat Billie Jean King 14–12, 11–9, to record the highest number of games played in a Wimbledon women's final.

5 JULY   *[187]*

National day of Venezuela.

1791 George Hammond was appointed the first Ambassador to the United States.

1803 George Borrow, English writer of works on travel and gypsies, born in East Dereham, Norfolk, the son of an army captain.

1810 (Phineas Taylor) P. T. Barnum, American showman extraordinary, born in Bethel, Connecticut.

1817 Sovereigns were first issued as coins in Britain.

1826 Sir Stamford Raffles, British colonial administrator and founder of Singapore in 1819, died in London.

1841 Thomas Cook arranged the first railway excursion in England, a temperance one, which ran from Leicester to Loughborough.

1853 Cecil Rhodes, British colonial administrator and financier, born the 7th of 11 children in Bishop's Stortford, Hertfordshire, where his father was vicar.

1854 The Republican Party of American politics was formally established.

1865 The world's first speed limit was imposed in Britain, under the Locomotives and Highway Act, which became known as the 'Red Flag Act'.

1872 Edouard Herriot, French statesman and Prime Minister, born in Troyes.

1879 Dwight Davis, American public official and donor of the Lawn Tennis Cup, born in St Louis, Missouri.

1902 Henry Cabot Lodge, US Republican Senator and Ambassador, born in Nahant, Massachusetts.

1911 Georges Pompidou, French statesman, Prime Minister and President, born in Montboudif, Auvergne.

1917 Joe Gormley, English mineworkers' union leader and President, born.

1924 The 8th Olympic Games opened in Paris.

1945 John Curtin, Australian Labour statesman and the 18th Prime Minister from 1941, died in office.

1946 The 'bikini' swimsuit, designed by Louis Reard, was first modelled, at a Paris fashion show.

1948 The National Health Service came into force in Britain.

1968 Rod Laver became the Wimbledon singles champion in the first year of open tennis.

1969 Tom Mboya, Kenyan politician influential in his country's independence movement, was assassinated in Nairobi.

1975 Arthur Ashe, in beating fellow American Jimmy Connors, became the first black tennis player to win the Wimbledon men's singles title.

1980 Bjorn Borg won the Wimbledon singles tennis championship for a record fifth consecutive time.

6 JULY   *[188]*

National day of Malawi.

1189 Death of King Henry II in Chinon, France—accession of his third son as Richard I, called Coeur de Lion.

1483 The coronation of King Richard III took place.

1535 Sir Thomas More, English statesman and Lord Chancellor, was executed on London's Tower Hill for high treason.

1553 Death of King Edward VI in Greenwich, having developed tuberculosis—accession of his half-sister Mary Tudor as Mary I, known as 'Bloody Mary'.

1685 The Battle of Sedgemoor in Somerset took place—the last on English soil—with victory for James II's Royalist forces over the rebels under the Duke of Monmouth.

1747 John Paul Jones, American naval officer, born in Kirkbean, Scotland, as John Paul, the son of a gardener.

1796 Nicholas I, Tsar of Russia, born the third son of Tsar Paul I.

1832 Emperor Maximilian, Austrian archduke and Emperor of Mexico, born in Vienna, the brother of Franz Joseph.

1886 Box numbers were first introduced in the classified advertisement columns of newspapers, by the *Daily Telegraph*.

1888 Glamorgan Cricket Club was founded at Cardiff, to become the youngest county club.

1893 King George V married Princess Mary of Teck, in St James' Chapel.

1907 Brooklands motor racing track near Weybridge in Surrey, was opened—closed in 1939.

1909 Andrei Gromyko, statesman and President of the USSR, born near Minsk of peasant stock.

1912 The 5th Olympic Games opened in Stockholm.

1919 The British airship *R34*, captained by Squadron Leader Scott, arrived at Mineola, New York, from East Fortune in Scotland, after 108 hours to become the first airship to cross the Atlantic.

1921 Nancy Reagan, wife of former American President Ronald, was born Nancy Davis.

1928 The first all-talking feature film, *Lights of New York*, was presented at the Strand Theatre in New York City.

1932 Kenneth Grahame, Scottish author of *The Wind in the Willows*, died.

1936 Dave Allen, Irish comedian, born as David O'Mahoney.

1946 The Young Conservatives political organisation was founded in Britain.
       Sylvester Stallone, American actor, best known as star and writer of the film *Rocky*, born in New York City.

1952 The last London tram ran.

1960 Aneurin Bevan, British Labour party politician and minister responsible for introducing the National Health Service in 1948, died.

1962 William Faulkner, American novelist, notably *The Sound and the Fury*, and Nobel prizewinner in 1949, died.

1964 Malawi, formerly Nyasaland, became an independent State within the Commonwealth, having been a British Protectorate since 1891.

1966 Malawi became a Republic, with Dr Hastings Banda its President.

1968 Billie Jean King became the Wimbledon women's singles champion in the first year of open tennis.

1971 Louis Armstrong, 'Satchmo', American jazz trumpeter and bandleader, died.

1973 Otto Klemperer, German conductor, died aged 88.

1988 166 lives were lost in the *Piper Alpha* oil rig explosion in the North Sea—the worst in the history of the oil drilling industry.

1307 Death of King Edward I at Burgh-on-Sands near Carlisle on his march north—accession of his son as Edward II.

1816 (Richard Brinsley) R. B. Sheridan, Irish dramatist, who wrote *School for Scandal* and *The Rivals*, died in great poverty in London.

1854 George Ohm, German physicist, noted for his work on electricity, died in Munich.

1860 Gustav Mahler, Austrian composer and musical director, born in Kalist, Bohemia.

1909 Gottfried von Cramm, German international tennis player, born.

1921 Ezzard Charles, American heavyweight boxer, born in Lawrenceville, Georgia.

1927 Christopher Stone became the first 'disc jockey' on British radio when he presented his 'Record round-up' from Savoy Hill.

1930 Sir Arthur Conan Doyle, British writer and creator of the crime detective character 'Sherlock Holmes', died.

1940 Ringo Starr, the drummer of the 'Beatles' pop group, born in Liverpool as Richard Starkey.

1944 Tony Jacklin, English golf champion, born in Scunthorpe, Humberside.

1950 The first Farnborough air display took place.

1952 The American liner *United States* on her maiden voyage made the fastest-ever Atlantic crossing—doing the 2949 nautical miles from Ambrose Light Vessel to Bishop Rock Light in 3 days 10 hours 40 minutes.

1967 Francis Chichester was publicly dubbed Knight, at Greenwich, using Sir Francis Drake's sword.

1970 Sir Allen Lane, English publisher and founder of 'Penguin' paperback books in 1936, died.

1973 Veronica Lake, American film actress and leading lady in the 1940s, died.

1976 David Steel was elected leader of the Liberal Party.

1977 The Solomon Islands gained full independence within the Commonwealth, having been a British Protectorate since 1899.

1978 Martina Navratilova won the women's singles tennis title at Wimbledon for the first time.

1981 *Solar Challenger*, piloted by Steve Ptacek, became the first solar-powered aircraft to make a crossing of the English Channel, flying from Cormeille-en-Vixen, France, to Manston in Kent.

1984 Dame Flora Robson, British stage and film actress, made a DBE in 1960, died in Brighton.

1985 Boris Becker defeated Kevin Curren at Wimbledon to become the first unseeded champion and also the youngest male singles winner at 17.

1721 Elihu Yale, American philanthropist and patron of the University named after him in New Haven, died.

1822 (Percy Bysshe) P. B. Shelley, English poet, was accidentally drowned off Leghorn while sailing in his small schooner *Ariel* to his home on the Gulf of Spezia.

1836 Joseph Chamberlain, British Liberal statesman, born in London.

1838 Count Zeppelin, German pioneer and builder of airships, born in Constance.

1839 John D. Rockefeller, American industrialist and philanthropist, born in Richford, State of New York.

1870 Richard Bennett, Canadian Conservative statesman, born in Hopewell, New Brunswick.

1882 Percy Grainger, Australian composer and pianist, born in Melbourne, capital of the State of Victoria.

1884 NSPCC, the National Society for Prevention of Cruelty to Children, was founded in London.

1889 John L. Sullivan defeated Jake Kilrain at Richburg in Mississippi after 75 rounds, in the last bareknuckle heavyweight world title contest.

1908 Nelson Rockefeller, American statesman and Vice-President to Gerald Ford, born in Bar Harbor, Maine—grandson of John D. above.

1914 Billy Eckstine, American singer, born.

1918 National Savings stamps went on sale in Britain.

1930 Sir Joseph Ward, New Zealand statesman and twice Liberal Prime Minister, died.

1933 Anthony Hope, British novelist, notably *The Prisoner of Zenda*, died.

1935 Steve Lawrence, American singer with wife Eydie Gorme, born in Brooklyn, New York, as Sidney Leibowitz.

1965 Horse racing starting stalls were introduced in Britain, in the Chesterfield Stakes, Newmarket.

1967 Vivien Leigh, British film actress, best known for her Academy Award winning performance as Scarlett O'Hara, in *Gone With the Wind*, died.

1973 Wilfred Rhodes, Yorkshire and England cricketer, a left-arm bowler and a right-hand batsman, died in Broadstone, Dorset, aged 95.

1978 Reinhold Messner and Peter Habeler made the first ascent of Everest entirely without oxygen.
Bjorn Borg won the Wimbledon men's singles title for the third year running.

1979 Michael Wilding, English stage and film actor, died.

1988 Judith Chisholm, British record-breaking aviator, died.

National day of Argentina.

1441 Jan van Eyck, Flemish portrait and religious painter, died.
1797 Edmund Burke, British statesman, political writer and orator, died.
1816 Argentina declared independence from Spanish rule, by the Congress of Tucuman, after a long campaign conducted by José de San Martin.
1819 Elias Howe, American inventor of the first practical sewing machine, born in Spencer, Massachusetts.
1850 Zachary Taylor, American military general, Whig statesman and 12th President for only 16 months, died in Washington, DC—the remainder of his term of office was completed by Millard Fillmore.
1877 Wimbledon staged its first lawn tennis championship, at its original site in Worple Road.
1888 Bruce Bairnsfather, British cartoonist, born in Murree, India.
Simon Marks, British retail and business innovator, born in Leeds.
1901 Barbara Cartland, British authoress of romantic novels, born.
1916 Edward Heath, British statesman and Conservative Prime Minister, born in Broadstairs, Kent.
1918 America suffered its worst train accident—101 killed in Nashville, Tennessee.
1932 King Camp Gillette, American inventor of the safety razor and blade, died.
1977 At Turnberry in Scotland, Tom Watson returned a British open record low aggregate of 268.
1984 The roof of York Minster was destroyed by fire.
1988 Barbara Woodhouse, British animal trainer and TV personality, died aged 78.

1509 John Calvin, French theologian who spread the Protestant Reformation, born in Noyon, Picardy.
1553 Lady Jane Grey was proclaimed Queen after the death of Edward VI.
1792 Frederick Marryat, English writer of novels on sea life, born in London, the son of a Member of Parliament.
1802 Robert Chambers, Scottish bookseller and publisher, born in Peebles.

1806 George Stubbs, English animal painter, especially of horses, died in London aged 81.

1834 James McNeill Whistler, American etcher and painter, born in Lowell, Massachusetts.

1890 Wyoming, the Equality State, became the 44th state of the Union.

1900 Metro, the Paris underground railway, the work of Fulgence Bienvenue, was opened.

1937 Australia beat England 5–4 in a soccer international played at Sydney. They created another upset ten days later at Newcastle winning by the odd goal of seven.

1943 The US 7th Army under 'Old Blood and Guts' General Patton and the British-Canadian 8th Army began the invasion of Sicily.
Arthur Ashe, American tennis player and Wimbledon champion, born in Richmond, Virginia.

1945 Virginia Wade, British tennis champion, born in Bournemouth, Dorset, the daughter of a clergyman.

1949 Sunil Gavaskar, Indian cricketer and holder of the record number of Test appearances, born.

1954 Gordon Richards rode his last mount—at Sandown—the 21 834th of his near-34-year career.

1958 Parking meters came into operation for the first time in England, in London's Mayfair.

1962 *Telstar I*, the world's first television telecommunications satellite, was launched in America.

1970 At Baule in France, David Broome became the first Briton ever to win the World Show Jumping Championship.

1973 The Bahama Islands in north West Indies attained full independence within the Commonwealth, having been a British colony since 1783.

1978 Joe Davis, British snooker player and world champion from 1927 to 1946, died in Grayshott.

1979 Arthur Fiedler, American conductor, especially of the Boston Symphony Pops Orchestra, died aged 84.

1985 Two explosions sank the Greenpeace campaign ship *Rainbow Warrior*, in Auckland, New Zealand.

---

11 JULY   *[193]*

National day of Mongolia.

1274 Robert the Bruce, King of Scotland and the first man to unite his country into a nation, born in Turnberry, Ayrshire.

1708 The Battle of Oudenarde in west Belgium ended, with victory of the Duke of Marlborough's forces over the French, led by Louis Vendôme, in the War of the Spanish Succession.

1767 John Quincy Adams, American statesman and 6th President, born in Braintree, Massachusetts, the son of John Adams, 2nd President.

1776 Captain Cook sailed from Plymouth in the *Resolution* accompanied by the *Discovery* on his third and last expedition.

1859 The chime of Big Ben in the clock tower of the Houses of Parliament was heard for the first time.

1911 Liverpool's Gladstone Dock was opened by King George V.

1916 Gough Whitlam, Australian Labour statesman and Prime Minister, born in Melbourne, Victoria.

1917 Yul Brynner, film actor in America, born in Sakhalin, off Siberia.

1935 Alfred Dreyfus, French Army officer who was accused of selling military secrets to Germany, imprisoned and later pardoned, died aged 75.

1937 George Gershwin, American composer, including *Rhapsody in Blue* and *Porgy and Bess*, died aged 38.

1950 BBC's children's television programme *Andy Pandy* was first transmitted.

1953 Leon Spinks, American heavyweight boxer and world champion, born.

1961 Terry Downes stopped Paul Pender in nine rounds at Wembley to win the world middleweight boxing title.

1962 American Fred Baldasare became the first to swim the English Channel underwater—from Cap Gris Nez to Sandwich in Kent—with 'scuba' (self-contained underwater breathing apparatus) equipment.

1979 America's *Skylab I* returned to earth after 34 981 orbits, since its launch on 14 May 1973.

1989 Laurence Olivier, English theatre and film actor, died aged 82.

12 JULY [194]

Orangeman's day in Northern Ireland.

1543 King Henry VIII married Catherine Parr—his sixth and last wife.

1730 Josiah Wedgwood, famous English potter, born in Burslem, Staffordshire.

1794 Nelson lost the sight of his right eye during an attempt to reduce the French garrison at Calvi.

1851 Louis Daguerre, French pioneer in photography, died.

1854 George Eastman, American pioneer in photography, born in Waterville, in the State of New York.

1870 London's Victoria Embankment, constructed by Sir J. W. Bazalgette, was opened by the Prince of Wales (later Edward VII).

1872 Lord Birkenhead, British Conservative statesman and law reformer, born as Frederick Edwin Smith.

1878 Cyprus was ceded by Turkey to Britain for administration.
1895 Kirsten Flagstad, Norwegian operatic soprano in Wagnerian roles, born in Hamar.
1895 Oscar Hammerstein, American librettist, famous for musicals created with composer Richard Rodgers, born in New York City.
1906 Frenchman Alfred Dreyfus was finally rehabilitated after lengthy imprisonment on Devil's Island.
1908 Milton Berle, American television comedian, born in New York City, as Milton Berlinger.
1910 Charles Stewart Rolls, aviator and co-founder of the engineering firm of Rolls-Royce, was killed in an air crash at Bournemouth in Dorset.
1920 President Wilson officially opened the Panama Canal.
1925 The first veteran car rally was held, at Munich.
1932 Hedley Verity, Yorkshire bowler, took all 10 wickets for 10 runs in 118 deliveries for his county against Nottinghamshire.
1947 Gareth Edwards, Welsh Rugby Union international, born.
1948 Six RAF De Havilland Vampires of Number 54 Squadron landed in Labrador to become the first jet-powered aircraft to fly across the Atlantic.

13 JULY [195]

1705 Titus Oates, English Protestant conspirator who fabricated a supposed Catholic plot to assassinate King Charles II and restore Catholicism, died.
1793 Jean Paul Marat, French revolutionary leader, was stabbed to death in his bath by Charlotte Corday.
1837 Queen Victoria became the first Sovereign to move into Buckingham Palace.
1860 The last naval execution at the yard-arm took place, aboard HMS *Leven* in the River Yangtse—the victim was Marine Private John Dalliger.
1865 Englishman Edward Whymper became the first to climb the 14 690-foot Matterhorn in the Alps, on the Swiss-Italian border.
1871 The first cat show was held at Crystal Palace, in London, organised by Harrison Weir.
1908 The 4th Olympic Games opened in London.
     Sir Alec Rose, English yachtsman, knighted for his round the world trip, born.
1919 The British airship *R34* under the command of Squadron Leader Scott, arrived back at Pulham in Norfolk after making the first Atlantic aerial round trip—having set out from East Fortune in Scotland on 2 July.

1930 The World Cup Football Competition was instituted—only 13 countries entered and the Cup was won by the hosts, Uruguay.

1942 Harrison Ford, American film actor, born in Chicago, Illinois.

1955 Ruth Ellis was hanged at Holloway for the murder of David Blakely, to become the last woman to be executed in Britain.

1956 Michael Spinks, a world heavyweight boxing champion, born in St Louis, Missouri, the younger brother of Leon.

1980 Sir Seretse Khama, President of the African Republic of Botswana since 1966, died in a London hospital.

1982 Kenneth More, English film actor, died at his home in Fulham, London.

1985 'Live Aid' pop concerts in Britain and America raised more than £50 million for famine victims in Africa.

---

14 JULY [196]

National day of both France and Iraq.

1789 The Bastille, a former State prison in Paris, was stormed by the citizens of Paris and razed to the ground, and so began the French Revolution.

1858 Emmeline Pankhurst, English suffragette, born in Manchester, with the maiden name of Goulden.

1867 Alfred Nobel first demonstrated the use of dynamite, at Merstham Quarry, Redhill, Surrey.

1887 Alfred Krupp, German manufacturer of arms at Essen in the Ruhr, died.

1893 Johannes Strijdom, South African statesman, born in Willowmore, Cape Province.

1904 Paul Kruger, South African statesman and Boer Leader, called 'Oom Paul', died in Switzerland.

1913 Gerald Ford, American Republican statesman and 38th President, born in Omaha, Nebraska, as Leslie King junior.

1918 Ingmar Bergman, Swedish film director, born in Uppsala.

1950 Bruce Oldfield, British fashion designer, born.

1958 King Faisal of Iraq was assassinated in a military coup led by General Kassem, and a Republic was established.

1959 Grock, world-famous Swiss clown, died.

1965 Adlai Stevenson, American politician and diplomat, died in London.

1986 A midget submarine landed on the *Titanic* and took pictures of the wreck.

St Swithin's Day.

1573   Inigo Jones, the first of the great English architects, born in London, the son of a clothmaker.

1606   Rembrandt, Dutch painter, born in Leyden, as Rembrandt Harmensz van Rijn, the son of a prosperous miller.

1685   The Duke of Monmouth, the illegitimate son of King Charles II and Lucy Walter, was beheaded on London's Tower Hill for leading a Protestant rebellion on the accession of James II.

1795   *La Marseillaise* was officially adopted as the French national anthem—was composed and written in 1792 by Rouget de Lisle.

1815   Napoleon surrendered to Captain Maitland of the *Bellerophon* at Rochefort.

1857   The Massacre of Cawnpore took place, in which English women and children of the garrison were killed (197) during the Indian mutiny.

1865   Lord Northcliffe, English journalist and newspaper proprietor, born near Dublin, as Alfred Harmsworth.

1869   Margarine was patented in France by Hippolyte Mège Mouriés of Paris.

1881   'Billy the Kid', the notorious American outlaw William H. Bonney, was shot by Sheriff Pat Garrett in New Mexico.

1883   'Tom Thumb', the tiny American showman who finally reached forty inches, died.

1904   Anton Chekhov, Russian dramatist and short story writer, died in Badenweiler.

1912   National insurance or social payment, devised by Lloyd George, began in Britain.

1918   The second Battle of Marne started, and ended when Ludendorff's advance was stopped by British, French and US troops.

1933   Julian Bream, British guitarist and lutenist, born in London.

1946   Linda Ronstadt, American pop and rock singer, born in Tucson, Arizona.

1948   John Pershing, commander of the US Army in France in World War I, nicknamed 'Black Jack', died in Washington, DC.
        'Alcoholics Anonymous' was founded in London, having been in existence in America since 1935.

1965   US *Mariner 4* sent back the first close-up pictures of Mars.

1975   *Apollo 18* was launched, with Vance Brand, Thomas Stafford and Donald Slayton.

1377   The coronation of King Richard II of England took place.
1557   Anne of Cleves, the fourth wife of King Henry VIII, died.
1723   Sir Joshua Reynolds, English portrait painter, born near Plympton, Devon, the 7th son of a clergyman.
1790   Washington, DC, was established as the seat of Federal Government.
1821   Mary Baker Eddy, American religious leader and founder of the Christian Science movement, born in Bow, New Hampshire.
1827   Josiah Spode, English potter and creator of a type of bone china bearing his name, died.
1867   Reinforced concrete was patented by Joseph Monier of Paris.
1872   Roald Amundsen, Norwegian explorer and first to reach the South Pole, in 1911, born in Borge.
1896   Trygve Lie, Norwegian statesman and Secretary-General of the United Nations, born in Oslo.
1907   Barbara Stanwyck, American film actress, born in Brooklyn, New York, as Ruby Stevens.
1910   Stan McCabe, Australian Test cricketer, born.
1911   Ginger Rogers, American dancer, film actress and Oscar winner for *Kitty Foyle* (1940), born in Independence, Missouri, as Virginia Katherine McMath.
1918   The last Tsar, Nicholas II, was murdered at Ekaterinburg with his five children—daughters, Olga, Tatiana, Marie, Anastasia and son Alexis.
1935   Parking meters, devised by Carlton Magee, came into service in America—in Oklahoma City.
1942   Margaret Court, Australian international lawn tennis champion, born in Albury, New South Wales, with the maiden name Smith.
1945   The first atomic bomb, produced at Los Alamos under the direction of Robert Oppenheimer, was detonated at Alamogordo Air Base in New Mexico.
1950   199 850 watched the Brazil *v.* Uruguay World Cup final in Rio—a world record for a football match.
1953   Hilaire Belloc, Anglo-French writer and poet, died.
1960   Albert Kesselring, German air commander on all fronts in World War II, condemned as a war criminal, died.
1965   The seven-mile Mont Blanc road tunnel was opened, linking France with Italy.
1969   *Apollo 11* was launched, with Neil Armstrong, Edwin Aldrin and Michael Collins.

1761 The Bridgewater Canal, from Worsley to Manchester, built by James Brindley, was opened.

1790 Adam Smith, Scottish economist and writer of *Wealth of Nations*, died in Edinburgh.

1841 The first issue of the English magazine *Punch* was published in London.

1876 Maxim Litvinov, Soviet statesman, born a Polish Jew in Bielostok.

1889 Erle Stanley Gardner, American crime novelist and creator of the detective character 'Perry Mason', born in Malden, Massachusetts.

1899 James Cagney, American film actor, dancer and Oscar winner, born in New York City.

1903 James McNeill Whistler, expatriate American artist whose 'Mother' hangs in the Louvre, died in London.

1909 Hardy Amies, dressmarker to the Queen, born.

1912 Art Linkletter, Canadian-American broadcaster, born in Moose Jaw, Saskatchewan, as Arthur Gordon Kelley.

1917 The British Royal family adopted the name 'House of Windsor' in place of 'House of Saxe-Coburg-Gotha'.
Phyllis Diller, American comedienne and stand-up comic, born in Lima, Ohio, as Phyllis Driver.

1945 The Potsdam Conference of Allied leaders Truman, Stalin and Churchill (later replaced by Attlee) began.

1951 Baudouin became King of the Belgians, on the enforced abdication of his father, King Leopold III.

1959 Billie Holiday, American jazz-blues singer, died as a result of drug addiction.

1961 Ty Cobb, probably the greatest player in baseball history, nicknamed the 'Georgia Peach', died.

1964 Donald Campbell attained a world speed record of over 403 m.p.h.—by a wheel-driven car *Bluebird*—on the salt flats at Lake Eyre in South Australia.

1975 A US *Apollo* spacecraft and a Russian *Soyuz* craft successfully docked while in orbit.

1981 The Queen formally opened the Humber Estuary Bridge—the longest single-span structure in the world—it having been opened to traffic on 24 June.

National day of Spain.

1635   Robert Hooke, English physicist, born in Freshwater, on the Isle of Wight.

1721   Antoine Watteau, French rococo painter, died.

1792   John Paul Jones, Scottish-born naval hero of the American Revolution, died in Paris.

1811   William Makepeace Thackeray, English novelist, born in Calcutta, where his father was in the service of the East India Company.

1817   Jane Austen, English novelist, author of *Pride and Prejudice* and *Emma*, died in a lodging in College Street, Winchester, Hampshire.

1848   (William Gilbert) W. G. Grace, famous England cricketer, born in Downend, near Bristol.

1864   Philip Snowden, British Labour statesman, born near Keighley, Yorkshire.

1887   Vidkun Quisling, Norwegian diplomat and later traitor, born in Fyresdal.

1892   Thomas Cook, English travel agent pioneer and founder of the agency bearing his name, died.

1895   Sir Henry Irving received a knighthood from Queen Victoria at Windsor.

1904   Work began on Liverpool's Anglican Cathedral—the largest in the British Isles—was completed in October 1978.

1918   Nelson Mandela, South African black nationalist and human rights leader, born.

1921   John Glenn, astronaut and first American to orbit the earth, born in Cambridge, Ohio.

1925   Shirley Strickland, Australian athlete and an Olympic champion, born.

1934   The 2.13-mile Mersey road tunnel was opened by King George V.

1936   The Spanish Civil War between Fascists and Republican forces began.

1947   The first night horse-racing meeting in Britain, under official rules, was held at Hamilton Park.

1949   Dennis Lillee, Australian Test cricketer, born in Perth.

1950   Richard Branson, head of the Virgin companies, born.

1951   Jersey Joe Walcott won the world heavyweight boxing title at Pittsburgh, knocking out Ezzard Charles in round seven to become the oldest winner of the crown.

1955   Disneyland, the amusement resort at Anaheim in California, was opened.

1957 Nick Faldo, British and international golf champion, born.
1966 Spacecraft *Gemini 10* was launched with John Young and Michael Collins.
1973 Jack Hawkins, British film actor, died.
1976 The 21st Olympic Games opened at Montreal in Quebec.
1986 Sir Stanley Rous, British and international football administrator, died aged 91.

19 JULY

1545 *Mary Rose*, the pride of Henry VIII's battle fleet, suddenly heeled over and sank in the Solent—was raised on 11 October 1982, ready to be taken to Portsmouth Dockyard.
1553 Mary Tudor was proclaimed Queen and Lady Jane Grey, a convinced Protestant, was sent to the Tower.
1814 Matthew Flinders, English explorer who surveyed and charted the coasts of Australia, died aged 40.
     Samuel Colt, American inventor and patentee in 1835 of a revolver that bears his name, born in Hartford, Connecticut.
1821 The coronation of King George IV took place in Westminster Abbey.
1834 Edgar Degas, French Impressionist painter and sculptor, born in Paris.
1837 Brunel's 236-foot *Great Western* was launched at Patterson's Yard at Bristol.
1843 Brunel's 320-foot *Great Britain*, the first all-metal liner was launched from London's Wapping Dock, by Prince Albert.
1860 Lizzie Borden, the alleged axe murderess, born in Fall River, Massachusetts.
1865 Charles Mayo, American surgeon who with his brother was founder of the Mayo Clinic, born in Rochester, Minnesota.
1877 The first men's Wimbledon tennis final took place, and was won by Spencer Gore.
1896 (Archibald Joseph) A. J. Cronin, British novelist, born in Cardross, Scotland.
1911 The Liver Building at Liverpool was opened.
1930 Marjorie Foster became the only woman to win the King's/Queen's Prize for rifle shooting at Bisley.
1932 London's Lambeth Bridge, leading from Lambeth Palace to Millbank over the Thames, was opened.
1942 Vikki Carr, American pop singer, born in El Paso, Texas.
1946 Ilie Nastasie, Romanian international tennis player, born in Bucharest.
1952 The 15th Olympic Games opened in Helsinki, Finland.

1969 John Fairfax arrived at Fort Lauderdale in Florida after 180 days, having rowed the Atlantic alone from Las Palmas in the 22-foot *Britannia*—the first to make such a crossing.

1980 The 22nd Olympic Games opened in Moscow.

20 JULY [202]

National day of Colombia.

1837 Euston Railway Station, the first in London, was opened.

1845 Charles Sturt became the first white man to enter Simpson's Desert in Central Australia.

1858 The first baseball match to charge admission took place at the Fashion Race Course, Long Island—Brooklyn against New York All Stars—about 1500 spectators paid the 50 cents entry fee.

1871 The English Football Association Challenge Cup competition was formed.

1885 Professional football was legalised in England.

1900 Maurice Leyland, Yorkshire and England cricketer, born in Harrogate.

1903 Leo XIII (Gioacchino Vincenzo Pecci), Pope since 1878, died aged 93.

1919 Sir Edmund Hillary, the first conqueror of Mount Everest in 1953 with Tenzing Norgay, born in Auckland, North Island, New Zealand.

1937 Guglielmo Marconi, Italian physicist and inventor who pioneered the use of wireless telegraphy, died in Rome.

1938 Natalie Wood, American film actress, born in San Francisco, as Natasha Gurdin.

1940 Singles-record charts were first published, in America, by *Billboard*.

1944 An assassination attempt on Hitler's life was made by a German staff officer, Count Claus Schenk von Stauffenberg, at Rastenberg, East Prussia.

1962 The first regular Hovercraft passenger service was inaugurated, on the Dee estuary between Wallasey and Rhyl.

1969 *Eagle*, the lunar module of *Apollo 11*, landed on the Moon, on the Sea of Tranquillity.

1970 Ian MacLeod, British politician, died.

1976 *Viking 1*, the American unmanned spacecraft, touched down on Mars after an 11-month journey.

National day of Belgium.

1796 Robert Burns, Scottish national poet, died aged 37, in Dumfries, and is buried there.

1797 Nelson had his right elbow shattered by a grapeshot, and had his arm amputated, as a result of an unsuccessful attempt to seize a richly laden Spanish ship at Santa Cruz de Tenerife.

1798 The Battle of the Pyramids took place, in which Napoleon, soon after his invasion of Egypt, defeated an army of some 60000 Mamelukes.

1816 Paul von Reuter, German founder of the world news agency that bears his name, born in Kassel as Israel Beer Josaphat.

1831 Prince Leopold became Leopold I, King of Belgium on its separation from the Netherlands.

1861 The first Battle of Bull Run took place, when Union troops, under McDowell, were defeated by the Confederates under Beauregard.

1873 The James–Younger gang carried out a train robbery near Adair in Iowa—the first in the American West.

1890 Battersea Bridge over the Thames was opened by the Earl of Rosebery.

1897 The Tate Gallery in London was officially opened—built on the site of the Millbank Prison.

1899 Ernest Hemingway, American novelist, born in Oak Park, Illinois, the son of a country doctor.

1928 Ellen Terry, English Shakespearean stage actress, died in Hythe, Kent, aged 81.

1944 Guam, in the western Pacific, was retaken by US Marines, having been in Japanese hands since December 1941.

1945 John Lowe, world-ranked British darts champion, born.

1947 Viscount Lee, British politician, benefactor and patron of the arts, died in his Gloucestershire home at Avening.

1959 The first nuclear merchant ship, US *Savannah*, was launched at Camden in New Jersey by Mrs Mamie Eisenhower.

1960 Mrs Sirimavo Bandaranaike took up office as Prime Minister of Ceylon, and became the world's first woman to hold such a position.

1961 Runcorn Bridge over the River Mersey—the longest steel arch bridge in the United Kingdom—was opened.

1967 Basil Rathbone, English film actor, synonymous with Sherlock Holmes, died.

1969 Neil Armstrong, command pilot of *Apollo 11*, left the lunar module *Eagle* and set foot on the moon, on the Sea of Tranquillity.

1988 David Gower played in his 100th Test match, at Headingley against the West Indies.

National day of Poland.

1812 The Battle of Salamanca took place in west Spain, the scene of the Duke of Wellington's victory over the French in the Peninsular War.

1822 Gregor Mendel, Augustine monk, botanist and pioneer of modern genetics, born in Heinzendorf, near Odrau, in Austrian Silesia.

1844 Reverend William Spooner, British educationalist and originator of 'spoonerisms', born in London.

1928 Jimmy Hill, British TV sports presenter and an ex-professional footballer, born in Balham, London.

1932 Florenz Ziegfeld, American theatrical producer and impresario, died in Hollywood.

1933 Wiley Post became the first to fly solo round the world—with 10 stops from Floyd Bennett Field in New York City and back, via the Arctic Circle, in a Lockheed Vega monoplane *Winnie Mae*—the journey took 7 days 18 hours 49½ minutes.

1934 John Dillinger, American bank robber and public enemy, was gunned down by law officers in front of the Biograph Theatre in Chicago.

1946 Bread rationing began in Britain.

1950 Mackenzie King, Canadian statesman and Liberal Prime Minister on three occasions, died in Kingsmere, Province of Quebec.

1976 Sir Mortimer Wheeler, British archaeologist and broadcaster, died.

National day of both Ethiopia and The United Arab Republic.

1759 Work commenced on the Royal Navy's 104-gun battleship HMS *Victory*, at Chatham in Kent—constructed from the wood of some 2200 oak trees.

1875 Isaac Singer, American inventor of the modern sewing machine, died in Torquay, Devon.

1885 Ulysses Grant, American commander of the Union Army, Republican statesman and 18th President from 1869 to 1877, died of cancer in Mount McGregor, near Saratoga, State of New York.

1886 Sir Arthur Whitten Brown, British aviator and companion of Alcock on the first transatlantic flight, born in Glasgow.

1888 Raymond Chandler, American detective story writer, creator of the character 'Philip Marlowe', born in Chicago.
1891 Haile Selassie, Emperor of Ethiopia, born in the Harar Province, as Tafari Makonnen.
1912 Michael Wilding, English actor, born in Westcliff-on-Sea, Essex.
1913 Michael Foot, British politician and one-time Labour Party leader, born.
1916 Sir William Ramsay, Scottish chemist and Nobel Prize winner in 1904, who discovered 'inert' gases—argon, helium, neon, krypton and xenon—died in High Wycombe, Buckinghamshire.
1930 Glenn Curtiss, American inventor and successful aeroplane builder, died.
1948 D. W. Griffith, American film producer, director and pioneer in the industry, died.
1949 Brian Close became England's youngest Test cricketer when he played against New Zealand at Old Trafford.
1951 Marshal Pétain, Army marshal and Head of State of Vichy France from 1940 to 1944, died in prison at Île d'Yeu, aged 95, serving a life sentence for collaboration.
1953 Graham Gooch, Essex and England Test cricketer, born.
1955 Cordell Hull, American statesman, diplomat and Nobel Peace Prize winner in 1945, died aged 83.
1973 'Eddie' Rickenbacker, American aviator and most celebrated US air ace in World War I, died aged 82.
1986 Prince Andrew married Miss Sarah Ferguson in Westminster Abbey, and was created Duke of York.

24 JULY [206]

1704 Admiral Sir George Rooke captured Gibraltar from the Spaniards—ceded to Britain by the 1713 Treaty of Utrecht.
1775 Eugène Francois Vidocq, the first police detective and founder of the Sûreté, born in Arras, Northern France, the son of a baker.
1783 Simon Bolivar, South American revolutionary leader and liberator of South America from Spanish Imperial control, born in Caracas, the capital city of Venezuela.
1802 Alexandre Dumas *père* (senior), French writer, notably *The Count of Monte Cristo* and *The Three Musketeers*, born as Alexandre Dumas Davy de la Pailleterie.
1824 The result of the first public opinion poll was published in the *Harrisburg Pennsylvanian*, conducted at Wilmington to determine voters' intentions in the 1824 Presidential election.
1862 Martin van Buren, American Democrat statesman and 8th President from 1837 to 1841, known as 'the little magician', died in Kinderhook, New York.

1883 Matthew Webb, the first man to swim the English Channel, in 1875, was drowned attempting to swim the rapids above the Niagara Falls.
1898 Amelia Earhart, American aviator, born in Atchison, Kansas.
1926 Belle Vue, Manchester, was opened for greyhound racing, by Brigadier Critchley.
1927 The Menin Gate, a memorial at Ypres to the armies of the British Empire, was unveiled by Lord Plumer.
1936 The 'Speaking Clock' was introduced by the GPO at the suggestion of Eugene Wender of Hampstead—was known as 'TIM' from the dial letters.
1974 Sir James Chadwick, English physicist, discoverer of the neutron and Nobel Prizewinner, died aged 82.
1980 Peter Sellers, English film actor and entertainer, died.

25 JULY [207]

1603 The coronation of King James I took place.
1834 (Samuel Taylor) S. T. Coleridge, English poet, who wrote *Kubla Khan* and *The Rime of the Ancient Mariner*, died.
1843 Charles Macintosh, Scottish chemist who developed and patented waterproof fabric in 1823, died near Glasgow.
1848 (Arthur James) A. J. Balfour, British statesman and Conservative Prime Minister, born in East Lothian, Scotland.
1909 Louis Blériot flew his *Blériot XI* monoplane across the English Channel, from Les Baraques near Calais to Northfall Meadow near Dover Castle, in 36½ minutes.
1934 Engelbert Dollfuss, Chancellor of Austria, was assassinated in Vienna by rebelling Austrian Nazis—Otto Planetta was convicted and hanged.
1943 Benito Mussolini resigned as Dictator of Italy, and the Fascist regime was abolished.
1954 Walter Payton, the American football legend, born in Columbia, Mississippi.
1957 Tunisia abolished the monarchy and became a Republic, with Habib Bourguiba, elected as President.
1959 The Hovercraft, the *SRN 1* as it was called, made its first English Channel crossing—from Dover to Calais—in a little over two hours.
1966 Billy Smart, British circus proprietor, died performing at his circus in Ipswich.
1969 Sharon Adams of the US put in at San Diego Harbour to become the first woman to sail the Pacific alone.
1978 The first test-tube baby in Britain was born—Louise Joy Brown, at Oldham General Hospital, Lancashire.

1984 A Soviet cosmonaut became the first woman to 'walk' in space.
1987 The *London Daily News* closed down five months after it was launched.

26 JULY [208]

National day of Liberia.

1745 The first recorded women's cricket match took place, at Gosden Common, near Guildford in Surrey—when '11 maids from Hambledon' beat '11 maids from Bramley'.
1788 New York, the Empire State, became the 11th state of the Union.
1845 Brunel's 320-foot iron ship *Great Britain* left Liverpool for New York on her maiden voyage.
1847 Liberia became the first African colony to secure independence.
1856 George Bernard Shaw, Irish dramatist and critic, born in Dublin.
1863 Sam Houston, American politician as President and Governor of Texas, and soldier as leader winning independence for Texas, died.
1866 The Canoe Club was formed in England by John MacGregor.
1875 Carl Jung, Swiss analytic psychologist, born in Kesswil.
1881 George Borrow, English writer of books of travel and gypsies, author of *Lavengro*, died.
1886 Emil Jannings, German-US film actor, born in Brooklyn, New York.
1908 The Federal Bureau of Investigation was established in Washington, DC.
1922 Blake Edwards, American film director, born in Tulsa, Oklahoma, as William Blake McEdwards.
1928 Stanley Kubrick, American film maker, producer and director, born in New York City.
1943 Mick Jagger, English rock singer and leader of 'The Rolling Stones', born in Dartford.
1945 Clement Attlee became Britain's Prime Minister after a Labour landslide in the general election.
1952 King Farouk was forced to abdicate as a result of a *coup d'état* carried out by General Neguib.
1954 Vitas Gerulaitas, American tennis player, born.
1956 President Nasser took over Egypt and nationalised the Suez Canal.
1958 Her Majesty the Queen created her eldest son, Charles, Prince of Wales.
      Debutantes were presented at the Royal Court in Britain for the last time.
1963 Severe earthquakes occurred at Skopje in Yugoslavia, with 1100 deaths.

1965 The Maldive Islands in the Indian Ocean, south-west of Sri Lanka, achieved independence, having been under British protection since 1887.
1971 *Apollo 15* was launched, with David Scott, James Irwin and Alfred Worden—Scott and Irwin making the 4th moon landing.
1979 Sir Charles Clore, English financier, died.
1986 Averell Harriman, American statesman, diplomat and Governor of New York, died aged 94.

27 JULY [209]

1689 The Battle of Killiecrankie took place near Pitlochry in Scotland, in which King William's forces, led by Mackay, were defeated by the Jacobites under John Graham of Claverhouse—who was killed.
1694 The Bank of England was founded with Government backing.
1824 Alexandre Dumas *fils* (junior), French playwright, especially *La Dame aux Camélias*, born in Paris.
1844 John Dalton, English chemist and physicist who developed the modern atomic theory and pioneer in meteorology, died.
1866 The *Great Eastern* arrived at Heart's Content in Newfoundland having successfully laid the transatlantic telegraph cable.
1870 Hilaire Belloc, English writer and poet, born in St Cloud, near Paris, the son of a French barrister.
1882 Sir Geoffrey de Havilland, English aircraft designer and manufacturer, born in Woburn, Buckinghamshire.
1904 Anton Dolin, English ballet dancer and choreographer, born in Slinfold, Sussex, as Patrick Healey-Kay.
1921 The first insulin was isolated by Canadians Sir Frederick Banting and his assistant Charles Best, at the University of Toronto, thus providing an effective treatment for diabetes.
1923 The BBC radio station 'Daventry' opened.
1929 Jack Higgins, English author of suspense novels, born in Newcastle, as Harry Patterson.
1930 Shirley Williams, British politician and co-founder of the Social Democratic Party, born the daughter of novelist Vera Brittain.
1942 Dennis Ralston, American international tennis player, born in Bakersfield, California.
 The first Battle of El Alamein ended after 27 days, with the British Army, under Auchinleck, having held the German and Italian forces and prevented their advance into Egypt.
1944 Bobby Gentry, American singer and songwriter, born in Chickasaw County, Mississippi.

1949 The world's first jet-propelled airliner built in UK—the De Havilland DH 106 *Comet*—first flew at Hatfield.
1953 The Korean Armistice was signed at Panmunjom.
1955 Alan Border, Australian cricketer and Test captain, born.
1958 Christopher Dean, ice skating star of the Torvill and Dean ice-dance team, born in Nottingham.
1964 Sir Winston Churchill made his last appearance in the House of Commons.
1969 Irishman Tom McClean of the Parachute Regiment arrived at Blacksod Bay in County Mayo, after rowing solo across the Atlantic for 71 days, from St John's, in 20-feet *Super Silver*.
1970 Antonio Salazar, Portuguese statesman and Prime Minister from 1932 to 1968, died in Lisbon, aged 81.
1972 Work began on the Humber Estuary Bridge—the world's longest main span at 4626 feet. Opened by the Queen on 17 July 1981.
1980 The Shah of Iran died in Egypt in exile.
1984 James Mason, English film actor, died in Switzerland.
1986 Sir Osbert Lancaster, British artist and cartoonist, died.

28 JULY [210]

National day of Peru.

1586 The first potatoes arrived in Britain in Plymouth, brought from Colombia by Sir Thomas Harriot.
1655 Cyrano de Bergerac, French novelist and playwright, died.
1741 Antonio Vivaldi, Italian violin virtuoso and composer, notably of *The Four Seasons*, died in Vienna.
1750 Johann Sebastian Bach, German composer, almost totally blind, died of apoplexy.
1794 Maximilien Robespierre, French leader of the Jacobins during the Revolution, was guillotined in Paris.
1809 The Battle of Talavera in the Peninsular War ended, with the Duke of Wellington victorious over French Marshal Soult.
1821 San Martin and his forces liberated Peru, and proclaimed its independence from Spain.
1866 Beatrix Potter, English author and illustrator of children's books and creator of 'Peter Rabbit', born in South Kensington, London.
1868 The Fourteenth Amendment to the US Constitution was ratified, dealing with citizenship rights.
1901 Rudy Vallee, American singer, born in Island Pond, Vermont.
1904 Selwyn Lloyd, British Conservative politician, born in Liverpool.
1917 The formation of the Royal Tank Corps in the British Army was authorised.
1928 The 9th Olympic Games opened in Amsterdam.

1929 Jacqueline Onassis, widow of President Kennedy, born in Southampton, New York State, as Jacqueline Lee Bouvier.

1934 Marie Dressler, US film actress and Oscar winner in 1930 for her role in *Min and Bill*, died.

1936 Garfield Sobers, West Indian Test cricketer, born in Bridgetown, capital of Barbados.

1938 The British liner *Mauretania* was launched at Birkenhead, Merseyside.

1939 William James Mayo, American surgeon and co-founder of the Mayo Clinic Foundation, died aged 78.

1967 The steel industry was re-nationalised in Britain.

1976 Vic Feather, British trade union leader, created Baron Feather in 1974, died.

1977 Ian Botham made his Test cricket debut, against Australia at Trent Bridge, Nottingham.

1984 The 23rd Olympic Games opened in Los Angeles.
George Gallup, whose name became synonymous with opinion polls, died in Switzerland, aged 82.

29 JULY [211]

1565 Mary, Queen of Scots married her cousin Lord Darnley in the Old Abbey Chapel of Holyrood Palace in Edinburgh.

1588 The Spanish Armada, a fleet of some 130 ships, sent by Philip II in an attempt to invade England, and led by Medina Sidonia, was defeated by the English fleet under Howard and Drake, off Plymouth.

1833 William Wilberforce, English philanthropist who played a large part in the abolition of the slave trade in 1807 and of slavery in the British Empire in 1833, died.

1856 Robert Schumann, German composer and director of music, died in an asylum near Bonn.

1883 Benito Mussolini, Italian statesman and Fascist dictator, born in Predappio, near Forli, the son of a blacksmith.

1887 Sigmund Romberg, Hungarian composer of musical comedies, notably *The Student Prince*, born in Szeged.

1890 Vincent van Gogh, famous Dutch painter, died after prolonged insanity—having shot himself in the chest two days earlier.

1900 Umberto I, King of Italy from 1878, was assassinated at Monza by anarchists.

1905 Dag Hammarskjöld, Swedish Secretary-General of the United Nations, born in Jönköping.

1907 The first Boy Scout movement originated with an experimental camp held on Brownsea Island, near Poole, Dorset, by Robert Baden-Powell—ended on 9 August.

1913 Jo Grimond, British politician and a leader of the Liberal Party, born.
1945 The BBC 'Light Programme' began broadcasting.
1948 The 14th Olympic Games opened in London.
     Bread rationing ended in Britain.
1949 BBC televised the first regular weather forecast.
1952 Joe Johnson, English snooker player and a world champion, born.
1970 Sir John Barbirolli, English conductor and musical director, died.
1981 The Prince of Wales and Lady Diana Spencer were married at Westminster Abbey.
1983 David Niven, British actor, died.

30 JULY

1718 William Penn, English Quaker leader and founder of the US state of Pennsylvania, died aged 73.
1771 Thomas Gray, English poet, noted for his 'Elegy written in a country churchyard', died in London.
1818 Emily Brontë, English novelist, author of *Wuthering Heights*, born in Thornton, Yorkshire.
1856 Viscount Haldane, British Liberal politician and statesman, born in Edinburgh.
1863 Henry Ford, American motor car engineer and manufacturer, born in Dearborn, Michigan, the son of a farmer.
1874 Billy Meredith, Welsh international footballer, born.
1898 Otto von Bismarck, Prussian statesman, founder and Chancellor of the German empire, died in Friedrichsruh, aged 83.
     Henry Moore, English abstract sculptor, born in Castleford, Yorkshire, the son of a coal miner.
1932 The 10th Olympic Games opened in Los Angeles.
1935 'Penguin' paperback books, founded by Sir Allen Lane, went on sale in Britain.
1938 The first edition of the *Beano* comic went on sale.
1941 Paul Anka, pop singer and composer, born in Ottawa, Canada.
1947 Sir Joseph Cook, Australian Liberal statesman and 9th Prime Minister from 1913 to 1914, died.
1948 The world's first radar station was opened, to assist shipping at the port of Liverpool.
1958 Daley Thompson, British athlete, notably in the decathlon, was born and christened Francis Morgan.
1960 Walter Lindrum, an international billiards champion, died.
1966 England won the World Cup at football, beating West Germany 4–2 at Wembley Stadium, London.

1983 Raymond Massey, Canadian-born film actor, died in Beverly Hills, California, aged 86.

---

31 JULY [213]

1556 Ignatius Loyola, Spanish soldier, priest and founder of the Society of Jesus (Jesuits), died.

1875 Andrew Johnson, American Democrat statesman and 17th President from 1865 to 1869, died in Carter County, Tennessee.

1878 Northamptonshire County Cricket Club was founded.

1886 Franz Liszt, Hungarian pianist, composer and director of music, died in Bayreuth, West Germany, aged 74.

1910 Dr Crippen, the murderer, was arrested aboard the SS *Montrose* just before docking in Quebec to become the first criminal to be captured by the use of wireless.

1912 Milton Friedman, American economist and Nobel Prize winner, born in Brooklyn, New York.

1929 The World Boy Scouts' Jamboree at Arrowe Park, Birkenhead, was opened.

1931 Cleveland Municipal Stadium, the home of the Cleveland Indians, was opened, and is the largest baseball stadium.

1943 Hedley Verity, Yorkshire and England cricketer, died when a prisoner of war in Italy, as a result of wounds received in action.

1951 Evonne Goolagong, Australian international tennis champion, born in Barellan, New South Wales.

1954 K2 in the Himalayas at 8611 metres, otherwise known as Mount Godwin-Austen, was first climbed by an Italian expedition of six climbers, led by Ardito Desio.

1956 At Old Trafford, Manchester, Jim Laker took all 10 Australian wickets in the second innings for 53 runs, after a first inings haul of 9 for 37.

1964 Jim Reeves, American 'country' singer, killed in an air crash.

1965 The advertising of cigarettes on British television was banned.

1971 Astronauts David Scott and James Irwin became the first to ride on the moon, in their Lunar Roving Vehicle.

---

1 AUGUST [214]

National day of Switzerland.

1714 Queen Anne, the last Stuart sovereign died—George I was proclaimed King of Britain under the Act of Settlement (1701), none of her children having survived her.

1779   Francis Scott Key, American poet who wrote *The Star-Spangled Banner*, which became the official US national anthem in 1931, born in Carroll County, Maryland.
1793   The kilogram was introduced in France as the first metric weight.
1798   Nelson, in the flagship *Vanguard*, was victorious in the Battle of the Nile at Aboukir Bay near Alexandria, against the French under Brueys aboard *L'Orient*, and thus isolated Napoleon and his army in Egypt.
1815   Richard Dana Jnr, American novelist and lawyer, born in Cambridge, Massachusetts.
1819   Herman Melville, American novelist, author of *Moby Dick*, born in New York City.
1831   New London Bridge, designed by John Rennie, was opened.
1876   Colorado, the Centennial State, became the 38th state of the Union.
1883   Parcel post was introduced in Britain.
1907   Eric Shipton, English mountaineer, born.
1921   Jack Kramer, tennis champion and promoter, born in Las Vegas, Nevada.
1924   Frank Worrell, West Indian Test cricketer, born in Bridgetown, Barbados.
1930   Lionel Bart, British composer, lyricist and playwright, born as Lionel Begleiter.
1936   The 11th Olympic Games opened in Berlin, where the Olympic flame was carried from Greece for the first time.
       Yves St Laurent, French fashion designer, born in Oran, Algeria.
1944   Post codes were first introduced, in Germany.
1968   The *Princess Margaret* inaugurated the English Channel Hovercraft service between Dover and Boulogne.
1969   The British pre-decimal halfpenny ceased to be legal tender.
1979   Queen Elizabeth The Queen Mother was installed as Lord Warden of the Cinque Ports, the first woman to hold the position.
1987   Eve Jackson completed the first microlight plane flight from Britain to Australia.

2 AUGUST   [215]

1100   King William II, called Rufus, was accidentally killed by an arrow while hunting in the New Forest—was succeeded by his brother as Henry I.
1776   The first signatures appeared on the US Declaration of Independence, adopted 29 days earlier in Philadelphia.
1784   The first specially constructed Royal Mail coach ran, from Bristol to London.

1788 Thomas Gainsborough, English painter of landscapes and portraits, including *The Blue Boy*, died.

1876 (James Butler) 'Wild Bill' Hickok was shot by Jack McCall while playing poker in a saloon in Deadwood, South Dakota.

1891 Sir Arthur Bliss, English composer, born in London.

1894 Death duties were introduced in Britain.

1905 Myrna Loy, American film actress, born in Helena, Montana as Myrna Williams.

1921 Enrico Caruso, internationally famous Italian operatic tenor, died in Naples.

1922 Alexander Graham Bell, Scottish-born inventor of the telephone in 1876, died at his home near Baddeck, Nova Scotia, aged 75.

1923 Warren Harding, American Republican statesman and 29th President from 1921, died in San Francisco on his return from a trip to Alaska—the remainder of his term of office was completed by Calvin Coolidge.

1925 Alan Whicker, television's most travelled reporter, born in Cairo, Egypt.

1932 Peter O'Toole, Irish actor, born in Connemara.

1934 Paul von Hindenburg, German military and political leader and President from 1925, died aged 86.

1936 Louis Blériot, French aviator and first to fly across the English Channel in 1909, died.

1945 Pietro Mascagni, Italian opera composer, best known for his *Cavalleria Rusticana*, died aged 81.

1970 During disturbances in Belfast the British Army fired rubber bullets for the first time.

---

3 AUGUST [216]

1492 Christopher Columbus left Palos de la Frontera in SW Spain on his famous westward voyage, in command of the small *Santa Maria*, attended by the *Pinta* and the *Nina*.

1721 Grinling Gibbons, English woodcarver, notably in St Paul's Cathedral, died.

1778 The famous Opera House La Scala in Milan, the work of Giuseppe Piermarini, was opened.

1792 Sir Richard Arkwright, English inventor who developed the mechanical cotton spinning process, died.

1801 Sir Joseph Paxton, English landscape gardener, architect and designer of the Crystal Palace, born in Milton Bryant, near Woburn, Bedfordshire.

1811 Elisha Graves Otis, American inventor, born in Halifax, Vermont.

1856 Alfred Deakin, Australian statesman and Prime Minister, born in Melbourne.

1858 Lake Victoria, the source of the Nile, was discovered by the English explorer John Speke.

1867 Stanley Baldwin, British statesman and three times Conservative Prime Minister, born in Bewdley, a market town on the river Severn.

1872 King Haakon VII of Norway, born in Charlottenlund.

1881 William George Fargo, co-founder of the Wells-Fargo Express Traffic service in 1852, died.

1887 Rupert Brooke, English poet, born in Rugby, the son of a housemaster at the public school.

1916 Sir Roger Casement, Irish nationalist, was hanged in London for treason, because of his attempts to induce Germany to support the cause of Irish independence.

1921 The first aerial crop spraying took place, at Troy, Ohio, to dust a grove infested with leaf caterpillars.

1924 Joseph Conrad, Polish-born novelist, author of *Lord Jim*, died.

1926 Tony Bennett, American singer and entertainer born in Astoria, New York as Anthony Benedetto.

1929 Emile Berliner, American inventor of the flat phonograph record, died.

1934 The German cabinet joined the offices of President and Chancellor and made Hitler 'Der Führer'.

1938 Terry Wogan, television broadcaster, born in Limerick, Ireland.

1956 The name of Bedloe's Island, the site of the Statue of Liberty, was changed to Liberty Island on the approval of President Eisenhower.

1958 The US submarine *Nautilus*, commanded by William Anderson, became the first ship to cross the North Pole beneath the ice.

1963 Michel Darbellay, Swiss climber, completed the first successful solo climb of the north wall of the Eiger.

1970 Miriam Hargrave, of Wakefield, Yorkshire, passed the driving test at the record 40th attempt and after 212 lessons.

1977 Archbishop Makarios, religious leader and President of Cyprus, died.

1988 Mathias Rust was freed from prison in Russia after serving 14 months of his four year sentence for landing his plane in Red Square.

---

4 AUGUST [217]

1265 The Battle of Evesham took place, in which Simon de Montfort was defeated and killed by Royalist forces led by the future King Edward I, during the Barons' War.

1792 (Percy Bysshe) P. B. Shelley, English romantic poet, born in
      Warnham, near Horsham, Sussex.
      John Burgoyne, British general in the War of American Independ-
      ence, who was forced to surrender at Saratoga in 1777 to General
      Gates, died.
1870 The Red Cross Society was founded in Britain by Lord Wantage.
      Sir Harry Lauder, Scottish comic singer and entertainer of the
      music hall, born in Portobello, near Edinburgh.
1875 Hans Christian Andersen, Danish writer of fairy tales, including
      The Ugly Duckling, died in Copenhagen.
1892 Lizzie Borden killed her stepmother and father by hacking them
      to death with an axe. She was tried later and found not guilty.
1900 Queen Elizabeth The Queen Mother, was born in St Paul's
      Waldenbury, Hertfordshire, as Elizabeth Angela Marguerite
      Bowes-Lyon, the ninth of ten children.
1908 Osbert Lancaster, English artist and cartoonist, born.
1913 Adrian Quist, Australian tennis champion, born in Medinia,
      South Australia.
1914 German troops invaded Belgium, in violation of the terms of the
      Treaty of London.
      Britain declared war on Germany.
1917 Captain Noel Chavasse, of the Royal Army Medical Corps, the
      second of only three to be awarded a bar to the Victoria Cross,
      died from his wounds.
1938 Pearl White, American actress and silent-film star, died in the
      American Hospital, Paris.
1939 British transatlantic airmail service was inaugurated by BOAC
      between Southampton and Montreal/New York; two flying boats
      maintaining a weekly service.
1942 David Lange, New Zealand Labour statesman and Prime
      Minister, born.
1958 Mary Decker, American athlete and record holder, born.
1961 Sir Sidney Holland, New Zealand statesman and Prime Minister
      from 1949 to 1957, died.

---

5 AUGUST   *[218]*

The oyster season opens.

1583 Sir Humphrey Gilbert founded the first English colony in North
      America, and called it St John's, Newfoundland.
1729 Thomas Newcomen, English inventor of the first atmospheric
      steam engine in 1705, died in London.
1754 James Gibbs, Scottish architect, especially responsible for St
      Martin's-in-the-Fields, died.

1792 Lord North, British Tory statesman and Prime Minister from 1770 to 1782, died.
1799 Richard Howe, British admiral and distinguished naval commander, died.
1815 Edward John Eyre, British explorer in Australia, born the son of a Yorkshire clergyman.
1852 The re-erection of the Crystal Palace began, at Sydenham, South London.
1858 The first transatlantic cable was completed by Cyrus Field, laid by USS *Niagara* and HMS *Agamemnon*, was opened by Queen Victoria and President Buchanan exchanging greetings.
1891 The first American Express travellers' cheque was cashed.
1895 Friedrich Engels, German Socialist, political writer and co-founder with Karl Marx of modern Communism, died in London.
1906 John Huston, American film director, born in Nevada, Missouri.
      Joan Hickson, English actress noted for her portrayal of 'Miss Marple', born.
1908 Harold Holt, Australian Liberal statesman, born in Sydney.
1911 Robert Taylor, American film actor, born in Filley, Nebraska as Spangler Arlington Brugh.
1914 The first electric traffic lights were erected, in Cleveland, Ohio.
1930 Neil Armstrong, American astronaut and first man on the moon, born in Wapakoneta, Ohio.
1960 Arthur Meighen, Canadian Conservative statesman and Prime Minister from 1920 to 1921, died.
1962 Marilyn Monroe, American film actress and sex symbol, tragically died in Los Angeles aged 36.
1986 Princess Anne rode her first winner, 'Gulfland' at Redcar, in her 13th ride as an amateur jockey.

6 AUGUST [219]

National day of Bolivia.

1623 Anne Hathaway, wife of William Shakespeare, died.
1637 Ben Jonson, English dramatist and poet, died in London.
1660 Diego Velasquez, Spanish painter, died in Madrid.
1775 Daniel O'Connell, Irish nationalist leader, born in County Kerry in the Republic of Ireland.
1809 Alfred, Lord Tennyson, English poet and Poet Laureate, born in Somersby rectory, Lincolnshire.
1825 Bolivia was proclaimed an independent Republic, free from nearly 300 years of Spanish rule, with Antonio Sucre its first President.

1866 John Mason Neale, English hymn writer, notably 'Jerusalem the golden' and 'O happy band of pilgrims', died in East Grinstead, Sussex.

1881 Sir Alexander Fleming, Scottish bacteriologist and discoverer of penicillin, born in Loudon, Ayrshire.

1890 The electric chair was used for the first time in America, at Auburn Prison, New York—the victim was murderer William Kemmler.

1891 William Slim, British Army field marshal, born in Bristol.

1893 The 3½-mile Corinth Canal of Southern Greece was opened.

1911 Lucille Ball, American comedy film actress, born in Jamestown, New York.

1916 Dom Mintoff, Labour politician and Prime Minister of Malta, born.

1917 Robert Mitchum, American film actor, born in Bridgeport, Connecticut.

1922 Freddie Laker, British airline operator, born.

1926 Gertrude Ederle of America became the first woman to swim the English Channel, crossing from Cap Gris Nez to Deal in 14½ hours.

1928 Andy Warhol, American pop artist, born in Pennsylvania.

1932 The first film festival was inaugurated, held in the Hotel Excelsior, Venice.

1934 Chris Bonington, British mountaineer and conqueror of Everest, born.

1945 An atom bomb was dropped on the Japanese city of Hiroshima, from a Boeing B29 bomber *Enola Gay*.

1949 John Haigh, the 'acid bath' murderer, was executed.

1962 Jamaica became independent after being a British colony for over 300 years.

1964 Sir Cedric Hardwicke, stage and film actor, knighted in 1934, died in New York.

1970 Kevin Murphy became the first Briton to swim the English Channel both ways non-stop, occupying 35 hours and 10 minutes swimming time.

1978 Pope Paul VI (Giovanni Battista Montini), died aged 80.

---

7 AUGUST [220]

1657 Robert Blake, one of the greatest of Britain's naval commanders, died as his ship entered Plymouth harbour.

1831 Dean Farrar, English clergyman and writer of school stories, notably *Eric, or Little by Little*, born in Bombay.

1834 Joseph Jacquard, French silk weaver and inventor of the first loom to weave patterns, died.

1858 The rules for Australian Football were formulated.
     Ottawa, the choice of Queen Victoria, was made the capital of the
     Dominion of Canada.
1876 Mata Hari, Dutch dancer, courtesan and spy, born in Leeu-
     warden as Margarete Gertrude Zelle.
1925 Summer time or daylight saving, introduced in Britain on 21 May
     1916 by William Willett, was made permanent.
1926 The first British Motor Racing Grand Prix was held, at the
     Brooklands track, over a distance of 110 laps and 287 miles.
1942 Guadalcanal, in the southern Solomon Islands, was assaulted by
     US Marines in one of the most costly Pacific campaigns of World
     War II. Was finally won the following January.
1948 Greg Chappell, Australian Test cricketer and captain, born.
1957 Oliver Hardy, of Laurel and Hardy fame, died.
1970 Syd Buller, one of the world's leading cricket umpires, collapsed
     and died during the break in play in the county championship at
     Edgbaston, Warwickshire.

8 AUGUST [221]

1827 George Canning, British Tory statesman, but Prime Minister for
     just over three months, died in Chiswick, London.
1870 The first America's Cup race, open to challenge by any nation's
     yachts, took place—*Magic* of the United States beating the British
     challenge of *Cambria*.
1876 Frank Richards, English author associated with the character
     'Billy Bunter', born in Ealing as Charles Hamilton.
1880 Sir Earle Page, Australian statesman, born.
1900 The Davis Cup for tennis, presented by Dwight Filley Davis, was
     contested for the first time, at Brookline, Massachusetts—won by
     USA on 10th.
1901 Ernest Orlando Lawrence, US physicist, born in Canton, South
     Dakota.
1914 The first British troops landed in France.
1919 (Frank Winfield) F. W. Woolworth, American merchant and
     founder in 1879 of the store that bears his name, died.
1931 America's airship *Akron* was launched by Mrs Hoover.
1937 Dustin Hoffman, American film actor and winner of two Oscars,
     for *Kramer vs Kramer* (1979) and *Rainman* (1989), born in Los
     Angeles, California.
1938 Connie Stevens, American singer, born in Brooklyn as Concetta
     Ingolia.
1940 The Battle of Britain began, countering the German air attack.
1953 Nigel Mansell, English motor racing champion, born.

1963 The Great Train Robbery took place at Sears Crossing at Mentmore, near Cheddington, Buckinghamshire, on the Glasgow to London mail train. The haul was over 2½ million pounds in bank notes on their way for destruction.

1974 Richard Nixon announced his resignation as US President—the first to do so—because of his implication in the Watergate scandal.

1979 Nicholas Monsarrat, English novelist of the sea, notably *The Cruel Sea*, died.

1988 The Duchess of York gave birth to a daughter in London's Portland Hospital. She was named Princess Beatrice of York.

---

9 AUGUST [222]

1593 Izaak Walton, English writer, author of *The Compleat Angler* on the pleasures of fishing, born in Stafford.

1631 John Dryden, English poet and critic, born at the vicarage of Aldwinkle All Saints, Northamptonshire.

1757 Thomas Telford, Scottish engineer of roads, canals and bridges, born in Westerkirk, near Langholm, the son of a shepherd.

1809 William Travis, Texas revolutionary army officer, born in Red Banks, South Carolina.

1848 Frederick Marryat, English writer of sea adventure novels, notably *Mr Midshipman Easy*, died in Langham, Norfolk.

1902 The coronation of King Edward VII took place—having been put back some six weeks because of the need of an emergency appendicitis operation.

1938 Rod Laver, Australian tennis champion, born in Rockhampton, State of Queensland.

1943 Ken Norton, a world heavyweight boxing champion, born in Jacksonville, Illinois.

1945 The second atom bomb of the war was dropped on the Japanese city of Nagasaki.

1965 Singapore seceded from the Federation of Malaysia and became an independent republic within the Commonwealth.

1974 Gerald Ford was sworn in as the 38th President of America, on the resignation of Richard Nixon—the first to serve without being chosen by the people in a national election.

1975 Dmitri Shostakovich, Soviet composer, died.

National day of Ecuador.

1675 Greenwich Observatory was established by King Charles II, and its foundation stone laid.

1810 Count Cavour, Italian statesman, primarily responsible for the unification of his country, born in Turin.

1821 Missouri, the Show Me State, became the 24th state of the Union.

1846 The Smithsonian Institution was established in Washington, DC, by the bequest of British scientist James Smithson.

1874 Herbert Hoover, American Republican statesman and 31st President, born in West Branch, Iowa, the son of a blacksmith.

1885 The first electric street-railway in the United States was opened in Baltimore by Leo Daft.

1896 Otto Lilienthal, German engineer and gliding pioneer, died as a result of a glider crash the previous day.

1897 Britain's Royal Automobile Club was founded, under the name of 'The Automobile Club of Great Britain'.

1904 Geraldo, English dance-band leader, born in London as Gerald Bright.

1928 Eddie Fisher, American singer, born in Philadelphia, Pennsylvania.

1966 America's first moon satellite, *Orbiter I*, was launched.

1976 Bert Oldfield, Australian wicket-keeper and Test cricketer, died aged 81.

1711 The first Royal Ascot horserace meeting took place—attended by Queen Anne.

1873 Bertram Mills, English circus proprietor, born in London.

1890 Cardinal Newman, English churchman and leader of the Oxford Movement which intended to restore high-Church ideals, died in Edgbaston, Warwickshire aged 89.

1897 Enid Blyton, English writer of children's books, born in East Dulwich, South London.

1919 Andrew Carnegie, Scottish-born American steel industrialist and philanthropist, died in Lennox, Massachusetts aged 83.

1921 Alex Haley, American author of the best seller *Roots*, born in Ithaca, New York.

1922 Ron Grainer, composer, born in Atherton, Australia.

1942 The New Waterloo Bridge over the Thames opened to traffic.

1952 King Hussein succeeded as King of Jordan on the deposition of his father, King Talal, because of mental illness.
1956 Jackson Pollock, American painter, leader of Abstract Expressionist movement and later initiator of the Op art movement of the 1950s and 1960s, died.
1960 Chad, a member state of the French Community in Northern Africa, became an independent Republic.
1965 Bill Woodfull, Australian cricketer in 35 Tests, died.

12 AUGUST [225]

The grouse shooting season opens in Britain.

1762 King George IV born in St James's Palace in London's Pall Mall, the eldest son of George III.
1774 Robert Southey, English poet and Poet Laureate, born in Bristol.
1827 William Blake, English poet and artist, died in London.
1848 George Stephenson, English engineer who constructed the *Rocket* and the first railway in 1825, from Stockton to Darlington, died in Tapton, near Chesterfield, Derbyshire.
1863 Hampshire County Cricket Club was founded in Southampton.
1881 Cecil B. De Mille, American film producer, noted for his biblical epics, born in Ashfield, Massachusetts.
1918 Guy Gibson, British Air Force pilot and commander, born in Simla, India.
1922 Arthur Griffith, Irish statesman, founder of the Sinn Fein and President of the Irish Free State, died.
1925 Norris and Ross McWhirter, editors and compilers of the *Guinness Book of Records*, born.
1944 'PLUTO'—'Pipe Line Under The Ocean'—supplying petrol across the English Channel to the allied forces in France, went into operation, from Shanklin on the Isle of Wight.
1953 It was reported that Russia exploded her first hydrogen bomb, in the Pacific—was announced from Moscow on 20 August.
1955 Thomas Mann, German novelist and Nobel Prize winner, died in Zurich aged 80.
1958 The US nuclear submarine *Skate*, commanded by James Calvert, became the second ship to make an underwater crossing of the North Pole.
1960 The first communications satellite was launched—America's *Echo I*.
1964 Ian Fleming, English author and creator of the hero 'James Bond' died.
1979 Sir Ernst Chain, English biochemist who shared the Nobel Prize in 1945, died in Ireland.
1982 Henry Fonda, American film actor, died aged 77.

1704   The Battle of Blenheim took place in southern Germany, in which an Anglo-Austrian army under Marlborough and Prince Eugene decisively defeated the French and Bavarian armies in the War of the Spanish Succession.

1818   Lucy Stone, American feminist and reformer, born in West Brookfield, Massachusetts.

1826   René Laennec, French physician who invented and named the stethoscope in 1819, died.

1860   Annie Oakley, American entertainer as a marksman with rifle and shotgun, born in Patterson, Ohio as Phoebe Anne Oakley Mozee.

1877   Birkenhead, on Merseyside, became a borough, with John Laird its first Lord Mayor.

1888   John Logie Baird, Scottish pioneer of television, born in Helensburgh, on the Firth of Clyde.

1896   Sir John Millais, English painter and a founder member of the Pre-Raphaelite Brotherhood, died, and was buried in St Paul's Cathedral.

1898   Jean Borotra, French tennis champion, born.

1899   Alfred Hitchcock, American film producer and master of suspense, born in Leytonstone, London, the son of a greengrocer.

1907   Sir Basil Spence, Scottish architect, designer of the new Coventry Cathedral, born in India.

1910   Florence Nightingale, English nurse in the Crimean War and founder of modern nursing, died in London aged 90.

1912   Ben Hogan, American golfing champion, born in Stephenville, Texas.

1913   Archbishop Makarios, President of Cyprus, born near Paphos, the son of a farmer.

1919   George Shearing, British blind pianist, born in London.

1927   Fidel Castro, Cuban revolutionary and political leader, born near Biran, the son of a sugar planter.

1946   (Herbert George) H. G. Wells, English writer and pioneer in science fiction, died in London aged 79.

1959   Work on the cable suspension Verrazano–Narrows Bridge project across the entrance to New York City harbour began.

1961   The border between East and West Berlin was sealed off by East Germany with the closure of the Brandenburg Gate to stop the exodus to the West.

1964   The last hangings in Britain took place—Peter Allen at Walton Gaol, Liverpool and John Walby at Strangeways Gaol, Manchester.

1977   Henry Williamson, English author, notably *Tarka the Otter* and *Salar the Salmon*, died.

1986 Jack Nicklaus won the US Masters golf championship for a record sixth time.

14 AUGUST [227]

1778 Augustus Toplady, English clergyman and hymn writer, especially 'Rock of Ages', died.

1816 Tristan da Cunha, a group of four islands in the South Atlantic were annexed to and garrisoned by Britain.

1867 John Galsworthy, English novelist, playwright and Nobel Prize winner, born in Combe, Surrey.

1893 France became the first country to introduce motor vehicle registration plates.

1895 Jack Gregory, New South Wales and Australian Test cricketer, born.

1908 The first international beauty contest in Britain was held, at the Pier Hippodrome in Folkestone, Kent.

1913 Fred Davis, English snooker player and three times world champion, born in Chesterfield, the younger brother of Joe.

1920 The 7th Olympic Games opened in Antwerp.

1922 Lord Alfred Harmsworth, British newspaper publisher who launched the *London Evening News*, *Daily Mail*, *Daily Mirror* and *The Times*, died.

1945 Japanese surrendered, ending World War II—the formal surrender took place aboard USS *Missouri* on 2 September.

1951 William Randolph Hearst, American newspaper owner and publisher, died aged 88.

1982 Barclay's Bank opened on Saturday for the first time in 13 years.

1988 Enzo Ferrari, racing pioneer and Italy's greatest sports car builder, died at his home in Modena aged 90.

15 AUGUST [228]

1769 Napoleon Bonaparte, French military leader and Emperor, born in Ajaccio, capital of the Mediterranean island of Corsica, the son of a lawyer.

1771 Sir Walter Scott, Scottish novelist and poet, born in Edinburgh.

1856 Keir Hardie, Scottish Labour leader and one of the founders of the Labour Party, born near Holytown, Lanarkshire.

1872 The first Parliamentary election held by secret ballot in Britain took place in Pontefract, Yorkshire.

1879 Ethel Barrymore, American stage and screen actress, the first lady of the American theatre, born in Philadelphia as Ethel Blythe.
1885 Sir Montague Burton, English multiple tailor, born of Jewish parents in Lithuania.
1888 (Thomas Edward) T. E. Lawrence, British soldier and writer who became known as 'Lawrence of Arabia', born in Tremadoc, Wales.
1914 The first ship, the SS *Ancon*, passed through the Panama Canal.
1917 Jack Lynch, Irish statesman and Prime Minister, born.
1925 Oscar Peterson, jazz pianist, born in Montreal, Canada.
1930 Tom Mboya, Kenyan politician and leader in his country's struggle for independence, born.
1935 Wiley Post, American aviator, was killed in a plane crash in Alaska—with passenger, American humorist, Will Rogers.
1947 India became independent, with Pandit Nehru its first Prime Minister.
1948 South Korea became independent and was formally proclaimed as the Republic of Korea, with Syngman Rhee its first President.
1950 Princess Anne (Anne Elizabeth Alice Louise) was born in Clarence House, London, the second child and only daughter of Queen Elizabeth II.
1971 Paul Lukas, US film actor and winner of an Oscar in 1943 for his role in *Watch on the Rhine*, died aged 80.
1972 Pat Pocock took seven wickets in 11 balls for Surrey v Sussex at Eastbourne.
1987 Septuplets, four girls and three boys, were born to Susan Halton in Liverpool's Oxford Street Hospital, with a combined weight of 9½ pounds. None survived, the last one dying on 31 August.

---

16 AUGUST

1743 The earliest prize-ring code of boxing rules was formulated in England by the champion pugilist Jack Broughton.
1819 The Peterloo massacre took place in St Peter's Fields, Manchester. The large meeting held there, petitioning for Parliamentary reform, was dispersed by the Army—killing 11.
1899 Robert Bunsen, German chemist, physicist and inventor of the gas burner that bears his name, died aged 88.
1912 Ted Drake, Arsenal and England footballer, born.
1930 Ted Hughes, English Poet Laureate, born in Mytholmroyd, West Yorkshire.
1948 George Herman 'Babe' Ruth, the legendary American baseball player, died in New York City.

1950 Jeff Thomson, Australian cricketer and fast bowler, born.

1952 Severe thunderstorms in Somerset and North Devon caused rivers to flood, bringing devastation to the town of Lynmouth.

1956 Bela Lugosi, Hungarian-American film actor, best known for horror films, especially *Dracula*, died.

1958 Madonna, American singer and actress, born in Bay City, Michigan as Madonna Louise Veronica Ciccone.

1960 Cyprus became an independent Republic, with Archbishop Makarios its first President.

1977 Elvis Presley, American rock-and-roll singer and film actor, died in Memphis, Tennessee.

1979 John George Diefenbaker, Canadian Conservative politician and Prime Minister from 1957 to 1963, died aged 83.

17 AUGUST [230]

National day of Indonesia.

1786 Frederick the Great, military leader and King of Prussia since 1740, died in Potsdam.
Davy Crockett, American frontiersman and later Congressman, born in Limestone, Tennessee.

1807 Robert Fulton made the first practical steamboat trip, 150 miles in *Clermont* from New York City to Albany.

1892 Mae West, American film actress and sex symbol, born in Brooklyn, New York, the daughter of a boxer.

1896 The first gold was discovered in the Klondike.

1921 Maureen O'Hara, Irish-American film actress, born in Dublin as Maureen Fitzsimmons.

1938 Henry Armstrong won the lightweight boxing title, and so became the only man in the ring's history to hold three world titles at different weights, at the same time.

1945 Indonesia was proclaimed independent, following Japanese occupation.

1951 Alan Minter, British middleweight boxing champion, born in Penge, London.

1952 Nelson Piquet, a world champion Grand Prix motor racing driver, born in Brazil.

1957 Robin Cousins, British ice skating champion, born in Bristol.

1958 Kirk Stevens, Canadian international snooker player, born.

1961 The construction of the Berlin Wall by the Russians began, separating East and West.

1978 Three Americans, Ben Abruzzo, Maxie Anderson and Larry Newman, made the first balloon crossing of the North Atlantic. They floated for five days in *Double Eagle II* on its 3200-mile trip.

1983 Ira Gershwin, American lyricist and elder brother of George, died in Beverly Hills, California.
1987 Rudolf Hess committed suicide in allied hands in Spandau Prison, at the age of 93.

18 AUGUST   [231]

1587 Virginia Dare became the first child born of English parents in the New World—on Roanoke Island, North Carolina—seven days after Sir Walter Raleigh's second expedition landed.
1774 Meriwether Lewis, American explorer, born in Albemarle County, Virginia.
1809 Matthew Boulton, English engineer and partner of James Watt, died in Soho, London.
1850 Honoré de Balzac, French novelist, died in Paris.
1857 Work began on the 7½ mile Mont Cenis rail tunnel linking France and Italy.
1875 Somerset County Cricket Club was founded.
1917 Caspar Weinberger, US Republican statesman and Secretary of Defence, born in San Francisco.
1920 Godfrey Evans, Kent and England cricketer, born in Finchley.
1922 Shelley Winters, American film actress, born in St Louis, Missouri as Shirley Schrift.
1927 Rosalynn Carter, wife of America's 39th President, born in Plains, Georgia as Rosalynn Smith.
1932 Scottish aviator Jim Mollison made the first westbound transatlantic solo flight, from Portmarnock, Ireland to Pennfield, New Brunswick.
1933 Roman Polanski, French film director, born in Paris.
1937 Robert Redford, American film actor, born in Santa Monica, California.
1948 Lester Piggott, aged 12, rode his first winner, on only his seventh ride.
1960 The birth control pill was launched in America.

19 AUGUST   [232]

1274 The Coronation of Edward I took place.
1646 John Flamsteed, English astronomer and first Astronomer Royal, born in Denby near Derby.
1662 Blaise Pascal, French philosopher and mathematician who invented the first digital calculator, died in Paris.

1743 Comtesse du Barry, the last mistress of Louis XV, born in Vaucouleurs as Marie Jeanne Bécu, the daughter of a dressmaker.

1745 After travelling from France to claim the throne of Britain, Bonnie Prince Charlie raised his father's standard at Glenfinnan.

1808 James Nasmyth, Scottish engineer who invented the first steam hammer, born in Edinburgh.

1819 James Watt, Scottish engineer and inventor of the modern steam engine under a patent of 1769, died in Heathfield Hall, near Birmingham aged 83.

1871 Orville Wright, American pioneer aviator, born in Dayton, Ohio, the younger of the two brothers.

1883 'Coco' Chanel, French fashion designer, born near Issoire as Gabrielle Chanel.

1897 The first taxi-cab, with limited range, began operating in Britain, in the City and West End of London.

1902 Ogden Nash, American poet known for his humorous verse, born in New York.

1928 Viscount Haldane, British statesman who re-organised the Army and founded the Territorials in 1908, died in London.

1929 Sergei Diaghilev, Russian ballet impresario and director, died.

1931 Willie Shoemaker, American champion jockey, the first to ride over 8000 winners, born near Fabens, Texas.

1942 Canadian and British Commandos raided the French port of Dieppe in Normandy—was called 'Operation Jubilee'.

1943 Billy J. Kramer, English pop singer, born.

1944 Sir Henry Wood, English conductor and co-founder of the Promenade Concerts in 1895, died in Hitchin, Hertfordshire.

1976 Alastair Sim, British comedy actor, died.

1981 Jessie Matthews, English stage and radio star, died in a London hospital.

1987 The Hungerford massacre took place, when gun-crazy Michael Ryan shot dead 16 people in the Berkshire town—and then himself.

1988 Sir Frederick Ashton, British dancer, choreographer and Director of the Royal Ballet, died in his Suffolk home, aged 83.

---

20 AUGUST [233]

1833 Benjamin Harrison, American Republican statesman and 23rd President, born in North Bend, Ohio, the son of a member of Congress and grandson of the 9th President.

1905 Jack Teagarden, American trombonist and orchestra leader, born in Vernon, Texas.

1906 'Bunny' Austin, English international tennis champion, born in London.

1912 William Booth, English social reformer, evangelist, founder and 'General' of the Salvation Army, died aged 83.

1921 Jacqueline Susann, American novelist, notably *Valley of the Dolls*, born in Philadelphia, Pennsylvania.

1924 Jim Reeves, American singer and entertainer, born in Panola County, Texas.

1940 Leon Trotsky, Russian revolutionary, was assassinated in Coyoacan near Mexico City—the killer was identified as Ramon Mercador del Rio.

1944 Rajiv Gandhi, younger son of Prime Minister Indira Gandhi, born.

1945 Lend-lease Act of 1941, whereby the US Congress offered military supplies to Britain and her allies, was officially terminated after the cessation of hostilities of World War II.

1956 Calder Hall in Cumbria, the world's first large-scale atomic power station, began generating.

1965 Clive Inman, Leicestershire batsman, scored 50 in a record eight minutes, at Trent Bridge cricket ground.

1968 Russian and troops of other Communist countries invaded Czechoslovakia.

1974 Nolan Ryan, at Anaheim Stadium, California, was measured to pitch a baseball at a record 100.9 m.p.h.

1975 *Viking I* was launched, on its way to Mars.

1977 Julius or 'Groucho' Marx, American comedian of the famous Marx Brothers, died in Los Angeles.
The *Voyager I* spacecraft was launched on its journey via Jupiter and Saturn to become the first man-made object to leave the Solar system.

1980 Italian mountaineer Reinhold Messner became the first to complete an entire climb of Everest solo.

---

21 AUGUST [234]

1754 William Murdock, Scottish engineer and inventor of coal-gas lighting in 1792, born in Auchinleck, Ayrshire.

1765 King William IV, the 'Sailor King', born in Buckingham Palace, the third son of King George III and Queen Charlotte.

1808 The Battle of Vimiero in the Peninsular War took place in Portugal, with Wellington defeating General Junot's French forces.

1879 An apparition of the Blessed Virgin was reported in the village of Knock, County Mayo, in the Republic of Ireland for the first time.

1904 Count Basie, American jazz pianist and band leader, born in Red Bank, New Jersey as William Basie.

1911 Leonardo da Vinci's painting of the *Mona Lisa* was stolen from the Louvre in Paris by an Italian waiter Vicenzo Perruggia—was recovered in 1913.

1930 Princess Margaret born in Glamis Castle in Angus, Scotland, the younger sister of Queen Elizabeth II.

1936 Wilt Chamberlain, American basketball player, born in Philadelphia, Pennsylvania.

1944 Meetings started at Dumbarton Oaks in Washington, DC, building the foundations of the charter of the United Nations—ended on 7 October.

1951 Constant Lambert, English composer and conductor, died in London two days before his forty-sixth birthday.

1959 Hawaii, the Aloha State, became the 50th state of the Union.
Sir Jacob Epstein, British sculptor, died.

1962 *Savannah*, the world's first nuclear-powered merchant ship, went on her maiden voyage.

1965 Spacecraft *Gemini 5* was launched, with Gordon Cooper and Charles Conrad.
K. Peacock became the first substitute to be called on in a Football League match, for Charlton Athletic at Bolton.

---

22 AUGUST [235]

1485 The Battle of Bosworth Field, the last of the Wars of the Roses, took place near Market Bosworth, Leicestershire, in which Richard III was defeated and killed by the forces of Henry VII.

1642 The Civil War in England began, between the supporters of Charles I (Royalists or Cavaliers) and of Parliament (Roundheads), when the King raised his standard at Nottingham.

1788 The British settlement in Sierra Leone was founded, the purpose of which was to secure a home in Africa for freed slaves and homeless Africans from England.

1806 Jean Fragonard, French painter, died.

1818 Warren Hastings, British administrator and first Governor-General of British India, died in Worcestershire aged 85.

1845 Surrey County Cricket Club was founded at a meeting at The Horns, Kennington.

1847 John Forrest, Australian explorer and politician, born in Bunbury, Western Australia.

1862 Claude Debussy, French romantic composer, born in St Germain-en-Laye near Paris.

1892 Percy Fender, Surrey and England cricketer, born in Balham, London.

1897 Bill Woodfull, Australian Test cricketer, born.

1922 Michael Collins, Irish politician and revolutionary, was assassinated by extremist Republicans in an ambush between Bandon and Macroom in Ireland.

1933 The first boxing match was televised in Britain, at Broadcasting House in London.

1940 Sir Oliver Lodge, English physicist and pioneer of wireless telegraphy, died.

1942 Michel Fokine, Russian dancer and choreographer, died.

1957 Steve Davis, world number one snooker player, born in Plumstead, London.

1963 Viscount Nuffield, British motor car magnate and philanthropist, died.

1964 Mats Wilander, Swedish international tennis player, born.

1978 Jomo Kenyatta, Kenyan leader and his country's first President in 1964, died.

1988 All-day drinking in England began, by a new law allowing pubs, wine bars and clubs to serve drinks from 11 a.m. to 11 p.m. every day except Sunday.

23 AUGUST [236]

National day of Romania.

1305 William Wallace, Scottish patriot and leader against the English to obtain his country's independence, was hanged in London.

1628 The Duke of Buckingham, British statesman and favourite of King James I, was assassinated at Portsmouth by a subaltern, John Felton.

1754 Louis XVI, King of France, born at Versailles, the only son of Louis XV.

1793 By decree France introduced the first national conscription, claiming all unmarried men aged 18 to 25.

1866 The Treaty of Prague was signed, ending the war between Austria and Prussia.

1905 Constant Lambert, composer and musician, born in London.

1912 Gene Kelly, American film actor and dancer in Hollywood musicals, born in Pittsburgh, Pennsylvania.

1913 Bob Crosby, American musician and bandleader, born in Spokane, Washington, the younger brother of Bing.

1914 The Battle of Mons, in Belgium near the French frontier, took place—the first important engagement fought by the British Expeditionary Force commanded by Sir John French.

1926 Rudolph Valentino, American film actor and romantic idol, died suddenly in a New York hospital at the age of 31.

1929 Peter Thomson, Australian golfing champion, born in Melbourne.

221

1938 Len Hutton completed an innings of 364, lasting 13 hours 17 minutes, for England against Australia in the fifth Test at the Oval, out of a record score of 903.

1944 Paris was liberated—having been captured and occupied by German forces since 14 June 1940.

1949 Geoff Capes, British Olympic shot-putter and international strong man, born in Holbeach, Lincolnshire.

1960 Oscar Hammerstein II, American lyricist, known for his collaboration with Richard Rodgers, died.

---

24 AUGUST   [237]

---

79 The cities of Pompeii, Herculaneum and Stabiae were destroyed by the eruption of Vesuvius, a volcano presumed extinct.

1572 The St Bartholomew's Day massacre took place in Paris—the massacre of thousands of French Huguenots, by order of the Catholic French court.

1680 Colonel Blood, Irish adventurer, noted for his attempt to steal the Crown jewels from the Tower of London in 1671, died.

1724 George Stubbs, English anatomist and painter of animals, especially horses, born in Liverpool.

1759 William Wilberforce, English philanthropist and anti-slavery campaigner, born in Hull on Humberside, the son of a merchant.

1814 The Capitol and the White House at Washington were burned by British troops under General Ross.

1862 The British flag was pulled down on the ship *Enrica*, and when the Confederate flag was raised, the *Alabama* was born.

1872 Sir Max Beerbohm, English writer and caricaturist, born in London.

1892 Goodison Park, the home of Everton Football Club in Liverpool, was opened.

1903 Graham Sutherland, English artist, born in London.

1958 Johannes Strijdom, South African statesman and Prime Minister from 1954, died in office.

---

25 AUGUST   [238]

National day of Uruguay.

1530 Ivan the Terrible, Tsar of Russia, born.

1819 Allan Pinkerton, American founder of the national detective agency in Chicago that bears his name, born in Glasgow, Scotland.

1822   Sir William Herschel, German-born English astronomer who
        discovered the planet Uranus in 1781, died.
1825   Uruguay gained independence from Spain under José Artigas.
1867   Michael Faraday, English physicist and founder of the science of
        electro-magnetism, died in Hampton Court, London.
1875   Captain Matthew Webb became the first to swim the English
        Channel, swimming breaststroke from Admiralty Pier, Dover to
        Calais in just under 22 hours.
1918   Leonard Bernstein, American composer and conductor, born in
        Lawrence, Massachusetts.
        Richard Greene, British film actor, born in Plymouth, Devon.
1919   George Wallace, American Democrat politician and Governor,
        born in Clio, Alabama.
        Daily air service began between London (Hounslow) and Paris
        (Le Bourget).
1927   Althea Gibson, the first black person to win a major honour at
        tennis, notably the US and Wimbledon Ladies' singles titles, born
        in Silver, South Carolina.
1928   Anfield's famous Kop terracing at Liverpool's football ground
        was opened. It was most likely named after the Battle of Spion
        Kop in the Boer War (1899–1902). The word 'Kopje' means small
        hill.
1930   Sean Connery, British film actor, born in Edinburgh as Thomas
        Connery.
1938   Frederick Forsyth, English novelist, notably *The Day of the Jackal*
        and *The Odessa File*, born.
1940   The first air raid on Berlin took place, with 'Whitleys', 'Hamp-
        dens' and 'Wellingtons'.
1942   The Duke of Kent, the son of King George V, was killed on active
        service.
1956   Alfred Charles Kinsey, American sexologist, died.
1960   The 17th Olympic Games opened in Rome.
1967   Paul Muni, Austrian-born American film actor and Academy
        Award (Oscar) winner in 1936 for his role in *The Story of Louis
        Pasteur*, died.
        Stanley Bruce, Australian Nationalist statesman and 12th Prime
        Minister from 1923 to 1929, died.
1968   Stan McCabe, Australian cricketer in 39 Test matches, died.
1979   Stan Kenton, American musician and orchestra leader, died.

26 AUGUST   [239]

1346   The Battle of Crécy took place, 32 miles south of Boulogne, the
        scene of Edward III's victory over Philip VI of France in the
        Hundred Years War—the first use of the English longbow in
        continental warfare.

1676   Sir Robert Walpole, statesman regarded as the first British Prime Minister, born in Houghton Hall, Norfolk.

1743   Antoine Lavoisier, French founder of modern chemistry, born in Paris.

1819   Albert, German prince and Consort of Queen Victoria, born in Rosenau near Coburg, Bavaria.

1875   John Buchan, Scottish novelist and statesman, born in Perth.

1884   Earl Biggers, American novelist, born in Warren, Ohio.

1920   The right to vote was given to women in America, by the 19th amendment.

Percy Fender, Surrey cricketer, scored a century in a record 35 minutes, at Northampton.

1930   Lon Chaney, American silent-screen actor known as the 'man of a thousand faces', died.

1936   Leslie Mitchell became the first television announcer in Britain when he announced the BBC's programme at Olympia.

1952   A Canberra bomber flew from Aldergrove, Northern Ireland to Gander, Newfoundland, and returned the same day, covering 4146 miles in eight hours.

1958   Ralph Vaughan Williams, English composer, died in London aged 85.

1972   Sir Francis Chichester, English aviator and round-the-world yachtsman, died in Plymouth, Devon.

The 20th Olympic Games opened in Munich.

1974   Charles Lindbergh, American aviator noted for being the first to fly the Atlantic solo non-stop in 1927, died.

1978   Charles Boyer, French romantic actor, died two days before his 79th birthday.

Cardinal Albino Luciani of Venice was elected as Pope John Paul I.

27 AUGUST   [240]

1576   Titian, one of the greatest Venetian painters, died in Venice.

1856   The first Australian Parliamentary election held by secret ballot took place in Victoria, Australia.

1859   The first commercially productive oil well was drilled, near Titusville, Pennsylvania, by Edwin Drake of Seneca Oil.

1877   Charles Stewart Rolls, aeronaut and partner of Rolls Royce fame, born in London.

1879   Sir Rowland Hill, English pioneer in postal services and deviser of the Penny Post in 1840, died.

1882   Sam Goldwyn, American film producer and pioneer in the film industry, born of Jewish parents in Warsaw as Samuel Goldfish (Gelbfisch).

1883 Krakatoa, a volcanic island in the Sunda Strait between Sumatra and Java, erupted with thousands killed by the resulting tidal waves.

1886 Eric Coates, English violinist and composer of light orchestral works, born in Hucknall, Nottinghamshire.

1899 (Cecil Scott) C. S. Forester, English novelist, creator of 'Captain Horatio Hornblower', born in Cairo, Egypt.

1908 Sir Donald Bradman, Australian cricketer of distinction, born in Cootamundra, New South Wales.
     Lyndon Baines Johnson, American Democrat statesman and 36th President, born in Johnson City, Texas.

1910 Mother Teresa of Calcutta, nun dedicated to the relief of the poor in India, born in Skopje, now in Yugoslavia, of Albanian parents. Her community is called Missionaries of Charity.

1919 Louis Botha, South African Boer general, statesman and first Prime Minister of the Union in 1910, died.

1928 The Kellogg-Briand Peace Pact, renouncing war, was signed in Paris.

1939 The world's first jet-propelled aeroplane, the Heinkel 178, with engine designed by Dr Von Ohain, made its first flight, at Marienehe, North Germany.

1957 Bernhard Langer, international golfing champion, born in Germany.

1958 Ernest Orlando Lawrence, US physicist and Nobel Prize winner, died.

1962 The US spacecraft *Mariner II* was launched to make the first interplanetary space-shot.

1966 Francis Chichester left Plymouth in *Gipsy Moth IV* on his single-handed voyage around the world—arriving back at Plymouth on the following 28 May.

1967 Brian Epstein, who managed the Beatles to rock stardom, died in a swimming pool accident.

1975 Haile Selassie, the deposed Emperor of Ethiopia, nicknamed 'The Lion of Judah', died in exile.

1979 Earl Mountbatten was murdered by members of the IRA, in a fishing boat off Mullaghmore, County Sligo.

28 AUGUST [241]

1207 Liverpool was created a borough by King John.

1749 Johann Goethe, German poet and novelist, author of *Faust*, born in Frankfurt-am-Main, the son of a lawyer.

1828 Count Leo Tolstoy, Russian novelist and philosopher, born of noble family in Tula Province.

1840 Ira Sankey, American hymn writer and evangelist with Dwight Moody, born in Edinburgh, Pennsylvania.

1899 Charles Boyer, French romantic actor, born in Figeac.

1913 Lindsay Hassett, Australian Test cricketer, born in Geelong in the State of Victoria.

1933 The BBC made the first broadcast appeal on behalf of the police, for Stanley Hobday, wanted for murder.

1944 David Soul, American film actor, best known as star of *Starsky and Hutch*, born in Chicago as David Solberg.

1962 Paul Allen, at 17, the youngest player to take part in an FA Cup final, born.

1972 Prince William of Gloucester was killed in an air crash.

---

29 AUGUST   [242]

1782 The 100-ton battleship HMS *Royal George* sank while at anchor at Spithead, with the loss of more than 900 lives, including Admiral Kempenfelt.

1835 Melbourne in Australia was founded, and was named after Lord Melbourne, the Prime Minister of Britain at the time. The city on the river Yarra was designed by Robert Russell.

1842 The Treaty of Nanking was signed, ending the Opium War (1839–42) between China and Britain, ceding Hong Kong to Britain.

1862 Andrew Fisher, Australian Labour statesman, born in Crosshouse, Kilmarnock.

1877 Brigham Young, American Mormon leader and founder of Salt Lake City, Utah, died.

1882 England cricketers lost to Australia in England for the first time, and from an epitaph that appeared in the *Sporting Times* the word 'Ashes' came into being.

1885 The first motorcycle was patented, built by Gottlieb Daimler in Cannstatt, Germany.

1895 The Rugby League was formed at a meeting in the George Hotel in Huddersfield, with 21 representatives of the leading Lancashire and Yorkshire Rugby Union clubs—the present title of 'Rugby League' was adopted in 1922.

1897 'Chop-suey', the most famous Chinese dish, was devised by a New York chef to appeal to Chinese and American tastes.

1898 Walter Lindrum, world billiards champion, born in Australia.

1904 The 3rd Olympic Games opened in St Louis, Missouri.

1909 The first air race took place at Reims, France, 'The Gordon Bennett', and was won by Glenn Curtiss.

1915 Ingrid Bergman, American film actress and twice Oscar winner, born in Stockholm.

1920 Charlie Parker, American jazz alto-saxophonist, born in Kansas City.
1923 Richard Attenborough, English film actor, producer and director, born in Cambridge.
1924 Dinah Washington, American blues singer, born in Tuscaloosa, Alabama as Ruth Jones.
1930 William Spooner, British scholar and originator of 'spoonerisms', died.
1940 Gary Gabelich, American driver and land speed record holder, born in San Pedro, California.
1946 Bob Beamon, American record long-jumper, born.
1947 James Hunt, British motor racing champion driver, born in Belmont, Surrey.
1958 Michael Jackson, international singing star, born in Gary, Indiana.
1975 Eamon de Valera, Irish statesman, three times Prime Minister and President from 1959 to 1973, died aged 92.
1982 Ingrid Bergman, Swedish-born American film actress and Oscar winner for *Gaslight* (1944) and *Anastasia* (1956), died in London on her 67th birthday, after a long illness.

30 AUGUST

1797 Mary Shelley, English novelist, best known as the author of *Frankenstein*, born in London.
1860 The first tramway in Britain opened, at Birkenhead on Merseyside.
1862 The second Battle of Bull Run took place, when Union forces, under Pope, were crushed by Lee's Confederate forces, reinforced by Jackson.
1871 Lord Rutherford, British physicist, eminent in the field of atomic research, born in Spring Grove, near Nelson on the southern island of New Zealand.
1896 Raymond Massey, American film actor, born in Toronto, Canada.
1907 Shirley Booth, American film actress and Oscar winner, born in New York City as Thelma Booth Ford.
1908 Fred MacMurray, American film actor, born in Kankakee, Illinois.
1917 Denis Healey, British Labour politician and statesman, born.
1923 Victor Seixas, American lawn tennis champion, born.
1924 Sir Peter Parker, British industrialist and company chairman, born.
1931 John Swigert, American astronaut, born in Denver, Colorado.
1937 Tommy Farr became the first boxer to take Joe Louis the full distance in a title fight.

1940 Sir J. J. Thomson, English physicist who discovered the electron in 1897, died in Cambridge, and was buried near Isaac Newton in the nave of Westminster Abbey.

1941 The siege of Leningrad by German forces began—ended in January 1943.

1943 Jean-Claude Killy, French alpine skier and an Olympic champion, born in St Cloud.

1945 Hong Kong was re-occupied by the British after four years of Japanese occupation.

31 AUGUST [244]

National day of both Malaysia and Trinidad and Tobago.

1422 King Henry V of England died in Vincennes, France, struck down with dysentery—was succeeded by his 9-month-old infant son as Henry VI.

1688 John Bunyan, religious writer, author of *The Pilgrim's Progress*, died at the house of a friend in Holborn, London.

1880 Wilhelmina, Queen of the Netherlands, born.

1881 The first US tennis championship was started in Newport, Rhode Island.

1888 Mary Ann 'Polly' Nichols, the first victim of Jack the Ripper, was found mutilated in Buck's Row in the early hours of the morning.

1889 'Bombardier' Billy Wells, British heavyweight boxer, born.

1897 Fredric March, American film actor and Oscar winner for *Dr Jekyll and Mr Hyde* (1932) and *The Best Years of our Lives* (1946), born in Racine, Wisconsin as Frederick McIntyre Bickel.

1900 Roland Culver, British actor, born.

1913 Sir Bernard Lovell, English astronomer and a leader in the development of radio astronomy, born in Gloucestershire.

1918 Alan Jay Lerner, American lyric writer of musical comedies in collaboration with Frederick Loewe, born in New York City.

1924 Buddy Hackett, rotund American comedian, born in Brooklyn as Leonard Hacker.

1928 James Coburn, American film actor, born in Laurel, Nebraska.

1930 Larry Grayson, English comedian and entertainer, born in Banbury as William White.

1936 Elizabeth Cowell, Britain's first woman TV announcer, made her debut at Alexandra Palace.

1942 Isao Aoki, Japanese international golfer, born.

1944 Clive Lloyd, West Indian cricketer, born in Georgetown, the capital of Guyana.

1955 Ed Moses, 400 metres hurdles champion for many years, born in Dayton, Ohio.

1957 Malaya achieved independence.
1962 Trinidad and Tobago in the West Indies became independent, having been a British possession since 1802.
1963 The 'hot line', linking the Kremlin with the White House, went into service.
1968 Gary Sobers of Nottinghamshire became the first cricketer to score six sixes off an over, at Swansea against Glamorgan—bowled by Malcolm Nash.
1969 Rocky Marciano, American world heavyweight boxing champion from 1952 to 1956, who retired undefeated, was killed in an air crash in central Iowa.
1973 John Ford, American film director, best known for his westerns, including *Stagecoach*, died.
1986 Henry Moore, English abstract sculptor, died aged 88.
     Urho Kekkonen, Finnish statesman, Prime Minister and President from 1956 to 1982, died aged 85.

1 SEPTEMBER   [245]

National day of Libya.
The partridge shooting season begins.

1159 Adrian IV, the only Englishman, Nicholas Breakspear, to be elected Pope, died.
1557 Jacques Cartier, French explorer of the North American coast and the St Lawrence river, died in St Malo.
1715 King Louis XIV of France, called the 'Sun King', died in Versailles, after reigning for just over 72 years—the longest in European history.
1834 Amilcare Ponchielli, Italian composer, notably *La Gioconda*, born near Cremona in Lombardy, the son of the town organist.
1854 Engelbert Humperdinck, German composer, born in Siegburg, near Bonn.
1859 Pullman (sleeping cars) carriages were introduced, on the Bloomington to Chicago line.
1864 Sir Roger Casement, British civil servant and Irish nationalist, born in Kingstown near Dublin.
1866 James Corbett, American heavyweight boxing champion known as 'Gentleman Jim', born in San Francisco.
1875 Edgar Rice Burroughs, American novelist best known for the series of 'Tarzan' books, born in Chicago.
1878 Emma Nutt made history when she started work as the first woman telephone operator at the exchange in Boston, Massachusetts.
1905 Violet Carson, English actress and pianist, born in Manchester.

1923 Rocky Marciano, American boxer and world heavyweight champion, born in Brockton, Massachusetts as Rocco Marchegiano.
An earthquake took place in Japan, leaving the cities of Tokyo and Yokohama in ruins and a total of nearly 100 000 deaths.
1924 Yvonne de Carlo, film actress in America, born in Vancouver, Canada as Peggy Middleton.
1931 Cecil Parkinson, British Conservative politician, born.
1933 Conway Twitty, American country singer, born in Friarspoint, Mississippi as Harold Jenkins.
1939 The BBC 'Home Service' on the radio began.
Hitler declared war on and invaded Poland, provoking World War II.
1946 Barry Gibb, the eldest member of the Bee Gees pop group, born in Douglas on the Isle of Man.
1969 Qaddhafi or Gadafy became Head of State of Libya, after leading a military coup overthrowing King Idris I.
1971 The British penny and the threepenny piece coins ceased to be legal tender.
1972 Iceland extended her fishing limits from 12 to 50 miles.

2 SEPTEMBER [246]

1666 The Great Fire of London began in Pudding Lane, in the bakehouse of Thomas Farriner, burnt itself out on 6th.
1834 Thomas Telford, Scottish engineer, road, bridge and canal builder, died in London and was buried in Westminster Abbey.
1898 The Battle of Omdurman took place, with victory for Kitchener's Anglo-Egyptian forces over the Khalifa's forces—winning back the Sudan for Egypt.
1910 Henri Rousseau, French primitive painter known as 'Le Douanier' because of his job as a customs official, died in Paris.
1916 The last of the famous Blaydon races in Northumberland were held.
1925 Russ Conway, British pop pianist, born as Trevor Stanford.
1937 Pierre de Coubertin, reviver of the Olympic Games in 1896, died.
1945 The formal Japanese surrender to the Allies was signed on board the US battleship *Missouri*.
1952 Jimmy Connors, American tennis champion, born in East St Louis, Illinois.
1971 Egypt discontinued the title of the United Arab Republic and reverted to its original name.
1973 J. R. R. Tolkien, South African-born English author, notably *The Lord of the Rings*, died in Bournemouth, Dorset.

1189 The coronation of King Richard I, the Lion Heart, took place at Westminster Abbey.

1658 Oliver Cromwell, statesman, Puritan leader and Lord Protector of England from 1653, died in Whitehall, London of pneumonia— was succeeded by his son Richard, as Protector.

1783 The peace ending the War of American Independence was signed in Paris.

1877 Adolphe Thiers, French statesman, Prime Minister and President, died of apoplexy in St Germain-en-Laye, near Paris.

1897 Cecil Parker, English film actor, born in Hastings, Kent as Cecil Schwabe.

1899 Sir Frank Burnet, Australian physician and Nobel Prize winner, born.

1900 Urho Kekkonen, Finnish statesman, Prime Minister and President, born.

1913 Alan Ladd, American film actor, born in Hot Springs, Arkansas.

1916 The first German airship was shot down by Captain Robinson in Cufley, Hertfordshire, for which he was awarded the Victoria Cross.

1918 John Forrest, Australian explorer, politician and colonial surveyor, died.

1925 The US dirigible *Shenandoah*, the first airship to use helium gas, broke apart in Caldwell, Ohio.

1939 Great Britain and France declared war on Germany.

1948 Eduard Beneš, Czech statesman and President until the Communist takeover, died.

1962 The Trans-Canada highway, 4800 miles from St John's, Newfoundland to Victoria, British Columbia, was opened.

1966 Captain Ridgway and Sergeant Blyth became the first Britons to row across the Atlantic; the journey in *English Rose III* took 91 days.

1967 Sweden switched to driving on the right of the road.

1969 Ho Chi Minh, Vietnamese leader and one of the most influential Communist leaders, died aged 79.

1976 *Viking* 2 set down on Mars's Utopia Plains after a journey lasting six days short of one year.

4 SEPTEMBER [248]

1870 Emperor Napoleon III, nephew of Bonaparte, deposed.

1886 Geronimo, Apache chief and leader of the last great American Red Indian rebellion, finally surrendered in Arizona to General Nelson Miles.

1907 Edvard Grieg, Norwegian composer, best known for his 'Peer Gynt Suite', died in Bergen.

1909 The first Boy Scout rally took place, in Crystal Palace, London.

1929 The German airship *Graf Zeppelin* completed its 20-day round-the-world trip, from Friedrichshafen, on the shore of Lake Constance, via Tokyo, Los Angeles and Lakehurst.

1931 Mitzi Gaynor, American dancer and film actress, born in Chicago as Francesca Mitzi von Gerber.

1937 Dawn Fraser, Australian Olympic swimming champion, born in Sydney.

1939 The British liner *Athenia* was sunk by a German submarine off the coast of Ireland.

1942 Raymond Floyd, American international golfer, born in Fort Bragg, North Carolina.

1948 Wilhelmina abdicated as Queen of the Netherlands in favour of her daughter Juliana.

1949 Tom Watson, American golfing champion, born in Kansas City, Missouri.
Britain's largest-ever aircraft, the 130-ton 8-engined *Bristol Brabazon*, had its first flight.

1955 Richard Baker presented the late-night summary on BBC to become the first television newscaster to be seen in vision.

1961 The Initial Teaching alphabet system was introduced in 19 schools throughout England.

1963 Robert Schuman, French statesman, Prime Minister and Foreign Minister, died.

1964 The Forth road bridge, 6156 ft long, and with a centre span of 3300 ft, was opened by Her Majesty the Queen.

1965 Albert Schweitzer, French medical missionary, noted organist and Nobel Prize winner in 1952, died aged 90 in Lambaréné, Gabon, where he set up a native hospital in 1913.

1972 At the Munich Games, Mark Spitz, US swimmer, won his seventh gold medal, a record for one Olympiad.

1984 Brian Mulroney won a decisive victory over John Turner in the Canadian General Election to become Prime Minister.

1985 The wreck of the *Titanic* on the Atlantic seabed off Newfoundland was photographed by remote control.

---

5 SEPTEMBER

1174 Canterbury Cathedral was destroyed by fire.

1638 Louis XIV, King of France, known as the 'Sun King', born in St Germain-en-Laye, an outer suburb of Paris.

1781 The Battle of Chesapeake Bay took place off the east coast of America, between French and British fleets.

1826 John Wisden, Sussex cricketer and compiler of the record books that bear his name, born in Brighton, Sussex.

1847 Jesse James, American outlaw and robber, born near Excelsior Springs in Clay County, Missouri, the son of a Baptist minister.

1857 Auguste Comte, French philosopher, sociologist and founder of Positivism, died.

1902 Darryl F. Zanuck, American film producer, born in Wahoo, Nebraska.

1905 The Treaty of Portsmouth was signed, ending the Russo-Japanese war.

1929 Bob Newhart, American comedian, born in Oak Park, Illinois.

1939 'Clay' Regazzoni, motor racing champion, born in Lugano, Switzerland.

1942 Raquel Welch, American film actress and sex symbol, born in Chicago, Illinois, with the maiden name of Jo-Raquel Tejada, of a Bolivian father.

1972 Alan Kippax, Australian cricketer in 22 Test matches, died.
Arab terrorists, members of the Black September Group, killed eleven Israelis at the Munich Olympic Games.

1975 An assassination attempt was made on US President Ford in Sacramento by Lynette Fromme, a Charles Manson follower.

1977 The *Voyager 2* spacecraft was launched to complement *Voyager 1*'s information on Saturn. It continues to Uranus and then to Neptune in September 1989, its last planetary stop.

1980 The ten-mile St Gotthard road tunnel, the longest in the world, was opened.

1982 Douglas Bader, British pilot of distinction and leader of 'the few' in the Battle of Britain, died in the early hours of the morning.

---

6 SEPTEMBER [250]

1522 Ferdinand Magellan's ship the *Vittoria*, under the command of Del Cano, arrived in San Lucar, Spain after completing the first circumnavigation of the world—Magellan himself was killed on the island of Mactan in the Philippines.

1666 The Great Fire of London came to an end—having started in Pudding Lane on 2nd.

1701 King James II died after a stroke in St Germain, France.

1757 Lafayette, French soldier, statesman and hero of the American Revolution, born in Chavagnac.

1766 John Dalton, English chemist and physician, born in Eaglesfield near Cockermouth in Cumbria, the son of a Quaker weaver.

1873 Austin Reed, men's outfitter, born in Newbury, Berkshire.

1880 England played Australia at the Oval in London, in the first cricket Test match in England.

1888 Joseph Patrick Kennedy, American financier, father of John, Robert and Edward, born in Boston, Massachusetts.

1901 American President McKinley was shot by anarchist Leon Czolgosz at a public reception in Buffalo—he died on 14th.

1915 The first military tank, called *No. 1 Lincoln*, modified and renamed *Little Willie*, and had its first run.

1939 The first air raid of the war on England took place.

1940 King Carol II of Romania abdicated in favour of his son Michael.

1942 Britt Ekland, Swedish film actress, born in Stockholm.

1948 Queen Juliana became Queen of the Netherlands, on the abdication of her mother, Queen Wilhelmina.
John Derry, piloting a De Havilland DH 108, and in a dive, became the first to fly supersonic in Britain.

1952 Gertrude Lawrence, British actress and associate of Noel Coward, died in New York.

1966 Hendrik Verwoerd, South African statesman and Prime Minister since 1958, was assassinated in Parliament in Cape Town, by Dimitric Tsafondas.

1968 Swaziland became an independent Kingdom within the Commonwealth.

1988 Thomas Gregory of Eltham, South London, became the youngest person to swim the English Channel at the age of 11 years and 11 months. He came ashore at Shakespeare Beach, Dover, 12 hours after setting off from France.

---

7 SEPTEMBER [251]

National day of Brazil.

1533 Queen Elizabeth I, born at Greenwich Palace in London, the daughter of Henry VIII and his second wife, Anne Boleyn.

1548 Catherine Parr, the sixth wife of Henry VIII, died in childbirth, by then the wife of Lord Seymour, at Sudeley Castle near Cheltenham, Gloucestershire.

1812 The Battle of Borodino took place 70 miles west of Moscow, in which Russian forces under Kutuzov failed to stop Napoleon's march to the capital.

1822 Brazil proclaimed its independence from Portugal, with Pedro I acclaimed Emperor.

1836 Sir Henry Campbell-Bannerman, British statesman and Liberal Prime Minister, born in Glasgow.

1838 Grace Darling made the famous rescue of the crew of the *Forfarshire*, shipwrecked near the Farne Islands off the Northumberland coast.

1871 George Hirst, Yorkshire cricketer, born in Kirkheaton.

1892 'Gentleman' James J. Corbett beat John L. Sullivan in 21 rounds in New Orleans, and became the first world heavyweight boxing champion under Queensberry rules—with gloves and three-minute rounds.

1893 Leslie Hore-Belisha, British Liberal politician, born in Devonport.

1895 The first Rugby League matches were played.

1910 Holman Hunt, English painter and co-founder of the Pre-Raphaelite Brotherhood, known for his religious works, died in London.

1913 Anthony Quayle, British Shakespearean actor, born in Lancashire.

1917 Sir John Cornforth, Australian chemist and the 1975 Nobel Prize winner, born.

1921 The first Miss America beauty contest was held in Atlantic City. The winner was 15-year-old blonde, Margaret Gorman of Washington, DC.

1930 King Baudouin of the Belgians, born at Stuyenberg Castle, the elder son of King Leopold III and Queen Astrid.

1932 J. Paul Getty II, American philanthropist, born.

1936 Buddy Holly, American singer and guitarist, born in Lubbock, Texas as Charles Harden Holley.

1943 Italy surrendered during World War II.

1956 C. B. Fry, English cricketer, footballer, rugby player and athlete, died in Hampstead, London, aged 84.

1986 Desmond Tutu was enthroned as Archbishop of Cape Town, South Africa.

---

8 SEPTEMBER [252]

1157 King Richard I was born in Oxford, the third son of Henry II and Eleanor of Aquitaine—called Richard the Lion Heart (Coeur de Lion).

1664 The Dutch settlement of New Amsterdam was seized by the English and re-named New York, in honour of James Duke of York, the future King James II.

1784 Ann Lee, religious leader and founder of the American sect of Shakers, died.

1831 The coronation of King William IV took place.

1841 Antonin Dvorak, Czech composer, born near Prague, the son of a butcher.

1888 English Football League matches were played for the first time.
Jack the Ripper claimed his second victim, Annie Chapman, found disembowelled at 29 Hanbury Street, London.

1901 Hendrik Verwoerd, Prime Minister of South Africa responsible for apartheid policy, born in Amsterdam in the Netherlands.

1921 Harry Secombe, British comedian, born in Wales.

1925 Peter Sellers, English comedian and film actor, born in Southsea, Hampshire.

1933 Faisal I or Feisal I, King of Iraq since 1921, died.

1944 The first German V2 flying bombs fell in Britain.

1946 Communists took power in Bulgaria, abolishing the monarchy.

1949 Richard Strauss, German composer, known for the opera *Der Rosenkavalier*, died.

1966 The Severn bridge over the Severn estuary, between Haysgate and Almondsbury, carrying the M4 motorway, was opened by Her Majesty the Queen.

1967 Uganda became a Republic, with Milton Obote its first President.

9 SEPTEMBER [253]

1087 William the Conqueror died in Rouen, France, from injuries received when his horse stumbled.

1513 The Battle of Flodden Field took place near Branxton in Northumberland, in which James IV of Scotland was defeated and killed by English troops under Thomas Howard, the Earl of Surrey.

1583 Sir Humphrey Gilbert, English explorer who established a Newfoundland colony at St John's, was drowned when the *Squirrel* went down off the Azores with all on board, during his voyage home.

1585 Cardinal Richelieu, French statesman and chief Minister of Louis XIII, born near Chinon.

1737 Luigi Galvani, Italian scientist and anatomist, born in Bologna.

1754 William Bligh, British captain of the *Bounty* at the time of the mutiny, born in Plymouth, Devon.

1850 California, the Golden State, entered the Union as the 31st state.

1894 Bert Oldfield, Australian Test cricketer, born.

1900 James Hilton, English novelist, author of *Lost Horizon* and *Goodbye, Mr Chips*, born in Leigh, Lancashire.

1901 Toulouse-Lautrec, the stunted, bespectacled French painter, died in Malromé from a paralytic stroke.

1903 Emile Littler, British theatrical impresario, born in Ramsgate, Kent.

1914 The first Battle of Marne ended when Von Moltke's advance on Paris was halted by the British Expeditionary Force and the French under Joffre and Foch.

1925 Cliff Robertson, American film actor and Oscar winner, born in La Jolla, California.

1938 The Auxiliary Territorial Service (ATS), the female branch of the Army, was formed by Royal Warrant.

1943 Allied forces landed in Salerno, south-west Italy.

1948 Following the Russian withdrawal North Korea became independent, as the People's Democratic Republic of Korea.

1949 John Curry, English skating champion, born.

1950 Soap rationing ended in Britain.

1976 Mao Tse-Tung, Chinese revolutionary leader and founder of the Communist State, died aged 82.

1985 Massive earthquakes in Mexico resulted in more than 4700 killed and 30 000 injured.

---

10 SEPTEMBER   [254]

1753 John Soane, English architect who designed the Bank of England, born in Goring, Oxfordshire, the son of a mason.

1771 Mungo Park, Scottish surgeon and explorer in West Africa, born in Foulshiels near Selkirk.

1890 Sir Mortimer Wheeler, British archaeologist, born in Glasgow.

1897 London taxi-driver George Smith became the first motorist to be convicted of drunken driving.

1929 Arnold Palmer, American international golfing champion, born in Youngstown, Pennsylvania.

1934 Roger Maris, American baseball player, born in Hibbing, Minnesota.

1945 Vidkun Quisling, the 'Puppet' Premier of Norway, was sentenced to death for collaboration—was executed on 24 October.
Jose Feliciano, singer, composer and guitarist, born in Larez, Puerto Rica.

1948 Bob Lanier, American basketball player, born in Buffalo, New York.

1960 The first English Football League match to be televised—Blackpool v Bolton Wanderers.

1966 Sir Seretse Khama became President of the new Republic of Botswana.

1967 The referendum held in Gibraltar resulted in an overwhelming vote to stay with Britain.

1709 The Battle of Malplaquet took place in Northern France near Mons, with the Duke of Marlborough and Prince Eugène in a costly victory over the French in the War of the Spanish Succession.

1777 The Battle of Brandywine Creek in the American War of Independence took place, in which the British under General Howe defeated George Washington.

1855 In the Crimean War Sebastopol was taken by the Allies after capitulation by the Russians.

1885 (David Herbert) D. H. Lawrence, English novelist, born in Victoria Street, Eastwood in Nottinghamshire, the son of a miner.

1895 During the night the original FA Cup was stolen from the shop window of William Shillcock, a firm of football outfitters of Newton Row, Birmingham, where it had been on display.

1915 The Women's Institute organisation was founded in Britain in Anglesey, Wales—founded originally in Canada in 1897.

1945 Franz Beckenbauer, German international footballer, born in Munich.

1950 Barry Sheene, English motorcycle racing champion, born in Holborn, London.
Jan Smuts, South African Boer War guerrilla leader, statesman and twice Prime Minister, died in Irene, aged 80.

1971 Nikita Khruschev, Soviet Communist leader and Premier from 1958 to 1964, died near Moscow.

1972 The BBC television quiz programme *Mastermind* was first transmitted.

1987 Lorne Greene, Canadian actor, died aged 72.

1609 Henry Hudson sailed the sloop *Half Moon* into New York harbour and up to Albany to discover the river named after him.

1818 Richard Gatling, American inventor of the revolving battery gun, born in Winton, North Carolina—his name is the origin of the slang 'gat', meaning a gun.

1819 Gebhard von Blücher, Prussian field marshal and contributor to the allied victories against Napoleon, died in Silesia.

1852 Herbert Henry Asquith, British statesman and Liberal Prime Minister, born in Morley, Yorkshire.

1878　'Cleopatra's Needle', an ancient Egyptian obelisk 68½ feet high in red granite presented to Britain, was erected on the Thames Embankment.

1888　Maurice Chevalier, French singer, musical comedy star and film actor, born in Paris.

1908　Winston Churchill married Clementine Hozier.

1910　The first policewoman was appointed, Alice Wells of the Los Angeles Police Department.

1913　Jesse Owens, American athlete, born in Danville, Alabama as John Cleveland Owens—the name Jesse was used because of its similarity to his initials J. C.

1918　Sir George Reid, Australian statesman and 4th Prime Minister from 1904 to 1905, died.

1940　A party of boys discovered a cave in Lascaux, south-west France in the Dordogne, the walls of which contained fine examples of early man's art.

1953　John F. Kennedy married Jacqueline Lee Bouvier.

1960　MOT tests on motor vehicles were introduced in Britain.

1972　William Boyd, American film actor renowned as Hopalong Cassidy, died.

1974　Ethiopian Emperor Haile Selassie was deposed by leaders of the armed forces.

1977　Steven Biko, the black South African leader, died while detained in police custody.

---

13 SEPTEMBER　　　　　　　　　　　　　　　　　　　[257]

1759　General Wolfe, British military commander, was killed in battle defeating Montcalm and the French forces on the Plains of Abraham, near Quebec—Montcalm died the following day from his wounds.

1806　Charles James Fox, British Liberal statesman, died in Chiswick, London.

1845　The first baseball club, the Knickerbockers Club, was formed in New York City.

1860　John Pershing, American commander-in-chief of the US Army in France in World War I, born in Linn County, Missouri.

1894　(John Boynton) J. B. Priestley, English author and playwright, born in Bradford, Yorkshire.

1902　The first conviction in Britain on the evidence of fingerprints was secured by the Metropolitan Police at the Old Bailey, in the case against Harry Jackson.

1905　Claudette Colbert, American film actress and Oscar winner for *It Happened One Night* (1934), born in Paris as Lily Claudette Chauchoin.

239

1916 Roald Dahl, British short story and children's-book writer, born in Llandaff, Wales.

1922 A record temperature of 136.4°F or 58°C was recorded in El Azizia, Libya.

1925 Mel Torme, American singer, born in Chicago, Illinois.

1944 Heath Robinson, English artist known for his drawings of complex machinery which performed simple tasks, died.

1966 Johannes Vorster was sworn in as Prime Minister of the Republic of South Africa.

1977 Leopold Stokowski, London-born American conductor and musical director, died in Hampshire, aged 95.

14 SEPTEMBER [258]

1735 Robert Raikes, English founder of the Sunday School system in 1780, born in Gloucester, the son of a printer.

1752 The Gregorian calendar, a reformed version of the Julian calendar, was adopted in Britain. Over the centuries, the measurement of a year (365.25 days) gradually got out of line with the real length which is slightly shorter, so 11 days had to be dropped at the changeover. Pope Gregory's calendar in use today has a Leap Year every fourth year, except every century, thus the year 2000 will not be one.

1812 Napoleon entered Moscow in his disastrous invasion of Russia.

1814 The US national anthem, *The Star-Spangled Banner*, was written by Francis Scott Key—set to the tune *Anacreon in Heaven*.

1851 James Fenimore Cooper, American novelist, author of *Last of the Mohicans*, died.

1852 The Duke of Wellington, English military commander, victor at Waterloo, statesman and Tory Prime Minister, died aged 83 at Walmer Castle in Kent, as Lord Warden of the Cinque Ports.
Augustus Pugin, English architect and co-designer of the Houses of Parliament at Westminster with Sir Charles Barry, died in Ramsgate, Kent.

1886 Jan Masaryk, Czech statesman, born in Prague, the son of the country's President.

1891 The first penalty kick was awarded in an English Football League match, taken by Heath of Wolves against Accrington.

1901 William McKinley, America's 25th President, died of wounds inflicted by anarchist Leon Czolgosz, in Buffalo on 6th.
Theodore Roosevelt was elected as the 26th President of the US, and the youngest at 42.
Alex James, Scottish footballer, born in Mossend, Bellshill in Lanarkshire.

1909 Peter Scott, English naturalist, born in London, the son of the famous Antarctic explorer.

1910 Jack Hawkins, British film actor, born in London.
1927 Isadora Duncan, American ballet dancer, was accidentally killed when her scarf caught in the wheel of her car.
1937 Thomas Masaryk, Czech statesman and his country's first President in 1918, died aged 87.
1938 The largest rigid airship ever built, the 803-ft German *Graf Zeppelin II*, made her maiden flight—was dismantled in April 1940.
1957 The last Liverpool tram ran—the 6A from the Pier Head to Bowring Park, full of civic dignitaries.
1959 The first direct hit on the moon was achieved by the Soviet space probe *Lunik II*, near the Mare Serenitatis.
The Aqueduct horseracing course, New York, opened.
1964 The British daily newspaper *Daily Herald* ceased publication, and was replaced by the *Sun*.
1975 Mother Elizabeth Seton, the first US-born saint, was canonised.
1982 Princess Grace died in Monaco's hospital without regaining consciousness, after a car crash the previous day.

15 SEPTEMBER [259]

Battle of Britain day.
National day of Costa Rica.

1649 Titus Oates, English religious agitator against Roman Catholics, born in Oakham, Leicestershire.
1789 James Fenimore Cooper, American novelist of stories of the sea and Red Indians, born in Burlington, New Jersey.
1830 William Huskisson, British statesman, was run down by Stephenson's *Rocket* at Parkside at the opening of the Liverpool and Manchester Railway—he died the same night.
1857 William Howard Taft, American Republican statesman and 27th President, born in Cincinnati, Ohio.
1859 Isambard Kingdom Brunel, British engineer of railways, steamships and docks, died in Westminster, London.
1864 John Speke, English explorer in Africa, who discovered Lake Victoria, accidentally shot himself while partridge shooting.
1877 Crazy Horse, Sioux chief and one of the leaders in the victory at Little Big Horn in 1876, died.
1879 Joseph Lyons, Australian Labour statesman, born in Stanley, Tasmania.
1891 Agatha Christie, English detective story writer, born in Torquay, Devon.

1916 Military tanks, originated by Sir Ernest Swinton, were first used by the British Army, at Flers in the Somme offensive.
Margaret Lockwood, British actress, born in Karachi, India as Margaret Day.
1923 Hank Williams, American country music singer and songwriter, born in Georgiana, Alabama.
1936 Ashley Cooper, Australian international tennis player, born in Melbourne.
1940 The Battle of Britain ended with a British victory. 1733 German planes were destroyed: the RAF lost 915.
1960 Traffic wardens were first introduced in London.
1964 The British daily newspaper the *Sun* began publication, having replaced the *Daily Herald*.
1973 Gustavus VI, King of Sweden since 1950, died aged 90.
1978 Muhammad Ali regained the world heavyweight boxing title for the second time, beating Leon Spinks in New Orleans.
Wilhelm Messerschmitt, German aviator engineer and designer, died aged 80.
1984 Prince Harry (Henry Charles Albert David) was born to Diana, Princess of Wales.
1985 Europe defeated America's golfers at The Belfry, to win the Ryder Cup.

---

16 SEPTEMBER [260]

National day of Mexico.

1387 King Henry V was born at Monmouth Castle in Wales, the eldest of six children of Henry IV.
1620 The 101 Pilgrim Fathers set sail from Plymouth in the *Mayflower*, captained by Myles Standish.
1736 Gabriel Fahrenheit, German physicist, who devised the scale of temperature that bears his name, died.
1810 The Mexican Revolution began for independence from Spanish rule.
1812 Moscow was burnt by the French under Napoleon.
1824 Louis XVIII, King of France, died.
1858 Andrew Bonar Law, British statesman and Conservative Prime Minister, born in Kingston, New Brunswick, Canada.
1861 The Post Office Savings Bank was instituted in Britain.
1893 Sir Alexander Korda, British film producer and director, born in Turkeye, Hungary as Sandor Corda.
1924 Lauren Bacall, American film actress, born in New York City as Betty Joan Perske.
1925 Charles Haughey, Irish Fianna Fail statesman and Prime Minister, born.

1927 Peter Falk, American TV actor who portrays detective 'Columbo', born in New York City.
1945 Count John McCormack, Irish-born American operatic tenor, died near Dublin.
1953 Jerry Pate, American international golfer, born.
1963 The name of Malaysia was adopted for the Federation of Malaya when joined by Singapore and Sarawak.
1966 Britain's first Polaris submarine *Resolution* was launched.
      The new Metropolitan Opera House at Lincoln Center, New York was opened.
1968 'Two-tier' postal system began in Britain.
1977 Maria Callas, American prima donna operatic soprano, died in Paris.
1981 In the Assembly in Llandudno, Wales the Liberals entered into an alliance with the Social Democratic Party, which had recently been formed on 26 March by a group of former Labour politicians.

---

17 SEPTEMBER   *[261]*

1771 Tobias Smollett, Scottish novelist, author of *Roderick Random*, died in Leghorn, Italy.
1787 The Constitution of the United States of America was signed.
1827 Wides in cricket were first scored as such in the Sussex v Kent game at Brighton.
1871 The 7½-mile Mont Cenis tunnel, carrying the main railway from Lyons to Turin, was opened.
1877 William Henry Fox Talbot, English pioneer of photography, died in Lacock Abbey, Wiltshire.
1901 Sir Francis Chichester, English yachtsman and aviator, born in Barnstaple, Devon.
1904 Sir Frederick Ashton, British ballet choreographer and director, born in Guayaquil, Ecuador.
1908 Lt Thomas Selfridge of the US Army Signal Corps was killed in a crash with Orville Wright in Fort Meyer, Virginia, to become the first aeroplane fatality.
1928 Roddy McDowell, film actor in America, born in London.
1929 Stirling Moss, British motor racing champion, born in Paddington, London.
1930 Thomas Stafford, American astronaut, born in Weatherford, Oklahoma.
1931 33⅓ rpm long-playing records were first launched, with a demonstration held at the Savoy Plaza Hotel in New York City.
      Anne Bancroft, American film actress and Oscar winner, born in New York's Bronx as Anna Marie Italiano.

1934 Maureen Connolly, American international tennis champion, born in San Diego, California.
1940 The first women workers on London's underground railway started duty as ticket collectors and porters.
1944 The British airborne invasion of Arnhem and Eindhoven in the Netherlands took place—was called 'Operation Market Garden'.
1948 Count Folke Bernadotte, Swedish diplomat and UN mediator for Palestine, was ambushed and killed in Jerusalem by Jewish terrorists.
1981 Twelve divers began the successful operation of recovering the 431 gold ingots, valued at £40 million, from HMS *Edinburgh*, which was sunk in the Barents Sea off Northern Norway, in 1942.
1986 Pat Phoenix, British actress noted for her long-running role in TV's *Coronation Street*, died.
1988 The 24th Olympic Games opened in Seoul in South Korea.

---

18 SEPTEMBER [262]

National day of Chile.

1709 Samuel Johnson, English lexicographer and poet, born in Lichfield, Staffordshire, the son of a bookseller.
1777 In advance of the British Army's occupation the Liberty Bell was moved from Philadelphia in a baggage train to Allentown, Pennsylvania, where it was hidden in a church.
1793 The cornerstone of the north section of the Capitol Building, Washington, DC, was laid by President Washington.
1819 Jean Foucault, French physicist, born in Paris.
1851 The *New York Times*, founded by Henry Jarvis Raymond, began publication.
1876 James Scullin, Australian Labour statesman, born.
1879 The Lancashire holiday resort of Blackpool held its first annual illuminations.
1895 John George Diefenbaker, Canadian statesman and Conservative Prime Minister, born in Normanby Township, Ontario.
1905 Greta Garbo, Swedish film actress, born in Stockholm as Greta Lovisa Gustafsson.
1909 Kwame Nkrumah, Ghanaian statesman and his country's first Prime Minister, born in Ankroful.
1931 Japan seized Manchuria and set up a puppet state called Manchukuo—was returned to China in 1945 after World War II.
1949 Peter Shilton, English goalkeeper and holder of the record for the highest number of both international and Football League appearances, born in Leicester.

1961 Dag Hammarskjöld, Swedish Secretary-General of the United Nations and Nobel Prize winner, was killed in a plane crash near Ndola in Northern Rhodesia when flying from Leopoldville.

1964 Sean O'Casey, Irish playwright, author of *Juno and the Paycock*, died in Torquay, Devon, aged 80.

1967 Sir John Cockcroft, English nuclear physicist who split the atom with Ernest Walton, died.

1970 Jimi Hendrix, American singer and guitarist, died of a drug overdose.

1981 France abolished capital punishment.

---

19 SEPTEMBER [263]

1356 The Battle of Poitiers in the Hundred Years War took place in western France, in which Edward the Black Prince defeated John II, King of France.

1839 George Cadbury, English chocolate manufacturer and social reformer, born in Birmingham.

1851 Viscount Leverhulme, English soapmaker and philanthropist, born, the son of a grocer, in Bolton, Lancashire as William Lever.

1876 The first practical carpet-sweeper was patented by Melville Bissell of Grand Rapids in Michigan.

1881 James Abram Garfield, American Republican statesman and 20th President since 4 March this year, died in Elberon, New Jersey, after being shot on 2 July—the remainder of his term of office was completed by Chester Arthur.

1888 The first beauty contest was held, in Spa, Belgium.

1893 New Zealand became the first nation to grant its female citizens the right to vote—the first occasion on which they went to the polls was the General Election of 28 November.

1905 Thomas Barnardo, British social reformer and founder of homes for destitute children in 1867, died.

1922 Emil Zatopek, international long-distance runner known as the 'Bouncing Czech', born.

1928 Walt Disney's *Steamboat Willie*, featuring Mickey Mouse, was shown in New York, to become the first cartoon talking picture.

1934 Brian Epstein, English music-group manager, born in Liverpool.

1936 Al Oerter, American discus thrower and winner of gold medals at four consecutive Olympics, born in Astoria, New York.

1949 'Twiggy', English model, actress and singer, born in Neasden, London as Lesley Hornby.

1955 Juan Peron, Argentine Presidential dictator from 1946, resigned and went into exile.

1958 NASA, the US Government Agency was founded to co-ordinate non-military US space flight and research.

1963 Sir David Low, New Zealand-born political cartoonist, died in London.
1968 *TV Times*, the weekly magazine for British independent television, was first published.

---

20 SEPTEMBER [264]

1258 Salisbury Cathedral was consecrated.
1519 Ferdinand Magellan, with a fleet of five small ships (*Trinidad, San Antonio, Concepcion, Vittoria* and *Santiago*), sailed from Seville on his expedition around the world. One ship only, the *Vittoria*, returned on 6 September 1522.
1746 To escape capture in Scotland, Bonnie Prince Charlie sailed to safety in France aboard the French ship *L'Heureux*.
1803 Robert Emmet, Irish patriot, was hanged for his part as a leader in the uprisings.
1842 Sir James Dewar, Scottish physicist and chemist and inventor of the vacuum flask, born in Kincardine-on-Forth, Fife.
1854 The Battle of Alma took place in the Crimean War, in which six Victoria Crosses were won.
1863 Jacob Grimm, German philologist and collector of folk tales with his younger brother Wilhelm, died in Berlin.
1869 George Robey, English music hall comedian, born in Herne Hill as George Wade.
1906 The Cunard liner *Mauretania*, holder of the Blue Riband of the Atlantic for over twenty years, was launched on the river Tyne.
1914 Kenneth More, English film actor, born in Gerrards Cross, Buckinghamshire.
1926 Fred Winter, English jockey and successful trainer, born in Andover, Hampshire.
1927 Johnny Dankworth, British musician, born.
1931 British sterling currency was taken off the gold standard.
1934 Sophia Loren, Italian actress and Oscar winner for *Two Women* (1961), born as Sophia Scicoloni.
1944 Guy Gibson, British pilot and Victoria Cross winner for his action against the Mohne and Eder dams, was killed when his aircraft crashed in Holland on its way back to base.
1957 Jean Sibelius, Finnish composer, principally national music, notably *Finlandia*, died aged 91.
1959 The last fly-past of Hurricanes over London commemorating the Battle of Britain.
1967 The British liner *QE 2* or *Queen Elizabeth 2* was launched at Clydebank in Scotland.
1973 Billie Jean King beat Bobby Riggs at tennis in the 'battle of the sexes' in the Astrodome, Houston, Texas.

National day of Malta.

1327   King Edward II was murdered in Berkeley Castle, to be succeeded by his son as Edward III.

1745   The Battle of Prestonpans took place in Scotland, in which Bonnie Prince Charlie's Jacobite army gained a victory over English Royal forces led by Sir John Cope.

1756   John McAdam, Scottish surveyor who introduced 'Macadam' system of roadmaking, born in Ayr.

1784   The first successful daily newspaper in America, *The Pennsylvania Packet and General Advertiser*, was published.

1792   France was declared a Republic.

1832   Sir Walter Scott, Scottish novelist and poet, died in Abbotsford on the banks of the river Tweed, and is buried at Dryburgh Abbey.

1866   H. G. Wells, English novelist and science fiction pioneer, born in Bromley, Kent, the son of a professional cricketer.

1874   Gustav Holst, English composer, notably *The Planets*, born in Cheltenham, Gloucestershire as Gustavus Theodore von Holst, of Swedish origin.

1902   Sir Learie Constantine, West Indian Test cricketer, born in Port of Spain, Trinidad.
       Sir Allen Lane, English publisher and founder of 'Penguin' books, born in Bristol as Allen Lane Williams.

1908   Captain C. H. Upham, one of only three to have been awarded a bar to the Victoria Cross, born in Christchurch, New Zealand.

1912   Ian MacGregor, a chairman of British Steel and British Coal, born.

1923   Jimmy Young, British radio broadcaster, born in Gloucestershire with the christian names Leslie Ronald.

1931   Larry Hagman, American stage and TV actor, born in Fort Worth, Texas the son of actress Mary Martin.

1947   An American *Skymaster* flew from Wilmington in Ohio to Brize Norton in England without crew, under automatic control, guided by radio impulses.

1949   The first comprehensive school in Britain opened in Holyhead, Anglesey, with the amalgamation of two local schools.

1952   Sir Montague Burton, English multiple tailor, knighted in 1931, died in Leeds.

1957   Death of Norway's King Haakon VII, accession of his son as Olav V.

1962   The British TV quiz programme *University Challenge*, conducted by Bamber Gascoigne, was first transmitted.

1964   Malta became independent, after 164 years of British rule.

1965 British Petroleum (BP) became the first company to strike oil in the North Sea.

1974 Jacqueline Susann, American novelist, notably *Valley of the Dolls*, died.

1981 Belize, originally known as British Honduras, became independent.

---

22 SEPTEMBER [266]

1735 Sir Robert Walpole became the first Prime Minister to occupy 10 Downing Street.

1761 The coronation of King George III took place.

1776 Nathan Hale, American patriot, was hanged in New York City by the British for being a spy during the American Revolutionary War.

1791 Michael Faraday, English chemist and physicist, born in Newington Butts, near London, the son of a blacksmith.

1880 Christabel Pankhurst, English suffragette, born, the daughter of Emmeline.

1885 Joseph 'Ben' Chifley, Australian Labour statesman, born.
Erich von Stroheim, US film director and actor, born in Vienna as Erich Oswald Hans Carl Maria von Nordenwall.

1895 Paul Muni, film actor and Oscar winner, born in Lemberg, Austria as Muni Weisenfreund.

1902 The earliest British airship, 75 feet long and built by Stanley Spencer, made its maiden flight from Crystal Palace, London.

1927 Gene Tunney defeated Jack Dempsey on points over ten rounds, at the Soldier's Field Stadium in Grant Park, Chicago—a fight dubbed as 'the battle of the long count'.

1934 The Gresford pit disaster took place in North Wales, in which 265 miners lost their lives.

1948 Captain Mark Phillips, husband of Princess Anne, born in Tewkesbury, Gloucestershire.

1955 Commercial television began in Britain—with 'Gibbs SR toothpaste' the first commercial.

1961 Argentinian swimmer Antonio Abertondo landed in St Margaret's Bay to complete the first double crossing of the English Channel, with only a four-minute rest in France.

1975 An assassination attempt was made on US President Ford in San Francisco by Sara Jane Moore, a political activist.

1980 The Gulf War broke out when Iraq invaded Iran in an attempt to control the Shatt al Arab waterway on the north coast of the Persian Gulf.

National day of Saudi Arabia.

1779   John Paul Jones on the *Bonhomme Richard* defeated the British ship *Serapis* in an engagement in North Sea waters off Flamborough Head during the War of the American Revolution.

1806   Meriwether Lewis and William Clark arrived back from their successful expedition to the Pacific; the gruelling journey lasted two years and four months.

1846   The planet Neptune was discovered by the German astronomer Johann Galle, following predictions of Leverrier and Adams.

1848   Chewing-gum was first commercially produced by John Curtis on a stove in his home in Bangor, Maine, and sold under the name of the 'State of Maine Pure Spruce Gum'.

1865   Baroness Orczy, British novelist and writer of *The Scarlet Pimpernel*, born in Tarnaors, Hungary.

1870   Prosper Mérimée, French novelist, notably *Carmen*, died in Cannes.

1889   Wilkie Collins, English novelist and pioneer of detective fiction, died in London.

1897   A nine-year-old boy was crushed to death by a taxi in Hackney, London to become the first motoring fatality on the public highway.

1898   Walter Pidgeon, film actor, born in New Brunswick, Canada.

1920   Mickey Rooney, American film actor, born in Brooklyn, New York as Joe Yule.

1926   The famous Gene Tunney—Jack Dempsey fight took place in Philadelphia, with a record paid attendance of 120757 and a 10th-round victory for Tunney.

1930   Ray Charles, American singer and composer, born in Albany, Georgia as Ray Charles Robinson.

1939   Sigmund Freud, Austrian psychiatrist and founder of psychoanalysis and called the 'Copernicus of the mind', died in Hampstead, London, aged 83.

1940   The George Cross, the highest British civilian award for acts of courage, was instituted.

1943   Julio Inglesias, Spanish pop singer, born.

1949   Bruce Springsteen, American singer, songwriter and guitarist, born in Freehold, New Jersey.

1952   Rocky Marciano won the world heavyweight boxing title in Philadelphia, knocking out Jersey Joe Walcott in the 13th round.

1974   CEEFAX, the teletext service of the BBC was inaugurated.

1987   Bob Fosse, American choreographer and film director, died aged 60.

1852 Henri Giffard, a French engineer, made the first airship flight, steam-powered from Paris, travelling 17 miles at 6 m.p.h.

1853 The *Northern Daily Times* in Liverpool became the first provincial daily newspaper in England.

1869 An American financial disaster, called 'Black Friday', took place when Jay Gould, a shrewd and unscrupulous investor, attempted to corner gold.

1890 (Alan Patrick) A. P. Herbert, English writer and Member of Parliament, born.

1896 Scott Fitzgerald, American novelist and short story writer, born in St Paul, Minnesota.

1898 Sir Howard Florey, British pathologist and joint producer of penicillin with Sir Ernest Chain, born in Adelaide, Australia.

1899 Sir William Dobell, Australian artist, born in Newcastle, New South Wales.

1930 John Young, American astronaut whose craft made the fifth landing on the Moon, born in San Francisco, California.

1931 Anthony Newley, English actor, singer and composer, born in Hackney, London.

1953 The first film made in CinemaScope®, *The Robe*, was premiered in Hollywood.

1960 The first nuclear-powered aircraft carrier, USS *Enterprise*, was launched at Newport in Virginia.

1975 Everest was climbed by the south-west face for the first time, by Dougal Haston and Doug Scott.

1493 Columbus set sail on his second expedition with a fleet of 20 ships.

1513 Vasco Balboa, Spanish explorer, became the first European to sight the Pacific Ocean after crossing the Darien isthmus.

1849 Johann Strauss the elder, Austrian conductor and composer of the *Radetzky March*, died in Vienna.

1864 William 'Billy' Hughes, Australian statesman, born in Llandudno, North Wales.

1872 (Charles Blake) C. B. Cochran, British theatrical producer and impresario, born in Lindfield, Sussex.

1897 William Faulkner, American novelist notably *The Sound and the Fury* and Nobel Prize winner, born in New Albany, Mississippi.

1906 Dmitri Shostakovich, Russian composer, born in Leningrad.
1907 Raymond Glendenning, English journalist and sports commentator, born.
1915 The British forces used poison gas for the first time.
1921 Robert Muldoon, New Zealand statesman and Prime Minister, born in Auckland.
1927 Sir Colin Davis, English conductor and musical director, born in Weybridge.
1929 Ronnie Barker, English comedy actor, born in Bedford, the county town on the river Ouse.
1942 Henri Pescarolo, motor racing champion, born in Paris.
1959 Solomon Bandaranaike, Prime Minister of Sri Lanka from 1956, was shot by a Buddhist monk in Colombo, and died the following day.
1962 Sonny Liston won the world heavyweight boxing title, knocking out Floyd Patterson in the first round in Chicago.
1977 Freddie Laker's first Skytrain service began, flying between Gatwick and New York.
1984 Walter Pidgeon, American film actor, died two days after his 86th birthday.

---

26 SEPTEMBER [270]

1087 The coronation of King William II of England took place.
1580 Francis Drake and crew arrived back in Plymouth in the 100-ton *Golden Hind*—originally the *Pelican*—after 33 months, to become the first Englishmen to circumnavigate the world.
1750 Lord Collingwood, British naval officer, Nelson's second-in-command at Trafalgar, born in Newcastle-upon-Tyne.
1820 Daniel Boone, American pioneer and frontiersman, died aged 85.
1861 The first British Golf Open was held at Prestwick in Scotland, and won by Tom Morris.
1887 Barnes Wallis, English aircraft designer, noted for his work on airships and special bombs, born.
     The first gramophone invented by Emile Berliner, a German immigrant living in Washington, DC, was patented.
1888 T. S. Elliot, British poet notably *The Wasteland*, and Nobel Prize winner, born in St Louis, Missouri.
1897 Pope Paul VI, born in Concessio as Giovanni Battista Montini.
1898 George Gershwin, American composer of musicals, born in Brooklyn, New York.
1907 New Zealand became a Dominion.
1915 James Keir Hardie, British Socialist and one of the founders of the Labour Party, died.
1934 The British liner *Queen Mary* was launched at John Brown's Yard in Clydebank, Scotland.

1937 Bessie Smith, American singer known as 'the empress of the blues', died as a result of a car accident.
1942 Wilson Carlile, English clergyman and founder of the Church Army in 1882, died aged 95.
1943 Ian Chappell, Australian Test cricketer and older brother of Greg, born.
1945 Bela Bartok, Hungarian composer and pianist, died.
1947 Hugh Lofting, American writer and creator of the character 'Dr Dolittle', died.
1948 Olivia Newton-John, British singer and actress, born in Cambridge.
1953 Sugar rationing ended in Britain.
1959 Solomon Bandaranaike, Prime Minister of Sri Lanka, died from wounds received at the hands of an assassin the previous day.
1961 Peter Dawson, Australian baritone, died.
1972 A building at the base of the Statue of Liberty, housing the Museum of Immigration, was opened by President Nixon.
Norway voted in a referendum against joining the European Economic Community.
1983 *Australia II* beat *Liberty* in the deciding race off Newport, Rhode Island, to deprive the US of the America's Cup, which they had held since its inception.

27 SEPTEMBER [271]

1722 Samuel Adams, American statesman, organiser of the Boston Tea Party and a signatory of the Declaration of Independence, born in Boston, Massachusetts.
1821 Mexico achieved independence through the efforts of General Iturbide, who made himself Emperor, as Augustin I.
1825 The steam locomotive *Active* pulled the first public train—the 27 miles from Shildon through Darlington to Stockton. It was later re-named *Locomotion No. 1*.
1854 The Lady Isabella water wheel at Laxey on the Isle of Man, the largest (72 ft 6 ins diameter) in the British Isles, was completed. It was once used for draining a lead mine.
1862 Louis Botha, South African military commander, statesman and first Prime Minister of the Union in 1910, born near Greytown in Natal.
1895 George Raft, American film actor, best known for roles as gangsters, born in New York as George Ranft.
1907 Sir Bernard Miles, English character actor, born.
1917 Edgar Degas, French artist, died.
1919 Adelina Patti, Spanish-born Italian soprano, died.
1921 Engelbert Humperdinck, German composer whose chief work was the opera *Hansel and Gretel*, died of apoplexy in Neustrelitz.

1922 Constantine I abdicated as King of Greece.
1938 The British liner *Queen Elizabeth*, the largest passenger vessel ever built, was launched at Clydebank in Scotland by the Queen Mother.
1967 The liner *Queen Mary* arrived in Southampton at the end of her last transatlantic voyage.
1968 Antonio Salazar retired as Prime Minister of Portugal, having held the post for 36 years and 84 days, the longest term of office of any statesman.
1979 Dame Gracie Fields, English comedienne and music hall entertainer, died in retirement at her home on the Isle of Capri, aged 81.

28 SEPTEMBER   *[272]*

1745 The British national anthem, *God Save the King*, was first performed, at the Drury Lane Theatre.
1803 Prosper Mérimée, French novelist, author of *Carmen*, the basis of Bizet's opera, born in Paris, the son of a painter.
1841 Georges Clemenceau, French statesman and Premier, known as the 'Tiger', born in La Vendée.
1852 Sir John French, British Army commander, born in Ripple, Kent.
1865 Elizabeth Garrett Anderson qualified to become Britain's first practising woman doctor.
1887 Avery Brundage, American sports figure and a President of the International Olympic Committee, born in Detroit, Michigan.
1891 Herman Melville, American novelist, notably *Moby Dick*, died in New York City.
1894 The first Marks and Spencer's (Penny Bazaar) in Britain, opened in Cheetham Hill, Manchester.
1895 Louis Pasteur, French chemist and bacteriologist, died in Saint-Cloud near Paris.
1902 Ed Sullivan, American TV personality and newspaper columnist, born in New York City.
1905 Max Schmelling, German heavyweight boxer and world champion, born in Brandenburg.
1909 Al Capp, American cartoonist and creator of the *Li'l Abner* comic strip, born in New Haven, Connecticut as Alfred Gerald Caplin.
1913 Alice Marble, American international tennis champion, born in Plumas County, California.
1916 Peter Finch, English film actor and Oscar winner, born in Kensington, London.
1923 The British magazine *Radio Times* was instituted and first published.

1924 Lieutenants Smith and Nelson, in US Army Douglas airplanes, completed the first circumnavigation of the world, flying a total of 26 103 miles with 57 stops.

1934 Brigitte Bardot, French actress, billed as a 'sex kitten', born in Paris.

1948 The first British motor racing Grand Prix at Silverstone took place.

1961 Syria seceded from the United Arab Republic after an anti-Egyptian revolt.

1964 Arthur 'Harpo' Marx, the silent member of the Marx brothers, died aged 75.

1970 Gamal Abdel Nasser, Egyptian political leader and President since 1956, died.

1978 Pieter Botha became Prime Minister of South Africa.
Pope John Paul I died after only 33 days as Pontiff.

1986 Sir Robert Helpmann, Australian dancer and choreographer, knighted in 1968, died.

---

29 SEPTEMBER [273]

1399 Richard II became the first British monarch to abdicate—next day was deposed by Parliament, which chose Henry IV as his successor.

1518 Tintoretto, Venetian painter, born as Jacopo Robusti, the son of a dyer.

1725 Robert Clive, English soldier, statesman and administrator, born in Styche, near Market Drayton, Shropshire, the son of a lawyer and eldest of 13 children.

1758 Horatio Nelson, English naval commander, born in Burnham Thorpe rectory, one of 11 children of a Norfolk clergyman.

1810 Elizabeth Gaskell, English novelist, author of *Cranford*, born at Cheyne Row, Chelsea as Elizabeth Stevenson.

1892 The first American football game to be played under floodlights was played by Mansfield Teachers College v Wyoming Seminary at Mansfield in Pennsylvania.

1899 Billy Butlin, holiday camp pioneer in Britain, born in South Africa.

1902 Emile Zola, French novelist, died in Paris, accidentally suffocated by charcoal fumes—received a State funeral and was buried in the Pantheon in Paris.

1907 Gene Autry, American singing cowboy in Westerns, born in Tioga, Texas, the son of a Baptist minister.

1908 Greer Garson, British film actress and Oscar winner for *Mrs Miniver* (1942), born in Co. Down in Northern Ireland.

1911 Ellsworth Vines, American tennis champion, born in Los Angeles.
1916 Trevor Howard, English film actor, born in Cliftonville, Kent.
(Carl Ronald) Giles, English cartoonist, born.
1931 Anita Ekberg, Swedish film actress, born in Malmo.
1934 Lance Gibbs, West Indian cricketer, born in Georgetown, Guyana.
1935 Jerry Lee Lewis, American singer, pianist and songwriter, born in Ferriday, Louisiana.
1938 The Munich Pact, an agreement between England, France, Germany and Italy, was signed, under which the Sudetenland was surrendered to Nazi Germany.
1943 Lech Walesa, Polish leader of the trade union Solidarity, born in Popowo, the son of a carpenter.
1946 BBC's 'Third Programme', known as Radio 3, was instituted.
1956 Sebastian Coe, British international athlete and world record holder, born in Chiswick, London.
1959 Bruce Bairnsfather, British cartoonist famous for his character 'Old Bill', died.
1962 Canada launched her first satellite—*The Alouette*.
1978 Johannes Vorster became President of the Republic of South Africa.
1979 Pope John Paul II arrived in Ireland for the first ever Papal visit.
1981 Bill Shankly, famous Scottish soccer manager, died in a Liverpool hospital.
1983 The 3389th performance of *A Chorus Line* set the longest run record for any Broadway show.

30 SEPTEMBER [274]

National day of Botswana.

1772 James Brindley, English engineer who constructed the Bridgewater, Grand Trunk and Manchester Ship canals, died in Turnhurst, Staffordshire.
1788 Lord Raglan, British army field marshal responsible for the disastrous 'Charge of the Light Brigade' at Balaklava, born in Badminton, Gloucestershire.
1832 Lord Roberts, British field marshal and commander, born in Cawnpore, India.
1888 Jack the Ripper butchered two more women—Liz Stride, found behind 40 Berner Street and Kate Eddowes in Mitre Square, both London.
1913 Rudolf Diesel, German engineer and inventor of an internal combustion engine that bears his name, died—vanishing from an English Channel steamer.

1921 Deborah Kerr, British film actress, born in Helensburgh, Scotland.

1930 Lord Birkenhead, British Conservative statesman and law reformer, died.

1931 Angie Dickinson, American film and TV actress, born in Kulm, North Dakota.

1935 Johnny Mathis, American pop singer and entertainer, born in San Francisco.

1938 Neville Chamberlain returned from Munich waving a piece of paper on which Hitler's signature appeared, so guaranteeing peace.

1939 Identity cards were first issued in Britain.
The first American football to be televised was the Fordham University v Waynesburg College game at Randall's Island, New York.

1952 The first film in Cinerama®—*This is Cinerama*—was shown in New York.

1955 James Dean, American film actor and cult figure, died in a car crash in California, aged 24.

1966 Bechuanaland became fully independent, changing its name to Botswana—with Sir Seretse Khama its first President.

1967 BBC's Radio 1 went on the air for the first time, with Tony Blackburn introducing *The Breakfast Show*.

1978 Edgar Bergen, American ventriloquist with dummy Charlie McCarthy, died.

1985 Charles Richter, American seismologist and deviser of the Richter scale, died.

---

1 OCTOBER [275]

National day of Nigeria, China and Cyprus.
The pheasant shooting season begins in Britain.

1207 King Henry III was born in Winchester, Hampshire, the son of King John.

1792 Money orders were introduced in Britain.

1843 The English Sunday newspaper *News of the World* began publication.

1865 Paul Dukas, French composer, best known for *The Sorcerer's Apprentice*, born in Paris.

1868 St Pancras Station, the London terminus of the Midland Railway, was formally opened.

1870 The first official issue of the postcard was made in Britain by the Post Office, together with the introduction of the halfpenny postage stamp.

1873 Sir Edwin Landseer, English animal painter noted for his *Monarch of the Glen*, died in London and was buried in St Paul's Cathedral.

1890 Stanley Holloway, English singer and comedy actor, born in London.

1904 Vladimir Horowitz, American concert pianist, born in Kiev, Russia.

1908 The first Ford model T motor car rolled off the production line at Detroit.

1910 Bonnie Parker, American outlaw of the Bonnie and Clyde duo, born in Rowena, Texas.

1920 Walter Matthau, American film actor, born in New York City, as Walter Matuschanskayasky.

1924 James Earl (Jimmy) Carter, American Democrat statesman and 39th President, born in Plains, Georgia.

1931 The Waldorf Astoria on New York's Park Avenue, the world's largest commercial hotel building, was opened.

1933 Richard Harris, British actor, born in Co. Limerick, Republic of Ireland.

1935 Julie Andrews, English film actress and singer, born in Walton-on-Thames, Surrey, as Julie Wells.

1936 General Franco took office as Head of the Nationalist (Insurgent) Government.

1949 The People's Republic was founded in China, with Mao Tse-Tung its chairman.

1955 O'Hare International, Chicago, the world's busiest airport, opened to scheduled traffic.

1960 Nigeria achieved independence within the Commonwealth.

1963 Nigeria became a Republic.

1966 Speer and von Schirach, were released from Spandau, leaving Rudolf Hess the sole prisoner.

1970 The funeral of President Nasser of Egypt took place in Cairo.

1971 'Disney World', the world's largest amusement resort, in central Florida, was opened.

1974 John Conteh won the vacant world light-heavyweight boxing title, outpointing Jorge Ahumada at Wembley.

1977 Pele retired from competitive football after 1363 games, in which the Brazilian scored 1281 goals.

1982 Internal telegrams in Britain were abolished.
Helmut Kohl became Chancellor of West Germany, succeeding Helmut Schmidt.

1452 Richard III was born in Fotheringhay Castle, Northamptonshire, the youngest brother of Edward IV.

1608 The first telescope was demonstrated by the Dutch lens maker, Hans Lippershey.

1803 Samuel Adams, American patriot, statesman and one of the signatories of the Declaration of Independence, died aged 81.

1836 HMS *Beagle*, with naturalist Charles Darwin aboard, returned after a near five-year scientific survey of South American waters.

1847 Paul von Hindenberg, German military leader and President of the Republic, born in Posen.

1851 Ferdinand Foch, French military commander, born in Tarbes.

1852 Sir William Ramsay, British chemist and discoverer of inert gases, born in Glasgow.

1869 Mohandas 'Mahatma' Gandhi, Indian political and religious leader, born in Porbander.

1871 Cordell Hull, American statesman and diplomat, born in Overton, Tennessee.

1890 'Groucho' Marx, American actor and comedian of the Marx Brothers, born in New York City, as Julius Marx.

1895 Bud Abbott, American comedy actor, born in Asbury Park, New Jersey.

1901 The first Royal Navy submarine, built by Vickers, was launched at Barrow.

1904 Graham Greene, English novelist notably *The Power and the Glory*, and short-story writer, born in Berknamsted, Hertfordshire.

1909 The first Rugby match at Twickenham was played—Harlequins *v.* Richmond.

1921 Robert Runcie, the 102nd Archbishop of Canterbury, born.

1931 Sir Thomas Lipton, British grocer, yachtsman and philanthropist, died in London.

1942 The British cruiser *Curacao* sank immediately off the coast of Donegal with the loss of 338 lives, after a collision with the Cunard liner *Queen Mary*.

1945 Don McLean, American guitarist, singer and songwriter, born in New Rochelle, New York State.
The first installation of fluorescent lighting in Britian was made on a platform of the Piccadilly Circus underground station.

1948 Trevor Brooking, English international footballer, born.

1950 Legal aid became effective in Britain.

1958 The Republic of Guinea in West Africa opted for full independence, and France withdrew all aid.
Marie Stopes, English pioneer of birth control, died.

1972 Sweden voted in favour of joining the European Economic Community.

1973 Paavo Nurmi, Finnish distance running champion, died aged 76.
1983 Neil Kinnock was elected leader of the Labour Party in Britain.
1985 Rock Hudson, American film actor, died.

3 OCTOBER [277]

1811 The first women's county cricket match started, Hampshire *v.* Surrey at Newington.
1867 Elias Howe, American inventor of the first practical sewing machine in 1846, died.
1906 SOS was established as an international distress signal at the Berlin Radio Conference—replacing the call sign CQD.
1914 The first national flag-day was held in England, in aid of the Belgian Relief Fund.
1916 James Herriot, Scottish author of best-selling books about the life of a rural Scottish vet, born in Glasgow as James Alfred Wight.
1921 Ray Lindwall, Australian fast bowler, born in Sydney.
1925 Gore Vidal, American novelist, playwright and critic, born in West Point, New York State.
1933 Neale Fraser, Australian international tennis champion, born in St Kilda, Melbourne.
1935 Italian forces invaded Abyssinia.
1939 The sunken British submarine *Thetis* was eventually beached.
1941 Chubby Checker, American singer and entertainer, born in Philadelphia, as Ernest Evans.
1952 Britain detonated her first atomic bomb, aboard a naval vessel in Monte Bello Islands off north-west Australia.
1959 The post code, required in the addressing of mail for mechanical sorting was first used in Britain in Norwich.
1961 Antony Armstrong-Jones, as the husband of Princess Margaret, was created Earl of Snowdon.
1967 Sir Malcolm Sargent, English conductor, especially of Promenade Concerts, died.
1987 Jean Anouilh, French playwright, died aged 77.
Catherine Bramwell-Booth, Salvation Army Commissioner, died aged 104.
Sir Peter Medawar, medical scientist and Nobel laureate for Britain, died aged 72.
1988 Sir Alec Issigonis, designer of the Mini motor car, knighted in 1969, died at his home in Edgbaston, Birmingham, aged 81.

National day of Lesotho.

1582 St Teresa (of Avila), Spanish nun and religious reformer, died—was canonised in 1622.

1626 Richard Cromwell, born the third son of Oliver Cromwell.

1669 Rembrandt, famous Dutch painter, died in Amsterdam.

1814 Jean Francois Millet, French painter of rural scenes, born in Grouchy, near Gréville, the son of a farmer.

1821 John Rennie, Scottish civil engineer and designer of bridges, died in London.

1822 Rutherford Hayes, American Republican statesman and 19th President, born in Delaware, Ohio, the son of a farmer.

1853 Turkey declared war on Russia, thus starting the Crimean War.

1878 The first Chinese Embassy to Washington was established.

1883 The Boys' Brigade organisation was founded in Glasgow, by Sir William Alexander Smith.

1884 Damon Runyon, American short-story writer, born in Manhattan, Kansas.

1892 Engelbert Dollfuss, Austrian statesman, Chancellor and dictator, born.

1895 'Buster' Keaton, American comedy actor of the silent film era, born in Piqua, Kansas, as Joseph Francis Keaton.
The first official American Golf Open took place, at Newport, Rhode Island—won by Horace Rawlins.

1911 Britain's first escalators were introduced, connecting the District and Piccadilly platforms at Earls Court underground station.

1924 Charlton Heston, American film actor and Oscar winner, for *Ben Hur* (1959), born in Evansville, Illinois.

1931 Basil D'Oliveira, Worcestershire and England cricketer, born in Cape Town.
Sir Terence Conran, British industrialist and company chairman, born.

1939 Ivan Mauger, world speedway champion, born in Christchurch, New Zealand.

1943 Owen Davidson, Australian international tennis champion, born.

1948 Sir Arthur Whitten Brown, British aviator of Alcock and Brown fame, died.

1957 Russia's *Sputnik 1*, the first space satellite, weighing 180 lbs, was launched from Tyuratam, a site some 170 miles east of the Aral Sea.

1962 'Patsy' Hendren, Middlesex and England cricketer, died.

1965 Pope Paul VI visited New York City, the first Papal visit to America.

1966 Basutoland became an independent Kingdom, having been a British Protectorate since 1868—now called Lesotho.

1983 Richard Noble reached a world record speed of 633½ m.p.h. in his jet-powered car *Thrust II*, at Black Rock Desert, Nevada.

---

5 OCTOBER [279]

1830 Chester Arthur, American Republican statesman and 21st President, born in Fairfield, Vermont, the son of a Baptist minister.

1880 Jacques Offenbach, German-born French composer of operettas and the opera *Tales of Hoffman*, died in Paris.

1919 Donald Pleasence, English actor, born in Worksop.

1923 Glynis Johns, British film actress, born in Durban, South Africa.

1930 The 777-foot British airship *R101*, captained by Flight Lieutenant Irwin, crashed at the edge of a wood near Beauvais in France, on its way from Cardington to India—killing 48 of the 54 passengers and crew.

1933 Diane Cilento, film actress, born in Queensland, Australia.
English champion jockey Gordon Richards rode his 12th consecutive winner in three days—11 at Chepstow following one at Nottingham.

1936 The Jarrow March of unemployed shipyard workers from Jarrow to London started on its southward journey, led by Labour MP Ellen Wilkinson.

1954 Bob Geldof, rock musician and singer with the 'Boomtown Rats' and international fundraiser, born in Dublin.

1967 The first majority verdict taken in Britain, by 10 to 2, at Brighton Quarter sessions.

1972 The Congregational Church in England and Wales and the Presbyterian Church of England combined to form the United Reform Church.

---

6 OCTOBER [280]

1536 William Tyndale, English religious reformer and translator of the Bible, was burned at the stake as a heretic, in Vilvarde, Brussels.

1820 Jenny Lind, Swedish international operatic soprano, born in Stockholm, as Johanna Maria Lind.

1829 Trials began at Rainhill, near Liverpool, for a locomotive for use on the Liverpool and Manchester Railway—won by Stephenson's *Rocket*. The other four entrants were *Cycloped*, *Sans Pareil*, *Perseverance* and *Novelty*.

1846   George Westinghouse, American engineer and inventor of the railway air brake, born in Central Bridge, State of New York.

1883   The Orient Express completed its maiden run from Paris to Constantinople (now Istanbul) in nearly 78 hours.

1891   Charles Stewart Parnell, Irish politician and leader for Home Rule, died in Brighton, Sussex.
        W. H. Smith, English newsagent, bookseller and politician, died.

1892   Alfred, Lord Tennyson, English poet and Poet Laureate from 1850, died in Aldworth, Surrey.

1895   The Promenade Concerts were founded by Sir Henry Wood.

1905   Helen Wills-Moody, American tennis champion, born in Centerville, California.

1906   Janet Gaynor, American film actress, born in Philadelphia, as Laura Gainer.

1911   Barbara Castle, British Labour politician, born.

1914   Thor Heyerdahl, Norwegian adventurer and leader of the *Kon Tiki* expedition, born in Larvik.

1919   Tommy Lawton, English international footballer, born.
        Alfred Deakin, Australian statesman and three times Prime Minister, died.

1927   Warner Bros' *The Jazz Singer*, the first successful talking feature film, opened in New York.

1928   Chiang Kai-Shek became President of Nationalist China.

1930   Richie Benaud, Australian cricketer and commentator, born in Penrith, New South Wales.

1946   Tony Greig, cricketer for Sussex and England and sports commentator in Australia, born in South Africa.

1949   The Berlin air lift ended. It carried on from May despite the Russians lifting the blockade.

1959   A record 92 706 attended the fifth game of the baseball World Series at the Memorial Coliseum, Los Angeles, between Los Angeles Dodgers and Chicago White Sox.

1969   Walter Hagen, American champion golfer, died aged 76.

1978   The first woman train driver started work on London's underground.

1981   Anwar Sadat, Egyptian political leader and President since 1970, was assassinated during a military parade in Cairo.

1985   Nigel Mansell won his first Grand Prix, the European at Brands Hatch, a circuit near Farningham, Kent.
        Nelson Riddle, American musician, bandleader and composer, died.

1986   A new British national daily newspaper *The Independent*, went into circulation.

1571 The naval Battle of Lepanto took place in the Gulf of Corinth, resulting in the destruction of the Turkish Fleet, commanded by Ali Pasha.

1769 Captain Cook reached New Zealand.

1799 The ship *Lutine* sank off the island of Vlieland in Holland—its salvaged bell was presented to Lloyd's of London.

1806 A patent for the first carbon paper was secured by its inventor Ralph Wedgwood of London—'for producing duplicates of writings'.

1849 Edgar Allan Poe, American writer of mysterious and macabre stories, died in Baltimore, Maryland.

1876 The first greyhound race with an artificial hare, the Hendon Cup, was run at Welsh Harp, Hendon, Middlesex.

1900 Heinrich Himmler, German Nazi leader and notorious chief of police, born in Munich.

1918 Sir Hubert Parry, English composer and musical historian, died in Rustington, Sussex.

1919 KLM, the national airline of the Netherlands and the oldest existing, was established—opening its first scheduled service on the following 17 May.

1922 Marie Lloyd, English music hall entertainer, died after collapsing on the stage of the Alhambra Theatre.

1923 June Allyson, American film actress, born in Lucerne, State of New York, as Ella Geisman.

1927 Al Martino, American pop singer, born in Philadelphia, as Alfred Cini.

1931 Desmond Tutu, Anglican priest in South Africa, born.

1939 Clive James, author and television presenter, born in Australia.

1949 The State of East Germany, or the German Democratic Republic, was formed.

1952 Graham Yallop, Victoria and Australian Test cricketer, born.

1953 Liverpool's Liver clock first chimed at 2.30 p.m.

1956 Clarence Birdseye, American inventor of a process for deep-freezing foodstuffs, died.

1957 Jayne Torvill, ice skating star of the Torvill and Dean ice-dance team, born in Nottingham.

1959 Mario Lanza, American tenor singer and actor, died aged 38.
      The first photograph of the far side of the moon was transmitted from Russia's *Lunik III*.

1754   Henry Fielding, English novelist, author of *Tom Jones*, died.

1793   John Hancock, American politician, governor and the first signer of the Declaration of Independence, died.

1869   Franklin Pierce, American Democrat statesman and 14th President from 1853 to 1857, died in Concord, New Hampshire.

1871   The Great Fire of Chicago broke out—ending on 11th—supposedly started in Mrs O'Leary's barn in DeKoven Street, by a cow upsetting a lantern.

1890   'Eddie' Rickenbacker, American aviator, born in Columbus, Ohio.

1891   The first street collection for charity in Britain took place in Manchester and Salford, for Lifeboat Day.

1895   Juan Peron, Argentinian general, statesman and nationalist dictator, born in Lobos.

1896   The Dow-Jones average index of selected stocks on the New York Stock Exchange was instituted.

1917   Billy Conn, an American world light-heavyweight boxing champion, born in Pittsburgh.

1923   Ron Randell, Australian actor, born in New South Wales.

1928   Neil Harvey, Australian cricketer, born in Melbourne, Victoria.

1932   Ray Reardon, six times world snooker champion, born in Tredegar, Wales.

1938   Fred Stolle, Australian international tennis champion, born in Hornsby, New South Wales.

1941   Jesse Jackson, American civil rights leader and Baptist minister, born in Greenville, North Carolina.

1944   Wendell Wilkie, American politician and Presidential candidate, died.

1953   Kathleen Ferrier, English international contralto singer, died.

1965   The 580-foot Post Office tower, in Maple Street, off Tottenham Court Road, London, was opened.

1967   Clement Attlee, British statesman and Labour Prime Minister from 1945 to 1951, died aged 84.
        The first breathalyser test took place in Britain, administered to a motorist at Flax Bourton in Somerset.

1973   London Broadcasting, the first commercial radio station on the British mainland, began transmitting.

1978   Ken Warby in *The Spirit of Australia* created the official water speed record, on Blowering Dam, New South Wales, with a speed of 319.627 m.p.h.

1987   Roger Lancelyn Green, British author, notably of children's books, died aged 68.

National day of Uganda.

1835   Camille Saint-Saëns, French composer, pianist and music critic, born in Paris.

1874   The Universal Postal Union was established, with headquarters in Berne, Switzerland.

1888   The 555-foot white-marble Washington Monument, designed by Robert Mills, was opened.

1900   Alastair Sim, Scottish comedy film actor, born in Edinburgh.

1907   Lord Hailsham, British Conservative statesman and Attorney-General, born as Quintin Hogg.

1909   Donald Coggan, English prelate and 101st Archbishop of Canterbury, born.

1934   Alexander, King of Yugoslavia from 1921, was assassinated by Croatian terrorists, in Marseilles.

1940   John Lennon, songwriter and musician of the 'Beatles' group, born in Liverpool, the son of a ship's steward.

1955   Steve Ovett, British international athlete, born.

1958   Pope Pius XII (Eugenio Pacell), died at the Castel Gandolfo, the Papal summer residence, some 27 kilometres south-east of Rome, aged 82.

1962   Uganda became independent after nearly 70 years of British rule, with Milton Obote its first Prime Minister.

1967   Ernesto 'Che' Guevara, Argentinian-born guerrilla leader and revolutionary, was murdered in Bolivia.

1968   Harold Wilson met Ian Smith for further talks about Rhodesia's independence, on HMS *Fearless* off Gibraltar, but again failed to resolve the situation.

1684   Antoine Watteau, French rococo painter, born in Valenciennes.

1731   Henry Cavendish, English scientist and chemist who discovered what is now known as hydrogen, born in Nice, France.

1813   Giuseppe Verdi, Italian opera composer, born in Le Roncole, near Busseto, the son of a tavern keeper.

1825   Paul Kruger, South African statesman and Boer leader, born in Colesberg, Cape Colony.

1861   Fridtjof Nansen, Norwegian Polar explorer, born near Oslo.

1877   Lord Nuffield, English car manufacturer and philanthropist, born in Worcestershire, as William Morris.

1886 The dinner jacket made its first appearance in public when worn by its creator at a ball at the Tuxedo Park Country Club, New York. Its later name being derived from the name of the club.
1900 Helen Hayes, American actress and Oscar winner, born in Washington, DC, as Helen Brown.
1911 The Imperial Dynasty of China was forced to a 'voluntary' abdication, and a republic was proclaimed at Wuchang, under Sun Yat-Sen.
1914 Dorothy Lamour, American actress known for the 'Road' films, born in New Orleans, as Dorothy Kaumeyer.
1930 The Tyne Bridge at Newcastle was opened.
     Harold Pinter, British dramatist, born.
1937 Bruce Devlin, Australian international golfer, born.
1940 Sir William Grenfell, English medical missionary in Labrador, died.
1961 Volcanic eruption on the South Atlantic island of Tristan da Cunha—the whole population was evacuated to Britain.
1964 Eddie Cantor, American film actor and entertainer, died aged 72.
     The 18th Olympic Games opened in Tokyo.
1970 Fiji became an independent member of the Commonwealth, having been a British colony since 1874.
     Edouard Daladier, French statesman and Prime Minister, died aged 86.
1972 Sir John Betjeman was appointed Poet Laureate.
1981 Richard Noble in his jet-engined *Thrust II*, attained a British record speed of 418 m.p.h., at Bonneville Salt Flats, Utah.
1983 Sir Ralph Richardson, English stage and film actor, died in London, aged 80.
1985 Yul Brynner, US film actor and winner of an Oscar in 1956 for *The King and I*, died.
     Orson Welles, American actor, director and producer, died of a heart attack after a TV chat show.

11 OCTOBER [285]

1727 The coronation of King George II took place.
1797 The naval Battle of Camperdown took place off the north Holland coast, with a British victory over a Dutch fleet which had threatened British naval supremacy.
1809 Meriwether Lewis, American explorer associated with William Clark, died.
1821 George Williams, English social reformer and founder of the YMCA in 1844, born in Dulverton, Somerset.
1844 H. J. Heinz, American food-products manufacturer, born of German parents in Pittsburgh, Pennsylvania.

1884 Eleanor Roosevelt, wife and cousin of Franklin D. Roosevelt, born in New York City.
1889 James Joule, English physicist who established the first law of thermodynamics, died.
1899 The South African Boer War began, between the British Empire and the republics of the Orange Free State and the Transvaal.
1906 Bob Danvers-Walker, English newsreel commentator, born in Cheam, Surrey.
1927 James Prior, British Conservative politician, born.
1930 Sir Michael Edwardes, British industrialist and company chairman, born.
1937 Bobby Charlton, English international footballer and scorer of a record 49 goals for his country, born in Ashington, Northumberland.
1939 Maria Bueno, Brazilian international tennis champion, born in Sâo Paulo.
1956 A Test cricket slow-scoring record was set. Australia scored 80 and Pakistan 15 for the loss of two wickets in a full day's play at Karachi.
1957 The radio telescope at Jodrell Bank in Cheshire, planned by Sir Bernard Lovell, went into operation.
1958 The BBC television sports programme *Grandstand*, the idea of Paul Fox, was first transmitted.
1961 'Chico' Marx, the piano-playing member of the Marx Brothers comedy team, died.
1963 Edith Piaf, French singer and legendary international cabaret star, died.
1968 *Apollo 7* was launched with Walter Schirra, Don Eiselle and Walter Cunningham.

---

12 OCTOBER [286]

1492 Columbus sighted his first land in discovering the New World, calling it San Salvador.
1537 King Edward VI was born in the Palace of Hampton Court, the son of Henry VIII and his third wife, Jane Seymour.
1845 Elizabeth Fry, English social worker and prison reformer, died.
1859 Robert Stephenson, English rail and civil engineer, died in London.
1860 Elmer Sperry, prolific American inventor, notably the gyroscopic compass, born in Cortland, State of New York.
1866 Ramsay MacDonald, British statesman and Labour Prime Minister, born in Lossiemouth, Morayshire, Scotland.
1870 Robert E. Lee, American general and outstanding Confederate military leader during the Civil War, died in Lexington, Virginia.

1872 Ralph Vaughan Williams, English composer, born in Down Ampney, Gloucestershire.

1899 Mafeking was besieged by the Boers and was gallantly defended by Baden-Powell until it was relieved 217 days later by Colonel Plumer.

1915 Edith Cavell, English nurse, was executed by a German firing squad in Brussels, for helping allied prisoners escape over the Dutch frontier.

1928 The first iron lung was used, at Boston Children's Hospital in Massachusetts.

1929 Magnus Magnusson, British writer and television presenter, born in Reykjavik, Iceland.

1935 Luciano Pavarotti, Italian operatic tenor, born.

1940 Tom Mix, American film actor in over 400 Westerns, died.

1944 Angela Rippon, British television presenter, born in Plymouth.

1946 Joseph Stilwell, American Army commander in the China-India theatre of war, known as 'Vinegar Joe', died.

1948 The first Morris Minor car, designed by Alex Issigonis, came off the production line at Cowley, Oxfordshire.

1965 Paul Müller, Swiss chemist who formulated the insecticide DDT in 1939, died in Basle.

1968 The 19th Olympic Games opened in Mexico City.

1969 Sonja Henie, former world skating champion and film actress, died.

1971 Dean Acheson, American politician and Secretary of State, died.

1984 The Grand Hotel in Brighton was bombed by the IRA in an attempt to murder the British Cabinet, during the Tory Party Conference there.

1986 Her Majesty The Queen arrived in China, the first British monarch to visit the country.

13 OCTOBER [287]

1399 The coronation of King Henry IV, the first King of the House of Lancaster, took place.

1792 The cornerstone of the US President's official residence—The White House in Washington, DC, designed by James Hoban—was laid.

1853 Lillie Langtry, British actress, born in Jersey with the forenames Emilie Charlotte, the daughter of the Dean of the island.

1884 Greenwich was adopted as the universal time meridian of longitude from which standard times throughout the world are calculated.

1892 At the by-election at Cirencester in Gloucestershire, the number of votes cast for Conservative and Liberal were found to have been equal—a new election was ordered.

1894 The first Merseyside 'derby' football match between Everton and Liverpool was played at Goodison Park—Everton winning 3–0.

1903 At their Hurlington Avenue grounds Boston Red Sox won 5–3 against Pittsburg Pirates to become the first baseball World Series winners.

1905 Sir Henry Irving, English actor and first in the profession to receive a knighthood, in 1895, died in Bradford from a heart attack outside his hotel.

1925 Mrs Thatcher, Conservative politician and Britain's first woman Prime Minister, born in Grantham, as Margaret Roberts, the daughter of a grocer.

1927 Britain's first veteran car rally, organised by the *Daily Sketch*, took place in London with 43 starters.
The horseracing course at Arlington Park, Illinois, opened.

1942 Art Garfunkel, American singer and songwriter with Paul Simon, born in New York City.

1959 Marie Osmond, American singer, born in Ogden, Utah, the younger sister of Donny.

1972 Bank rate was abolished, to be called instead minimum lending rate.

1974 Ed Sullivan, American television presenter, died.

1984 John Lowe achieved the first televised 501 score in nine darts in a major event, in the quarter finals of the World Match Play championship in Slough.

---

14 OCTOBER [288]

National day of Madagascar.

1066 The famous Battle of Hastings took place on Senlac Hill, near Pevensey (seven miles from Hastings), in which King Harold was slain and the English army routed.

1633 King James II was born at St James's Palace, the second son of Charles I and Henrietta Maria.

1644 William Penn, English Quaker leader and founder of Pennsylvania, born in London, the son of an admiral.

1830 Belgium was proclaimed an independent kingdom—having formed part of the 'Low Countries'.

1854 The first baby show was held, at Springfield, Ohio.

1878 The first football match was played under floodlights, at Bramall Lane, Sheffield.

1882 Eamon de Valera, Irish statesman, Prime Minister and President, born in Manhattan, New York City.

1890 Dwight Eisenhower, American military commander, Republican statesman and 34th President, born in Denison, Texas.

1896 Lillian Gish, American film actress of the silent screen, born in Springfield, Ohio, as Lillian de Guiche.

1912 Former President Theodore Roosevelt was shot and seriously wounded by a demented man in Milwaukee.

1913 Britain's worst pit disaster took place at Universal Colliery, Senghenydd, Glamorgan—killing 439.

1920 Degrees were first open to women at Oxford University, though they had been allowed previously to sit for examinations.

1928 Roger Moore, English film actor, born in Stockwell, London, the son of a policeman.

1929 Britain's largest airship, the 777-foot *R101*, built at Cardington, flew on its first trial.

1939 The Royal Navy battleship *Royal Oak* was torpedoed and sunk in Scapa Flow, with the loss of 810 lives.

1940 Cliff Richard, English singer and entertainer, born in Lucknow, India, as Harry Webb.

1947 The first supersonic flight was achieved over Edwards Air Base at Muroc, California.

1959 Errol Flynn, Tasmanian-born actor in action-adventure films, died.

1960 Steve Cram, English middle-distance runner and holder of world records, born.

1968 New Euston station in London was opened.

1969 The 50p decimal coin was first issued in Britain.

1976 Dame Edith Evans, British actress, known principally for stage appearances, especially Shakespearean roles, died aged 88.

1977 Bing Crosby, American singer, actor and Academy Award (Oscar) winner in 1944 for his part in *Going My Way*, died on a golf course in Madrid.

1982 The largest mass wedding ceremony took place in Seoul, South Korea, when 5837 couples were married simultaneously.

15 OCTOBER [289]

1608 Evangelista Torricelli, Italian mathematician and scientist who devised the barometer, born in Faenza.

1851 The Great Exhibition at Crystal Palace in London's Hyde Park closed—having opened on 1 May.

1858 John L. Sullivan, American world heavyweight boxing champion, known as the 'Boston Strong Boy', born in Roxburgh, Massachusetts.

1880 Marie Stopes, scientist and sex education reformer, born in Edinburgh.

1881 (Pelham Grenville) P. G. Wodehouse, English comic novelist, born in Guildford, Surrey.

1887 Preston North End scored a record number of goals in an FA Cup tie. Every player except the goalkeeper scored in their 26–0 win over Hyde.

1895 The first motor show in Britain was held at the Agricultural Showground in Tunbridge Wells, Kent.

1917 Mata Hari, Dutch spy, was shot in Paris, having been found guilty of espionage for the Germans.

1920 Mario Puzo, US novelist, author of *The Godfather*, born in New York City.

1928 The German airship *Graf Zeppelin*, captained by Hugo Eckener, crossed the Atlantic from Friedrichshafen to Lakehurst in New Jersey.

1945 Pierre Laval, French leader of the Vichy Government's collaboration with the Germans, was executed for treason.

1946 Hermann Goering, Nazi war criminal, poisoned himself in Nuremberg Prison a few hours before he was scheduled to be hanged.

1948 President Gerald Ford married widow Elizabeth Bloomer Warren.

1951 The Liberals held the first BBC televised Party Political broadcast— given by Lord Samuel.
      Roscoe Tanner, American international tennis player, born in Cincinnati, Ohio.

1959 Sarah, Duchess of York, born Sarah Margaret Ferguson.

1964 Cole Porter, American prolific composer and lyricist, died.

---

16 OCTOBER   *[290]*

1555 Hugh Latimer and Nicholas Ridley, the English Protestant reformers and Oxford martyrs, were burned at the stake for heresy.

1758 Noah Webster, American lexicographer and originator of the dictionary that bears his name, born in West Hartford, Connecticut.

1793 Marie Antoinette, Queen of France as wife of Louis XVI, was convicted of treason and guillotined in Paris.

1803 Robert Stephenson, English civil engineer, born in Willington Quay, Northumberland, the son of a famous father, George Stephenson.

1815 Napoleon was exiled to the Atlantic island of St Helena.

1834 The Palace of Westminster was burned down—firemen managed to save Westminster Hall and St Stephen's Chapel.

1846 Doctor Warren performed the first major surgical operation using ether as an anaesthetic, when he removed a tumour at Massachusetts General Hospital.

1854 Oscar Wilde, Irish playwright and dramatist, born in Dublin, the son of a surgeon.

1859 John Brown, American abolitionist, with 21 followers seized the US armoury at Harper's Ferry in Virginia—an action for which he was later hanged.

1863 Sir Austen Chamberlain, British statesman, born in Birmingham.

1869 Girton College, the oldest women's college of Cambridge University, was opened.

1881 The British newspaper *The People* began publication.

1886 David Ben-Gurion, statesman and first Prime Minister of Israel in 1948, born in Plonsk, Poland as David Green—he chose the name of 'Ben-Gurion' for its biblical flavour.

1888 Eugene O'Neill, American playwright, notably *Long Days' Journey Into Night*, born in New York City, the son of an actor.

1890 Michael Collins, Irish politician and revolutionary, born near Clonakilty in County Cork.

1902 The first Borstal Institution was opened in the village of Borstal, near Rochester, Kent.

1908 The first aeroplane flight in England was made, at Farnborough in Hampshire, by American Samuel Franklin Cody.

1920 Gordon Richards rode the first of his 21 834 mounts, at Lingfield Park.

1922 The world's longest main-line tunnel, the Simplon II under the Alps, was completed, after four years work.
Max Bygraves, English singer and entertainer, born in Rotherhithe, London.

1925 Angela Lansbury, actress and star of several Broadway musicals, born in London.

1932 Ingemar Johansson, Swedish heavyweight boxer and a world champion, born in Gothenburg.

1945 The Food and Agricultural Organization (FAO) was established to raise levels of nutrition and standards of living.

1946 The Nuremberg executions took place.

1947 Terry Griffiths, British snooker player and a world champion, born.

1959 George Marshall, American soldier and statesman who formulated the Marshall Aid Plan for post-war European relief, died in Washington, DC.

1964 Harold Wilson of the Labour Party became the British Prime Minister.

1973 Gene Krupa, American drummer and bandleader, died.

1978 Pope John Paul II was elected—the first non-Italian to be elevated to the Papacy since 1522.

1981 Moshe Dayan, Israeli military leader, died in Tel Aviv.

1987 Hurricane force winds hit southern Britain, killing 19 and causing hundreds of millions of pounds worth of damage.

1727 John Wilkes, English political agitator and advocate of freedom of the Press, born in Clerkenwell, London, the son of a distiller.

1777 The Battle of Saratoga took place, with victory for the American colonists under General Horatio Gates, over John Burgoyne's British troops during the War of American Independence.

1849 Frédéric Chopin, Polish pianist and composer, died of tuberculosis in Paris, aged 39.

1854 The siege of the fortress of Sebastopol began by British and French forces.

1860 The first professional golf tournament was held, at Prestwick, Scotland, and won by Willie Park.

1908 Jean Arthur, American film actress, born in New York City as Gladys Greene.

1915 Arthur Miller, American dramatist, notably *Death of a Salesman*, born in New York City.

1918 Rita Hayworth, American dancer and film actress, born in New York City as Margarita Carmen Cansino.

1938 Evel Knievel, American stunt motorcyclist, born in Butte, Montana.

1953 A memorial at Cooper's Hill, near Runnymede, to members of the Commonwealth Air Forces who lost their lives and have no known grave, was unveiled by Queen Elizabeth II.

1956 Calder Hall in Cumbria, Britain's first large-scale atomic energy station, was formally opened by the Queen, when power was first fed into the grid system.

1960 The British daily newspaper *News Chronicle* ceased publication, and was incorporated into the *Daily Mail*.

1970 Anwar Sadat succeeded Nasser as President of Egypt.

1977 Sir Michael Balcon, English film producer knighted in 1948, died in Hartfield, Sussex aged 81.
The US Supreme Court ruled that Concorde could use New York's Kennedy airport.

1697 Canaletto, Italian painter of cityscapes, born in Venice as Giovanni Antonio Canal.

1826 The last state lottery was held in Britain.

1865 Lord Palmerston, British Whig statesman and twice Prime Minister, died at Brocket Hall, Welwyn, Hertfordshire.

1873 Rules for American football were formulated in New York, by Columbia, Princeton, Rutgers and Yale delegates.

1884   Emanuel Shinwell, British Labour politician and Minister, born in Spitalfields, London.

1893   Charles Gounod, French composer of operas, including *Faust*, died in St Cloud, a suburb of Paris.
Lucy Stone, American reformer and leader in the women's rights movement, died.
Sir Sidney Holland, New Zealand statesman, born in Greendale, Canterbury on South Island.

1898   America took formal possession of Puerto Rico from Spain.

1919   Pierre Trudeau, Canadian statesman and Liberal Prime Minister, born in Montreal, Quebec.

1926   Bing Crosby made his first commercial recording—*I've got the girl*.

1927   George C. Scott, American film actor who refused the Oscar award in 1970 for his portrayal of 'Patton', born in Wise, Virginia.

1931   Thomas Alva Edison, American inventor of the phonograph and the electric lamp, died aged 84.

1939   Lee Harvey Oswald, American assassin, born in New Orleans.

1956   Martina Navratilova, world champion tennis player, born in Prague.

1958   Denis Law of Huddersfield Town became the youngest footballer to play for Scotland—being 18 years 7 months in the game against Wales at Cardiff.

1963   Harold Macmillan resigned as Prime Minister, and was succeeded by Sir Alec Douglas-Home.

1966   Elizabeth Arden, American cosmetics company founder, died.

1968   Bob Beamon created a world long jump record of 8.9 metres or 29 feet 2½ inches, at the Mexico Olympic Games.

1978   Frank Woolley, all-round cricketer for Kent and 64 times for England, died in Halifax, Nova Scotia aged 91.

1978   Anatoly Karpov regained the world chess championship, defeating Viktor Korchnoi.

1982   Elizabeth Truman, widow of Harry S. Truman, died.

---

19 OCTOBER [293]

1216   John, King of England from 1199, died of fever at Newark, and was buried in Worcester Cathedral.

1745   Jonathan Swift, Anglo-Irish satirist best known for his masterpiece *Gulliver's Travels*, died aged 77.

1781   Lord Cornwallis surrendered to General Washington at Yorktown in Virginia, and marked the end of fighting in the American War of Independence.

1812   Napoleon's army began the retreat from Moscow.

1859   Alfred Dreyfus, French army officer noted for the 'Dreyfus Treason Affair', born in Alsace of Jewish parents.

1864 The Battle of Cedar Creek took place during the American Civil War, with General Sheridan gaining victory over the Confederates.

1872 The Holtermann nugget, the largest gold-bearing nugget ever found, weighing 630 lbs, was mined at Hill End, New South Wales, Australia.

1875 Sir Charles Wheatstone, English physicist and pioneer of telegraphy, died in Paris.

1897 George Pullman, American manufacturer of sleeping-cars and dining-cars that bear his name, died in Chicago, Illinois.

1900 William Ponsford, Australian Test cricketer, born in North Calton, Melbourne.

1931 John le Carré, British author, especially spy books, born as David John Cornwell.

1937 Lord Rutherford, New Zealand-born atomic physicist, founder of modern atomic theory and Nobel Prize winner in 1908, died in Cambridge.

1954 Britain and Egypt signed their agreement concerning the Suez Canal base.

1963 Sir Alec Douglas-Home became Britain's Conservative Prime Minister.

1987 Jacqueline du Pré, British cellist, died aged 42.
Ian Woosnam, by beating Sandy Lyle, became the first Briton to win the Suntory World Matchplay Golf Championship, held at Wentworth, Surrey.

20 OCTOBER [294]

1524 Thomas Linacre, English physician to Henry VII and Henry VIII and founder of the Royal College of Physicians in 1518, died.

1632 Sir Christopher Wren, English astronomer, best known as the architect of St Paul's Cathedral, born in East Knoyle, Wiltshire, the son of a dean.

1714 The coronation of King George I took place.

1784 Lord Palmerston, British statesman and twice Prime Minister, born at 20 Queen Anne's Gate, Westminster, as Henry John Temple.

1818 The 49th parallel was established by USA and Britain as the boundary between Canada and USA.

1822 Thomas Hughes, English author of *Tom Brown's Schooldays*, born in Uffington, Berkshire.
The British newspaper *Sunday Times* began publication.

1842 Grace Darling, English heroine renowned for saving the ship-wrecked crew of the *Forfarshire* in 1838, died.

1884 Bela Lugosi, actor best known for horror films, born in Hungary as Bela Lugosi Blasko.

1890 Sir Richard Burton, British explorer, writer and translator of the *Arabian Nights* tales, died.
1891 Sir James Chadwick, English physicist who discovered the neutron in 1932, born in Manchester.
1904 Anna Neagle, English stage and film actress, born in Forest Gate, London as Marjorie Robertson.
George Woodcock, British trade unionist, born.
1931 Mickey Mantle, the legendary New York Yankee baseball player, born in Spavinaw, Oklahoma.
1941 Britain's largest ever and last battleship, HMS *Vanguard*, was laid at Clydebank—was launched on 30 November 1944.
1961 Ian Rush, Welsh international and Liverpool footballer, born.
1964 Herbert Hoover, American Republican statesman and 31st President from 1929 to 1933, died in New York City aged 90.
1968 Bud Flanagan, English comic and one of the Crazy Gang, died.
1988 Sheila Scott, British aviator and holder of many speed and endurance records, died in a London hospital.

---

21 OCTOBER [295]

1772 S. T. Coleridge, English poet whose works include *The Rime of the Ancient Mariner*, born the son of a vicar of Ottery St Mary, Devon.
1805 Lord Nelson, English hero and victor in many naval battles, was killed in one such battle off Cape Trafalgar in south-west Spain.
1824 Portland cement was patented by Joseph Aspdin of Wakefield, Yorkshire.
1833 Alfred Nobel, Swedish chemist and inventor of dynamite in 1867, born in Stockholm.
1868 Sir Ernest Swinton, British soldier and one of the originators of the military tank, born in Bangalore in India.
1912 Sir Georg Solti, conductor, born in Budapest.
1917 Dizzy Gillespie, US jazz trumpeter, born in Cheraw, North Carolina with the christian names John Birks.
1937 Michael Landon, American film actor, director and producer, born in New York City as Eugene Maurice Orowitz.
1940 Geoff Boycott, Yorkshire and England cricketer, born near Pontefract, Yorkshire.
1958 The first women peers were introduced to the House of Lords.
1960 Britain's first nuclear-powered submarine, *Dreadnought*, was launched at Barrow, Lancashire.
1964 Terry Venables played for England against Belgium at Wembley to complete a unique collection of England football caps – youth, amateur, under-23 and full.

1966 The Aberfan disaster occurred, when a coal tip slid down upon that mid-Glamorgan mining village, killing 144, including 116 children.
1973 The Sydney Opera House, designed by the Danish architect Joern Utzon, was opened by Queen Elizabeth II.
1974 Liverpool's Radio City first went on the air.

22 OCTOBER [296]

1797 The first parachute descent was made, over the Parc Monceau in Paris, by André-Jacques Garnerin from a balloon.
1806 Thomas Sheraton, English furniture-designer and cabinet-maker, died.
1811 Franz Liszt, Hungarian composer and piano virtuoso, born in the village of Raiding near Oedenburg.
1844 Sarah Bernhardt, French dramatic actress, born in Paris as Henriette Rosine Bernard.
1878 The first rugby match under floodlights took place, Broughton v Swinton, at Broughton, Lancashire.
1883 The Metropolitan Opera House in New York was opened.
1906 Paul Cézanne, French painter, died.
1910 American-born Dr Hawley Crippen was convicted at the Old Bailey of poisoning his wife Cora, and was subsequently hanged—23 November—at Pentonville Prison, London.
1917 Joan Fontaine, American film actress and Oscar winner, born in Tokyo, Japan as Joan de Havilland, the younger sister of Olivia de Havilland, who was also an Oscar winner.
   Bob Fitzsimmons, the only British boxer to have won the world heavyweight title, died in Chicago.
1928 Andrew Fisher, Australian Labour statesman and three times Prime Minister, died.
1933 The first all-European world heavyweight title fight took place in Rome when Italy's Primo Carnera fought and beat Spain's Paulino Uzcudun.
1973 Pablo Casals, Spanish cellist, composer and conductor, died aged 96.

23 OCTOBER [297]

1642 The Battle of Edgehill, in the Cotswolds, took place—the first major conflict of the Civil War, between Charles I's Cavaliers and the Parliamentary Roundheads.

1844   Robert Bridges, English poet and Poet Laureate in 1913, born in Walmer, Kent.
1900   Douglas Jardine, Surrey and England cricketer, born in Bombay.
1906   Gertrude Ederle, American swimmer who, in 1936, was the first woman to swim the English Channel, born in New York.
1915   W. G. Grace, the legendary English cricketer, died in Eltham, Kent.
1921   John Boyd Dunlop, Scottish veterinary surgeon and inventor of the pneumatic tyre, died.
1922   A. Bonar Law became British Prime Minister, to be replaced by Stanley Baldwin the following 22 May, for the shortest term of office in the 20th century.
1925   Johnny Carson, American TV chat show host, born in Corning, Indiana.
1931   Diana Dors, English film actress, born in Swindon, Wiltshire as Diana Fluck.
1939   Zane Grey, American writer of cowboy and western stories, notably *Riders of the Purple Sage*, died.
1940   Pelé, Brazilian footballer, born at Bauru as Edson Arantes do Nascimento.
1942   The Battle of El Alamein began.
1946   The first New York meeting of the General Assembly of the United Nations Organization took place.
1950   Al Jolson, American singer and entertainer, famous for his *Mammy* and *Sonny Boy*, died in California.
1970   American Gary Gabelich achieved a world record speed of over 631 m.p.h.—for a rocket-engine car—on Bonneville Salt Flats in Utah.

24 OCTOBER [298]

National day of Zambia.

1601   Tycho Brahe, Danish royal astronomer, died in Benatky near Prague, Czechoslovakia.
1648   The Treaty of Westphalia was signed, ending the Thirty Years' War.
1857   A number of Cambridge University Old Boys formed the first football club, at Sheffield.
1861   The Pony Express Mail Service in America, running from St Joseph in Missouri to Sacramento in California, ended after operating for just over 18 months.
1882   Sybil Thorndike, English stage and film actress, born in Gainsborough, Lincolnshire.
1894   Jack Warner, English character actor, born as Jack Waters.

1915   Tito Gobbi, Italian international operatic baritone singer, born in
        Bassano del Grappa.
1922   George Cadbury, English chocolate manufacturer and social
        reformer, died in Birmingham aged 83.
1923   Sir Robin Day, television interviewer and reporter, born in London.
1945   The United Nations formally came into existence.
        Vidkun Quisling, Norwegian Premier and Nazi collaborator,
        executed by a firing squad at Akershus Fortress, Oslo.
1948   Franz Lehar, Hungarian composer of operettas including *The Merry
        Widow*, died in Vienna.
1957   Christian Dior, French fashion designer and creator of the 'New
        Look', died.
1964   Northern Rhodesia became the Republic of Zambia, with
        Kenneth Kaunda its first President.
1977   The transatlantic liner *France* was sold to Saudi Arabia for use as a
        floating luxury hotel.
1988   The death of Henry Armstrong, the triple world boxing champion
        of the late 1930s was announced in Los Angeles.

25 OCTOBER   [299]

St Crispin's day.

1400   Geoffrey Chaucer, English poet and master storyteller, known
        for his unfinished *The Canterbury Tales*, died.
1415   The Battle of Agincourt took place, 20 miles inland from
        Boulogne, during the Hundred Years' War, with Henry V's
        longbowmen victorious over the French knights.
1647   Evangelista Torricelli, Italian mathematician and physicist who
        devised the barometer or 'Torricellian Tube', died in Florence.
1760   King George II died suddenly at Kensington, London—was
        succeeded by his grandson, as George III.
1825   Johann Strauss the younger, Austrian composer and 'waltz
        king', best known for *The Blue Danube*, born in Vienna.
1838   Georges Bizet, French composer, notably the opera *Carmen*, born
        in Paris.
1839   *Bradshaw's Railway Companion* became the first national railway
        timetable to be published.
1854   The infamous Charge of the Light Brigade took place at Balaklava
        during the Crimean War, led by Lord Cardigan.
1881   Pablo Picasso, Spanish painter and creator of Cubism, born in
        Malaga, Andalusia.
1888   Richard Byrd, American naval officer and Polar explorer, born in
        Winchester, Virginia.
1921   King Michael of Romania born, the son of King Carol II.

1941 Helen Reddy, Australian singer and songwriter, born in Melbourne.

1951 The British General Election was won by the Conservative Party with a small majority, and Winston Churchill was made Prime Minister the following day.

---

26 OCTOBER [300]

National day of both Iran and Austria.

1759 Georges Danton, French statesman and revolutionary leader, born in Arcis-sur-Aube.

1764 William Hogarth, English painter and engraver, died in London, and was buried in Chiswick churchyard.

1825 The Erie Canal—or properly named the New York State Barge Canal—linking Niagara river with the Hudson river, was opened to traffic.

1863 The English Football Association was formed at a meeting at Freeman's Tavern in Great Queen Street, London.

1879 Leon Trotsky, Russian Communist leader and one of the founders of the Soviet state, born in Yanovka in the Ukraine as Lev Davidovich Bronstein.

1902 Elizabeth Stanton, American leader of the women's suffrage movement, died aged 86.
Jack Sharkey, a world heavyweight boxing champion, born in Binghampton, New York State.

1906 Primo Carnera, Italian heavyweight boxer, born in Sequals.

1907 The Territorial Army, a British volunteer force, was established by Richard Haldane, when Secretary of State for War.

1913 Hugh Scanlon, British trade unionist, born.

1914 Jackie Coogan, American film actor, born in Los Angeles, California as John Leslie.

1916 François Mitterrand, French statesman and President, born.

1950 The re-built chamber of the House of Commons was opened by King George VI, having been destroyed by bombing in 1941.

1972 Igor Sikorsky, Russian-born American aeronautical engineer who developed the first successful helicopter in 1939, died in Easton, Connecticut.

1987 The City Airport opened in London's docklands for short landing and take-off aircraft.

1728 Captain James Cook, English naval officer and explorer, born in Marton, Cleveland, Yorkshire, the son of a farmer.
1782 Niccolo Paganini, Italian violin virtuoso and composer, born in Genoa, the son of a porter.
1811 Isaac Singer, American inventor and manufacturer of sewing machines, born in Pittsdown in the State of New York.
1854 Sir William Smith, Scottish founder of the Boys' Brigade movement in Glasgow in 1883, born.
1858 Theodore Roosevelt, American Republican statesman and 26th President, born in New York City, the son of a collector of the port.
1879 The *Liverpool Echo* printed its first copy.
1904 The first section of the New York subway was opened.
1914 Dylan Thomas, Welsh poet, born in Swansea, the son of a schoolmaster.
1923 Roy Lichtenstein, American painter and a leader of the Pop Art movement, born in New York City.
1931 David Bryant, English bowls champion, born.
1936 Mrs Wallis Simpson obtained a divorce from her second husband, and became free to marry King Edward VIII.
1939 John Cleese, English comedy actor, born in Weston-super-Mare.
1944 The Japanese fleet was crushingly defeated in the world's largest naval battle of Leyte Gulf, which started on 22nd and involved a total of 231 ships and 1996 aircraft.
1957 Glen Hoddle, Monaco and England footballer, born in Hayes, Middlesex.
1958 The first edition of the BBC television programme *Blue Peter* was transmitted.
1971 The Republic of the Congo changed its name to the Republic of Zaire.
1986 It was 'Big Bang' day in the Stock Exchange of the city of London, a shambles as the computer failed.

1636 Harvard University, America's oldest university, was founded at Cambridge in Massachusetts, and named after the English-born Puritan minister John Harvard.
1792 John Smeaton, English civil engineer, noted for his novel design for the third Eddystone lighthouse, died.
1846 Escoffier, the famous French chef known as the 'King of Cooks', born at Villeneuve-Loubet.

1886 The Statue of Liberty, presented by France to mark the 100th anniversary of the Declaration of Independence and designed by the French sculptor Auguste Bartholdi, was unveiled by President Grover Cleveland—having taken more than nine years to complete.

1893 The Royal Navy's first destroyer, HMS *Havock*, went on trials.

1903 Evelyn Waugh, English novelist including *Brideshead Revisited*, born in London.

1914 Jonas Salk, American microbiologist and discoverer of the antipoliomyelitis vaccine, born in New York City of Polish-Jewish immigrant parents.

1927 Cleo Laine, English singer and entertainer, born in Southall, London, as Clementina Campbell.

1936 Carl Davis, American composer, born in New York City.

1952 William 'Billy' Hughes, Australian statesman and Prime Minister from 1915 to 1923, died aged 88.

1965 The stainless steel 'Gateway to the West' arch in St Louis, Missouri was completed to commemorate the westward expansion.

1975 Georges Carpentier, French boxer and world light heavyweight champion from 1920 to 1922, died.

1987 Woody Herman, American band leader, died aged 74, at the Cedars Sinai Medical Centre in Los Angeles.

29 OCTOBER [303]

National day of Turkey.

1618 Sir Walter Raleigh, English navigator, courtier and favourite of Elizabeth I, was executed at Whitehall for treason.

1740 James Boswell, Scottish diarist and biographer, born in Edinburgh, the son of a judge.

1814 The US Navy launched the *Demologos* at New York, the first steam-driven warship, designed by Robert Fulton.

1863 The International Red Cross was founded by Henri Dunant, as a result of his witnessing the tending of the wounded at the Battle of Solferino, near Mantua, Northern Italy.

1877 Wilfred Rhodes, Yorkshire and England cricketer, born in Kirkheaton.

1879 Franz von Papen, German politician and ambassador, born in Werl, Westphalia.

1886 Fred Archer rode 'Blanchland' at Newmarket—the last of his 2 746 winners in his brief 16 years in the saddle.

1891 Fanny Brice, American singer and comedienne, born in New York City.

1897 Joseph Goebbels, German political leader and Nazi propagandist, born in Rheydt, the son of a factory foreman.
1901 Anarchist Leon Czolgosz was electrocuted for the assassination of President McKinley.
1911 Joseph Pulitzer, American newspaper publisher who gave his name to annual prizes, died.
1923 The Turkish Republic was proclaimed, with Mustafa Kemal (or Kemal Ataturk) becoming its first President.
1927 Frank Sedgman, Australian tennis champion, born in the state of Victoria.
1929 The New York Stock Exchange in Wall Street 'crashed'—was known as 'Black Tuesday'.
1932 The French passenger liner *Normandie* was launched at St Nazaire, at the mouth of the river Loire.
1933 The Falange Party, a Spanish breed of Fascism, was founded by José Antonio Primo de Rivera.
1947 Richard Dreyfus, American film actor and Oscar winner, born in New York City.
1950 Gustav V, King of Sweden from 1907, died aged 92.
1964 The name of Tanzania was officially adopted.
1985 Lester Piggott rode 'Full Choke' at Nottingham, to record his 4349th winner and the last of his career in Britain.
1986 The final section of the M25 motorway around London was opened.
       John Braine, British novelist, notably *Room at the Top*, died.
1987 Thomas Hearns won the world middleweight title in Los Angeles, and so became the first boxer to have won world titles at four different weights.

30 OCTOBER   [304]

1650 'Quakers', the more common name for the religious Society of Friends, came into being during a court case, at which George Fox, the founder, told the magistrate to 'quake and tremble at the word of the Lord'.
1735 John Adams, American Federalist statesman and 2nd President, born in Braintree, Massachusetts, the son of a farmer.
1751 R. B. Sheridan, Irish playwright and dramatist, born in Dublin, the son of a teacher of elocution.
1823 Edmund Cartwright, English inventor of the power loom in 1785 and wool-combing machines, died in Hastings, Sussex aged 80.
1910 Henri Dunant, Swiss philanthropist who inspired the foundation of the International Red Cross in 1863, died.
1915 Sir Charles Tupper, Canadian Conservative statesman and Prime Minister in 1896, died.

1918 Czechoslovakia was proclaimed a republic, under the leadership of Jan Masaryk and Eduard Beneš.
1923 Andrew Bonar Law, Canadian-born British Conservative statesman and Prime Minister, died.
1932 Ralph Reader presented the first Gang Show, at the Scala Theatre in London.
1939 Henry Armstrong defended his world welterweight title for the fifth time in 21 days, four of which were won inside the distance.
1959 Jim Mollison, Scottish aviator and holder of many flying records, died.
1974 Muhammad Ali knocked out George Foreman in round eight in Kinshasa, Zaire, to regain the world heavyweight title.
1979 George Woodcock, British trade unionist, died in Epsom.
Sir Barnes Wallis, English aeronautical engineer, aircraft designer and inventor, died aged 92.

---

31 OCTOBER [305]

1485 The coronation of King Henry VII took place.
1620 John Evelyn, English diarist and author, born in Wotton, near Dorking, Surrey.
1632 Jan Vermeer, Dutch painter, born in Delft, the son of an art dealer.
1795 John Keats, one of the foremost English romantic poets, born in London, the son of an innkeeper.
1828 Sir Joseph Swan, English chemist and inventor of an electric lamp independently of Edison, born in Sunderland.
1864 Nevada, the Sagebrush or Battle Born State, became the 36th state of the Union.
1887 Chiang Kai-Shek, Chinese military and political leader, born in Fenghwa, Chekiang Province.
1903 Hampden Park, Queen's Park Football Club's home ground, Glasgow, was opened.
1916 Charles Taze Russell, American religious leader whose sect 'The Russellites' formed the nucleus of the Jehovah's Witnesses, died.
1920 Dick Francis, British author and ex-jockey, born near Tenby, South Wales.
1922 Benito Mussolini became Prime Minister and dictator of Italy.
1926 Harry Houdini, the famous American escape artist, whose real name was Erich Weiss, died in a Detroit hospital.
Jimmy Savile, British television and radio broadcaster, born in Leeds, Yorkshire.
1929 Eddie Charlton, Australian snooker player, born.
1930 Michael Collins, American astronaut and pilot of the command module during the first moon landing, born in Rome, Italy.

1951 Zebra crossings came into effect in Britain.
1952 United States detonated her first hydrogen bomb, at Eniwetok Atoll, in the Marshall Islands in mid-Pacific.
1961 Augustus John, Welsh portrait painter of many leading personalities of his day, died in Fordingbridge, Hampshire aged 83.
1968 Ramon Novarro, American romantic film actor, died.
1982 The Thames barrier was raised for the first time.
1984 Mrs Indira Gandhi, the Prime Minister of India, was murdered in Delhi by Sikh members of her bodyguard. Her son Rajiv was sworn in as Prime Minister some 12 hours later.

1 NOVEMBER [306]

National day of Algeria.
Fox-hunting begins in Britain.

1695 The Bank of Scotland was founded.
1755 A great earthquake occurred in Lisbon, resulting in an estimated 60 000 deaths.
1793 Lord George Gordon, British anti-Catholic agitator and leader of the 'Gordon Riots' in 1780, died in Newgate Prison, London.
1848 W. H. Smith's first railway bookstall was opened, in London's Euston Station.
1884 Standardisation of Gaelic football came with the formation of the Gaelic Athletics Association in Thurles, Ireland.
1887 (Laurence Stephen) L. S. Lowry, English artist of the Lancashire industrial scene, born in Rusholme, Manchester.
1895 The first motoring association, the 'American Motor League', was founded in Chicago, Illinois.
1922 Licences for radios were introduced in Britain, at ten shillings (50p) per annum.
1924 The British Empire Exhibition at Wembley closed.
1929 The Pony Club movement was founded in Britain.
1935 Gary Player, South African golfer, born in Johannesburg in the Transvaal.
1950 An attempt was made to assassinate President Truman by two members of a Puerto Rican nationalist movement.
1956 Premium Bonds first went on sale in Britain.
1978 The English newspaper the *Daily Star* was launched in the north and midlands.
1982 British television's Channel 4 began transmitting.
1985 Phil Silvers, American comedy actor noted for his character part as Sergeant Bilko, died.

1734 Daniel Boone, American frontiersman and hunter, born in Pennsylvania.

1755 Marie Antoinette, Austrian Princess and Queen Consort of Louis XVI of France, born in Vienna.

1766 Joseph Radetsky, Austrian field marshal and national hero, born in Trebnitz near Tabor.

1785 The first insubmersible lifeboat was patented by Lionel Lukin, a London coachbuilder.

1795 James Polk, American Democrat statesman and 11th President, born in Mecklenburg County, North Carolina.

1865 Warren Harding, American Republican statesman and 29th President, born near Corsica (now called Blooming Grove), Ohio, the son of a country physician.

1871 All prisoners in Great Britain were photographed, thereby starting the 'Rogues Gallery'.

1877 Victor Trumper, Australian Test cricketer, born in Sydney.

1887 Jenny Lind, Swedish international operatic soprano, known as the 'Swedish nightingale', died.

1889 North Dakota, the Sioux or Flickertail State, became the 39th state of the Union.
South Dakota, the Sunshine or Coyote State, became the 40th state of the Union.

1899 Ladysmith in Natal was beseiged by the Boers—until relieved by Sir Redvers Buller the following 28 February.

1903 The British newspaper *Daily Mirror* was first published in London.

1913 Burt Lancaster, American film actor and Oscar winner, born in New York City.

1920 The first regular radio programme was broadcast, KDKA, in Pittsburgh.

1924 The first crossword appeared in a British newspaper—sold to the *Sunday Express* by C. W. Shepherd.

1929 The Embassy in New York was opened as the first News Theatre cinema.

1930 Haile Selassie was crowned as Emperor of Ethiopia.

1934 Ken Rosewall, Australian tennis player, born in Sydney.

1936 The first British high definition TV broadcast took place, from the BBC studios in Alexandra Palace, North London.

1944 Erwin Rommel, German military commander in North Africa, known as the 'Desert Fox', died by self-administered poison in Herringen.

1950 George Bernard Shaw, British playwright and Nobel Prize winner in 1925, died in Ayot St Lawrence, Hertfordshire aged 94.

1959 The main section of the M1, London to Birmingham motorway, was officially opened.
1960 Said Ouita, athlete and world record breaker, born in Morocco.
1961 James Thurber, American cartoonist, humorous writer and creator of 'Walter Mitty', died in New York City.
1964 King Faisal ascended the throne of Saudi Arabia, succeeding his brother.
1981 CB or citizen's band radio became legal in Britain.
1986 Britain's first artificial heart transplant operation was performed at Papworth Hospital, Cambridgeshire.

3 NOVEMBER [308]

National day of Panama.

1493 Columbus, on his second expedition, sighted the island of Dominica in the West Indies.
1706 A violent earthquake occurred in Abruzzi, Italy, destroying the town and killing some 15 000 inhabitants.
1843 The 17-foot 16-ton statue of Lord Nelson was hauled up to the top of the column in Trafalgar Square, London—in two pieces—the top half was hoisted the following day.
1901 Leopold III, King of the Belgians from 1934, born the son of King Albert I.
1903 After a revolt Panama declared its independence from Colombia.
1926 Annie Oakley, American entertainer as a markswoman with rifle and shotgun in Buffalo Bill's Wild West Show, died.
1936 Roy Emerson, Australian international tennis champion, born in Blackbutt, Queensland.
1945 Gerd Müller, West German international footballer, born.
1949 Larry Holmes, a world heavyweight boxing champion, born in Cuthbert, Georgia.
1954 Henri Matisse, French painter and sculptor, died in Nice aged 84.
1957 The dog 'Laika' was launched into space in Russia's *Sputnik II*.
1961 Viscount Linley, son of Princess Margaret, sister of the Queen, and the Earl of Snowdon, born.

4 NOVEMBER [309]

1650 William III, King of England, Scotland and Ireland, born in The Hague, Holland, the posthumous son of William II of Orange.
1677 King William III married his cousin Princess Mary, the eldest daughter of King James II and Anne Hyde.

1740 Augustus Toplady, English writer of hymns, the best known of which is *Rock of Ages*, born in Farnham, Surrey.

1841 The first emigrant wagon train for California reached Stanislaus River—having left Independence, Missouri on 1 May.

1842 President Abraham Lincoln married Mary Todd in Springfield.

1847 Felix Mendelssohn, German composer and pianist, died in Leipzig.

1852 The building of the new House of Commons was completed, after the fire of 1834, to the designs of Sir Charles Barry and Augustus Pugin.

1862 Richard Gatling patented his revolving battery gun with 10 parallel barrels, firing some 1200 shots a minute.
Eden Phillpotts, English novelist, born in Mount Aboo, India.

1870 Derbyshire County Cricket Club was founded at a meeting in the Guildhall, Derby.

1879 The first cash register was patented, by saloon owner James Ritty of Dayton, Ohio.

1890 The first electrified underground railway system, now the City branch of the Northern Line in London, was officially opened by the Prince of Wales. Passenger service commenced the following 18 December.

1918 Art Carney, American film actor and Oscar winner, born in Mt Vernon, New York State.

1942 The second battle of El Alamein ended after 12 days, with Montgomery sending Rommel's army into full retreat.

1946 The United Nations Educational, Scientific and Cultural Organisation (UNESCO) was established, with headquarters in Paris.

---

5 NOVEMBER [310]

1605 The Gunpowder Plot of Guy Fawkes to blow up King James I and Parliament was foiled when 36 barrels of gunpowder were found in Parliament's cellar.

1854 The Battle of Inkerman in the Crimean War took place, with a French and British victory over the Russians.

1905 Joel McCrea, American film actor, born in Los Angeles, California.

1909 The first Woolworth's store in Britain was opened, in Liverpool's Lord Street.

1911 After numerous stops C. P. Rodgers landed in Pasadena and completed the first transcontinental aeroplane flight, having left New York on 17 September and spending 82 hours and 4 minutes in the air.

1912 Roy Rogers, American singing cowboy film actor, born in Cincinnati, Ohio as Leonard Slye.

1913 Vivien Leigh, British film actress and Oscar winner, born in Darjeeling, India, as Vivien Hartley.
1914 Cyprus was annexed to Britain on the outbreak of war with Turkey.
1927 The first automatic traffic lights in Britain began functioning, at Prince Square crossroads in Wolverhampton.
1935 Lester Piggott, English champion jockey, born in Wantage, Berkshire.
1940 HMS *Jervis Bay* was lost defending an Atlantic convoy from the German warship *Admiral Scheer*.
1956 The weekly British TV programme *What the papers say* was first transmitted.
1960 Mack Sennet, American film producer and creator of the 'Keystone Kops', died in Richmond, Canada.
1963 Tatum O'Neal, American film actress, born in Los Angeles, California, the daughter of Ryan O'Neal.
1977 Guy Lombardo, Canadian bandleader, playing 'the sweetest music this side of heaven', died.
1987 Eamonn Andrews, British broadcaster, died.

6 NOVEMBER [311]

1429 The coronation of King Henry VI of England took place.
1632 Gustavus II, King of Sweden from 1611, was killed in victory in the battle of Lutzen near Leipzig.
1796 Catherine the Great, German-born Empress of Russia from 1762, died.
1814 Adolphe Sax, Belgian musical instrument maker and designer of the saxophone and the saxhorn, born.
1854 John Philip Sousa, American bandmaster and composer of many marches, including *Stars and Stripes Forever*, born in Washington, DC.
1869 Blackfriars Bridge over the Thames in London was opened.
1872 General George Meade, of the Union Army and victor at Gettysburg, died.
1892 Sir John Alcock, English aviator of Alcock and Brown fame as the first to make the Atlantic crossing, born in Manchester.
1893 Tchaikovsky, famous Russian composer, died of cholera in St Petersburg.
     Edsel Ford, American car executive, born in Detroit the only child of Henry Ford.
1901 Kate Greenaway, English artist and illustrator of children's books, died.
1926 Frank Carson, stand-up comedian, born in Belfast.
1956 Work began on the Kariba High Dam on the river Zambesi, between Zambia and Zimbabwe.

National day of Russia.

1783 John Austin, a forger, became the last of some 50 000 to be executed at Tyburn.

1867 Marie Curie, Polish-French scientist, born in Warsaw as Marie Sklodowska.

1872 The 282 ton brigantine *Marie Celeste* set sail from New York on her ill-fated journey.

1885 The last spikes were driven in at Craigellachie in British Columbia to complete the Canadian Pacific Railway, after 4½ years' work.

1910 Leo Tolstoy, Russian novelist, notably *War and Peace* and *Anna Karenina*, died in a siding of Astapovo railway station.

1917 The Bolshevik Revolution, led by Lenin, overthrew Prime Minister Alexander Kerensky's government.

1918 Billy Graham, American Baptist evangelist, born in Charlotte, North Carolina, the son of a dairy farmer.

1926 Joan Sutherland, Australian operatic soprano singer, born in Sydney.

1935 Sir Charles Kingsford Smith, Australian pilot of distinction, knighted in 1932, passed over Calcutta on a flight from England and was never seen again.

1944 Franklin D. Roosevelt was re-elected American President, for a record fourth time.

1959 Victor McLaglen, English-born film actor and Academy Award (Oscar) winner in 1935 for his part in *The Informer*, died.

1962 Eleanor Roosevelt, niece of Theodore and wife of Franklin Delano, called 'The First Lady of the World', died aged 78.

1967 Henry Cooper beat Billy Walker and became the first and only boxer to win three Lonsdale belts outright.

1975 Cardinal Heenan, English Roman Catholic Archbishop of Westminster, died.

The *Scottish Daily News* closed down after six months.

1978 Gene Tunney, the legendary American heavyweight boxing champion, died aged 80.

1988 'Sugar' Ray Leonard knocked out Canadian Donny Lalonde in Las Vegas to complete an incredible collection of world titles at five different weights.

1656 Edmond Halley, English astronomer and mathematician, born in London.

1674 John Milton, English poet, blind since 1652 and author of *Paradise Lost*, died in Chalfont St Giles, Buckinghamshire.

1847 Bram Stoker, Irish novelist and creator of 'Count Dracula', born in Dublin.

1866 Herbert Austin, English motor mechanic, born in Little Missenden.

1868 Viscount Lee of Fareham, who gave the Buckinghamshire country-house Chequers to the nation in 1921, born.

1884 Steve Donoghue, English jockey of distinction, born in Warrington.

1886 Fred Archer, English champion jockey, shot himself at his house in Newmarket, aged 29.

1889 Montana, the Treasure State, became the 41st state of the Union.

1895 At Würzburg, Wilhelm Röntgen discovered electro-magnetic rays which he called X-rays.

1922 Dr Christiaan Barnard, South African surgeon and heart-transplant pioneer, born in Beaufort West, Cape Province.

1923 Hitler made his attempted Putsch at Munich.

1927 Ken Dodd, English comedian, born in Liverpool.
      Patti Page, American pop singer, born in Claremore, Oklahoma as Clara Anne Fowler.

1942 British and American troops invaded North Africa—in French Algeria, with Eisenhower in command—called 'Operation Torch'.

1958 British album record charts were first published by *Melody Maker*, with the *South Pacific* film track at number one.

1967 Radio Leicester, the first local radio station, was opened by the Postmaster General, Edward Short.

1973 The 'cod war' between Britain and Iceland ended.

1974 After 300 years in central London, Covent Garden market moved to its new site at Nine Elms.

1976 Gottfried von Cramm, German tennis star of the thirties, died in Egypt.

National day of Cambodia.

1841 King Edward VII, second child and eldest son of Queen Victoria, born in St James's Palace, London.

1869   Marie Dressler, Canadian-US film actress, born in Coburg, Ontario as Lelia Von Koerber.
1888   Jack the Ripper's fifth and last victim was Mary Jane Kelly, found in her room at 13 Miller's Court, London.
1908   Britain's first woman Mayor, Elizabeth Garrett Anderson, was elected at Aldeburgh, Suffolk.
1909   Katharine Hepburn, American film actress and Oscar winner on four occasions, born in Hartford, Connecticut.
1915   Hedy Lamarr, American film actress, born in Vienna, Austria as Hedwig Kiesler.
1918   Spiro Agnew, American politician and vice-President to Richard Nixon, born in Baltimore, Maryland.
       Kaiser William, Emperor of Germany, abdicated and fled to Holland.
1934   Carl Sagan, American astronomer, born in New York.
1937   Ramsay MacDonald, British statesman and the first Labour Prime Minister in 1924, died at sea while on a cruise for his health.
1940   Neville Chamberlain, British statesman and Prime Minister from 1937 to 1940, died.
1942   Tom Weiskopf, American golfer, born.
1951   Sigmund Romberg, Hungarian-born composer of operettas, notably *The Student Prince*, died.
1953   Dylan Thomas, Welsh poet, notably *Under Milk Wood*, died in New York City aged 39.
1965   An act abolishing capital punishment in Britain came into force.
1968   Wally Grout, Australian cricketer and wicket-keeper in 51 Tests, died.
1970   Charles de Gaulle, French general, statesman and President from 1958 to 1969, died of a heart attack in Colombey-les-deux-Eglises.
1980   Jimmy White became the youngest world amateur snooker champion at 18½, in Launceston, Tasmania.

10 NOVEMBER   [315]

1483   Martin Luther, German religious reformer, leader of the Protestant reformation, born in Eisleben, the son of a miner.
1683   George II, King of England, born in Hanover, Germany, the only son of George I.
1697   William Hogarth, English painter and engraver, born in Smithfield, London, the son of a teacher.
1728   Oliver Goldsmith, Irish poet and novelist, notably *The Vicar of Wakefield*, born the son of a curate.
1775   The United States Marine Corps was formed.

1871 Stanley met Livingstone at Ujiji, on the eastern shore of Lake Tanganyika—now in Tanzania.

1880 Jacob Epstein, British sculptor of Russo-Polish descent, born in New York City.

1889 Claude Rains, stage and film character actor, born in London.

1919 Britain's first regular civil airmail service was inaugurated, flying between Hounslow and Paris.

1925 Richard Burton, British dramatic actor, born as Richard Jenkins in Pontrhydfen, South Wales.

1938 Kemel Ataturk, statesman, founder and first President of the Turkish Republic in 1923, died.

1944 Tim Rice, English songwriter, born in Amersham, Buckinghamshire.

1959 Randy Mamola, American motorcycling champion, born.
     Lupino Lane, English comedian and theatre manager, died in London.

1971 Kenny Dalglish made his soccer international debut for Scotland, as a substitute against Belgium.

1982 Leonid Brezhnev, Soviet politician and President since 1964, died aged 75.

1985 Gary Kasparov, aged 22, became world chess champion when he beat Anatoly Karpov in Moscow.

1986 Sir Gordon Richards, 26 times champion jockey, died aged 82.

11 NOVEMBER [316]

1821 Fyodor Dostoyevsky, Russian novelist, born in Moscow, the son of a surgeon.

1830 Mail was first carried by railway, on the newly opened Liverpool to Manchester line.

1880 Ned Kelly, Australian bushranger and notorious bank robber, was hanged in Old Melbourne Gaol in Russell Street in his mid-twenties.

1882 Gustaf VI, King of Sweden, born the elder son of Gustaf V.

1885 George Patton, American military commander in World War II, born in San Gabriel, California.

1887 The first sod of the Manchester Ship Canal was cut.

1889 Washington, the Evergreen State, became the 42nd state of the Union.

1918 The Armistice was signed in Marshal Foch's railway coach, near Compiègne.
     Stubby Kaye, American actor and singer, born in New York City.

1920 Roy Jenkins, British politician and Labour Member of Parliament, born in Abersychan, Wales.
     The 35-foot Cenotaph War Memorial in Whitehall, London, designed by Sir Edwin Lutyens, was unveiled by King George V.

1921 The British Legion held its first Poppy Day.
1936 Sir Edward German, English composer, notably *Merrie England*, died.
1940 The Italian fleet at Taranto was crippled by naval planes of the Fleet Air Arm.
1945 Jerome Kern, American composer of Broadway shows and numerous songs, died.
1946 Stevenage in Hertfordshire became the first 'new town' to be designated in Britain.
     Alan Jones, Australian motor racing driver, born.
1947 Rodney Marsh, Australian cricketer, born.
1953 BBC's television programme *Panorama* was first transmitted by Patrick Murphy.
1965 Ian Smith, Prime Minister of Rhodesia, announced his country's unilateral declaration of independence (UDI).
1971 Sir Alan P. Herbert, created CH in 1970, died.
1975 Angola gained independence from Portugal.

---

12 NOVEMBER [317]

1671 Thomas Fairfax, British general and leader of the Parliamentary Army in the Civil War, died in Nunappleton, Yorkshire.
1815 Elizabeth Stanton, American reformer, born in Johnstown, New York State.
1833 Alexander Borodin, Russian composer, born in St Petersburg.
1840 Auguste Rodin, French sculptor, born in Paris, the son of a clerk.
1842 Lord Rayleigh, English physicist and Nobel Prize winner, born in Witham near Maldon, Essex.
1865 Elizabeth Gaskell, English novelist, notably *Cranford*, died near Alton, Hampshire.
1866 Sun Yat-Sen, Chinese nationalist and revolutionary leader, born in Tsuiheng near Canton.
1903 Jack Oakie, American film actor, born in Sedalia, Missouri as Lewis Delaney Offield.
1916 Percival Lowell, American astronomer who predicted the existence of the planet Pluto prior to its 1930 discovery, died in Flagstaff, Arizona.
1918 The Republic of Austria was declared, thus ending the Hapsburg dynasty.
1919 Brothers Ross and Keith Smith set out from Hounslow on the first aeroplane flight to Australia—reaching Darwin in their Vickers Vimy on 13 December.
1927 The first veteran car rally from London to Brighton, sponsored by the *Daily Sketch*, took place, and was won by John Bryce from an entry of 51.

1929 Princess Grace of Monaco was born in Philadelphia, Pennsylvania as Grace Patricia Kelly.

1944 The German battleship *Tirpitz* was sunk in Tromso Fjord, by Lancaster bombers of the RAF.

1947 Baroness Orczy, novelist noted for *The Scarlet Pimpernel* and the character 'Sir Percy Blakeney', died.

1951 The BBC television programme *Come Dancing* was first transmitted.

1961 Nadia Comaneci, Romanian international gymnast, born in Onesti.

1972 Rudolf Friml, American composer of operettas, notably *Rose Marie* and *The Vagabond King*, died aged 92.

1981 The US shuttle *Columbia* became the first space vehicle to make a second trip.

1982 Yuri Andropov became the new Soviet leader in succession to Brezhnev.

1983 The Lord Mayor's Show in London was an historic occasion, with its first Lady Lord Mayor, Dame Mary Donaldson.

---

13 NOVEMBER [318]

1312 King Edward III was born in Windsor Castle, the son of Edward II.

1687 Nell Gwyn or Gwynne, British actress and principally remembered as the mistress of Charles II by whom she had two sons, died in London aged 37.

1850 Robert Louis Stevenson, Scottish author, notably *Treasure Island* and *Kidnapped*, born at 8 Howard Place, Edinburgh, the son and grandson of famous lighthouse builders.

1851 The telegraph service between London and Paris was opened.

1854 John Peel, English squire, the subject of the old hunting song, died in Caldbeck in the Lake District.

1868 Gioacchino Rossini, Italian composer of operas, notably *The Barber of Seville* and *William Tell*, died in Passy, France aged 76.

1906 Hermione Baddeley, English character actress of stage and films, born in Broseley, Shropshire.

1914 The bra was patented in America by heiress Mary Phelps Jacob.

1916 The Battle of the Somme, which had the object of driving the Germans north towards the coast, ended at a cost of some 60 000 allied lives, having started on 1 July.

1922 Charles Bronson, American film actor, born in Ehrenfield, Pennsylvania as Charles Buchinsky.

1942 With Rommel's army in full retreat Tobruk was re-captured.

1969 Quins were born to Mrs Irene Hanson of Rayleigh, Essex.

1982 Chesney Allen, co-founder and last surviving member of the 'Crazy Gang', died aged 88.

1765 Robert Fulton, American engineer and inventor of the first steamboat, born of Irish parents in Pennsylvania.

1770 The source of the Blue Nile—Lake Tana in NW Ethiopia—was discovered by the British explorer James Bruce.

1840 Claude Monet, French Impressionist painter, born in Paris.

1863 Leo Baekeland, American chemist and inventor of 'Bakelite®', one of the first plastics, born in Ghent, Belgium.

1889 Pandit Nehru, statesman and first Prime Minister of India on its independence, born in Allahabad.

1891 Sir Frederick Banting, Canadian co-discoverer of insulin with Macleod and Best in 1922, born in Alliston, Ontario.

1896 Mamie Eisenhower, wife of America's 34th President, born in Boone, Iowa as Mamie Doud.

1900 Aaron Copland, American composer, born in Brooklyn, New York.

1904 Harold Larwood, English cricketer and fast bowler, born in Nurcargate, Nottinghamshire.

1905 Robert Whitehead, English engineer who invented the naval torpedo in 1866, died in Berkshire.

1908 Joe McCarthy, American politician and lawyer noted for his purge against Communism, born in Grand Chute, Wisconsin.

1910 Pilot Eugène Ely, in a Curtiss biplane, made the first take-off from a ship, the US light cruiser *Birmingham*, at anchor in Chesapeake Bay.

1914 Lord Roberts, British soldier and Boer War commander, died while visiting troops in the field in France.

1918 John Bromwich, Australian international tennis player, born in Kogarah, New South Wales.

1919 Veronica Lake, American film actress, born in Lake Placid, New York as Constance Ockleman.

1922 The BBC transmitted its first regular radio programme—a news bulletin from 2LO in London's Strand.

1933 Fred Haise, American Astronaut, born in Biloxi, Mississippi.

1934 Arsenal had seven of their players in the England soccer team against Italy.

1935 King Hussein of Jordan was born in Amman, the son of King Talal.

1940 Coventry Cathedral was destroyed by enemy action.

1941 Britain's aircraft carrier *Ark Royal* was sunk.

1946 Manuel de Falla, Spanish composer of the ballet *The Three-Cornered Hat*, died.

1948 Prince Charles (Charles Philip Arthur George), Prince of Wales, born in Buckingham Palace.

1952 Charts for single records were first published in Britain, by *New Musical Express*.

1959 The Dounreay fast reactor went into operation.

1963 The island of Surtsey off Iceland was 'born' by the eruption of an under-water volcano.

1969 *Apollo 12* was launched, with Charles Conrad, Richard Gordon and Alan Bean—Conrad and Bean making the 2nd moon landing.
Colour programmes began on British TV.

1973 Princess Anne married Captain Mark Phillips in Westminster Abbey.
Bobby Moore made his 108th football international appearance for England, against Italy at Wembley Stadium.

1983 The first cruise missiles arrived at the Greenham Common base in Newbury, Berkshire.

---

15 NOVEMBER   *[320]*

1708 William Pitt the Elder, British statesman and orator, born in Westminster, London.

1738 Sir William Herschel, English astronomer who discovered the planet Uranus in 1781, born in Hanover, Germany.

1802 George Romney, English portrait painter, died in Kendal, Cumbria.

1837 Pitman's system of shorthand was published, under the title *Stenographic Sound-Hand*.

1889 Dom Pedro was dethroned as Emperor, and a republic was proclaimed in Brazil.

1891 Averell Harriman, American administrator and ambassador, born in New York City.
Erwin Rommel, German Army field marshal and commander of the Afrika Korps, born in Heidenheim.

1897 Aneurin Bevan, British politician and Labour Party leader, born in Tredegar, Monmouth, one of 13 children of a miner.

1905 Mantovani, Italian conductor, born in Venice.

1908 The State of the Congo, founded in 1885, became a Belgian colony.

1927 Wallace Rowling, New Zealand Labour statesman and Prime Minister, born in Motueka.

1934 Petula Clark, British singer and actress, born in Ewell, Surrey.

1954 Lionel Barrymore, American film actor and Academy Award (Oscar) winner in 1931 for his part in *A Free Soul*, died aged 76.

1958 Tyrone Power, American film actor and leading man, died.

1965 American, Norman Breedlove achieved a world record speed of almost 614 m.p.h. for a jet-engined car—on Bonneville Salt Flats in Utah.
1968 The British liner *Queen Elizabeth* ended her last passenger voyage.
1974 Dr Donald Coggan succeeded Dr Michael Ramsey as Archbishop of Canterbury.
1977 A son, Peter Mark Andrew, was born to Princess Anne and Captain Mark Phillips.
1985 The Anglo-Irish Agreement was signed in Belfast by Mrs Thatcher and Dr Fitzgerald.

16 NOVEMBER [321]

1272 Death of King Henry III in Westminster, resulting in the accession of his elder son as Edward I.
1665 The *London Gazette*, originally called the *Oxford Gazette*, was first published.
1724 Jack Sheppard, English highwayman, hanged at Tyburn.
1811 John Bright, British Radical statesman and orator, born in Rochdale, Lancashire, the son of a Quaker cotton spinner.
1824 Hamilton Hume discovered the Murray River in Australia.
1896 Sir Oswald Mosley, British politician and Fascist leader, born in London.
1907 Oklahoma, the Sooner State, became the 46th state of the Union.
1942 Willie Carson, English champion jockey, born in Stirling, Scotland.
1960 Gilbert Harding, British television personality, collapsed and died on the steps of the BBC studios in London.
Clark Gable, American film actor and Academy Award (Oscar) winner in 1934 for his part in *It Happened One Night*, died.
1961 Frank Bruno, British heavyweight boxing champion, born.
1965 William Cosgrave, Irish statesman and President of the Irish Free State, died.
1982 Arthur Askey, Liverpool-born comedian, died in London aged 82.

17 NOVEMBER [322]

1558 Mary I, Queen of England, called Mary Tudor and 'Bloody Mary', died in St James's Palace in London—accession of her half-sister as Queen Elizabeth I.
1755 Louis XVIII, King of France after the fall of Napoleon, born in Versailles.

1858   Robert Owen, social reformer and early trade unionist, died aged 87.

1869   The 100-mile Suez Canal from Port Said to Port Tewfik, the work of Ferdinand de Lesseps, was opened at Port Said—work having begun on 25 April 1859.

1887   Viscount Montgomery, British soldier and commander of distinction in World War II, born the son of a vicar in Kennington, South London.

1917   Auguste Rodin, French sculptor whose works include *The Thinker* and *The Kiss*, died at Meudon near Paris aged 77.

1925   Rock Hudson, American film actor, born in Winnetka, Illinois as Roy Scherer.

1934   President Lyndon Johnson married Claudia Taylor, affectionately called 'Lady Bird'.

1970   Russia's *Luna 17* landed on the Sea of Rains on the moon and released the first moon-walker vehicle.

18 NOVEMBER [323]

1626   St Peter's Church in Rome was consecrated.

1786   Carl von Weber, German composer, born in Eutin near Lübeck of an Austrian family.

1789   Louis Daguerre, French artist and pioneer in photography, born near Paris.

1836   Sir W. S. Gilbert, English writer of comic operas, of Gilbert and Sullivan fame, born in London's Strand.

1852   The funeral of the Duke of Wellington took place in St Paul's Cathedral.

1860   Paderewski, Polish pianist, statesman and his country's first Prime Minister, born in Kurylowka.

1880   The Irish Football Association was formed.

1886   Chester Alan Arthur, American Republican statesman and 21st President from 1881 to 1885, died in New York City.

1899   Eugene Ormondy, US conductor and music director, born in Budapest, Hungary.

1901   George Gallup, American public opinion statistician who evolved the Gallup Polls, born in Jefferson, Iowa.

1903   Panama granted the canal strip to the US, by treaty ratified on 26 February 1904.

1909   Johnny Mercer, American lyricist and composer, born in Savannah, Georgia.

1918   The country of Latvia gained independence from Russia (by then under Lenin's rule) later to be the Soviet Union.

1923   Alan Shepard, the first American astronaut in space, born in East Derry, New Hampshire.

1935 Economic sanctions against Italy went into effect by members of the League of Nations, because of her invasion of Ethiopia—ended on 15 July 1936.

1941 John Watson, Australian Labour statesman, the country's 3rd Prime Minister in 1904 and the world's first Labour Prime Minister, died.

1963 The Dartford-Purfleet tunnel, linking Kent and Essex under the Thames, was opened.

1969 Joseph Patrick Kennedy, American diplomat and ambassador, died aged 81.

1983 Six girls were born to Janet Walton in the Liverpool Maternity Hospital—the only surviving sextuplets in Britain—Hannah, Ruth, Sarah, Lucy, Kate and Jenny.

1987 Fire broke out at King's Cross Underground station on London's Piccadilly line; the inferno resulted in the deaths of 31 travellers.

19 NOVEMBER [324]

1493 Puerto Rico was discovered by Christopher Columbus.

1600 King Charles I, born in Dunfermline Palace in Scotland, the second son of James I and Anne of Denmark.

1805 Ferdinand de Lesseps, French diplomat and engineer, best known as the builder of the Suez Canal, born in Versailles.

1828 Franz Schubert, Austrian composer, died in Vienna of typhus.

1831 James Garfield, American Republican statesman and 20th President, born near Orange, Ohio.

1850 Alfred, Lord Tennyson was appointed Poet Laureate—an appointment he held until his death in 1892.

1863 Abraham Lincoln delivered his famous address at the dedication of the military cemetery in Gettysburg, Pennsylvania.

1893 The first newspaper colour supplement was a four-page section published in the *New York World*.

1900 Anton Walbrook, actor in British films, born in Vienna as Adolf Wohlbruck.

1905 Tommy Dorsey, American trombonist, band leader and younger of the musical brothers, born in Shenandoah, Pennsylvania.

1917 Indira Gandhi, Indian stateswoman and first woman Prime Minister of her country, born in Allahabad, the daughter of Jawaharlal Nehru.

1969 Pelé, Brazilian footballer, scored the 1000th goal of his brilliant career.

1976 Sir Basil Spence, architect of the new Coventry Cathedral, knighted in 1960, died in Eye, Suffolk.

1759 The naval battle of Quiberon Bay took place—British Admiral Hawke destroying the French invasion fleet under Admiral Conflans, during the Seven Years War.

1841 Sir Wilfrid Laurier, Canadian Liberal statesman, born in St Lin, Quebec.

1885 Albert Kesselring, German air force commander, born in Markstedt.

1894 Anton Rubinstein, Russian pianist, composer and musical director, died in Peterhof.

1908 Alistair Cooke, English-American journalist and broadcaster, born in Salford, Manchester.

1917 Bobby Locke, South African golfing champion, born in Germiston in the Transvaal.

1920 Gene Tierney, American film actress, born in Brooklyn, New York.

Dulcie Gray, British actress, born as Dulcie Bailey.

1925 Robert Kennedy, American politician and younger brother of the 35th President, born in Brookline, Massachusetts.

Queen Alexandra, wife of King Edward VII, died.

1935 Admiral Jellicoe, British commander at the Battle of Jutland, created an Earl in 1925, died in London and is buried in St Paul's Cathedral beside Nelson.

1945 The Nuremberg war crimes tribunal began, with the trials of 24 Nazi leaders.

1947 Queen Elizabeth II, as Princess Elizabeth, married Prince Philip in Westminster Abbey.

1954 Clyde Cessna, American aircraft manufacturer, died.

1970 The Bank of England ten-shilling note went out of circulation.

1973 Allan Sherman, American comedian and composer of satirical songs, died.

1975 General Franco, Spanish statesman and Head of State from 1936, died.

1980 The solar-powered *Solar Challenger* was flown for the first time, entirely under solar power.

1694 Voltaire, French philosopher and writer, born in Paris as Jean Francois-Marie Arouet.

1695 Henry Purcell, English composer, died in London from tuberculosis.

1783 History was made when Francois de Rozier and Marquis
     d'Arlandes lifted off from the Bois de Boulogne in their hot air
     balloon and flew for 25 minutes, covering just over three
     kilometres.
1787 Samuel Cunard, Canadian shipowner, born in Halifax, Nova
     Scotia.
1789 North Carolina, the Tar Heel or Old North State, became the 12th
     state of the Union.
1843 Vulcanised rubber was patented in England by Thomas Hancock.
1918 The mighty German High Seas Fleet was handed over to the
     British Fleet for internment, at Scapa Flow in the Orkneys.
1931 Malcolm Williamson, composer, pianist and Master of the
     Queen's Music, born in Australia.
1936 The first television gardening programme was broadcast by the
     BBC—*In Your Garden* with Mr Middleton.
1941 Juliet Mills, English actress, born in London the elder daughter of
     Sir John Mills.
1942 James Hertzog, South African soldier, statesman and anti-British
     Premier, died.
1945 Goldie Hawn, American actress and giddy comedienne, born in
     Washington, DC.
1949 Max Baer, American heavyweight boxer and world champion
     1934/35, died in Hollywood.
1953 The Piltdown skull, 'discovered' by Charles Dawson in Sussex in
     1912, was found by anthropologists to be a hoax.
1958 Work began on the construction of the Forth Road Bridge in
     Scotland—to be the longest suspension bridge in Europe.
1960 Jacques Laffite, French motor racing driver, born.
1964 The Verrazano-Narrows Bridge (until the Humber Bridge the
     world's longest single span) across the entrance to New York
     City harbour was opened to traffic.

22 NOVEMBER [327]

National day of Lebanon.

1497 Vasco da Gama became the first to round the Cape of Good
     Hope—his fleet comprised the *St Gabriel*, the *St Raphael*, the *Berrio*
     and a store ship.
1718 Edward Teach, English pirate known as 'Blackbeard', was killed
     off the coast of North Carolina.
1774 Robert Clive, English soldier and British administrator in India,
     died from an overdose of opium.
1808 Thomas Cook, English travel agent pioneer, born in Melbourne,
     Derbyshire.

1819 George Eliot, English novelist, author of *The Mill on the Floss*, born near Nuneaton, Warwickshire as Mary Ann or Marian Evans, the daughter of an estate agent.
1890 Charles de Gaulle, French soldier, statesman and President, born in Lille.
1899 'Hoagy' Carmichael, American pianist and composer, born in Bloomington, Indiana.
Wiley Post, American aviator, born in Grand Saline, Texas.
1900 Sir Arthur Sullivan, English composer of comic operas in conjunction with W. S. Gilbert, died in London.
1913 Benjamin Britten, English composer, born in Lowestoft, Suffolk.
1914 Gardnar Mulloy, American tennis champion, born in Miami, Florida.
1916 Jack London, American novelist, notably *Call of the Wild* and *White Fang*, died in California.
1930 The first Irish Sweep—a sweepstake organised by the Irish Hospitals Trust with the backing of the government of the Republic of Ireland, was held, on the Manchester November Handicap horse race.
Sir Peter Hall, British theatre manager, born in Bury St Edmunds, Suffolk.
1943 Billie-Jean King, American tennis champion, born in Long Beach, California.
Lorenz Hart, American lyricist in collaboration with Richard Rogers, died.
1954 Andrei Vyshinsky, Soviet politician and Foreign Minister, died in New York City.
1956 The 16th Olympic Games opened in Melbourne.
1963 John F. Kennedy, American Democrat statesman and 35th President from 1961, was assassinated in Dallas allegedly by Lee Harvey Oswald—the remainder of his term of office was completed by Lyndon Johnson.
1967 Boris Becker, German tennis player and youngest male winner of the singles title at Wimbledon, born.
1975 King Juan Carlos II became Head of State in Spain—two days after the death of General Franco.
1980 Mae West, American film actress and sex symbol, died aged 88.
1986 Mike Tyson became the youngest ever, at 20 years old, heavyweight boxing champion when he defeated Trevor Berbick in Las Vegas.

23 NOVEMBER   *[328]*

1499 Perkin Warbeck, Flemish imposter claiming to be Richard of York, son of Edward IV, was executed in the Tower of London.

1804　Franklin Pierce, American Democrat statesman and 14th President, born in Hillsborough, New Hampshire.

1852　Britain's first pillar boxes, erected in St Helier, Jersey, were brought into public use.

1859　Billy the Kid, American outlaw and gunman, born in New York City as William H. Bonney.

1876　Manuel de Falla, Spanish composer of the ballet *The Three-cornered Hat*, born in Cadiz.

1887　Boris Karloff, film actor best known for horror roles, born in Dulwich, London as William Henry Pratt.

1888　'Harpo' Marx, of the Marx brothers comedy team, born in New York City.

1889　The first jukebox was installed, in the Palais Royal Saloon in San Francisco.

1910　American Dr Hawley Crippen was executed in London's Pentonville prison for the murder of his wife, Cora.

1934　Lew Hoad, Australian international lawn tennis player, born.

1963　The BBC television programme *Dr Who* was first broadcast, with William Hartnell playing the role of the Doctor.

1964　The first British commercial radio station—Manx—was opened.

1979　Merle Oberon, Australian-born actress in Hollywood, died.

---

24 NOVEMBER　　　　　　　　　　　　　　　　[329]

1572　John Knox, Scottish religious leader and founder of Scottish Presbyterianism, died.

1642　Abel Tasman, Dutch navigator, discovered Van Diemen's Land, which was renamed Tasmania in 1853.

1713　Laurence Sterne, Irish clergyman and novelist, author of *The Life and Opinions of Tristram Shandy*, born in Clonmel in the county of Tipperary, the son of an Army officer.

1784　Zachary Taylor, American soldier, Whig statesman and 12th President, born in Orange County in the state of Virginia.

1815　Grace Darling, heroine of a rescue in the North Sea in 1838, born in Bamburgh, Northumberland, the daughter of the lighthouse keeper.

1848　Lord Melbourne, British statesman and Whig Prime Minister on two occasions died near Welwyn, Hertfordshire.

1859　Cass Gilbert, American architect, born in Zanesville, Ohio.

1864　Toulouse-Lautrec, French painter, born in Albi.

1868　London's Smithfield meat market was opened by the Lord Mayor.
　　　Scott Joplin, American pianist and composer, born in Texarkana, Texas.

1894 Herbert Sutcliffe, Yorkshire and England cricketer, born in Pudsey, near Leeds.
1916 Sir Hiram Maxim, English-born American inventor of the machine gun in 1883 that bears his name, died in London.
1929 Georges Clemenceau, French statesman and twice Premier, known as the 'Tiger', died.
1955 Ian Botham, Worcestershire and England all-round cricketer, born in Cheshire.
1963 Lee Harvey Oswald, the alleged assassin of President Kennedy, was shot by Jack Ruby.

25 NOVEMBER [330]

1748 Isaac Watts, English hymn writer, notably *O God, our help in ages past* and *When I survey the wondrous cross*, died.
1823 The chain pier at Brighton was opened.
1835 Andrew Carnegie, American industrialist and philanthropist, born in Dunfermline, Scotland, the son of a weaver.
1844 Karl Benz, German engineer and pioneer of early motor cars, born in Karlsruhe.
1881 Pope John XXIII, born in Sotto il Monte, near Bergamo, Italy, as Angelo Giuseppe Roncalli, the son of a peasant.
1903 British-born boxer Bob Fitzsimmons won the world light-heavyweight title, and so became the only boxer to have won the three heaviest titles.
1912 Francis Durbridge, English writer of mystery novels, born.
1914 Joe Dimaggio, American baseball player, born in Martinez, California.
1937 The first British quiz programme, an inter-regional spelling competition, was broadcast.
1941 The Royal Navy battleship HMS *Barham* was sunk.
     Tina Turner, American rock singer, born in Brownsville, Tennessee as Annie Mae Bullock.
1952 The long-running play *The Mousetrap* by Agatha Christie opened in London, at the Ambassador's Theatre.
     Imran Khan, Pakistan Test cricketer, born.
1957 Sir Ernest Oppenheimer, diamond mining magnate and philanthropist, knighted in 1921, died.
1965 Dame Myra Hess, British concert pianist, died in London aged 75.
1970 Peter Shilton won the first of his many England soccer caps, playing against East Germany at Wembley.
1974 U Thant, Burmese diplomat and Secretary-General of the United Nations from 1962 to 1971, died.
1975 Surinam, a republic of NE South America—previously called Dutch Guiana—became fully independent.

1731 William Cowper, English poet, born in Berkhamsted, Hertford-shire, the son of a rector.
1789 The first national Thanksgiving Day in the USA, celebrating the 1621 harvest of the Pilgrim Fathers, was held. Is now held on the fourth Thursday in November.
1832 Trams were first introduced by John Mason in New York City, between Prince Street and 14th Street.
1836 John McAdam, Scottish engineer who introduced the 'macadam-ising' system of road-making, died.
1851 Nicolas Soult, French general under Napoleon, died in Soultberg aged 82.
1905 Emlyn Williams, British playwright and actor, born in Mostyn, North Wales.
1917 Sir Leander Jameson, British colonial administrator and leader of the 'Jameson' raid into the Transvaal, died.
1922 The tomb of the king Tutankhamun was discovered by Howard Carter and his patron, Lord Carnarvon.
       Charles Schulz, American cartoonist and creator of the comic strip *Peanuts*, born in Minneapolis, Minnesota.
1924 Pat Phoenix, actress, born in Portnum, County Galway, Ireland.
1933 Robert Goulet, American actor and singer, star of Broadway musicals, born in Lawrence, Kansas.
1956 Tommy Dorsey, American trombonist and key figure in the big band era, died.
1966 The world's first major tidal power station, at the Rance estuary in the Golfe de St Malo in Brittany, was officially opened by President de Gaulle.
       Harold Holt won the Australian General Election to become the country's Liberal Prime Minister.

1582 William Shakespeare, at 18, married Anne Hathaway.
1701 Anders Celsius, Swedish astronomer who devised the centigrade temperature scale in 1742, born in Uppsala.
1811 Andrew Meikle, Scottish agricultural engineer, inventor of the threshing machine in 1786, died in Dunbar, East Lothian.
1895 Alexandre Dumas (*fils*), French playwright, author of *La Dame aux Camélias*, died.
1914 On completion of their training Britain's first policewomen went on duty, in Grantham, Lincolnshire.

1921 Alexander Dubcek, Czechoslovakian statesman and political leader, born in Uhrovek.
1925 Ernie Wise, of Morecambe and Wise comedy team, born in Leeds, Yorkshire as Ernest Wiseman.
1942 The French fleet in the harbour was scuttled when German forces entered Toulon.
Jimi Hendrix, American singer and guitarist, born in Seattle, Washington.
1953 Eugene O'Neill, American playwright and Nobel Prize winner in 1936, died in Boston, Massachusetts.
1970 Pope Paul II was unharmed by a knife-wielding assailant dressed as a priest at Manila airport.
1975 Ross McWhirter, co-editor and compiler of the *Guinness Book of Records*, killed.

28 NOVEMBER [333]

1757 William Blake, English poet, born in London.
1820 Friedrich Engels, German Socialist and associate of Karl Marx, born in Barmen.
1829 Anton Rubinstein, Russian pianist and composer, born in Wechwotynetz.
1837 John Wesley Hyatt, American inventor of celluloid, born in Starkey in the State of New York.
1859 Washington Irving, American author, notably *Rip Van Winkle* and *The Legend of Sleepy Hollow*, died.
1883 Andrei Vyshinsky, Soviet politician, born in Odessa of Polish origin.
1905 Sinn Fein Irish political party was founded in Dublin by Arthur Griffith.
1919 Keith Miller, Australian Test cricketer, born in Melbourne, the capital of Victoria.
1920 Cecilia Colledge, British ice skating champion, born.
1934 'Baby Face' Nelson, American bank robber and a member of the John Dillinger gang, was killed in a gun battle with law officers.
1935 The Miles quads (Ann, Ernest, Paul, and Michael) were born in St Neots, Cambridgeshire.
1943 Randy Newman, American singer and songwriter, born in Los Angeles.
1945 Dwight Davis, American donor of the Davis Cup for international tennis, died.
1959 The dockyard at Hong Kong closed, after 80 years.
1962 Wilhelmina, Queen of the Netherlands from 1890 to 1948, died.
1968 Enid Blyton, English writer of children's books, died.

1976 Len Harvey, British light-heavyweight and heavyweight boxing champion, died in London.

Rosalind Russell, American film and stage actress, died in Beverly Hills, California.

29 NOVEMBER [334]

National day of Yugoslavia.

1530 Cardinal Wolsey, English churchman, statesman and Lord Chancellor, died on his way from his York diocese to London.

1780 Maria Theresa, Empress of Austria and Queen of Hungary and Bohemia, died in Vienna.

1832 Louisa M. Alcott, American novelist, author of *Little Women*, born in Germanstown, Philadelphia.

1864 The Sand Creek massacre took place—the tribes were waiting to surrender—of Cheyenne and Arapahoe Indians by soldiers under the command of Colonel Chivington.

1872 Horace Greeley, American newspaper editor and founder of the *New York Tribune*, died.

1895 Busby Berkeley, US actor and choreographer, born in Los Angeles as William Berkeley Enos.

1924 Giacomo Puccini, Italian opera composer, notably *La Bohème* and *Madame Butterfly*, died in a hospital in Brussels of cancer of the throat.

1929 Richard Byrd, American admiral, explorer and aviator, made the first flight over the South Pole, with Pilot Bernt Balchen.

1932 Jacques Chirac, French statesman and Prime Minister, born in Paris.

1945 Yugoslavia was proclaimed a communistic Republic.

1954 Sir George Robey, English comedian, dubbed the 'Prime Minister of mirth', died.

1974 James J. Braddock, American heavyweight boxer and world champion from 1935 to 1937, died in North Bergen, New Jersey.

1975 Graham Hill, British racing driver and Grand Prix winner, was killed in a plane crash at Arkley, Hertfordshire.

30 NOVEMBER [335]

St Andrew's Day—national day of Scotland.

1667 Jonathan Swift, Irish clergyman and writer, author of *Gulliver's Travels*, born in Dublin.

1835 Mark Twain, American author and humorist, born near Florida, Missouri as Samuel Langhorne Clemens.

1872 The first football international took place, Scotland and England drawing 0–0 in Partick, Glasgow.

1874 Sir Winston Churchill, British statesman and Prime Minister, born in Blenheim Palace, Woodstock, Oxfordshire.

1900 Oscar Wilde, Irish poet and dramatist, notably *The Importance of Being Ernest*, died in poverty and exile in Paris, having adopted the name of Sebastian Melmoth.

1901 Edward John Eyre, Australian explorer into the centre of the country and later in turn the Governor of New Zealand, St Vincent and Jamaica, died aged 86.

1920 Virginia Mayo, American film actress, born in St Louis, Missouri as Virginia Jones.

1924 Allan Sherman, American comedian, born in Chicago as Allan Copelon.

1936 Crystal Palace, a building of glass and iron, designed by Joseph Paxton to house the Great Exhibition of 1851, was burned down on its new site in Sydenham.

1944 Britain's largest ever and last battleship, HMS *Vanguard*, was launched in Clydebank, Scotland—having been laid down on 20 October 1941.

1955 Floodlights were used for the first time at Wembley Stadium, London, towards the end of the soccer international against Spain.

1956 Floyd Patterson became the youngest boxer ever at 21 years and 10 months to win the world heavyweight title when he knocked out Archie Moore in Round five in Chicago for the title left vacant by Rocky Marciano. Mike Tyson, the current world heavyweight titleholder has now broken this record.

1957 Beniamino Gigli, Italian operatic tenor, died.

1966 Full independence was proclaimed in Barbados.

1972 Compton Mackenzie, British writer knighted in 1952, died in Edinburgh aged 89.

1977 Terence Rattigan, English playwright, notably *French Without Tears* and *The Winslow Boy*, died.

1979 'Zeppo' Marx, the agent of the Marx Brothers, died.
Joyce Grenfell, actress, entertainer and broadcaster, died in London.

1986 Cary Grant, US film actor, died aged 82.

1987 James Baldwin, American writer, died aged 63.

1 DECEMBER   [336]

1135 Death of King Henry I of England near Rouen—accession of his nephew Stephen.

1655 Samuel Pepys married Elizabeth St Michel in St Margaret's, Westminster.

1822 Dom Pedro was crowned Emperor of recently independent Brazil.

1844 Queen Alexandra, wife of Edward VII, born, the eldest daughter of King Christian of Denmark.

1895 Henry Williamson, English novelist and nature writer, notably *Tarka the Otter*, born in Bedfordshire.

1910 Alicia Markova, English prima ballerina, born in London as Lilian Alicia Marks.

1913 Mary Martin, American actress and singer, born in Weatherford, Texas.

1919 Nancy, Viscountess Astor, Member of Parliament for the Sutton division of Plymouth, became the first woman Member to take her seat in the House of Commons.

1925 The Locarno Pact was signed in London, guaranteeing peace and frontiers in Europe.

1928 Keith Michell, Australian actor, born in Melbourne.

1935 Woody Allen, American comedian, writer and film director, born in Brooklyn, New York, as Allen Stewart Königsberg.
Lou Rawls, American rhythm-and-blues singer, born in Chicago.

1939 Lee Trevino, American international golf champion, born near Horizon City in Texas.

1942 The Beveridge Report on Social Security was issued; it formed the basis of the welfare state in Britain.

1947 Samuel Courtauld, silk and rayon manufacturer and patron of the arts, died in London.

1966 Britain's post offices issued the first special Christmas stamps.

1973 David Ben-Gurion, Israeli statesman, his country's first Prime Minister, often called the 'Father of the Nation', died.

---

2 DECEMBER

1547 Hernando Cortez, Spanish conqueror of Mexico in 1521, died near Seville.

1697 The re-built St Paul's Cathedral was formally opened.

1804 Napoleon Bonaparte was crowned Emperor in Paris, by Pope Pius VII.

1805 The Battle of Austerlitz took place near Brunn in Moravia, in which Napoleon defeated the Austro-Russian force under the command of Kutuzov—is sometimes called the 'Battle of the Three Emperors'.

1823 The Monroe Doctrine was declared, opposing European attempts to interfere.

1849 Queen Adelaide, wife of William IV, died.
1859 John Brown, American anti-slavery campaigner, was hanged for treason, in Charlestown, West Virginia.
1899 Sir John Barbirolli, English conductor and musical director, born in London of Italian parents.
1901 King Camp Gillette patented the first safety razor.
1903 Jim Sullivan, Wigan's international Rugby League footballer, born.
1916 The lights of the Statue of Liberty were turned on by President Wilson.
1942 The world's first nuclear chain reaction took place at Stagg Field at the University of Chicago, under physicists Enrico Fermi and Arthur Compton.
1966 British Prime Minister Harold Wilson met Ian Smith on HMS *Tiger* off Gibraltar for talks on the independence of Rhodesia.
1969 Stephen Potter, English radio producer and writer of humorous books, died in London.
1972 Gough Whitlam became Labour Prime Minister of Australia.
1987 Peter Darrell, CBE, founder-director of Scottish Ballet and choreographer, died aged 58.

3 DECEMBER [338]

1753 Samuel Crompton, English inventor of the spinning-mule, which substituted machinery for hand work in the cotton industry, born in Firwood near Bolton, Lancashire, the son of a farmer.
1795 Sir Rowland Hill, English educator and pioneer in postal services, born in Kidderminster, Worcestershire.
1818 Illinois, the Prairie State, became the 21st state of the Union.
1854 Miners fought with police and troops in Ballarat, in a battle known as the Eureka Stockade, opposing a method of licensing.
1857 Joseph Conrad, English novelist notably *Nostromo*, born in Berdichev of Polish parents as Teodor Jozef Konrad Korzeniowski.
1894 Robert Louis Stevenson, Scottish novelist, author of *Treasure Island* and *Kidnapped*, died on the island of Samoa in the Pacific.
1905 Leslie Ames, Kent and England cricketer, born in Elham.
1910 Mary Baker Eddy, American religious leader and founder of the Christian Science movement, died.
1917 The Quebec Bridge, the world's longest cantilever, over the St Lawrence river, was opened to traffic—87 lives were lost during its construction.
1919 Pierre Auguste Renoir, French Impressionist painter, died in Cagnes-sur-Mer.
1930 Andy Williams, American singer and entertainer, born in Wall Lake, Iowa.

1953 Franz Klammer, Austrian skier and downhill racing champion, born.

1967 Christiaan Barnard performed the first heart transplant operation—Louis Washansky received the heart of traffic victim Denise Darvali, at Groote Schuur Hospital in Cape Town, but died 18 days later.

1969 Marshal Voroshilov, Soviet political leader and army marshal, died.

1980 Sir Oswald Mosley, English politician and leader of the British Union of Fascists, died in exile in his home near Paris.

1984 A leakage of poisonous gas from the pesticides factory in Bhopal, India killed over 2500 and blinded many thousands.

---

4 DECEMBER [339]

1154 Nicolas Breakspear became the only English Pope—as Adrian IV.

1642 Cardinal Richelieu, French statesman and chief minister to Louis XIII from 1624, died in Paris.

1732 John Gay, English poet and playwright, notably *The Beggar's Opera*, died in London.

1791 *The Observer*, the oldest Sunday newspaper in the United Kingdom, was first published.

1795 Thomas Carlyle, Scottish historian and writer, born in Ecclefechan, Dumfriesshire, the son of a master mason.

1798 Luigi Galvani, Italian scientist and anatomist who researched into animal electricity, or galvanism, died.

1835 Samuel Butler, English novelist and satirist, known especially for his utopian satire, *Erewhon*, born in Langar rectory, near Bingham, Nottinghamshire.

1850 William Sturgeon, English physicist who built the first electro-magnet, died in Prestwich, Lancashire.

1865 Edith Cavell, English nurse and patriot, born the daughter of the rector of Swardeston in Norfolk.

1875 Edgar Wallace, English writer of detective thrillers and playwright, born.

1892 General Franco, Spanish dictator and Head of State, born in El Ferrol.

1922 Deanna Durbin, singer and film actress, born in Winnipeg, Manitoba, Canada.

1930 Ronnie Corbett, British actor, comedian and partner of Ronnie Barker, born in Edinburgh.

1937 The character 'Desperate Dan' first appeared in *The Dandy* comic.

1965 *Gemini 7* was launched, with Frank Borman and James Lovell.

1969 Jack Payne, British dance band leader, died.

1976 Benjamin Britten, English composer, died in Aldeburgh, Suffolk.

National day of Thailand.

1594 Gerard Mercator, Flemish geographer and cartographer, died in Duisberg.

1697 The first Sunday service was held in the new St Paul's Cathedral.

1766 Christie's, famous auctioneers of London, held their first sale.

1782 Martin van Buren, American Democrat statesman and 8th President, born in Kinderhook in the State of New York, the son of a Dutch farmer.

1791 Wolfgang Amadeus Mozart, Austrian composer, died of typhus in Vienna, and was buried in the common ground of St Mark's churchyard.

1839 George Armstrong Custer, American cavalry commander in the West, born in Harrison County, Ohio.

1859 Admiral Jellicoe, British naval commander, born in Southampton, the son of a sea captain.

1870 Alexandre Dumas the elder, French novelist, best known for *The Three Musketeers* and *The Count of Monte Cristo*, died in Dieppe.

1872 *Marie Celeste*, an American brig, captained by Benjamin Briggs, was found by the *Dei Gratia* abandoned in the Atlantic on its way to Genoa with a cargo of alcohol.

1879 Clyde Cessna, American aircraft manufacturer, born in Hawthorne, Iowa.

1899 Sir Henry Tate, English businessman, philanthropist and founder of the Tate Gallery in London, died aged 80.

1901 Walt Disney, American cartoon film producer, born in Chicago, Illinois.

1906 Otto Preminger, American film director, born in Vienna, Austria.

1908 The first American football game in which players were numbered was the University of Pittsburgh v Washington and Jefferson, at Pittsburgh.

1926 Claude Monet, French painter and one of the founders of the Impressionist movement, died as a recluse in Giverny.

1933 Prohibition in America was repealed by the 21st Amendment— having come into effect on 16 January 1920.

1958 The first STD telephone service in Britain was inaugurated in Bristol, by the Queen calling up the Lord Provost of Edinburgh.
The first motorway in Britain, the 8½-mile Preston by-pass section of the M6, was opened by the then Prime Minister Harold Macmillan.

National day of Finland.

1421 Henry VI, born in Windsor Castle, the only child of Henry V.
1492 Haiti, a republic of the West Indies, was discovered by Columbus—was then named Hispaniola.
1732 Warren Hastings, British administrator and first Governor-General of India, born in Churchill, Oxfordshire.
1778 Joseph Gay-Lussac, French physicist and chemist, born in St Léonard.
1877 Thomas Edison demonstrated the first gramophone in West Orange, New Jersey, a recording of himself reciting *Mary Had a Little Lamb*.
1882 Anthony Trollope, English novelist, best known for his *Barchester Chronicles* of Victorian life, died in London, and was buried in Kensal Green, London.
1888 Will Hay, British music hall and film comedy actor, born in Stockton-on-Tees.
1889 Jefferson Davis, American political leader and President of the Confederate States, died aged 81.
1905 James J. Braddock, American heavyweight boxing champion, known as the 'Cinderella Man', born in North Bergen, New Jersey.
1907 America suffered its worst mine disaster, with 361 deaths in Monongah, West Virginia.
1908 'Baby Face' Nelson, American bank robber, born in Chicago.
1914 Cyril Washbrook, Lancashire and England cricketer, born.
1917 Finland proclaimed independence from Russian rule.
1920 Dave Brubeck, American pianist and composer, born in Concord, California.
1921 The Irish Free State was established after independence from the United Kingdom.

1732 The original Covent Garden Opera House in London, designed by Edward Shepherd, was opened.
1783 William Pitt the Younger became the youngest of Britain's Prime Ministers—aged 24.
1787 Delaware, the Diamond or First State, achieved statehood.
1815 Marshal Ney, French soldier, the most famous of Napoleon's marshals, was shot in Paris for high treason.
1817 Captain Bligh, captain of the *Bounty*, died in London.

1863 Pietro Mascagni, Italian composer, famous for his *Cavalleria Rusticana*, born in Leghorn, the son of a baker.
1879 Rudolf Friml, American composer, born in Prague, Czechoslovakia.
1894 Ferdinand de Lesseps, French diplomat, engineer and promoter of the Suez Canal, died aged 89.
1915 Eli Wallach, American film actor, born in Brooklyn, New York.
1916 David Lloyd George became head of the wartime coalition Government.
1941 Some 360 Japanese planes attacked the US Pacific Fleet anchored at Pearl Harbor in Hawaii.
1957 Geoff Lawson, New South Wales and Australia Test cricketer, born.
1962 Kirsten Flagstad, Norwegian operatic soprano, died.
1972 *Apollo 17* was launched, with Eugene Cernan, Ronald Evans and Dr Harrison Schmitt—Cernan and Schmitt making the 6th Moon landing.
1975 Thornton Wilder, American novelist, especially *The Bridge of San Luis Rey*, died.
1979 Charles Haughey was elected Prime Minister of the Irish Republic for the first time, on the resignation of Jack Lynch.

8 DECEMBER [343]

1542 Mary, Queen of Scots, cousin of Queen Elizabeth I, born in Linlithgow Palace, the daughter of James V of Scotland.
1765 Eli Whitney, American inventor who perfected the cotton-gin, which made cotton growing highly profitable, born in Westborough, Massachusetts.
1841 Prince Albert Edward was created Prince of Wales—later became King Edward VII.
1863 The first heavyweight boxing championship of the world took place, in Wodhurst, Kent—Tom King of England beating American John Heenan.
1864 Brunel's Clifton Suspension Bridge over the river Avon in Bristol was opened.
1865 Jean Sibelius, Finland's leading composer, noted for *Finlandia*, born in Hameenlinna, the son of a surgeon.
1894 James Thurber, American humorous artist, writer and creator of 'Walter Mitty', born in Columbus, Ohio.
1911 Lee J. Cobb, American film actor, born in New York City as Lee Jacoby.
1925 Sammy Davis junior, American singer and entertainer, born in New York City.

1934 The London to Australia airmail service was inaugurated.

1939 James Galway, British international flautist, born in Belfast.

1941 Britain and the United States declared war on Japan.

Geoff Hurst, the only scorer of three goals in a World Cup final, born in Ashton-under-Lyne, Greater Manchester.

1963 19 year old Frank Sinatra junior was kidnapped from his hotel room in Lake Tahoe, California. He was released three days later after his father paid the 240 000 dollar ransom.

1964 Simon Marks, successful retailer in conjunction with Thomas Spencer, knighted in 1944 and raised to the Peerage in 1961, died in London at his head office.

1978 Golda Meir, Israeli stateswoman and Prime Minister from 1969 to 1974, died.

1981 Arthur Scargill was elected leader of the National Union of Mineworkers in Britain in succession to Joe Gormley.

9 DECEMBER [344]

National day of Tanzania.

1608 John Milton, English poet, notably *Paradise Lost*, born in Cheapside, London, the son of a scrivener.

1641 Sir Anthony van Dyck, Flemish court painter to Charles I, died in his studio in Blackfriars, London, and was buried in Old St Paul's.

1837 Émile Waldteufel, French composer, notably of the *Skaters Waltz*, born in Strasbourg.

1848 Joel Chandler Harris, American writer and creator of 'Uncle Remus', born in Eatonton, Georgia.

1868 W. E. Gladstone became Prime Minister on the first of his four terms of office.

1874 Ezra Cornell, American capitalist, philanthropist and founder of Cornell University in Ithaca, died.

1886 Clarence Birdseye, American inventor of a process for deep-freezing foodstuffs, born in New York City.

1902 R. A. Butler, British Conservative politician, born in Attock Serai, India.

1909 Douglas Fairbanks junior, American film actor, born in New York City.

1911 Broderick Crawford, American film director, born in Philadelphia, Pennsylvania.

1915 Elizabeth Schwarzkopf, German international operatic singer, born in Jarotschin, Posen.

1918 Kirk Douglas, American film actor, born in Amsterdam, New York to Russian-Jewish parents as Issur Danielovitch Demsky.

1921 Sir Arthur Pearson, English newspaper owner and founder of *Pearson's Weekly* in 1890, died.

1929 Robert Hawke, Australian Labour statesman and Prime Minister, born in Bordertown, South Australia, the son of a Congregational minister.

1933 The London to Singapore airline service was inaugurated.

1957 Donny Osmond, American entertainer, born in Ogden, Utah.

1960 The first episode of British television's *Coronation Street* was screened.

1961 Tanganyika became independent.

1962 Tanzania became a republic within the Commonwealth, with Julius Nyerere its first President.

1980 John Lennon, British composer, of 'Beatles' fame, was murdered outside his Manhattan home, by Mark David Chapman.

---

10 DECEMBER [345]

Grouse shooting ends.

1768 The Royal Academy of Arts was founded, with Joshua Reynolds its first President.

1805 William Lloyd Garrison, American journalist and abolitionist, born in Newburyport, Massachusetts.

1817 Mississippi, the Magnolia State, became the 20th state of the Union.

1819 Felice Orsini, Italian nationalist and conspirator, born in Meldola.

1845 The first pneumatic tyres were patented by the Scottish civil engineer Robert Thomson.

1851 Melvil Dewey, American librarian who devised the system of classification for library cataloguing, born in Adams Centre, State of New York.

1865 Leopold I, King of the Belgians, the first sovereign on its separation from the Netherlands, died.

1868 The first edition of *Whitaker's Almanack* was published.
The first traffic lights, erected off London's Parliament Square, went into operation.

1878 Henry Wells, American transport partner of William Fargo, died.

1891 Earl Alexander, British army commander in North Africa and Italy in World War II, born in County Tyrone, Ireland.

1896 Alfred Nobel, Swedish chemist and philanthropist, inventor of dynamite and founder of the Nobel Prizes, died in San Remo, Italy.

1898 Cuba became an independent State—Spain giving up all claims after the short Spanish-American War.

1901 Nobel Prizes were first awarded.

1902 The Aswan dam, built to control the Nile flood, was opened.

1941 The British battleships *Repulse* and *Prince of Wales* were sunk off Malaya by Japanese aircraft.

1945 London's second Waterloo Bridge, designed by Sir Giles Gilbert Scott, was formally opened for full use, its half-width having been opened in 1942.

1946 Damon Runyon, American story writer, notably *Guys and Dolls*, died.

1958 The first domestic jet airliner passenger service in the US was opened by National Airlines, between New York and Miami.

1959 The raising of the British school leaving age to 16 was recommended by the Crowther Report.

1963 Zanzibar became independent, after being a British Protectorate since 1890.

Jahangir Khan, squash player and a world champion, born in Karachi.

1969 A sixth Nobel Prize was added, for Economics.

1987 Jascha Heifetz, American violin virtuoso and international celebrity, died in Los Angeles following a fall, aged 86.

---

11 DECEMBER   *[346]*

1803 Hector Berlioz, French composer, born in La Côte Saint André, near Grenoble, the son of a doctor.

1816 Indiana, the Hoosier State, became the 19th state of the Union.

1843 Robert Koch, German bacteriologist, born in Klausthal.

1883 Victor McLaglen, English-American film actor and Oscar winner for *The Informer* (1935), born in London.

1894 The first Motor Show opened in the Champs-Elysées, Paris, with nine exhibitors—closed on 25th.

1903 The first wildlife preservation society in Britain was founded, under the name of 'The Society for the Preservation of the Wild Fauna of the Empire'.

1913 Carlo Ponti, Italian film director, born in Milan.

1914 The Royal Flying Corps (later the Royal Air Force) adopted the roundel for aircraft identification.

1917 Sir Mackenzie Bowell, Canadian Conservative statesman and Prime Minister, died aged 93.

1918 Alexander Solzhenitsyn, Russian novelist, born in Rostov.

1931 The Statute of Westminster, recognising independence of the British Commonwealth, became law.

1936 Edward VIII abdicated as King, in favour of his brother, the Duke of York, who became George VI.

1965 Ed Murrow, American journalist, broadcaster and director of the US Information Agency, died in New York.

National day of Kenya.

1724 Samuel Hood, British admiral of distinction, born in Thorncombe, Dorset.
1787 Pennsylvania, the Keystone State, became the 2nd state of the Union.
1805 Henry Wells, American transportation executive, born in Thetford, Vermont.
1849 Sir Marc Isambard Brunel, French-born English engineer, builder of the Thames tunnel from Wapping to Rotherhithe, died in London, aged 80.
1889 Robert Browning, English poet, died.
1893 Edward G. Robinson, American film actor, born in Bucharest, Hungary as Emanuel Goldenburg.
1897 Hermione Gingold, English actress, born in London.
1901 The first transatlantic wireless signal, the letter 'S', was sent from Poldhu in Cornwall and received by Marconi at Signal Hill, St John's, Newfoundland.
1912 Henry Armstrong, American boxer, known as 'Homicide Hank', who held titles at three weights simultaneously, born in Columbus, Mississippi as Henry Jackson.
1915 Frank Sinatra, American entertainer, born in Hoboken, New Jersey.
The German Junkers J1, the first all-metal aeroplane, was test flown at Dessau.
1917 The world's worst train accident occurred in Modane, France, with 543 killed.
1925 The first motel opened, in San Luis Obispo, California.
1929 John Osborne, English playwright and actor, born in London.
1938 Connie Francis, American singer and actress, born in Newark, New Jersey.
1939 Douglas Fairbanks senior, American film actor famous for his swashbuckling hero parts, died.
1941 Dionne Warwick, American pop singer, born in East Orange, New Jersey.
1946 Emerson Fittipaldi, motor racing champion, born in Sao Paulo, Brazil.
1950 Peter Fraser, New Zealand Labour statesman and Prime Minister from 1940 to 1949, died.
1955 The hovercraft or air-cushion vehicle was patented by the British engineer Christopher Cockerell.
1963 Kenya attained independence, with Jomo Kenyatta its first Prime Minister.
1964 Kenya became a republic, with Jomo Kenyatta its President.

1968 Tallulah Bankhead, American actress renowned for her gravel voice, died in New York City.

1977 Lady Spencer Churchill, widow of Sir Winston, died in her 92nd year.

13 DECEMBER [348]

1577 Francis Drake began his famous voyage from Plymouth in the *Golden Hind* that was to take him around the world—returning on 26 September 1580.

1642 New Zealand was discovered by the Dutch navigator Abel Tasman.

1784 Dr Samuel Johnson, English writer and lexicographer known for his dictionary, died in London and was buried in Westminster Abbey.

1862 The Battle of Fredericksburg took place in the American Civil War in which Lee's Confederate forces defeated Major General Burnside's men.

1913 Archie Moore, US boxer, holder of the world light-heavyweight title for ten years, born as Archibald Lee Wright.

1915 Johannes Vorster, South African Nationalist statesman and Prime Minister, born in Jamestown, Cape Province.

1920 George Shultz, American Secretary of State, born in New York City.

1939 The Battle of the River Plate took place—a naval action between British cruisers *Exeter*, *Ajax* and *Achilles* and the German battleship *Graf Spee*, off the south-east coast of South America.

1952 John Francombe, British National Hunt champion jockey and rider of a record total of 1138 winners, born.

1973 A three-day work week was ordered by the British Government because of the Arab oil embargo and the coalminers' slowdown.

14 DECEMBER [349]

1546 Tycho Brahe, Danish astronomer and mathematician, born in Knudstrup.

1799 George Washington, American soldier, Federalist statesman and first President from 1789 to 1797, died in Mount Vernon on the south bank of the Potomac in Virginia.

1819 Alabama, the Heart of Dixie or Cotton State, entered the Union as the 22nd state.

1861 Albert, German Prince, consort and husband of Queen Victoria, died of typhoid in Windsor Castle.

1871 George Hudson, English 'Railway King', died. He was a speculative capitalist based in York who organised railway investment, notably the North Midland Railway and much of the East Coast main line. Eventually disgraced for financial fiddling.

1895 King George VI, the second son of George V and Mary, born in Sandringham, a Royal residence in Norfolk.

1911 Roald Amundsen, Norwegian explorer, in his ship *The Fram*, became the first to reach the South Pole—35 days ahead of Captain Scott.
Spike Jones, American musician and zany bandleader, born in Long Beach, California as Lindley Armstrong Jones.

1918 Women over 30 voted in a British General Election for the first time.
Women were first allowed to be candidates in a General Election in Britain. Seventeen contested seats, but only one was elected to the House of Commons.

1932 The first Rugby League match was played under floodlights, Leeds v Wigan at the White City Stadium in London.
Charlie Rich, American country singer, born in Forrest City, Arkansas.

1947 Stanley Baldwin, British Conservative statesman and three-times Prime Minister, who became Earl Baldwin of Bewdley, died.

1959 Archbishop Makarios was elected first President of Cyprus.
Bill Shankly began his brilliant career as manager of Liverpool FC.

1960 The cricket match between Australia and the West Indies at Woolloongabba, Brisbane became the first Test match to result in a tie.

1970 William Slim, British Army field-marshal, victor in Burma and Governor General of Australia, died.

1975 Malcolm Fraser gained a landslide election victory over Gough Whitlam.

1987 Allan Border, in the second Test match against New Zealand at Adelaide, completed a double century to become the most prolific run scorer in Australian cricket.

---

15 DECEMBER

1675 Jan Vermeer, Dutch painter, died.

1683 Izaak Walton, English writer, best known as the author of *The Compleat Angler* on pleasures of fishing, died in Winchester, aged 90.

1791 Ten original amendments to the US Constitution were added.

1832 Gustave Eiffel, French engineer, best known for his design of the tower built for the Paris exhibition of 1889 and which bears his name, born in Dijon.

1859 Ludwig Zamenof, Polish linguist and creator of the artificial language of Esperanto, born in Bielostock (Bialystok).

1890 Sitting Bull, Red Indian chief of the Sioux, was killed by police in South Dakota while resisting arrest.

1892 Paul Getty, American oil magnate, born in Minneapolis, Minnesota.

1906 The Piccadilly branch of the London Underground Railway system was opened.

1939 Nylon was first produced commercially, in Seaford, Delaware, and made up into stockings by various manufacturers.

1943 Fats Waller, American musician and jazz pianist, died.

1961 Adolph Eichmann, Nazi official responsible for the execution of millions of Jews, was sentenced to death after a four-month trial in Jerusalem.

1962 Charles Laughton, English-born film actor and Academy Award (Oscar) winner in 1933 for his part in *The Private Lives of Henry VIII*, died.

1966 Walt Disney, American film producer and leader in movie animation, died.

1968 Jesse Willard, American heavyweight boxing champion, died in Pacoimo, California, aged almost 87.

1969 City status was conferred on Swansea.

1982 Gibraltar's frontier with Spain was opened to pedestrians after 13 years.

---

16 DECEMBER [351]

1485 Catherine of Aragon, the first wife of King Henry VIII, born the fourth daughter of Ferdinand and Isabella.

1653 Oliver Cromwell became Lord Protector of England—ruling for over four years.

1742 Gebhard von Blucher, Prussian field marshal, born in the seaport of Rostock.

1770 Beethoven, German composer, born in Bonn, the son of an undistinguished tenor.

1773 The 'Boston Tea Party', promoted by Samuel Adams, took place off Griffin's Wharf in Boston harbour, as a protest against British taxation.

1775 Jane Austen, English novelist, born in Steventon, a remote hamlet in Hampshire, the seventh of eight children of the rector.

1809 The 13 year marriage between Josephine and Napoleon Bonaparte, being childless, was dissolved.

1838   The Zulu chief Dingaan was defeated by a small force of Boers at Blood River. Is celebrated in South Africa as 'Dingaan's Day'.

1859   Wilhelm Grimm, the younger of the two brother philologists who made a great collection of fairy tales, died in Berlin.

1882   Jack Hobbs, Surrey and England cricketer, born in Cambridge.

1899   Noel Coward, English actor, composer and playwright, born in Teddington near London.

1917   Arthur C. Clarke, English science fiction writer, born.

1921   Camille Saint-Saens, French composer, best known for *The Carnival of the Animals*, died in Algiers.

1925   Construction began on the building of the Mersey Road Tunnel— was opened on 18 July 1934.

1929   The British airship *R100*, designed by Barnes Wallis, first flew on trials.

1935   The Huey P. Long Bridge in Metairie, Louisiana, the world's longest railway bridge, was completed.

1944   Glenn Miller, American dance band leader and trombonist, was tragically killed in an aircraft accident.
        The 'Battle of the Bulge' began in the Ardennes region, with a violent counter-attack launched by 15 German divisions commanded by General von Rundstedt.

1952   Joel Garner, West Indian fast bowler, born.

1962   William Perry, American footballer known as 'the Refrigerator', born.

1965   W. Somerset Maugham, English novelist and short story writer, died in Nice in the south of France, aged 91.

1971   Bangladesh formally came into existence after East Pakistan surrendered in the war with India.

1977   The extension of the Piccadilly tube line to Heathrow airport in London was opened by HM The Queen.

---

17 DECEMBER   [352]

1778   Sir Humphry Davy, English chemist and inventor of the miners' safety lamp, born in Penzance, Cornwall, the son of a woodcarver.

1830   Simon Bolivar, South American statesman and revolutionary leader, called 'The Liberator', died from tuberculosis.

1874   Mackenzie King, Canadian statesman and Prime Minister, born in Kitchener, Ontario.

1891   Robertson Hare, British actor, born.

1894   Arthur Fiedler, American conductor, born in Boston, Massachusetts.

1895   Gerald Patterson, Australian international tennis player, born in Melbourne.

1903 Orville Wright made the first successful controlled flight in a powered aircraft, at Kill Devil Hill, near Kitty Hawk, North Carolina.

1907 Lord Kelvin, Irish-born physicist and inventor, died.

1909 Albert I succeeded his uncle Leopold II as King of the Belgians.

1933 For this day only the public was allowed to walk through the new Mersey Road Tunnel.

1936 Tommy Steele, British pop singer and entertainer, born in Bermondsey, London as Thomas Hicks.

1938 Peter Snell, New Zealand athlete and a world record holder, born in Opunake.

1939 The German battleship *Graf Spee*, captained by Langsdorf, was scuttled in the entrance of Montevideo harbour during the Battle of the River Plate. The anchor is still visible.

1967 Harold Holt, Australian Liberal statesman and 22nd Prime Minister, disappeared while swimming at Cheviot Beach near Melbourne.

1986 Mrs Davina Thompson created medical history when, at Papworth Hospital in Cambridge, Britain, she was given a new heart, lungs and liver.

---

18 DECEMBER [353]

1707 Charles Wesley, English evangelist and hymn writer, born in Epworth, Lincolnshire, the son of the rector.

1737 Antonio Stradivari, famous Italian violin-maker, died in Cremona, Lombardy.

1779 Joseph Grimaldi, British clown, born the son of an Italian actor.

1787 New Jersey, the Garden State, became the 3rd state of the Union.

1856 Sir J. J. Thomson, English physicist and discoverer of the electron, born in Cheetham Hill near Manchester, the son of a bookseller.

1865 Slavery was abolished throughout the United States of America, ratified by the 13th Amendment.

1886 Ty Cobb, American baseball player, born in Narrows, Georgia.

1890 Passenger service started on London's City and South London Railway (now the City branch of the Northern line), to become the first underground system to be electrified. It ran from King William Street to Stockwell, and had been officially opened on 4 November by the Prince of Wales.

1912 The Piltdown man 'discovery' in East Sussex by Charles Dawson was announced—was proved in 1953 to have been a hoax.

1913 Willy Brandt, German statesman and Chancellor, born in Lübeck as Karl Herbert Frahm.

1916 Betty Grable, American film actress and pin-up girl, born in St Louis, Missouri.

1919 Sir John Alcock, English aviator who first flew the Atlantic with Arthur Brown, died of injuries received in an aeroplane accident.
1947 Steven Spielberg, American film maker, born.
1957 Dorothy L. Sayers, English author of detective novels featuring hero 'Lord Peter Wimsey', died.
1969 The death penalty for murder was formally abolished in Britain.
1970 Divorce became legal in Italy.
1971 Stan Mellor, English National Hunt champion jockey, rode his 1000th winner—'Ouzo'—at Nottingham.
      Bobby Jones, American golfer and winner of many international championships, died.

19 DECEMBER [354]

1154 Henry II acceded as King of England on the death of Stephen on 24 October.
1741 Vitus Bering, Danish-born explorer for Russia, who gave his name to the Bering Strait and Bering Sea, died on Bering Island leading an expedition.
1848 Emily Brontë, English novelist, died aged 30.
1851 Joseph Turner, English painter of landscapes and sea pictures, notably 'The Fighting Téméraire', died in a lodging in Chelsea, under the assumed name of Booth.
1852 Albert Michelson, American physicist, born in Prussia.
1902 Sir Ralph Richardson, English stage and film actor, born in Cheltenham, Gloucestershire, the son of an art teacher.
1906 Leonid Brezhnev, Soviet political leader and President, born in Kamenskoye (now Dneprodzerzhinsk) in the Ukraine.
1922 Eamonn Andrews, television commentator and presenter, born in Dublin.
1946 Stan Smith, American tennis player, born in Pasadena, California.
1957 Air service between London and Moscow was inaugurated.
1980 Alexei Kosygin, Soviet Communist leader, died aged 77.
1981 The Penlee lifeboat, *Solomon Browne*, was lost with all of her crew of eight attempting to rescue the crew of the coaster *Union Star*.
1984 Ted Hughes was appointed Poet Laureate in succession to Sir John Betjeman.

20 DECEMBER [355]

1894 Sir Robert Menzies, Australian Liberal statesman and Prime Minister, born in Jeparit in the state of Victoria.

1904 Irene Dunne, American film actress, born in Louisville, Kentucky.
1905 Bill O'Reilly, Australian Test cricketer, born.
1914 The British Protectorate of Egypt was established, with Hussein Kamil as Sultan.
1926 Sir Geoffrey Howe, British Conservative statesman, born.
1937 Erich Ludendorff, German general who helped to formulate World War I strategy, died.
1942 Robert Lee Hayes, American athlete and international sprint champion, born.
1946 Uri Geller, Israeli known for his claims to psychic powers, born in Tel Aviv.
1954 James Hilton, English novelist, known for *Lost Horizon* and *Goodbye Mr Chips*, died in California.
1961 Sir Earle Page died, Australian statesman and the 15th Prime Minister, for 19 days in 1939, on the death of Joseph Lyons.
1968 John Steinbeck, American author, notably *The Grapes of Wrath*, *Of Mice and Men* and Nobel Prize winner in 1962, died in New York City.
1973 Bobby Darin, American singer of the rock-and-roll era, died.
1982 Artur Rubinstein, Polish-born American concert pianist, died at his home in Geneva, aged 95.

21 DECEMBER [356]

1375 Giovanni Boccaccio, Italian writer, best known for his *Decameron*, died in Certaldo.
1620 The Pilgrim Fathers landed at Plymouth, Massachusetts from the *Mayflower*—the family had increased to 103 with two births on the voyage.
1804 Benjamin Disraeli, British statesman and Tory Prime Minister, born at 22 Theobald's Road, London.
1844 The Rochdale Pioneers opened the first co-operative store, in Toad Lane.
1879 Joseph Stalin, Soviet political leader, born in Gori, Georgia as Joseph Vissarionovich Dzhugashvili, the son of a shoemaker.
1892 Walter Hagen, American golf champion, born in Rochester, State of New York.
1913 The first crossword puzzle was published in the weekend supplement of the *New York World*, compiled by Liverpool-born Arthur Wynne.
1918 Kurt Waldheim, Austria's President and former Secretary-General of the United Nations, born in the Danube town of Tulin.
1920 Kel Nagle, Australian golfer, born.

1937 Jane Fonda, American film actress, born in New York City, the daughter of Henry Fonda.
Walt Disney's *Snow White and the Seven Dwarfs* was shown in Los Angeles, to become the first full length cartoon talking picture.
1945 George Patton, American general and military commander in Europe, nicknamed 'Old Blood and Guts', died in Heidelberg, Germany.
Doug Walters, Australian Test cricketer, born.
1954 Christine Evert, American tennis champion, born in Fort Lauderdale, Florida.
1957 Eric Coates, English musician and composer of light orchestral music, especially the *London Suite*, died.
1958 Charles de Gaulle was elected as President of France.
1963 Sir Jack Hobbs, Surrey and England cricketer—the first in his sport to be knighted—died aged 81.
Leeds Rugby League Club, the first with undersoil heating, used it during a game against Dewsbury.
1968 *Apollo 8* was launched, with Frank Borman, James Lovell and William Anders.
1971 Kurt Waldheim succeeded U Thant as Secretary-General of the United Nations.

---

22 DECEMBER [357]

1135 The coronation of King Stephen took place.
1552 St Francis Xavier, Basque Jesuit missionary, called the 'Apostle of the Indies', died near Canton in China.
1715 James Stuart, the 'Old Pretender' landed at Peterhead after his exile in France.
1768 John Crome, English landscape painter, born in Norwich, the son of a poor weaver.
1858 Giacomo Puccini, Italian operatic composer of *Tosca*, *La Bohème* etc., born in Lucca, Tuscany.
1880 George Eliot, English novelist, author of *The Mill on the Floss*, died in Chelsea and was buried in Highgate Cemetery.
1894 Alfred Dreyfus, French artillery officer, found guilty of selling army secrets to Germany—was imprisoned on Devil's Island, but was later pardoned and completely exonerated.
1899 Dwight Moody, American evangelist and writer of gospel hymns with Ira Sankey, died.
1901 André Kostelanetz, American conductor, born in St Petersburg, now Leningrad.
1912 'Lady Bird' Johnson, wife of America's 36th President, born in Karnack, Texas.

1938 A fish identified as a coelacanth, then thought to be extinct, was dredged out of the sea off the coast of South Africa.

1943 Beatrix Potter, English writer of children's books and creator of 'Peter Rabbit', died.

1949 Maurice and Robin Gibb, twin members of the 'Bee Gees' pop group, born in Manchester.

1965 A 70 m.p.h. speed limit was introduced in Britain.
Richard Dimbleby, British television commentator, died.

1968 The captain and crew of the *Pueblo* were released by the North Koreans in Panmunjon.

1979 Darryl F. Zanuck, American film producer and executive, died.

1987 Sir Henry Cotton, MBE, British golfer, died aged 80.

---

23 DECEMBER [358]

1732 Sir Richard Arkwright, English inventor of mechanical spinning processes in the cotton industry, born in Preston, Lancashire, the youngest of 13 children.

1805 Joseph Smith, American religious leader and founder of The Church of Jesus Christ of Latter-day Saints (Mormons), born in Sharon, Vermont.

1834 Hansom cabs were patented by the English architect Joseph Hansom.

1888 J. Arthur Rank, British film magnate, born in Hull, Humberside.

1905 The final of the earliest recorded beauty contest in Britain took place, in Newcastle-upon-Tyne.

1913 The Federal Reserve, the Central banking system of the United States, was established.

1922 The BBC began daily news broadcasts.

1948 Hideki Tojo, Japanese Premier who provoked the American entry into the war by the bombing of Pearl Harbor, was hanged as a war criminal.

1959 Earl of Halifax, British Conservative statesman and Viceroy of India from 1926 to 1931, died.

1986 The US plane *Voyager*, piloted by Dick Rutan and Jeana Yeager, completed the first non-stop flight round the world without refuelling.

---

24 DECEMBER [359]

1167 King John, the sixth and youngest son of Henry II and Eleanor of Aquitaine, born in Oxford.

1491 Ignatius Loyola, Spanish priest and founder of the Society of Jesus (Jesuits), born in Azpeitia.

1524 Vasco da Gama, Portuguese explorer and navigator, died in Cochin on the Malabar coast of India.

1809 Christopher 'Kit' Carson, American frontiersman and guide, born in Madison County, Kentucky.

1814 The Treaty of Ghent was signed, ending the war of 1812 between America and Britain.

1818 James Joule, English physicist famous for his experiments with heat, born in Salford, Manchester.

1822 Matthew Arnold, English poet and critic, born in Laleham near Staines, Surrey.

1863 W. M. Thackeray, English novelist, best known for *Vanity Fair*, died in London.

1905 Howard Hughes, American industrialist and film producer, born in Houston, Texas.

1914 The first air raid on British soil took place—a single bomb on Dover, in the grounds of St James's Rectory.

1922 Ava Gardner, American film actress, born in Smithfield, North Carolina as Lucy Johnson.

1932 Colin Cowdrey, English Test cricketer, born in Bangalore, India.

1951 Libya became an independent monarchy, with Idris I as King.

1961 Frank Richards, writer of British boys' papers, notably the *Gem* and the *Magnet* which introduced 'Billy Bunter' and Greyfriars School, died near Broadstairs, aged 85.

25 DECEMBER [360]

Christmas Day.

1066 The coronation of William the Conqueror took place at Westminster Abbey.

1497 The South African province of Natal was discovered and named by the Portuguese explorer and navigator Vasco da Gama.

1642 Sir Isaac Newton, English mathematician and scientist, born in Woolsthorpe near Grantham, Lincolnshire, the son of a farmer.

1821 Clara Barton, American humanitarian, born in Oxford, Massachusetts.

1830 The first US regularly scheduled passenger train service using steam power began at Charleston on the South Carolina Railroad.

1864 The Christmas-day dip in the Serpentine in London's Hyde Park was inaugurated.

1870 The Mont Cenis tunnel through the Alps was completed.

1887 Conrad Hilton, American hotelier, born in San Antonio, New Mexico.

1891 Clarence Grimmett, Australian cricketer and the first to take 200 Test wickets, born in New Zealand.

1892 Rebecca West, British novelist and critic, born in County Kerry, Ireland as Cicily Isabel Fairfield.

1899 Humphrey Bogart, American film actor, born in New York City, the son of a doctor.

1906 Lew Grade, English impresario, born in Russia as Lewis Winogradsky.

1918 Anwar Sadat, Egyptian statesman and President, born in Talah Minufiya.

1926 Hirohito became Emperor of Japan. He died in January 1989 after 62 years as Emperor.

1934 The horseracing course at Santa Anita, California, opened.

1941 Hong Kong surrendered to the Japanese forces.

1944 Kenny Everett, British disc jockey and TV personality, born in Liverpool as Maurice Cole.

1946 W. C. Fields, American vaudeville and film comedian, died.

1950 The Stone of Scone or Stone of Destiny, the Scottish Coronation Stone, was stolen from Westminster Abbey by nationalists—was returned the following 13 April.

1957 The Queen made her first Christmas broadcast on television, to the peoples of the Commonwealth.

1974 Darwin, capital of Northern Territory in Australia, was devastated by cyclone 'Tracy'.

1977 Charlie Chaplin, American film actor and director, died.

---

26 DECEMBER [361]

1716 Thomas Gray, English poet, author of 'Elegy in a country churchyard', born in London, the son of a money broker.

1734 George Romney, English portrait painter, born in Dalton-in-Furness, Lancashire.

1797 John Wilkes, British radical politician and champion of freedom of the Press, died in London.

1891 Henry Miller, American novelist, born in New York City.

1893 Mao Tse-Tung, Chinese statesman and one of the founders of the Communist Party, born in Hunan the son of a peasant farmer.

1898 Radium was discovered and isolated by Pierre and Marie Curie and G. Bémont.

1908 Jack Johnson became the first coloured boxer to win the world heavyweight title, knocking out Tommy Burns in round 14 in Sydney, Australia.

1914 Richard Widmark, American film actor, born in Sunrise, Minnesota.

1931   Melvil Dewey, American librarian and pioneer in book classification, died.
1935   The League game at Prenton Park produced a record total of goals. Tranmere Rovers scored 13 and the visitors, Oldham Athletic, netted 4.
1943   The German battleship *Scharnhorst* was sunk off North Cape.
1957   Charles Pathe, French film pioneer who inaugurated newsreels, died in Monte Carlo.
1959   The first charity walk took place, along the Icknield Way, in aid of the World Refugee Fund.
1972   Harry S. Truman, American Democrat statesman and 33rd President from 1945 to 1953, died in Independence, Missouri, aged 88.
1974   Jack Benny, American comedian famed for his deadpan delivery, died aged 80.
1977   Howard Hawks, American film director, noted for his comedies and action dramas, died aged 81.
1983   Violet Carson, English actress, best remembered for her role as Ena Sharples in British TV's *Coronation Street*, died.

27 DECEMBER   *[362]*

1703   The Methuen Treaty was signed between Portugal and England, giving preference to the import of Portuguese wines into England.
1822   Louis Pasteur, French chemist and bacteriologist, born in Dôle.
1823   Sir Mackenzie Bowell, Canadian Conservative statesman, born in Rickinghall, Suffolk.
1831   The Admiralty survey ship HMS *Beagle*, with Charles Darwin aboard, set out from Plymouth on its famous scientific voyage round the world, which was to last five years.
1834   Charles Lamb, English essayist, died.
1879   Sydney Greenstreet, English actor, notably in the film *The Maltese Falcon*, born in Kent.
1901   Marlene Dietrich, film actress notably *The Blue Angel*, born in Berlin as Maria Magdalena von Losch.
1927   Leon Trotsky was expelled from the Communist Party.
1931   John Charles, Welsh international footballer, born in Swansea.
1945   The International Monetary Fund was established, with headquarters in Washington.
1957   Tim Witherspoon, a world heavyweight boxing champion, born in Philadelphia, Pennsylvania.
1965   The North Sea oil rig *Sea Gem* collapsed.
1972   Lester Pearson, Canadian statesman, Prime Minister from 1963 to 1968 and Nobel Prize winner in 1947, died.

1975 The Sex Discrimination and Equal Pay Acts came into force in Britain.
1979 Russian armed forces invaded the territory of neighbouring Afghanistan.

28 DECEMBER

1694 Queen Mary II died of smallpox, after which William III reigned alone.
1846 Iowa, the Hawkeye State, became the 29th state of the Union.
1856 Woodrow Wilson, American Democrat statesman and 28th President, born in Staunton, Virginia, the son of a Presbyterian minister.
1879 The Tay railway bridge, from Fife to Angus, designed by Thomas Bouch, collapsed, carrying the Edinburgh to Dundee train and its passengers into the water below—killing about 90.
1908 Messina, on the island of Sicily, was severely damaged by an earthquake.
Lew Ayres, American film actor, born in Minneapolis as Lewis Ayer.
1923 Alexandre Gustave Eiffel, French engineer and designer of the 300 metre tower in Paris that bears his name, died aged 91.
1926 Victoria scored the highest recorded cricket innings total of 1107 runs, against New South Wales, in Melbourne.
1932 Roy Hattersley, British Labour politician and a deputy leader of the Party, born.
1934 The first women's Test match at cricket took place in Brisbane, Australia v England.
Maggie Smith, British film actress and Oscar winner for *The Prime of Miss Jean Brodie* (1969), born in Ilford, Essex.
1937 Maurice Ravel, French composer of *Bolero*, died in a Paris hospital.
1947 Victor Emmanuel III, King of Italy from 1900 until he abdicated in 1946, died.
1950 The Peak District was designated as the first National Park in Britain.
1981 Hoagy Carmichael, American pianist and song writer, died of a heart attack in Palm Springs, California.

1170 Thomas à Becket, the 40th Archbishop of Canterbury, was murdered in his own cathedral by four knights—Reginald Fitzurse, William de Tracy, Hugh de Merville and Richard le Breton—acting on Henry II's orders.

1721 Madame de Pompadour, French mistress of King Louis XV of France, born in Paris as Jeanne Antoinette Poisson.

1766 Charles Macintosh, Scottish chemist and inventor of waterproof fabrics, born in Glasgow.

1800 Charles Goodyear, American inventor who developed the art of vulcanising rubber, born in New Haven, Connecticut.

1808 Andrew Johnson, American Democrat statesman and 17th President, born in Raleigh, North Carolina, the son of an inn porter.

1809 William Ewart Gladstone, British Liberal statesman and four times Prime Minister, born in Liverpool, the son of a wealthy Scottish merchant.

1813 Alexander Parkes, English chemist who invented celluloid, born in Birmingham.

1845 Texas, the Lone Star state, became the 28th state of the Union.

1860 Britain's first seagoing iron-clad warship, HMS *Warrior*, was launched.

1881 Jesse Willard, American heavyweight boxing champion, born in St Clere, Kansas.

1890 The Battle of Wounded Knee in South Dakota, the last major conflict between Red Indians and US troops, took place.

1895 The Jameson Raid into the Boer colony of Transvaal to support the Uitlanders—the European settlers—to overthrow Kruger's government, started.

1914 The first zeppelin appeared over the British coast.

1918 The British newspaper the *Sunday Express* began publication.

1931 The discovery of heavy water (deuterium) was publicly announced by the American chemist H. C. Urey.

1937 The Constitution of the Republic of Ireland went into operation.

1938 Harvey Smith, British international show jumper, born in Yorkshire.
Jon Voight, American film actor and Oscar winner for *Coming Home* (1978), born in Yonkers, New York.

1940 London's Guildhall was destroyed in an air raid.

1960 David Boon, Australian Test cricketer, born.
Eden Phillpotts, English novelist and playwright, died.

1967 Paul Whiteman, American musician and bandleader, died.

1972 *Life* ended publication after 36 years as the leading weekly pictorial magazine.

1691   Robert Boyle, British physicist and chemist who formulated Boyle's Law on gases, died.
1865   Rudyard Kipling, English story writer and poet, born in Bombay.
1876   Pablo Casals, Spanish cellist and conductor, born in Vendrell.
1894   Amelia Bloomer, American social reformer who campaigned for temperance and women's rights, died.
1906   Carol Reed, English film director, born in Putney, London.
1932   The London-Brighton line became electrified, and the *Southern Belle* was renamed the *Brighton Belle*.
1934   Barry Briggs, speedway champion rider, born in Christchurch, New Zealand.
1947   King Michael of Romania abdicated in favour of a Communist Republic.
1956   The last passenger train ran on the Liverpool Overhead Railway.
1961   Ben Johnson, Canadian athlete and disqualified Olympic sprint champion, born in Falmouth, near Jamaica's Montego Bay.
1968   Trygve Lie, Norwegian statesman and first Secretary-General of the United Nations from 1946 to 1952, died.
1970   'Sonny' Liston, American heavyweight boxer and world champion from 1962 to 1964, died.
1979   Richard Rodgers, American composer in collaboration with Lorenz Hart and Oscar Hammerstein, died.

31 DECEMBER [366]

1491   Jacques Cartier, French navigator and explorer of the North American coast and the St Lawrence River, born in St Malo on the Normandy coast.
1719   John Flamsteed, English astronomer, the first Astronomer Royal, for whom King Charles II built the Greenwich Observatory, died.
1720   Bonnie Prince Charlie was born in Rome, the elder son of James, the 'Old Pretender'.
1763   Villeneuve, French naval officer, born in Valensoles.
1815   George Meade, American Union Army general, born at Cadiz in Spain.
1869   Henri Matisse, French painter and sculptor, born in Le Cateau.
1880   George Marshall, American general and statesman who originated the Marshall Aid Plan for the post-war reconstruction of Europe, born in Uniontown in Pennsylvania.
1890   Ellis Island, in upper New York Bay, opened as the Immigration Depot on the closure of Castle Garden.

1923 The chimes of Big Ben were first broadcast.

1938 The first breath tests for drunken drivers were officially introduced by the Indianapolis Police Department—using a 'Drunko-meter', a type of breathalyser.

1943 John Denver, American singer and composer, born in Roswell, New Mexico as Henry John Deutschendorf.

1945 The Home Guard defence force was disbanded.

1948 Sir Malcolm Campbell, English racing driver and holder of world land and water speed records, died.

1951 Maxim Litvinov, Soviet politician and ambassador, died.

1960 After midnight British farthings ceased to be legal tender.

1968 Russia's *TU144* flew, thus becoming the first supersonic airliner.

1973 The three-day working week was introduced in Britain as a measure to conserve fuel during a miners' strike.
The five-day week was re-introduced on 9 March 1974.

1985 Rick Nelson, American singer and songwriter, died in a plane crash at the age of 45.

Index

The numbers after each entry refer to the day of the year rather than the page number in the book.

Benz, Karl **29-95-330**
Bergen, Candice **130**
Bergen, Edgar **47-274**
Bergerac, Cyrano de **66-210**
Bergman, Ingmar **196**
Bergman, Ingrid **242**
Bering, Vitus **354**
Berkeley, Busby **74-334**
Berle, Milton **194**
Berlin air lift **180-280**
Berlin air raids **66-238**
Berlin blockade **133-176**
Berlin, Irving **132**
Berliner, Emile **141-216**
Berlioz, Hector **68-346**
Berman, Shelley **34**
Bermuda **160**
Bernadotte, Count Folke **2-261**
Bernhard, Prince **7-181**
Bernhardt, Sarah **86-296**
Bernstein, Elmer **95**
Bernstein, Leonard **238**
Berry, Chuck **15**
Bessemer, Sir Henry **19-75**
Best, Charles **58-209**
Best, George **143**
Betjeman, Sir John **97-140-284**
Betting shops, GB **122**
Bevan, Aneurin **188-320**
Beveridge Report **336**
Bevin, Ernest **69-105**
Bhopal disaster **338**
Bhutto, Ali **95**
'Big Bang' **301**
'Big Ben' **101-152-193-366**
Biggers, Earl **96-239**
Bikini swimsuit **187**
Biko, Steven **256**
Billy the Kid **197-328**
Bird, 'Dickie' **110**
Birdseye, Clarence **66-281-344**
Birkenhead **226-243**
Birkenhead, Lord **194-274**
Birmingham Exhibition Centre **33**
Birth control pill **1-231**
Births, marriages and deaths **183**
Bismarck, battleship **148**
Bismarck, Otto van **92-212**
Bixby, Bill **22**
Bizet, Georges **155-299**
Black and White Minstrel Show **145**
Black, Cilla **148**
'Black Friday' **268**
Black Hole of Calcutta **172**
Blackfriars Bridge **311**
Blackpool illuminations **262**
Blackwall Tunnel **143**
Blackwell, Elizabeth **23-34-152**
Blake, Robert **220**
Blake, William **225-333**
Blanc, Mel **151**
Blanchard, Jean Pierre **7-67**
Blankers-Koen, Fanny **117**
Blaydon races, last **246**

Blenheim, Battle of **226**
Blériot, Louis **183-207-215**
Bligh, William **119-253-342**
Bliss, Sir Arthur **87-215**
Blondin, Charles **50-59-182**
Blood bank, US **75**
Blood, Colonel Thomas **130-237**
'Bloody Sunday', Londonderry **30**
'Bloody Sunday', Russia **22**
Bloom, Claire **46**
Bloomer, Amelia **148-365**
Blücher, Gebhard von **256-351**
Blue Nile, source **319**
Blue Peter, TV programme **301**
Blum, Léon **90-100**
Blyton, Enid **224-333**
'Bob-a-job' week **109**
Boccaccio, Giovanni **356**
Bodoni, Giambattista **47**
Boeing 747 **12-40**
Boer War **285**
Bogarde, Dirk **88**
Bogart, Humphrey **14-360**
Boleyn, Anne **25-140-251**
Bolivar, Simon **206-352**
Bolivia **219**
Bolshevik Revolution **312**
Bonaparte, Joseph **7**
Bonington, Chris **219**
Bonnie and Clyde **144**
Bono, Cher **47**
Book of Common Prayer **161**
Books of stamps **76**
Boon, David **364**
Boone, Daniel **270-307**
Boone, Pat **153**
Boot, Jesse **154-165**
Booth, John Wilkes **117-131**
Booth, Shirley **243**
Booth, William **101-233**
Borden, Lizzie **153-201-334**
Borden, Sir Robert **162-178**
Border, Alan **209-349**
Borg, Bjorn **158-187-190**
Borge, Victor **3**
Borgia, Lucrezia **109-176**
Borglum, Gutzon **66-85**
Borgnine, Ernest **24**
Borman, Frank **74**
Borodin, Alexander **59-317**
Borodino, Battle of **251**
Borotra, Jean **226**
Borrow, George **187-208**
Borstal Institution **290**
Boston massacre **65**
Boston Red Sox **287**
Boston Tea Party **351**
Boswell, James **140-303**
Bosworth Field, Battle of **235**
Botha, Louis **240-271**
Botha, Pieter **12-272**
Botham, Ian **210-329**
Bottomley, Horatio **133**
Boult, Sir Adrian **54-99**

Cole, Natalie   37
Coleridge, S. T.   207-295
Colledge, Cecilia   333
Collingwood, admiral   270
Collins, Joan   144
Collins, Michael   235-290
Collins, Michael   305
Collins, Wilkie   8-267
Colman, Ronald   40-140
Colorado   214
Colt, Samuel   10-201
Columbus, Christopher   141-216-269-
    286-308
Comaneci, Nadia   317
Come Dancing, first programme   317
Comet, jet airliner   209
Comic Cuts   138
Comiskey Park   183
Common Market   85-157
Commonwealth Day   145
Communications satellites   97-225
Como, Perry   139
Comprehensive school, first   265
Compton, Denis   144
Comte, Auguste   19-249
Concorde, supersonic airliner   9-21-62-
    100-291
Concrete, reinforced   198
Confederate States of America   39
Congo   301-320
Congress, US   64
Conn, Billy   282
Connecticut   9
Connery, Sean   238
Connolly, Maureen ('Little Mo')   173-261
Connors, Jimmy   246
Conrad, Charles   154
Conrad, Joseph   216-338
Conran, Sir Terence   278
Constable, John   91-163
Constantine I, King   271
Constantine II, King   66-154
Constantine, Sir Learie   183-265
Conteh, John   148-275
Convicts to Australia   26-134
Conway, Russ   246
Coogan, Jackie   300
Cook, Captain   17-18-45-119-193-281-301
Cook, Sir Joseph   212
Cook, Thomas   200-327
Cooke, Alistair   325
Cookson, Catherine   172
Coolidge, Calvin   5-186
Cooper, Alice   35
Cooper, Ashley   259
Cooper, Gary   128-134
Cooper, Henry   55-81-124-312
Cooper, James Fenimore   258-259
Co-operative store, first   356
Copenhagen, Battle of   93
Copernicus, Nicolaus   50-145
Copland, Aaron   319
Coral Sea, Battle of   129
Corbett, James J.   49-245-251

Corbett, Ronnie   339
Corinth Canal   219
Coronation Stone   104
Coronation Street, first   344
Cornell, Ezra   11-344
Cornforth, Sir John   251
Corps of Commissionaires   44
Cortez, Hernando   337
Corunna, Battle of   16
Cosgrave, William   321
Cossack, HMS   47
Costello, Lou   66
Cotton, Henry   26-357
Cotton, Joseph   136
Coubertin, Pierre de   1-246
Countess of Athlone   3-56
Court, Margaret   186-198
Courtauld, Samuel   128-336
Courtenay, Tom   56
Courtneidge, Cicely   92-117
Cousins, Robin   53-230
Cousteau, Jacques   163
Covent Garden market   313
Covent Garden Opera House   136-342
Coventry Cathedral   83-146-319
Coventry, HMS   146-173
Coward, Sir Noel   86-351
Cowdrey, Colin   359
Cowper, William   116-331
CQD, distress signal   7
Cram, Steve   288
Cramm, Gottfried von   189-313
Cranmer, Thomas   81-184
Crawford, Broderick   117-334
Crawford, Joan   83-131
Crawford, John   82
Crawford, Michael   19
Crazy Horse   259
Crécy, Battle of   239
Cremation, first GB   86
Cremation, municipal   2
Crenshaw, Ben   11
Crete   141
Cricket   10-11-129-136-163-168-174-208-
    233-239-277-363
Cricket, county   8-12-14-33-61-63-85-99-
    188-213-225-228-231-235-309
Cricket Tests   10-46-72-74-75-86-88-103-
    175-177-213-236-250-285-349
Crimean War   278
Crippen, Dr   31-213-296-328
Cripps, Sir Stafford   112-115
Cristofori, Bartolommeo   27-125
Crockett, Davy   66-230
Croix de Guerre   99
Crome, John   357
Crompton, Samuel   178-338
Cromwell, Oliver   116-247-351
Cromwell, Richard   278
Cronin, A. J.   6-201
Crosby, Bob   236
Crosby, Bing   123-288-292
Crossroads, TV show   95
Crosswords   307-356

Eisenhower, Mamie 319
Ekberg, Anita 273
Ekland, Britt 250
El Alamein 209-297-309
Election, first US 7
Election, Portugal 116
Election returns, first televised 54
Election, Spain 167
Electric chair 1-219
Electricity industry 92
Elgar, Sir Edward 54-154
El Greco 99
Eliot, George 327-357
Eliot, T. S. 4-270
Elizabeth I, Queen 15-84-119-165-251-286-322
Elizabeth II, Queen 37-112-126-154-325
Elizabeth, Queen Mother 214-217
Elliott, Herb 56
Ellis Island 366
Ellis, Jimmy 55-118
Ellsworth, Lincoln 133-147
Ely Cathedral 61
Emerson, Ralph Waldo 118-146
Emerson, Roy 308
Emigrant wagon, first 122-309
Emmet, Robert 264
Empire Day 145
Empire Exhibition 114-306
Employment agency, first 186
Empress of Britain, liner 163
Engels, Friedrich 218-333
English Channel, first balloon 7
English Channel, first double crossing swim 266
English Channel, first man swimmer 238
English Channel, first steamboat crossing 77
English Channel, first underwater swimmer 193
English Channel, first underwater swimmer, British 219
English Channel, first woman to fly 107
English Channel, first woman swimmer 219
English Channel, pedal crossing 164
English Channel, solar-powered crossing 189
English Channel, youngest swimmer 250
English counties, changes 92
English Table Tennis Association 115
Entebbe terrorists 185
Envelopes, reply-paid 109
Epiphany 6
Epping Forest 127
Epstein, Brian 240-263
Epstein, Sir Jacob 234-315
Ericsson, John 68
Erie Canal 186-300
Escalators 75-278
Escoffier 43-302
Ethiopia 277

Eureka stockade 338
European Cup, football 129-131-139-146-150-165
European song contest, first 145
Eurovision 158
Eurydice, submarine 64
Euston station 202-288
Evans, Dame Edith 39-288
Evans, Godfrey 231
Evelyn, John 58-305
Evening News 55
Everest, Mount 94-137-150-190-233-268
Everett, Kenny 360
Everly, Don 32
Everly, Phil 19
Evert, Chris 356
Evesham, Battle of 217
Expo 67 118
Eyck, Jan van 191
Eyre, Edward John 218-335

Fagg, Arthur 170
Fahrenheit, Gabriel 135-260
Fairbanks Jnr, Douglas 344
Fairbanks, Douglas 144-347
Fairfax, Thomas 17-317
Faisal, King 85-196-252-307
Faith, Adam 175
Falange 303
Faldo, Nick 200
Falk, Peter 260
Falkland Islands 93-96-166
Falla, Manuel de 319-328
Family allowance, GB 167
Fangio, Juan 176
FAO 290
Faraday, Michael 238-268
Fargo, William George 141-216
Farnborough Air Display 189
Farouk, King 42-78-119-170-208
Farr, Tommy 61-243
Farrar, Dean 82-220
Farrow, Mia 40
Farthings 366
Fascist Party 83-210-294
Father's Day 171
Faulkner, William 188-269
Fawkes, Guy 31
Faye, Alice 126
FBI 208
Feather, Vic 101-210
February Revolution 68
Federal Bureau of Investigation 208
Federal Reserve 358
Feliciano, Jose 254
Fellini, Federico 20
Fender, Percy 167-235-239
Fenway Park 111
Ferdinand, Archduke 180
Ferrari, Enzo 51-227
Ferrier, Kathleen 113-282
Festival of Britain 124
Feynman, Richard 46
Fiedler, Arthur 192-352

347

McEnroe, John 47
McGregor, Ken 154
McGuigan, Barry 59
McKenzie, Graham 176
McKern, Leo 76
McKinley, William 29-250-258-303
McLaglen, Victor 312-346
McLaren, Bruce 154
McLean, Don 276
McMahon, Sir William 54-91
McQueen, Steve 84
McWhirter, Norris 225
McWhirter, Ross 225-332
Meade, General George 311-366
Meads, Colin 155
Medawar, Sir Peter 277
Meighen, Arthur 168-218
Meikle, Andrew 332
Meir, Golda 71-124-343
Melba, Dame Nellie 54-140
Melbourne 242
Melbourne, Viscount 75-329
Mellor, Stan 101-170-353
Melville, Herman 214-272
Menai Tubular bridge 65-145
Mendel, Gregor 6-204
Mendelssohn, Felix 34-309
Mendes, Sergio 42
Menin Gate 206
Menuhin, Yehudi 113
Menzies, Sir Robert 136-355
Mercator, Gerardus 65-340
Mercer, Johnny 177-323
Merchant ship, nuclear 203-234
Meredith, Billy 75-110-212
Meredith, George 43-139
Mérimée, Prosper 267-272
Mermaid Theatre 149
Merman, Ethel 16
Mersey ferry 182
Mersey railway tunnel 20-124
Mersey road tunnels 176-200-351-352
Mesmer, Friedrich 65-144
Messerschmitt, Wilhelm 178-259
Messina earthquake 363
Meteorological Office 42
Meteorological satellite 92
Methuen Treaty 362
Métro, Paris 192
Metropolitan Opera House 260-296
Mexican earthquake 253
Mexico 260-271
Michael, King 299-365
Michelangelo 49-66
Michelin, André 16-95
Michell, Keith 336
Michelson, Albert 130-354
Michigan 26
Midsummer Day 176
Midway Island, Battle of 158
Miles, Sir Bernard 271
Military Academy, US 76
Military conscription, France 236
Military conscription, GB 40-118

Millais, Sir John 160-226
Milland, Ray 3-70
Miller, Arthur 291
Miller, Glenn 61-351
Miller, Henry 159-361
Miller, Johnny 120
Miller, Keith 333
Miller, Roger 2
Millet, Jean Francois 20-278
Milligan, Spike 107
Mills, Bertram 107-224
Mills, Hayley 109
Mills, John 53
Mills, Juliet 326
Milne, A. A. 18-31
Milton, John 313-344
Mini cabs 66
Minnelli, Liza 72
Minnelli, Vincente 59
Minnesota 132
Minter, Alan 230
Mintoff, Dom 173-219
Miss America 251
Mississippi 345
Mississippi River 138
Missouri 223
Miss World 110
Mitchum, Robert 219
Mitterrand, François 131-300
Mix, Tom 6-286
Mixed bathing 168
Mohne and Eder dams 137
Molière 15-48
Mollison, Jim 110-231-304
Molotov 69
Monaco Grand Prix 105
Mona Lisa, stolen 234
Mondale, Walter 5
Monet, Claude 319-340
Money orders 275
Monkhouse, Bob 153
Monmouth, Duke of 100-197
Monroe Doctrine 337
Monroe, James 119-186
Monroe, Marilyn 153-218
Mons, Battle of 236
Monsarrat, Nicholas 82-221
Mont Blanc road tunnel 6-198
Mont Cenis tunnel 231-261-360
Montana 313
Monte Carlo Rally, first 21
Montezuma 182
Montgomery, Viscount 84-322
Moody, Dwight 36-357
Moon, first direct hit 258
Moon, first photographs 2-281
Moon, first satellite 223
Moon, first 'soft' landing 34
Moon, soft landing, US 154
Moore, Archie 348
Moore, Bobby 103-135-141-319
Moore, Dudley 110
Moore, Garry 31
Moore, Henry 212-244

Northcliffe, Lord 197
Norton, Ken 162-222
Norway 159
Novak, Kim 44
Novarro, Ramon 37-305
Novello, Ivor 15-66
NSPCC 190
Nuclear chain reaction 337
Nuclear power station 123
Nuffield Foundation 44
Nuffield, Viscount 235-284
Nuremberg, executions 290
Nuremberg, tribunal 325
Nureyev, Rudolf 77
Nurmi, Paavo 165-276
Nylon 23-47-55-136-350

Oak apple day 150
Oakie, Jack 23-317
Oakley, Annie 226-308
Oates, Lawrence 77
Oates, Titus 195-259
Oberon, Merle 50-328
Obote, Milton 25
Observer, The 339
O'Casey, Sean 90-262
O'Connell, Daniel 136-219
Oerter, Al 263
Offenbach, Jacques 172-279
O'Hara, Maureen 230
O'Hare International 275
Ohio 61
Ohm, George 76-189
Oil rig disasters 46-188
Oil well, first 240
Okinawa invasion 92
Oklahoma 321
Olav V, King 184-265
Old Bailey 58
'Old Pretender' 1-162-357
Old Testament 76
Old Vic Theatre 132
Oldfield, Bert 223-253
Oldfield, Bruce 196
Olivier, Laurence 143-193
Olympic Games 97
Olympic Games: 2nd 184
   3rd 242
   4th 195
   5th 188
   7th 227
   8th 187
   9th 210
   10th 212
   11th 214
   14th 211
   15th 201
   16th 327
   17th 238
   18th 284
   19th 286
   20th 239
   21st 200
   22nd 201

   23rd 210
   24th 261
Olympics, first Winter 25
Olympics, Winter: 2nd 42
   3rd 35
   4th 37
   5th 30
   6th 45
   7th 26
   8th 49
   9th 29
   10th 37
   11th 34
   12th 35
   13th 44
   14th 39
   15th 44
Olympic killings 249
Ombudsman, first 61-92
Omdurman, Battle of 246
Onassis, Aristotle 15-75
Onassis, Jacqueline 210
O'Neal, Tatum 310
O'Neill, Eugene 290-332
O'Neill, Jonjo 104
Ono, Yoko 49
Oosterhuis, Peter 124
Open prison, first GB 148
Open University 3-175
Opera House, La Scala 216
'Operation Chariot' 88
'Operation Dynamo' 148-156
'Operation Jubilee' 232
'Operation Market Garden' 261
'Operation Overlord' 158
'Operation Torch' 313
Opium War 242
Oppenheimer, Sir Ernest 143-330
Oppenheimer, Robert 49-113
Orangeman's Day 194
Orbison, Roy 114
Orczy, Baroness 267
'Order of Merit' 175
Oregon 45
O'Reilly, Bill 355
Orient Express 141-280
Ormandy, Eugene 72-323
Orsini, Felice 14-73-345
Orwell, George 21-177
Osborne, John 347
Oscars, first 137
Osmond, Donny 344
Osmond, Marie 287
O'Sullevan, Peter 63
O'Sullivan, Maureen 138
Oswald, Lee Harvey 292-329
Otis, Elisha Graves 99-216
O'Toole, Peter 215
Oudenarde, Battle of 193
Oughtred, William 65-182
Ouita, Said 307
Ovett, Steve 283
Owen, David 184
Owen, Robert 135-322

Piltdown skull   326-353
Pinkerton, Alan   183-238
Pinter, Harold   284
Piquet, Nelson   230
Pitman, Isaac   4-12-320
Pitney, Gene   48
Pitt, William (elder)   132-320
Pitt, William (younger)   9-23-149-342
Pius IX, Pope   38-51
Pius XII, Pope   62-283
Pizarro, Francisco   178
Planetarium, UK first   81
Plassey, Battle of   175
Plate, Battle of River   348
Play, shortest run   71
Player, Gary   306
Pleasence, Donald   279
Plimsoll, Samuel   41-155
Plomley, Roy   20-29
PLUTO   225
Pluto, planet   73
Pneumatic tyres   345
Poe, Edgar Allan   19-281
Point-to-point, first   62
Poison gas   113-269
Poitier, Sidney   51
Poitiers, Battle of   263
Polanski, Roman   231
Polaris submarines   161-260
Police Training College   131
Policewomen, first   256-332
Polk, James Knox   167-307
Pollock, Jackson   28-224
Pompadour, Madame de   106-364
Pompidou, Georges   93-187
Ponchielli, Amilcare   16-245
Ponsford, William   293
Ponti, Carlo   346
Pony Club   306
Pony Express   94-298
Pop music chart, first   4
Pope, Alexander   142-151
Porter, Cole   161-289
Portland cement, patent   295
Portland Vase   38
Post, Wiley   204-228-327
Postal orders   1
Postal system, two-tier   260
Postcard, first issue   275
Post codes, GB   277
Post codes, Germany   214
Postmarks   110
Post Office, books of stamps   76
Post Office, savings bank   260
Post Office, speaking clock   206
Post Office Tower   282
Post Office, US   72
Potatoes, first import   210
Potsdam Conference   199
Potter, Beatrix   210-357
Potter, Dennis   138
Potter, Stephen   32-337
Powell, Enoch   168
Power, Tyrone   126-320

Preminger, Otto   114-340
Premium Bonds   153-306
Prescription NHS   32
Presley, Elvis   8-84-229
Press Association   181
Prestonpans, Battle of   265
Prévin, André   97
Price, Alan   110
Price, Vincent   148
Pride, Charley   78
Priestley, J. B.   257
Priestley, Joseph   37-73
Primrose Day   110
Prince Edward Island   183
Prince of Wales, HMS   124-345
Princeton, Battle of   3
Prior, James   285
Prison term, longest   128
Prohibition   16-340
Prokofiev, Sergei   65-114
Promenade Concerts   280
Prost, Alain   55
Public execution, last   147
Public execution, last woman   93
Public holiday   1
Public lavatories, first   33-42
Public opinion poll   206
Puccini, Giacomo   334-357
Pueblo, USS   23-357
Puerto Rico   102-292-324
Pugin, Augustus   258
Pulitzer, Joseph   101-303
Pullman carriages   153-245
Pullman, George   63-293
Punch magazine   199
Purcell, Henry   326
Pushkin, Alexander   41-147
Puttnam, David   56
Puzo, Mario   289
Pyramids, Battle of   203

Qaddhafi   245
Quads, Miles   333
'Quakers'   304
Quant, Mary   42
Quayle, Anthony   251
Quebec   185
Quebec Bridge   338
Queen Elizabeth, liner   9-271-320
Queen Elizabeth 2 (QE 2), liner   25-123-
   133-163-264
Queen Mary, liner   270-271-276
Quiberon Bay, Battle of   325
Quimby, Harriet   107
Quinn, Anthony   112
Quins   149-318
Quisling, Vidkun   200-254-298
Quist, Adrian   217
Quiz programmes, first   136-330

R34   188-195
R100   351
R101   279-288
Rabi, Isidor   11

Rachmaninov, Sergei **88-93**
Radar **57**
Radetsky, Joseph **5-307**
Radio Caroline **80**
Radio, first commercial GB **328**
Radio, first daily news **358**
Radio licences **306**
'Radio 1', BBC **274**
'Radio 3' BBC **273**
Radio programme, first **319**
Radio programme, first regular **307**
Radio request programme, British **140**
Radio Times **272**
Radium, discovery **361**
Raffles, Sir Stamford **187**
Raft, George **271**
Raglan, Lord **180-274**
Raikes, Robert **96-258**
Railway bookstall **306**
Railway excursion **187**
Railway mail, first **316**
Railway station, first **7**
Railway timetable, national **299**
Railway trials **280**
Railways, nationalisation **1**
Rainbow Warrior **192**
Rainer, Luise **12**
Rainier, Prince **110-130-152**
Rains, Claude **151-315**
Raleigh, Sir Walter **303**
Ralston, Dennis **209**
Ramillies, Battle of **144**
Ramsay, Sir William **205-276**
Ramsey, Sir Alf **22**
Ramsey, Dr Michael **24-179**
Randell, Ron **282**
Rank, J. Arthur **89-358**
Rantzen, Esther **174**
Raphael **88-97**
Rathbone, Basil **165-203**
Rattigan, Terence **162-335**
Ravel, Maurice **67-363**
Rawls, Lou **336**
Ray, Johnnie **10**
Rayleigh, Lord **182-317**
Reade, Charles **102-160**
Reagan, Nancy **188**
Reagan, Ronald **20-37-90**
Reardon, Ray **282**
Record charts **75-202-313-319**
Records, LP **261**
'Red Baron' **112-123**
Red Cross, International **48-303**
Red Cross Society **217**
Reddy, Helen **299**
Redford, Robert **231**
Redgrave, Sir Michael **80-81**
Redgrave, Vanessa **30**
Redpath, Ian **132**
Red River Colony **133**
Reed, Austin **126-250**
Reed, Sir Carol **116-365**
Reeves, Jim **213-233**
Regazzoni, Clay **249**

Regent's Park **118-154**
Reichstag, fire **58**
Reid, Beryl **169**
Reid, Sir George **56-256**
Rembrandt **197-278**
Rennie, John **159-278**
Renoir, Pierre Auguste **56-338**
Republican Party, US **59-187**
Republic of Ireland **109-183-364**
Repulse, battleship **345**
Reuter, Paul Julius **56-203**
Revere, Paul **1-109-131**
Reynolds, Burt **42**
Reynolds, Debbie **92**
Reynolds, Sir Joshua **54-198**
Rhine crossing **67**
Rhode Island **150**
Rhodes, Cecil **86-187**
Rhodes, Wilfred **103-190-303**
Rhodesia **62-108**
Rice, Tim **315**
Rich, Buddy **182**
Rich, Charlie **349**
Richard I, King **97-188-247-252**
Richard II, King **6-174-198-273**
Richard III, King **178-188-235-276**
Richard, Cliff **288**
Richards, Frank **221-359**
Richards, Sir Gordon **91-126-130-158-192-279-290-315**
Richards, Theodore **31-93**
Richards, Viv **67**
Richardson, Sir Ralph **284-354**
Richardson, Samuel **186**
Richelieu, Cardinal **253-339**
Richthofen, Manfred von **112-123**
Richter, Charles **274**
Richenbacker, 'Eddie' **205-282**
Riddle, Nelson **153-280**
Riebeck, Jan van **112**
Rifle shooting, Bisley **201**
Riggs, Bobby **56-264**
Rimsky-Korsakov **78-173**
Rippon, Angela **286**
Ritchie, Lionel **172**
Ritter, Tex **2-12**
Robbins, Harold **142**
Robert the Bruce **159-193**
Roberts, Lord **274-319**
Robertson, Cliff **253**
Robertson-Justice, James **167**
Robeson, Paul **23-100**
Robespierre, Maximilien **127-210**
Robey, Sir George **264-334**
Robinson, Edward G **26-347**
Robinson, Heath **152-257**
Robinson, Sugar Ray **124**
Robson, Bobby **49**
Robson, Bryan **11**
Robson, Dame Flora **88-189**
Roche, Tony **138**
'Rock around the Clock', record **103**
Rockefeller, John D. **144-190**
Rockefeller, Nelson **26-190**

Rodgers, Richard 180-365
Rodin, Auguste 317-322
Rodney, Lord 145
Rogers, Ginger 198
Rogers, Roy 310
'Rogues Gallery' 307
Rolls, Charles Stewart 154-194-240
Romberg, Sigmund 211-314
Rome liberation 156
Rommel, Erwin 307-320
Romney, George 320-361
Ronstadt, Linda 197
Röntgen, Wilhelm von 41-87-313
Rooke, Sir George 206
Rooney, Mickey 267
Roosevelt, Eleanor 285-312
Roosevelt, Franklin D. 20-30-46-103-312
Roosevelt, Theodore 6-258-288-301
Rorke's Drift 23
Rose, Sir Alec 186-195
Rose, Mervyn 23
Rosebery, Lord 128-142
Rosewall, Ken 307
Ross, Diana 86
Rossetti, Dante Gabriel 100-133
Rossini, Gioacchino 60-318
Rotary Club 54
Rotherhithe tunnel 164
Rouget de Lisle 178
Roundell, aircraft identification 346
Round-the-world flight, first 62
Round-the-world flight, first solo 204
Rous, Sir Stanley 116-200
Rousseau, Henri 142-246
Rousseau, Jean Jacques 180-184
Rowling, Wallace 320
Rowntree, Joseph 55-145
Royal Academy of Arts 345
Royal Air Force 36-92-185-346
Royal Albert Hall 89-141
Royal Ascot, first 224
Royal Automobile Club 223
Royal Canadian Mounted Police 32-144
Royal Chelsea Hospital 71
Royal College of Surgeons 173
Royal Command performance 183
Royal Exchange 23
Royal Flying Corps 135
Royal George, HMS 242
Royal Mail coach, first 215
Royal Military Academy 93-104
Royal Naval Air Service 175
Royal Naval Lifeboat Institution 64
Royal Oak, HMS 288
Royal Opera House 136
Royal Society 113
Royal Tank Corps 210
Royce, Sir Frederick 87-113
Rubber bullets, Belfast 215
Rubens, Peter Paul 151-181
Rubinstein, Anton 325-333
Rubinstein, Artur 28-355
Ruby, Jack 3-329
Rudolph, Wilma 175

Rugby 276
Rugby Football Union 26-172
Rugby internationals 87
Rugby League 242-251-349
Runcie, Robert 85-276
Runcorn Bridge 203
Runnymede memorials 135-291
Runyon, Damon 278-345
Rush, Ian 294
Rusk, Dean 40
Ruskin, John 20-39
Russell, Bertrand 33-139
Russell, Charles Taze 47-305
Russell, Jane 173
Russell, Ken 185
Russell, Rosalind 156-333
Russo-Japanese War 39-249
Russo-Turkish War 63
Ruth, 'Babe' 37-229
Rutherford, Lord 243-293
Rutherford, Margaret 132-143
Ryan, Nolan 31-233
Ryun, Jim 120

Saccharin 58
Sadat, Anwar 280-291-360
Sadler's Wells Ballet 16
Sadler's Wells Theatre 6
Sadowa, Battle of 185
Safety pin 101
Sagan, Carl 314
Saint, first US born 258
Saint-Saëns, Camille 283-351
St Andrew's Day 335
St Bartholomew's Day massacre 237
St Crispin's Day 299
St George's Day 114
St Gotthard road tunnel 249
St Gotthard tunnel 60
St Helena 142
St Helens volcano 139
St John's Ambulance 176
St Laurent, Ives 214
St Lawrence Seaway 116
St Nazaire raid 88
St Pancras station 275
St Paul's Cathedral 173-337-340
St Peter's Church, Rome 323
St Pierre, Martinique 129
St Swithin's Day 197
St Teresa 278
St Valentine's Day massacre 45
Salamanca, Battle of 204
Salazar, Antonio 119-209-271
Salerno landing 253
Salisbury Cathedral 264
Salk, Jonas 302
Salvation Army 184
Salyut space station 110
Sand Creek massacre 334
Sand, George 160-183
Sandwich Islands 18
San Francisco earthquake 109-110
Sankey, Ira 241

Notes